"Satisfying and impactful work for PhD holders can be found in a wide range of roles in today's colleges and universities—teaching and learning, diversity programs, academic affairs, faculty development, communications, institutional research, and career coaching, to name a few. This book provides inspiration for those exploring nonfaculty careers within academia. The authors of these first-person essays candidly describe their own journeys—from discovering new possibilities, to refashioning a professional identity, to thriving in a previously unimagined job. If you are expanding your view of what is possible, read this book for pragmatic advice and encouragement."

    CHRIS M. GOLDE, Career Coach for PhDs and
      Postdocs, Stanford Career Education

"This important book explores the 'constellation of possibilities' for PhDs within the higher education landscape, identifying not just the push away from faculty jobs, but also the pull toward work that can be joyful, flexible, and meaningful. Among its many powerful contributions, the collection reveals how these roles allow PhDs—who vary by academic discipline, race, gender, gender identity, class, and sexuality—to center values of equity and inclusion, creating communities of care in their workplaces. This is the rare book that offers hope as well as concrete approaches to creating a better life!"

    JOYA MISRA, President, American Sociological Association

"Too many doctoral students think their career choices are limited to a tenure-track job or leaving higher education. *Higher Education Careers Beyond the Professoriate* makes clear that higher education depends on PhDs in myriad ways—in advising, in deans' offices, in libraries, in DEI offices, and in many other functions. More importantly, the book offers advice that focuses not simply on the practicalities of plotting career paths, but also on the financial, family, emotional, and identity issues with which we all must wrestle when making choices about how to move consciously through our careers and our lives. Graduate schools should purchase multiple copies!"

    PAULA KREBS, Executive Director, Modern Language Association

"This book goes well beyond simply outlining career options for PhDs in higher education, providing substantive engagement with what those jobs look and feel like in a changing higher education landscape. Blending personal narrative and critical insight, the essays offer not only useful windows into particular kinds of work, but also new perspectives on living one's values over the course of a nonlinear career."

    DEREK ATTIG, Assistant Dean for Career and Professional Development, Graduate College, University of Illinois Urbana-Champaign

"Nothing teaches better than a story, and *Higher Education Careers Beyond the Professoriate* is filled with good ones, and with good data, too. Career diversity lies at the center of this splendid book, and the many inventive storytellers in its pages show that 'pracademia' leads to lives both creative and satisfying. Academics of all stripes—inside and outside the academy—should read this book."

    LEONARD CASSUTO, coauthor of *The New PhD: How to Build a Better Graduate Education*

Higher Education Careers Beyond the Professoriate

NAVIGATING CAREERS IN HIGHER EDUCATION

The success of diverse faculty entering institutions of higher education is shaped by varying factors at both the individual and institutional levels. Gender, race, class, ethnicity, and immigrant generation influence experiences and aspirations of faculty members and administrators. The Navigating Careers in Higher Education series utilizes an intersectional lens to examine and understand how faculty members and administrators navigate careers and their aspirations to succeed. The series will include books that adopt an interdisciplinary, scholarly approach as well as personal testimonies of individuals sharing their own lived experiences, including challenges faced and lessons learned. With a US or global focus, topics include addressing sexism, homophobia, racism, and ethnocentrism; the role of higher education institutions; the effects of growing non-tenure-track faculty; the challenge of research agenda that may be perceived as controversial; maintaining a life-work balance; and entering leadership positions. Additional topics related to careers in higher education are also welcome.

SERIES EDITOR
Mangala Subramaniam, Senior Vice Provost for Faculty Affairs
Virginia Commonwealth University

SERIES COEDITOR
M. Cristina Alcalde, Vice President for Institutional Diversity and Inclusion
Miami University

OTHER TITLES IN THIS SERIES

The Challenges of Minoritized Contingent Faculty in Higher Education
Edna Chun and Alvin Evans

Transforming Leadership Pathways for Humanities Professionals in Higher Education
Roze Hentschell and Catherine E. Thomas (Eds.)

*Dismantling Institutional Whiteness:
Emerging Forms of Leadership in Higher Education*
M. Cristina Alcalde and Mangala Subramaniam (Eds.)

Higher Education Careers Beyond the Professoriate

Edited by
Karen Cardozo, Katherine Kearns, and Shannan Palma

Purdue University Press • West Lafayette, Indiana

Copyright 2024 by Purdue University. All rights reserved.
Printed in the United States of America.

Cataloging-in-Publication Data is on file at the Library of Congress.
978-1-61249-895-9 (hard cover)
978-1-61249-896-6 (paperback)
978-1-61249-897-3 (epub)
978-1-61249-898-0 (epdf)

Cover: Composite image using the following assets: tiny-al/iStock via Getty Images; Inner_Vision/iStock via Getty Images; shironosov/iStock via Getty Images; Thinkstock/Stockbyte via Getty Images

CONTENTS

Foreword   ix
NATALIE LUNDSTEEN

Introduction: Navigating Disruption, Redefining Success   1
KAREN CARDOZO, KATHERINE KEARNS, AND SHANNAN PALMA

PART 1: CREATING, FINDING, AND OPENING CAREER DOORS   13

1. Let's Stop Saying "Career Path": Meandering Through a Career in Academia   17
   DAVID A. MCDONALD

2. "This Isn't What I Thought It Would Be": Building New Identities and Skills in the Academy   31
   HEATHER DWYER AND KATHARINE P. WALSH

3. Getting from Here to There: Navigating Career Crossroads as a Black Woman Scientist   49
   DIEDRA M. WRIGHTING

4. Contingencies and Possibilities   67
   ALYSSA STALSBERG CANELLI

PART 2: INTER/DISCIPLINARY TRANSFER   81

5. Applied Humanities at Work in STEM Graduate Education   85
   JESSICA A. HUTCHINS

6. From Humanities Tenure Track to Medical School Communications   101
   LEIGH TILLMAN PARTINGTON

7   PhDs Going Rogue: From the Bench to the Library and Beyond   115
    STACEY E. WAHL AND CARRIE L. IWEMA

8   Finding Neverland: From Chimpanzee Research to Career Services   131
    SARAH K. BARKS

PART 3: CRAFTING BLENDED POSITIONS AND IDENTITIES   139

9   Embracing Both/And: Reflections from a Boundary-Spanning Pracademic   143
    BARBARA JACOBY

10 On Our Own Terms: Becoming an Independent Researcher and Writer   159
    LEE SKALLERUP BESSETTE

11 Ambivalent in a Good Way: On Both Staying In and Leaving Academia   171
    CLARE FORSTIE

12 From Stuck to Satisfied: Creating a Joyful, Balanced Life   189
    KRISTINE LODGE

PART 4: CENTERING PERSONAL VALUES, CULTIVATING WORK-LIFE FULFILLMENT   205

13 Finding Your Place, Finding Your Voice   209
    ALEXIS BOYER

14 Well-Being as a Guiding Light Toward a Fulfilling Career   219
    KRISTINE M. SIKORA

15 Embracing Uncertainty: Following My Values Toward a Career in Faculty Development   233
    RYAN RIDEAU

PART 5: NAVIGATING INSTITUTIONAL STRUCTURES AND CULTURES   245

16 Horizontal Mentoring: The Positive Impact of a Diverse Graduate Student Professional Development Community   249
    MARISELLA RODRIGUEZ AND SARAH SILVERMAN

17 When One Door Closes, Another Door . . . Also Closes: The Rewards and Challenges of Work in Diversity, Equity, and Inclusion   261
    JACOB MCWILLIAMS

18 Cultivating Community as an Administrator   277
    SARAH CHOBOT HOKANSON

19 Queering Careers: LGBTQ+ Advocacy on Campus and Beyond   293
    KIMBERLY CREASAP AND DORIAN RHEA DEBUSSY

Afterword: Fostering Career Versatility in PhD Education   305
TREVOR M. VERROT

Appendix A. PhD Characteristics of Essay Contributors   319
Appendix B. Current Employment Characteristics of Essay Contributors   320
Appendix C. Personal Identities of Essay Contributors   322
Annotated Bibliography   325
About the Contributors   329
Index   339

FOREWORD

NATALIE LUNDSTEEN

My first career advising conversation with a doctoral student was over twenty-five years ago at the Stanford University Career Development Center (known today as Stanford Career Education) in a specialized role providing guidance on internships to undergraduate students. I am not sure how that first PhD student ended up on my appointment schedule, but I was terrified in advance of that meeting to advise someone who was working on a doctorate about their future. I remember feeling intimidated and uncertain. What knowledge could I (a higher education professional in my mid-twenties, just starting my career) possibly offer to this brilliant individual with deep academic expertise? To my surprise, it was an exciting conversation about possibilities that left both of us feeling optimistic about the future.

That graduate student, an art historian, was about to accept a great museum job offer in New York. Yet her biggest concern was not about negotiating the offer or any aspects of the new role; instead, she was anxious about breaking the news to her PhD advisor and needed an empathetic ear and some practical advice. Career advising at its core is about listening, guiding, and suggesting, so I provided this student with an objective hour where she could speak without judgment about the role she wanted to choose beyond academia and her feelings of failure over not taking the tenure-track job role to which everyone else in her program (and indeed, most of the faculty) aspired. We strategized about the best way to communicate her decision to her advisor, and together we practiced statements that gave her confidence and conveyed her certainty. I remember feeling relieved that the student didn't ask me anything "PhD-career-specific," although I now realize that there is no universal PhD career. I am certain she has continued to find career success (I do peek at her LinkedIn profile every once in a while), and I am equally certain she has no idea how that conversation catalyzed a crucial pivot in my own professional life.

At that time, I had launched a career in higher education administration but did not have a PhD and was unfamiliar with graduate research culture. That meeting opened my eyes to the world of graduate careers, especially the culture of secrecy around diverse career choices, in which graduate students lived when they did not want to pursue an academic career path. I was astonished by the uneven power dynamic between advisor and student and the mutual lack of knowledge about options. That first conversation gave me a foundation to continue meeting with graduate students without fear of looking naive and with growing confidence in my understanding of the curious culture of academia, which made it all the more important to offer career counseling tools and resources to support PhDs. I have since had countless career development meetings with graduate students, postdoctoral researchers, and PhD alumni at universities in the US and Europe. These varied sessions have only further confirmed the need for such affirmative support in rapidly changing times.

In the ensuing years I obtained my own PhD, studying knowledge transfer from academia to workplaces, and shifted from student and academic affairs to graduate career education work, currently as a dean of students in a medical school. My post-PhD shift into graduate career advising came about not just because I found the work fascinating, but also because I completed my doctorate in 2011 just as the economy was imploding and the shrinking availability of tenure-track jobs became more dire than it had ever been. There were also factors I could not ignore about how the changing PhD career landscape was affecting my own graduate study. My doctoral fieldwork entailed observing undergraduates navigating internships on an investment bank trading floor and watching them make decisions about whether or not to adopt that organizational culture and career choice. They needed to ask, *Am I the kind of person who will thrive in this culture and work environment?* For many, the answer was no, something I saw happening in my own graduate education as I and my peers observed our faculty as professional role models.

I returned from fieldwork to immerse myself in academic activities at my university, where I found most of my fellow students pondering whether or not their own identities aligned with following the tenure track, which was really the only option people could speak of then—at least within earshot of the faculty. I couldn't help but see how the odds were stacked against anyone pursuing the traditional academic career in research and/or teaching. Likewise, the process was equally fraught for those graduate students who—like the undergraduates I was observing—had not yet decided whether that path was, in fact, really right for them. The parallels were clear, and I knew I could use both my own doctoral training and career advising background to support a population that lacked perspective and resources.

National higher education conversations about how PhDs should be trained, how many PhDs should be trained, and what the purpose of doctoral education should be are central to my work. As a PhD career professional at research universities, I developed programs and resources for PhD students and postdocs that helped them transition to the next stage of their careers, while also setting a foundation for lifelong career management. I am currently dean of students in a medical school, but that is a very recent job transition. The bulk of my career has been spent advising across academic disciplines at research institutions in the US and UK. Graduate career education has gone through a period of immense change over the past decade, and I have been working on the inside, watching the ebbs and flows of PhD careers and changes in the way graduate education is structured.

Over the past thirty years, I have seen my profession evolve and expand exponentially, from what can only be called niche roles on campuses in the late 1980s, where often just one individual had responsibility for career advising thousands of graduate students out of a primarily undergraduate-focused career center, to the present time where a professional society of over 500 individuals across North America (and more around the globe!) support the career development of graduate students and postdoctoral researchers in myriad ways from roles based in graduate and professional schools, career centers, and academic departments.

I have been active in this rapidly expanding community for those who serve graduate students and postdocs in career and professional development roles, the Graduate Career Consortium (GCC). This community of practice has been a lifeline for me and others in the field since many of us work alone or in small teams at our institutions. When I joined the GCC in 2013, there were around 150 members; hitting the 500-member mark in 2021 was a testament to the growth in institutional support for graduate career education and institutional intentions to provide resources for PhD students to move beyond traditional tenure-track roles. However, after this period of growth and the feeling that things might be changing for the better in graduate education, there appear to be rough seas ahead for all of us in academia. The COVID-19 pandemic catalyzed change that was simmering below the surface, so many aspects of higher education systems are now being examined and reimagined. We are braced for change in graduate career work: resilience and growth have always been at the heart of what we do.

I was thrilled that the 2022 annual meeting of the GCC featured an opening keynote from Leonard Cassuto, who encouraged graduate career professionals to continue this important work supporting PhDs. As he and Robert Weisbuch make clear in *The New PhD*, the odds simply demand it. Of the entering cohorts now pursuing doctoral education, only a fraction will end up in what were traditionally conceived of as faculty careers. In addition, many who pursue graduate credentials increasingly do so with careers in other sectors in mind. As such, it is incumbent upon anyone who works with those pursuing advanced study to recognize the reality and range of PhD career outcomes. Listening to Cassuto reminded me of my first graduate advising session and the bewilderment I felt that doctoral students had to hide their preferences within a culture of resistance to diverse PhD career choices. Cassuto noted that changing our culture is difficult but not impossible and suggested necessities for strong and sustainable graduate education that include student-centeredness and acceptance of career diversity. Cassuto knows GCC members will amplify his message at our home institutions, and thanks to that keynote we are further inspired to impact change in graduate education.

The themes of this book mirror the work of PhD career professionals, reflecting how we provide an array of resources for those who are exploring and making authentic choices for their futures. In contrast to what some graduate students describe as inhospitable "home" departments that maintain a relatively narrow view of PhD careers, we operate in a positive, affirming space—developing skills, expanding knowledge of jobs both in and beyond academia, reframing perspectives, and urging everyone to claim their true identities and values. This book creates that space, and not only for graduate students: recent PhDs and mid-career professionals, too, will find significant value here to inspire and inform as they ponder their next steps. Indeed, if they were denied such opportunities in their own graduate training, some readers at more advanced career stages may find in this book an invitation to step back and consider who they really are and what they want to become.

The essays in this collection will amplify many of my observations from the firsthand perspective of those who have lived through such transitions, including the overarching new normal we find ourselves navigating as a result of the pandemic. With the benefit of hindsight and reflection, we are able to see significant inflection points across diverse trajectories that are often not visible in the moments as we are living through them. By retracing their journeys and describing pivotal experiences as well as how they came to consciousness about their own interests, strengths, and values, contributors illuminate the myriad ways that people with academic training can embrace greater authenticity and self-acceptance as they explore and embrace professional opportunities beyond the faculty, yet still within higher education. As I learned from my own experience, it is possible to go from feeling like the proverbial fish out of water to one swimming happily in its element. The lessons in this book highlight professional moves that provide a different view of the higher education pond, and maybe even other waters we might not have envisioned before.

For me, the most important theme of this book is the necessity of rigorous reflection and staying true to an authentic sense of self. This is a fundamental idea in career counseling theory, and something I myself experienced during the pandemic, recognizing that where I was situated career-wise was fine, but could be better. I believe many PhD students also have that aspirational sense but may not be able to readily find the mentoring to create better alignment between who they are and what they do for work. The essays in part 1 of this book focus on building a better understanding of self and then using that knowledge to find a way forward in more flexible, if uncharted, paradigms beyond a path or track mentality. Part 3 on blended roles and part 4 on leading with your values illuminate possibilities for new work–life configurations in answer to questions like *Who am I?* or *Am I happy with where I am?* And if the answer is no, then *What changes do I need to make to become the person I want to be and design a life in alignment with my values?* These are challenging questions for anyone, but especially for those leaving a familiar academic research trajectory and venturing into unknown territory. Fortunately, as part 2 on interdisciplinary transfer demonstrates, every PhD is equipped with skills that can be applied effectively to other roles and sectors.

Like the editors who have shepherded this collection into being, many of the authors in this book work in professional roles that support PhD students in their career exploration and other forms of professional development. As such, the book contains informed wisdom from both personal and professional experience, along with many exercises and resources that will be useful to readers across the disciplines and at all career stages. Particularly indispensable is the afterword, in which Trevor Verrot reviews challenges and opportunities for PhDs in the current landscape and discusses how the collection models key aspects of the career development process. Verrot's incisive analysis and advice, like the book as a whole, should be required reading for everyone involved in PhD education.

Although I have been in the field of PhD career development for almost three decades, this collection has illuminated how the past few years have impacted not only individual PhD students, but also academia as a system undergoing immense change amidst ongoing societal upheaval. It has helped me realize that uncertainty about the future will increasingly be the norm, including in higher education. Accepting this reality can be especially complicated for PhD students who still see a terminal degree as successful only if it ends in tenure-track employment. Moreover, the collection reveals significant links between career diversity and larger institutional conversations about diversity, equity, and inclusion. Here, the book brings forward thoughtful explorations of varied intersectional identities, understanding that who we are or strive to become is often closely allied to a sense of vocation. While the entire collection offers varied perspectives on this theme, part 5 is particularly devoted to an exploration of how work expresses our identities and commitments.

In conclusion, those who are pursuing or have completed their PhD should be encouraged to explore a range of fitting opportunities and reflect on their trajectories at all life stages, not just as they approach the finish line of their graduate program. Taken together, these reflective essays illuminate fundamental concepts of personal and professional development. I strongly encourage all stakeholders in the doctoral system to thoroughly familiarize yourself with the many eye-opening narratives in *Higher Education Careers Beyond the Professoriate*—whether to inform your own career development or to support those whom you mentor in more relevant and empathetic ways. No matter how well you think you know the terrain, you will gain new perspectives from these wide-ranging and thoughtful reflections by PhDs working in a variety of roles in higher education.

INTRODUCTION

Navigating Disruption, Redefining Success

KAREN CARDOZO, KATHERINE KEARNS, AND SHANNAN PALMA

Well before COVID-19 wreaked havoc around the globe, the evolution of capitalism had led to major shifts in the world of work, including increased automation, leaner organizations, casualization of labor, the rise of entrepreneurship, and hybrid or remote work arrangements. As Bruce Melman (2020) has noted, however, 2020 was unprecedented for the simultaneous manifestation of four "super-disruptors": a recession, mass protests, an intense US presidential election, and a global pandemic. Thus, in *Recalculating*, workplace expert Lindsey Pollak uses the GPS metaphor to explain the flexible mindset and more fluid career development process that most professionals now need to deploy: "When the navigation app is recalculating, it's demonstrating that there are multiple ways to get wherever you want to go.... And, if you decide to change your destination entirely, it can get you there as well" (2021, 6).

While recalculating can be challenging for anyone, it is especially difficult for those with doctoral training. Most PhDs have been socialized in a track mentality to pursue a relatively specialized academic career involving some combination of research, teaching, and institutional service. Yet amidst ongoing disruption, this mentality ignores the realities of capitalism, where greater adaptability and situational responsiveness are required to meet basic physiological and psychological needs for shelter and safety. In such a context, academia's emphasis on the traditional faculty track inverts Maslow's (1943) hierarchy of needs, framing self-actualization and ego through academic identity, knowledge production, and peer review as the foundation, with safety and security as a higher-echelon privilege earned through tenure. This inversion is sorely misaligned with current realities: as noted in *The New PhD* (Weisbuch and Cassuto), only about a quarter of aspiring PhDs will end up in faculty positions and the worldwide faculty majority (including, technically, those on the tenure track) work in precarious positions. In hopes of winning the academic lottery, many PhDs have lived on food stamps and foregone health insurance. Meanwhile, to protect the tenure system, many institutional policies put term limits on renewable non-tenure-track contracts beyond six years, as reasonable questions would be (and are) asked about why groups of faculty who share the same credentials and do similar work receive such disparate treatment within the neoliberal university. Even so, advocacy to meet the basic needs of academic professionals is often seen as somehow gauche, a failed commitment to the idealized life of the mind.

In this context, it can be difficult for recent PhDs or those pursuing advanced degrees to freely explore, or openly communicate their interest in, alternative careers. Moreover, many roles that are ripe for a PhD's skills are often not visible to those with doctoral training or, if known, may not appear viable because they are not explicitly related to the academic field of expertise. Yet ironically, many fruitful career pathways are right under the nose of every PhD and all around them: jobs in higher education. *Higher Education Careers Beyond the Professoriate* (*HECBP*) features compelling frameworks, practical advice, and both personal and professional reflections from diverse PhDs working in varied career fields at higher education institutions.

Designed for current and future doctoral students, faculty advisors, and PhDs at all career stages interested in higher ed positions beyond the faculty, this volume draws in its audience with engaging, highly reflective narratives from professionals with PhDs from a variety of academic disciplines, personal identities, and employing institution types. Together they show that myriad trajectories are possible within higher ed. Other significant audiences for this book include policymakers and leaders charged with institutional transformation, particularly efforts to advance diversity, equity, and inclusion. The collection reveals that the egregious inversion of Maslow's hierarchy of needs in academia's track mentality presumes a best-case scenario PhD candidate—one who does not have to earn a living from their labor, who does not have social or familial responsibilities outside of academia, and who is not persistently alienated by the various "isms" inherent to institutions forged by histories of colonization and patriarchal racial capitalism. Collectively, contributors to *HECBP* amass significant insight into the cultural and structural barriers that inhibit belonging within this limited sphere while obscuring fuller possibilities for PhD futures. We hope that all stakeholders in doctoral education will see the relevance of these issues to their own work, as many programs and organizations now do.

In recent years there have been increased calls for reforming doctoral education in ways that acknowledge and support PhD career diversity, including *The New PhD* (Weisbuch and Cassuto 2021) and *The Graduate School Mess* (Cassuto 2015). National initiatives supporting PhD career diversity include the Council of Graduate School's PhD Career Pathways Project (CGS 2022) and the Association of American Universities' PhD Education Initiative (AAU 2019). Yet, while numerous sources of advice and personal narratives exist for people interested in traditional faculty careers, only a handful of volumes focus on other PhD career paths, and most of those focus on transitions to industry. These sources include Caterine (2020), Fruscione and Baker (2018), Gallagher and Gallagher (2020), and Robbins-Roth (2005). These and other resources are itemized in the annotated bibliography we offer in this volume. The recognition of higher education as an industry that employs PhDs in capacities beyond faculty roles has only recently been noted, in *Going Alt-Ac: A Guide to Alternative Academic Careers* (Kelly, Linder, and Tobin, 2020). However, *Higher Education Careers Beyond the Professoriate* is the first book to offer reflective first-person essays on the growing range of professional opportunities for PhDs within colleges and universities. As such, it offers critical perspectives by diverse contributors highlighting different intersections of identity, who are trained in a range of disciplines and who now work in a variety of roles and units across campus.

For those actively interested in exploring and pursuing higher ed careers beyond the professoriate, as well as those aiming for an academic career but realizing that they may need to cultivate alternatives amidst ongoing academic precarity, this book offers possibilities, advice, and concrete strategies for building and succeeding in a wide range of higher ed career fields, including advising; academic or other program administration; diversity, equity and inclusion; faculty development; teaching and learning, including instructional technology; libraries; institutional research and data analysis; student affairs; business operations; advancement; enrollment; marketing and communications; and community relations or other predominantly external-facing or partnership functions.

Here, one of our contributors (Canelli) offers an apt metaphor for reframing career paradigms: *a constellation of possibilities*. Of the eighty-eight known stellar constellations,[1] one has a particular significance in this context. Circinus is a drafting compass metaphor that signals the capacity to pivot in a delimited space, which is just what all contributors to this volume have done. Moreover, Circinus is located next to a bright star, Alpha, which we may understand metaphorically as the shining faculty career that PhDs are supposed to be aiming for but may no longer want or find possible. Interestingly, this constellation is difficult to see in the north but in the south is readily visible year-round, yet another apt metaphor for the shift in perspectives this book offers. Indeed, myriad alternative roles within higher education are always available, just not necessarily visible based on one's standpoint. Thus, however subtly, our book's cover image alludes to these abiding constellations, reminding us to look up and around.

Our contributors provide a nuanced view of this landscape and the process of navigating it, including different pathways and the levels at which PhDs may enter alternative roles; when prior experience transfers and when they may have to start over in a new field; overcoming the paradoxical feeling of being simultaneously over/underqualified; adopting the growth mindset that fosters agility and resilience in exploring new options; and the challenges or benefits of switching roles within one's current institution or elsewhere. Many also call attention to well-being concerns: managing stress and health issues, negotiating insufficient flexibility for accommodating different neurotypes, seeking work–life integration, and finding belonging through an affirmative community. In short, they advocate for the real needs of diverse brains and bodies. They challenge the preeminence of faculty tracks in PhD career discourse and reject having to discard pieces of themselves—values, identities, desires—to fit into the narrow confines of what is, in actuality for most, contingent employment. At the same time, they acknowledge the challenges of deprogramming their own fixed mindsets and of negotiating change, grief, and inspiration when considering how to move forward and deciding which aspects of identity to claim and which to release upon transitioning into roles beyond the faculty.

Authors of the essays in this volume provide readers with a firsthand view of the process of moving into their current professional field. They share their decision-making and transition experiences, challenges and rewards of their professional fields, and practical advice for those interested in exploring those career fields. Imparting what they wish they had known during their own PhD journeys, the authors demystify the process of succeeding in one's choice of higher ed careers, pushing back against the notion that successful and rewarding careers for PhDs in higher ed are found exclusively among the faculty ranks. Their stories reveal that faculty careers continue to unfold most smoothly for those with normative identities and substantial privilege; indeed, all of our contributors note that the dissonance between their own identities and values and normative identities in academe was a significant factor in their decision to pursue careers beyond the faculty and make other significant life choices. Thus, the collection reveals that PhD career versatility must be understood within broader contexts and efforts to advance diversity, equity, belonging, and social justice.

Aligned with the vision of the Purdue University Press series Navigating Careers in Higher Education, the volume disrupts common myths about the career paths of PhDs who go on to careers in academia outside the faculty track. Throughout the book, contributors wrestle with the question of how academia is defined, and how the boundaries around the concept of the academic community shape career paths and experiences. Additionally, this multidisciplinary group of contributors (appendix A) located across institutional types (appendix B) bringing distinct intersectional identities (appendix C) helps us rethink received notions of successful PhD outcomes, demonstrating how and why values and goals other than securing a tenure-track position have been important to their own experiences of success and professional fulfillment. Across the collection, contributors discuss how their identities and values created points of alienation from their disciplines or a traditional faculty career path and led them to find and form new communities in other parts of the university where they felt more affinity. Contributors also intervene in discourses that favor linear, neatly organized career paths, illuminating the nuances and complexity of real-life PhD journeys as well as sharing strategies for navigating career trajectories that unfold beyond what many graduate students are often still socialized to expect from their careers. Their journeys speak to Pollak's point that many careers no longer unfold on a linear track and that ongoing recalculations may be necessary. Our contributors fully recognize that their current position may not be their last.

Indeed, as a microcosm of the broader society, this collection has been affected by the global pandemic and other disruptors in ways that have required our own ongoing adaptation. First, one of our original editors, Dr. Brandy Simula, had to leave the project for personal reasons. Fortunately, Dr. Karen Cardozo agreed to step in and contribute her unique blend of academic, administrative, and career development experience to shaping the volume. Second, several contributors left the project, citing inordinate work–life demands, while others joined, excited about the opportunity. Third, all three of the editors and several contributors have changed jobs while bringing this volume to fruition. Clearly, as we move through the pandemic, higher education is mirroring the destabilization happening in industry and the wider world. Since career planning across sectors is subject to ongoing disruption in current economic, cultural, and historical circumstances, a major contribution of this collection as a whole is its cumulative insight into how our readers can foster agility and resilience on their journeys.

When we solicited contributions, we asked authors to explicitly reflect on the following: how they were trained and what they had been anticipating when they matriculated into advanced study; key inflection points where they began to realize that their circumstances, needs, and/or goals had changed; the processes and people that helped them effect both personal and professional transitions; and what may have shifted even since they signed onto this book collection.

Thus, this book captures a historic moment on multiple levels: within the higher education sector, within individual institutions, and in personal experiences of living and working through a period of crisis and transformation. At the same time, by illuminating ongoing processes of assessment, change, exploration, risk, and reward, this book reveals how PhDs can navigate disruption to build satisfying careers and lives.

Collectively, the contributions to *HECBP* make three core arguments. First, the book *explodes the inside/outside-the-academy binary* that has long framed conversations about and research on PhD careers. By highlighting the numerous career fields beyond the faculty track within the academy, the book shifts the conversation about the range of occupations that can productively harness PhD training, as well as the ways doctoral training might be viewed more expansively considering these myriad outcomes. For instance, some chapters explore moving between academic and other roles, discussing how skills and experiences gained in administrative and other work before and during graduate school contributed to their academic work, as well as decisions to leave the faculty for an administrative, hybrid, or staff position. These contributors offer a both/and paradigm in which academic and other professional pursuits may coexist or alternate in evolving ways.

Second, the book demonstrates that *transferable skills, networking, and professional development, more than disciplinary specialization, are essential to career paths beyond the professoriate.* Across the volume, contributors emphasize how understanding and communicating the applicability of their skills to broader pursuits is key to both securing a position and succeeding in that position. For example, some note that relationship-building skills and experience leading teams were crucial to their career advancement, while others highlight the value of their analytic, writing, and research skills. All offer advice for identifying and building similar synergies between doctoral training and any number of career paths.

Third, the book, particularly the afterword by Trevor Verrot, argues that *we must change the culture and practice of graduate training, professional development, and career preparation.* While the contributors clearly demonstrate that PhDs can be and are successful in a wide range of higher ed career fields, their narratives also highlight the gaps they had to fill in their career preparation, as well as how the culture of graduate training at many institutions continues to stigmatize diverse career paths by focusing extensively on research faculty careers. Some describe their struggles with impostor syndrome, and how moving beyond a faculty role left them wondering: *Did I fail, or did the institution fail me?* Verrot and other contributors identify the cultural and structural shifts that graduate programs must engage to better support aspiring PhDs, while also highlighting strategies graduate students and postdocs can pursue, even in programs and institutions that don't provide sufficient professional development. Others emphasize their growing comfort with ambiguity and uncertainty, understanding that their narratives are still unfolding. All illuminate how to make sense of evolving career journeys, finding meaning and purpose in new kinds of work and redefining success on their own terms.

While many contributors address similar themes and concerns, we made the editorial decision to group them into five distinct parts in order to highlight different aspects of career exploration, professional development, and life design. Many other arrangements could have been possible, given the rich content in these multifaceted essays. For example, while many contributors discuss intentional career development strategies, happenstance is also a strong theme in identifying key inflection points in a career trajectory: we could have had a part that simply highlights lucky breaks. And, while part 5 discusses most explicitly how those with historically marginalized identities may be inclined to seek pathways into more affirming professional spaces, contributors in every part reflect thoughtfully on the intersections of the personal and the professional, on challenges faced by underrepresented minorities in the academy, and what it might take to build truly inclusive and equitable environments in higher education. Thus, we encourage you to explore the book fully, without assuming that any one part will be most relevant to your aspirations, current field, or career stage. Each part displays an array of disciplinary backgrounds, identities, and institutional experiences, and all offer excellent, actionable, and supportive advice, as well as perspective and wisdom gleaned from the journey. Having said that, we can now describe the primary emphases of each part.

Part 1, "Creating, Finding, and Opening Career Doors," provides a strong reframe of the traditionally linear, career track mentality that is still far too prominent in academic socialization and graduate advising. Contributors to this part echo the growing public acknowledgment that professional trajectories in disruptive global economies will be more fluid and unpredictable. Thus, these authors take a relatively balanced approach that encourages readers to be both intentional and strategic about their aims, while also becoming more adaptable and resilient in the face of changing circumstances or new discoveries. They highlight the paradox of being prepared to "make your own luck" and the flexibility that will be required if and when things don't go as planned. In empathizing with and illuminating the struggles of PhDs from historically marginalized groups in particular, they reveal the difficult yet necessary work of letting go of initial expectations in order to evolve into more capacious personal and professional identities. In distinct and salutary ways, each of the essays in part 1 offers a more realistic and holistic perspective along with empowering advice to suggest how those initially trained for an academic career might navigate successfully onto broader terrain by considering a fuller constellation of possibilities.

In part 2, "Inter/Disciplinary Transfer," contributors reflect on how the skills they honed in their doctoral training contribute to new roles and contexts. In making their career transitions, contributors in this part discuss how they opened new career doors and show how they crafted positions that aligned with their values and allowed them to take the parts of their disciplinary training they enjoyed most and turn them into something that better suited their needs. They also provide a window into organizational cultures beyond the faculty. They show how inextricable our five themes really are, while explicitly expanding readers' thinking about how disciplinary training and knowledge can be applied in professional spheres that may at first seem unrelated, as well as identifying which aspects of PhD training offer the most transferable skills. Authors in part 2 describe how research, writing, teaching, and data analysis skills show up in a variety of roles beyond the faculty and how disciplinary expertise yields insights into nominally unrelated areas. Those trained in the humanities may be especially interested in some of the examples of bringing writing and editing skills into STEM fields.

In part 3, "Crafting Blended Positions and Identities," contributors undermine academic/nonacademic binaries and productively complicate "leaving academe" discourse, revealing how it is possible to be both in and out of academe. In so doing they discuss how their personal and professional identities, along with their intellectual interests, shifted when they took up roles beyond the faculty. They reflect on how other affinities can coexist alongside academic work, while also describing ways to reclaim one's intellectual identity and voice when no longer working primarily as a faculty member. Contributors further emphasize the energizing and restorative aspects of integrating personal and professional identities through values-driven decision-making. Ultimately, while they do not shy away from the ambiguity or ambivalence of inhabiting uncharted waters and multifaceted identities, these authors show us how empowering and fulfilling it can be to cross boundaries and renegotiate the terms of success by prioritizing one's own needs and values for more holistic ways of living and working. Echoing part 1, these contributors remind us that career paths are not linear but informed by the ongoing negotiations of trying to meet personal and professional needs in shifting circumstances. They model how one can grow as a thinker, researcher, and writer while taking up new professional responsibilities. More than this, these profoundly humanizing essays show us what it means to grow in wisdom as a whole human being.

In part 4, "Centering Personal Values, Cultivating Work–Life Fulfillment," contributors model how to live more intentionally among competing personal and professional priorities. Through explorations of integrity and authenticity, these authors help readers think about higher education career decisions in the context of trying to create a life aligned with their own values. Moving from moments of misalignment to values clarification and discernment to greater role refinement, they reflect on career and life choices incorporating sociocultural factors and seeking to balance work, family, leisure, and rest in a life of purpose and fulfillment that brings value to the communities in which they live and serve. They also describe the challenges and tensions inherent in their journeys, including the effects of the burden shift in diversity, equity, and inclusion (DEI) work toward minority groups. These essays enable us to witness the authors healing from fragmentation by integrating their personal and professional selves and helping others to do similar restorative work.

In part 5, "Navigating Institutional Structures and Cultures," contributors describe how engaging in advocacy work became a means of claiming and integrating both personal and professional identities. Essays in this part share how the authors have worked to improve conditions and equity for marginalized others in higher education and thus provide what they did not have, spaces of belonging and traumatic recovery. They write about advocating for space and boundaries that maintain their own well-being as well as connecting with colleagues, mentors, peer groups, and other positive microstructures that help them combat the range of mental health challenges particularly prevalent among those who work in helping professions (Kolomitro, Kenny, and Le-May Sheffield 2020; van Dernoot, Lipsky, and Burk 2009). They share their experiences of working for systemic change and how institutions can both enable that advocacy work and act as a barrier. And they reflect on difficult decisions when they are proximal to projects that don't align with their values. Together, they demonstrate a collective commitment to disrupting normative, oppressive practices in higher education.

Taken together, the essays in *Higher Education Careers Beyond the Professoriate* authorize us to "stop saying career path" (McDonald). They normalize and validate the moments when we realize "this isn't what I thought it would be" (Dwyer and Walsh). As such, they can be read and returned to in any order, whenever you find yourself "at the crossroads" (Wrighting), exploring a constellation of both "contingencies and possibilities" (Canelli).

In reminding us that no part of our training is ever really wasted, they show us how it is possible to go from comparative literature to applied humanities work in STEM environments (Hutchins) and from the humanities to medical writing (Partington). They take us from being trained in academic departments to working in libraries (Wahl and Iwema) and from conducting chimpanzee research to managing the analytics for career services (Barks).

Some contributors further show us how it is possible to become "boundary-spanning pracademics" (Jacoby) who find creative ways to pursue intellectual interests "on our own terms" (Bessette). In the process, they suggest that we can learn to be "ambivalent in a good way" (Forstie), embracing doubts or difficult emotions as productive for growth. Others find that they can integrate various aspects of their identities in surprising and satisfying ways (Lodge), breaking free from self-limiting perceptions of personal and professional obligations (Sikora) in order to find and claim their own places and voices (Boyer).

Finally, these essays remind us of the importance of community in embracing uncertainty while running the marathon of academic training, especially for those whose identities are historically marginalized (Rideau). They show us that a supportive community can be created and built horizontally through peer mentoring (Rodriguez and Silverman) and through administrative contributions that foster belonging in spaces beyond the professoriate (Hokanson). They are also fearlessly honest about the limitations of diversity work and the perils of navigating exceedingly narrow professional pathways, especially for transgender and/or nonbinary professionals (McWilliams). Indeed, they productively queer the very notion of a career by highlighting the ways in which identity-driven values and a thirst for equity and justice may lead one to make different choices, break into new professional territories, and build new communities (Creasap and Debussy). Taken together, they illuminate the versatility of PhD pathways and expand our understanding of how to find meaningful work in a fulfilling life.

NOTE

1. For a full list of the eighty-eight constellations and their meanings, see Starchild Team (n.d.). For additional information on locating Circinus in particular, see Whitt (2022).

REFERENCES

AAU (Association of American Universities). 2019. "AAU Launches PhD Initiative with Pilot of Eight Universities." https://www.aau.edu/newsroom/press-releases/aau-launches-phd-initiative-pilot-eight-universities.

CGS (Council of Graduate Schools). 2022. *Shaping New Narratives About PhD Careers*. https://cgsnet.org/wp-content/uploads/2022/02/ShapingNewNarratives2020.pdf.

Kolomitro, Klodiana, Natasha Kenny, and Suzanne Le-May Sheffield. 2020. "A Call to Action: Exploring and Responding to Educational Developers' Workplace Burnout and Well-Being in Higher Education." *International Journal for Academic Development* 25 (1): 5–18. https://doi.org/10.1080/1360144X.2019.1705303.

Lipsky, Laura van Durnoot, and Connie Burk. 2009. *Trauma Stewardship: An Everyday Guide to Caring for Self While Caring for Others*. San Francisco: Berrett-Koehler.

Maslow, Abraham H. 1943. "A Theory of Human Motivation." *Psychological Review* 50 (4): 370–96. https://doi.org/10.1037/h0054346.

Melman, Bruce. 2020. *The Great Acceleration: How 2020 Is Bringing the Future Faster*. https://s3.documentcloud.org/documents/6988354/Great-Acceleration-Mehlman-Q3-2020.pdf?utm_source=newsletter&utm_medium=email&utm_campaign=newsletter_axiosam&stream=top.

Pollak, Lindsey. 2021. *Recalculating: Navigate Your Career Through the Changing World of Work*. New York: HarperCollins.

Starchild Team, The. n.d. "88 Officially Recognized Constellations." Accessed April 27, 2023. https://starchild.gsfc.nasa.gov/docs/StarChild/questions/88constellations.html.

Whitt, Kelly Kizer. 2022. "Circinus the Drawing Compass, Alpha Centauri's Neighbor." EarthSky. https://earthsky.org/constellations/circinus-the-drawing-compass/.

Part 1
CREATING, FINDING, AND OPENING CAREER DOORS

Part 1 provides a strong reframe of the traditionally linear career track mentality that is still too prominent in academic socialization and graduate advising. Contributor insights echo a growing literature indicating that professional trajectories in disruptive global economies will be more fluid and unpredictable. As such, career development across all sectors might be better aligned with a chaos theory of careers (Pryor and Bright 2011), the creative, iterative approach of life design (Burnett and Evans 2016, 2020), or the situationally responsive mode of recalculating (Pollak 2021).

Contributors to this part take a relatively balanced approach that encourages readers to be intentional and strategic about their aims, while also becoming more adaptable and resilient in the face of changing circumstances or new discoveries. They highlight the preparation required to make your own luck as well as the flexibility required when things don't go as planned. In various ways, they reveal the difficult necessity of letting go of initial expectations to evolve into more capacious personal and professional identities. In so doing, they empathize with and illuminate the challenges involved, particularly for PhDs from historically marginalized groups.

David McDonald opens the collection with a clear provocation: "Let's Stop Saying 'Career Path.'" In this essay, McDonald describes how he gradually became disenchanted with a research-intensive STEM trajectory and ultimately came to realize that many PhDs do not, in fact, end up in faculty positions. As indicated by his subtitle, "Meandering Through a Career in Academia," McDonald found himself organically moving into successively more satisfying positions beyond the professoriate while clarifying his own values, in part through prioritizing his queer identity and marriage. Drawing from varied experiences, including professional work in career services, McDonald shares some highly useful exercises by which readers can identify and assess their own skills and values in order to meander in fulfilling new directions.

Heather Dwyer and Katharine (Katie) Walsh elaborate on the idea that things often don't turn out as expected in "This Isn't What I Thought It Would Be: Building New Identities and Skills in the Academy." In an alternating dialogue and reflection format, the authors explore how common cultural and structural features of their training in STEM and humanities fields at two different institutions acted as push factors that led them to rethink their identities and future trajectories. Meanwhile, the stimulating work and affirming community they found while working as graduate students in centers for teaching acted as pull factors that led them both into careers in educational development. Because they were trained in different fields at different institutions, their comparative perspectives illuminate some of the structural factors that inhibit diversity, equity, and belonging while also highlighting the value of finding community and professional development beyond the home academic department. Dwyer and Walsh close their insightful essay with useful advice for both individuals and institutions.

Amplifying the theme of inhospitable factors that lead to changes of trajectory and attendant identity shifts, Diedra Wrighting offers the empowering metaphor of being in the driver's seat in "Getting from Here to There: Navigating Career Crossroads as a Black Woman in Science." Wrighting describes how she negotiated several key inflection points and offers readers substantive advice on how to do the same, from assessing one's strengths and searching for fitting job descriptions, to assembling robust mentoring networks, to making effective use of LinkedIn and informational interviewing to leverage those networks. Equally important, she discusses the attendant grief of relinquishing a long-held career aspiration and the emotional fallout from others' reactions to her decision to leave laboratory science and focus instead on supporting underrepresented minorities in STEM through professional development efforts. Wrighting closes with the affirming insight that, although she no longer works in a lab, she still identifies strongly as a principal investigator since her current work in faculty development taps into many of the same aptitudes and analytic, exploratory, and experimental activities on a daily basis.

Alyssa Stalsberg Canelli closes out part 1 with a compelling alternative framing to the limited notion of a career path. In "Contingencies and Possibilities," she describes how to imagine a fuller landscape or constellation within which one might, at any point, move in multiple directions. Canelli observes that doctoral training inevitably unfolds against a host of changing personal circumstances that will inevitably require most graduate students to reassess their priorities in a larger work–life context. Offering three pivotal snapshots of her own trajectory at different inflection points, she parses these moments insightfully through varied meanings of contingency. In a journey that seems nothing less than heroic, Canelli describes how a perfect storm of health issues and financial concerns while trying to build a queer family led her to transition from humanities study into higher education administration, where she now leads a major PhD career initiative. Canelli reminds us simply, yet profoundly, that "most of life is contingent" in promising neither the predictability nor necessity of any given outcome, but "we tend to forget these truths when deeply enculturated into academia." It is only when we acknowledge the inevitability of contingencies that we become correspondingly open to a fuller range of possibilities.

In distinct and salutary ways, each of the essays in part 1 offers a more holistic and realistic perspective on PhD career journeys, along with empowering advice to suggest how those initially trained for an academic career might navigate successfully onto broader terrain.

REFERENCES

Burnett, Bill, and Dave Evans. 2016. *Designing Your Life: How to Build a Well-Lived, Joyful Life*. New York: Knopf.

Burnett, Bill, and Dave Evans. 2020. *Designing Your Work Life: How to Thrive and Change and Find Happiness at Work*. New York: Knopf.

Pollak, Lindsey. 2021. *Recalculating: Navigate Your Career Through the Changing World of Work*. New York: HarperCollins.

Pryor, Robert, and Jim Bright. 2011. *The Chaos Theory of Careers: A New Perspective on Living and Working in the Twenty-First Century*. New York: Routledge.

1

LET'S STOP SAYING "CAREER PATH"

Meandering Through a Career in Academia

DAVID A. MCDONALD

Many of us say "career path" as a common turn of phrase, but that image can limit the way we think about our futures. It promises that by taking prescribed steps, we will arrive at our chosen destination. In academe, it is often implied that the only path after graduation is to do postdoctoral training, land that assistant professor position, secure tenure as an associate professor, attain a promotion as a full professor, and stay there forever. You may individualize this pattern to add titles of editor, director, or dean, but the pattern largely remains the same. You stick to the path through its various steps, heading off toward the sunset.

Today, most PhDs don't end up as tenured professors, so "career path" is a misleading phrase. Yet even as the academic job market became more competitive, requiring more experience and a more prestigious pedigree, many fields continue with "path" discourse. Graduate school should be a professional development opportunity to build skills that can transfer to any number of jobs and fields. It's time that we stop thinking about a career as a single, straightforward path. Instead, we should conjure the image of a career landscape in which we can go in whatever direction we choose and find many unique jobs along the way.

For many PhDs (anywhere from 50 percent to 90 percent depending on your field), careers are less prescriptive. We're blazing our own trail, and only in looking back can we see the path we created. This shift in thinking has been one of the most liberating realizations of my life. There's no singular way to work in academia, which can be both freeing and intimidating. If you don't know your next step and your timeline to get there, how do you build such a career? In addition, how do you seek out environments that allow you to express your identities and values?

When I started graduate school, I had the single-minded intention to be a faculty member at a research university. As I discovered that a faculty research career didn't actually fit my interests and values, I had to forge new professional identities. I first went on to a teaching postdoc position at a historically Black university to explore being faculty at a smaller college. After it became clear that a faculty role did not match the work–life balance I desired, I moved into student affairs and career counseling. In this position, I advised graduate students, taught workshops, and used my research skills to assess our impact. I grew in my abilities to build relationships with faculty and to manage a team.

From there, it became clear that in order to strengthen graduate education, I would have to be embedded in an academic unit, so I found a position as a PhD program director. With each change, my professional identity was evolving. I realized that I'm drawn to new opportunities to grow every few years, looking for ways to apply my talents in new ways while also developing new skills. I still leverage the research skills that I developed in graduate school, but now I use them to study how graduate students learn and develop.

As a gay, cisgender man, I also began to leverage my identity as a strength. I've come to appreciate that minoritized identities can be seen as strengths in higher education. My past few jobs in academia have been at offices with strong commitments to promoting DEI. One of them works to promote scientists from underrepresented groups. I was hesitant to out myself when interviewing for these jobs (and ultimately did not), but in hindsight, talking about my gay identity might have been an asset. I still needed to gain more knowledge and skills to do DEI work with students, but sharing my personal experiences might have been more of a benefit than a risk in those situations. Many institutions are asking how candidates engage with DEI issues, so everyone should think about how their identities, experiences, and training contribute to creating a welcoming space for all to be successful. Later in the essay I will reflect on this aspect of my own experience.

In what follows, I share my thought process at each career crossroad to show that you don't have to rigidly plan your whole journey. Along the way, I present my favorite reflective exercises because a deeper understanding of your interests, needs, limitations, and strengths can help you to think creatively about different work possibilities. Overall, I want to normalize the idea that you don't need a ten-year career plan. Some people are happy to get a job in an environment that fits their identities, do good work for a while, and then look for new opportunities to keep learning and growing.

FOLLOWING THE PRESCRIBED PATH

Like many PhDs, I went to graduate school with the intention of becoming faculty one day. It's more common now in some fields for graduate students to have a variety of career interests, but I was chasing the academic dream: pursuing new knowledge and sharing it with the world. As an undergraduate, I majored in biochemistry, which led me to apply to biomedical science PhD programs. I wasn't sure what I wanted to study at the graduate level, but I had curiosity, motivation, and the confidence of a twenty-two-year-old who had done well in classes and research as an undergraduate.

Starting graduate school came with many adjustments. The courses were more advanced, and I was expected to engage with original research more than textbooks. Even though I had put in twenty hours per week as an undergraduate research assistant, it was still jarring to go to lab anytime I wasn't in class. It was the first time I had to put in a full-time effort as a grad student compared to the flexible schedule of an undergraduate. My program required ten-week research rotations, so every couple of months I started over with new science in a new space with new colleagues. I was able to adjust quickly to keep up with the constant change and higher expectations.

Although I didn't recognize it at the time, I was already starting to shift my career interests in the first couple of years of my PhD studies. My research mentor and other faculty were presenting a more complete view of their working lives. While I had been initially inspired by the autonomy of faculty life, I realized it also comes with high levels of pressure and additional responsibilities. The publish or perish expectation was palpable—no matter the faculty level, your department and the university demanded more of your time. More publications, more grant funding, more committees, more service. By all of the typical academic metrics, I was a successful graduate student. I obtained two predoctoral fellowships, and I published multiple first-author papers. But it was increasingly clear that I didn't want a life like that of my research mentor. Faculty jobs are competitive and demanding in ways I found dispiriting. The career path I had been on for more than five years no longer looked as attractive. The path was starting to narrow, taking unexpected turns, and becoming filled with too many people who wanted it more than I did. I needed to start thinking about where else my skills could take me.

CHARTING YOUR SKILLS

Increasingly, graduate studies are becoming more of a professional development opportunity than just a credential for your curriculum vitae or résumé. Some slim subset of careers require a PhD, but many others require skills you build in a PhD program without necessarily requiring that credential. So it's worth paying attention to the skills you build in graduate school, because they can provide inspiration for exploring a range of careers and setting professional development goals.

One of my favorite reflection exercises with students is to chart your skills. A version of this approach originally appeared in Richard Bolles's classic career development book *What Color Is Your Parachute?* You can see a more recent version in its latest companion workbook (Bolles and Brooks 2021). Divide a piece of paper into four equal quadrants by drawing a horizontal line and a vertical line. The horizontal line (x-axis) represents the strength of a particular skill: on the far right are skills you are very good at, and on the far left are competencies you lack. The vertical line (y-axis) represents how much you like to use a skill: at the top are the skills you love to use, and at the bottom are those you would rather not deploy.

Fill the quadrants of your chart with any skills you can think of. They can be techniques, broad research skills, transferable skills, and even your hobbies. The goal is to brainstorm and observe patterns, so the more you add to your chart the better. You can either list skills in each quadrant (Q) or plot them like data points. In grad school, mine would have looked like this:

Q 1: Good at AND Like to Do
- understanding a topic well
- developing and implementing a plan

- working with people and on my own
- teaching adult students
- data management and analysis in Excel
- tailoring content to different audiences

Q2: Good at BUT Do Not Like to Do
- failing often
- genotyping
- sequencing for genetic mutations

Q3: Unskilled BUT Like to Do
- having an impact
- advocating for others, particularly underrepresented groups in academia
- innovating (applying existing ideas to new problems)
- creating websites

Q4: Unskilled AND Do Not Like to Do
- coding in R
- Western blots
- next gen sequencing
- handling animals for research
- inventing (coming up with brand new, unique ideas)

After you've created your own chart, you can look at each quadrant and consider what trends you see. Q1 contains your top interests as well as strengths, so you want to make sure that future jobs will give you the opportunity to act on those interests and use at least a few of these skills. Opposite this section, Q4 highlights your antipathies and/or weaknesses. You may want to avoid jobs that use these skills often: if you can't avoid such roles, then you'll have to commit to getting better at those skills.

By comparison, Q2 contains proven skills you can bring to a job, but since you don't enjoy those aspects, you may want to minimize how often you use them, or at least have more opportunities to use skills you like. Lastly, *Q3 is likely the section with the most opportunities for professional development.* How can you improve these skills to upgrade them to the more promising terrain of Q1?

TAKING A NEW DIRECTION

Over time, I realized that I enjoyed teaching, and I was becoming better at it. I had taught undergraduate-level chemistry labs in college, and I sought out more experience in grad school. I dedicated time each semester to teaching, taking classes on course design, and participating in a Preparing Future Faculty program. I was inspired by the student-focused, humanistic side of academic science. However, in the biomedical sciences, teaching is the weakest leg of the research–teaching–service trinity. Many faculty members use grant funds to buy out their teaching time. Graduate-level courses can also be nearly devoid of quality pedagogy. As I was ready to leave the research faculty career path, I could not envision many clear alternatives.

Some faculty would offer this common piece of career advice: you can do whatever you want as a faculty member after you obtain tenure. The idea is that associate and full professors could pursue interests in teaching and outreach, but before then you had to dedicate your full attention to getting a faculty job and attaining tenure. It's simple advice, but the reality of waiting ten years to use the skills you value most starts to feel like a dream deferred (see Langston Hughes's "Harlem" for how that ends).

While I was ready to examine other teaching careers in academia, I was stuck in that "primary path" mentality—that is, the idea that a PhD leads to just one kind of role. As such, I focused on near transfer, an analogous path to the one I was leaving: a career as a faculty member at a smaller, more teaching-focused college. Similar to research university faculty jobs, full-time teaching-intensive positions are quite competitive, so additional experience from postdoctoral training is increasingly required.

As I was starting to look at jobs after grad school, I did not fully comprehend the numbers game that I was facing. Postdoc positions are quite common across the US, but the vast majority are focused on research and not on teaching. Moreover, I had put down roots during graduate school and wanted to remain near my boyfriend's family and the local network of friends we had built. So the wide pool of postdoc positions shrank very quickly to two. Both were a combination of science research and teaching, one at a large research university (an Institutional Research and Academic Career Development Award [IRACDA] program) and the other at a nearby historically black university

(HBCU). I applied to both, and eventually I was hired at the HBCU. My postdoc position was set up as 75 percent biomedical research and 25 percent teaching and educational research. Funded by a grant from the Howard Hughes Medical Institute, the team I joined was studying how to incorporate authentic research experiences in an undergraduate biology laboratory course.

IDENTIFYING YOUR CAREER VALUES

An aspect of career development that students often overlook is better understanding the personal values that affect the work they want to do. We do discuss how much a job will pay or the working environment, but it can be illuminating to identify your values and establish priorities. Without knowing it while I was searching for postdoc positions, I was prioritizing location (staying near my future husband and his family) and professional development opportunities (building skills as a teacher and researcher). I had begun to identify my values.

Look through this list of values and consider which are in your top five or top ten. Then, reflect on what each value means to you and how it would look at your next job.

- Achievement
- Advancement opportunities
- Analytical thinking
- Attention to detail
- Autonomy
- Challenge
- Compensation
- Competition
- Consistency
- Creativity/innovation
- Diversity, equity, inclusion
- Empathy
- Expertise
- Family
- Geographic location
- Helping/service
- Leadership
- Learning
- Loyalty among colleagues
- Physicality (using your body)
- Prestige
- Professional development
- Relationships
- Respect
- Responsibility
- Risk
- Spirituality/religion
- Travel
- Using preferred skills
- Variety in the work
- Work environment
- Work–life harmony

American culture emphasizes compensation and promotional opportunities, but that may not align with your personal values and priorities. It's completely reasonable to pick a job that pays less than others if it will be more fulfilling in other ways or is located where you want to live. Conversely, it's also reasonable to pick a job that pays more and isn't your ideal workplace if it helps you meet a high priority of caring for your family. Looking back, I would add that I also wanted variety in the work and the ability to help others. Work–life harmony was important, too, and for me that meant that I would not bring work home with me. Lastly, I was seeking an environment that values diversity, equity, and inclusion where I could bring my full self to the work, being open with my co-workers and students about my personal life.

THE TICKING CLOCK OF THE FACULTY PATH

As soon as I started my postdoc position, a countdown clock started. Grad school is relatively flexible timewise. The stars may align, your research could go well, and you might finish your degree on the earlier side. Or, more commonly, you might hit unexpected roadblocks and toil on dead-end projects for too long. Either way, the nice part about grad school is that your timeline is malleable. Staying for one more year than you had originally thought can be frustrating, but at least it's a stable position.

In pursuing a faculty career, though, your life starts to revolve around more rigid timelines. Some systems in the US only allow an individual to be a postdoc for a total of five years, even if you change institutions. In that time, you have to create your research and/or teaching program that will get you a faculty job. Assistant professors have about six years to prepare their dossier for tenure, meaning they need to establish a track record of research and funding (and maybe teaching and service too). Associate professors have about another five to six years (depending on the institution) to demonstrate they're accomplished enough to be promoted to full professor. There have been numerous calls for more flexibility, particularly for individuals who want to start families, but progress has been inconsistent.

My postdoc position was funded for three years, though faculty at the HBCU were encouraging me to apply for faculty jobs after the first year. They were much more aware of the numbers game. If the number of faculty positions is low, then one approach is to maximize the number of applications you send out in every annual cycle. Even before I felt confident in my new research project and teaching responsibilities, I was being forced to think about next steps. The work itself was interesting and fulfilling. I was learning new science research skills to do experiments in cell culture. In the classroom, I co-led lab sections of an introductory biology course. We were improving the class by showing students how research really works. I found it gratifying to skip the cookbook-style labs and challenge students to hypothesize, test, and analyze. As part of our Howard Hughes Medical Institute–funded educational grant, we were assessing how this new lab experience was affecting student learning. In doing this work, I learned that I enjoy working in a relatively smaller field. Science research can be competitive, but in education research I felt I was finding more colleagues and collaborators. Though this HBCU wasn't as accepting of queer identities as I'd hoped, it was a place where I felt like I was starting to make an impact on students' lives.

However, like the tormented narrator in Edgar Allen Poe's *The Tell-Tale Heart*, I kept hearing the ticking of my career clock. Following the advice to start applying to faculty jobs, I started drafting my materials. CVs are relatively straightforward, and I felt knowledgeable enough to write a strong teaching statement. But every time I tried to write a research statement, I stared at a blank page, the blinking cursor marking the seconds slipping by. Slowly, I began to realize that I had writer's block for a reason: though I enjoyed teaching, I was not inspired by science research. I had already ventured from the career path of working at a large research institution to the side path of being faculty at a smaller institution. If that path ended abruptly, where would I go?

EXPLORING A VARIETY OF OPTIONS

One of the most powerful ways to spend your time in grad school is to regularly explore different job possibilities. In academia, this is relatively easy since many university offices have websites and most people in academia post their email address online. Start by poking around different sections of your local universities. Take notes on what sounds interesting (and why) and what doesn't (and why).

To get you started, here's a quick list of common university offices and positions (a longer version was posted on *Inside Higher Ed*'s *Carpe Careers* blog; McDonald 2018):

- Academic affairs and advising
- Academic administration: coordinating student programs (degrees, certificates, et al.)
- Professor of the practice roles: nontenured or tenure-like faculty roles that focus on teaching, research, or extension
- Teaching roles: lecturer, instructional development, online/hybrid curriculum designer
- Relationship building: alumni affairs, community outreach, corporate partnerships
- Diversity, equity, and inclusion: diversity officers, student centers
- Institutional research and assessment: how universities measure their effectiveness
- Library affairs
- Research administration: research integrity, development, technology transfer
- Student affairs: learning that happens outside the classroom

Importantly, any exploring needs to involve talking to a real-life human being. You can gain a surface-level understanding of jobs online, but a deeper understanding only comes from meeting people doing that work. You get to ask questions targeted toward your values. That's the beginning stages of networking—mutual exchanges of your experiences and interests. Many people enjoy helping others when they can, including sharing their stories and providing advice. At the end of every networking session, be sure to ask everyone, "Based on our conversation, who else do you think I should meet?"

A common refrain you may hear about how others landed their jobs is, "Well, I just got lucky." There's certainly some serendipity in every job search, but attributing success to luck makes it sound like you don't have any control. I prefer a quote often attributed to the Roman philosopher Seneca: "Luck is what happens when preparation meets opportunity." You don't have much control over when a job that fits your values will be posted or whether you'll get an interview. So, focus on areas under your control. Know your strengths and what you're looking for. Talk to a lot of people (aka network). Set ways to identify jobs of interest so you can apply quickly. When a colleague tells you that a fitting job at their institution is posting soon, you'll feel lucky too.

BLAZING YOUR OWN TRAIL

After the first year of my three-year postdoc, I started exploring different academic jobs in earnest. Looking for your next job while you're stably employed is much easier than waiting until your timeline is running out. Even if you're simply learning more about your options, explore as early as you can. I attended professional development workshops, browsed scientific journal career blogs, and analyzed LinkedIn profiles to understand what other PhDs were doing in academia (and beyond).

Job search sites ended up being a primary focus of my exploration. Databases such as Indeed give you a lot of filtering options so you can iteratively improve your searches. Here's an important lesson I learned: focus more on specific functions or skills, because job titles aren't consistent enough between universities to yield dependable results. You should also experiment with your search terms. For me "teach biology" generated a list of familiar lecturer and adjunct positions, but swapping "mentor" or "advise" for "teach" brought up many new options.

One option that came up was a career counselor position working with graduate students at my graduate alma mater. It aligned well with my desire to teach in group and individual settings. As much as I enjoy science, I had previously felt frustrated by students' lack of engagement with the class material. So teaching students about topics they care about (e.g., themselves, finding a job) was appealing. Plus, I had a strong knowledge of the institution and existing connections there. After some interviews and a teaching demonstration (leading a mock workshop), I officially left the tenure-track path and became a career counselor.

A few months into my new job, I realized that the ticking clock that haunted me had stopped. I was immensely relieved to be in a space where I felt like I could stay as long as I wanted. There were opportunities to utilize my understanding of the graduate student experience as well as my expertise in teaching. At the same time, I could learn new skills in developing advising relationships and program evaluation. I was also navigating a new side of academia; student affairs is more centralized and larger in scale compared to an academic department. When I saw new opportunities to gain experience, I tried to take them: joining a task force on assessing learning in higher education; change management in shifting my office and the students we serve to a new technology; managing a team.

I discovered that I could flip the script on what I knew of academic career transitions. I had been sticking to a path until I encountered a problem (and a simultaneous existential crisis). After stepping off that path, I could instead explore the rest of the untamed working world. Even in university career centers, the hierarchy of titles (assistant director, associate director, director, senior director) suggest another possible track. But I know now that I have the choice of following that path or continuing toward another destination. If you're not motivated by the pressure of a long-term plan and timeline, then just focus on doing your job well, developing new skills, and looking around to see where your next destination may be. Increasingly, the world is coming to view careers not as a linear, stepwise track but a more fluid and iterative process.

After working in career services for about three and a half years, I started feeling the itch for something new. As I got better at my work, my growth had slowed, and I was discovering that some of the best parts of advising grad students were hampered by the larger culture of academia. Similar to my previous transition, I started reflecting, exploring, and networking before I made my next move. I discovered a director-level position at a nearby school coordinating an umbrella PhD program for biomedical scientists. It offered me new ways to apply my current skills, manage a larger team, and work more with faculty while earning a higher salary. In my current role, I guide around a hundred PhD students through their first year of graduate school, serving as the guide that I didn't have through courses and research rotations. The five employees on my team provide the administrative support to my program and a few others in our office. I also lead mentor training opportunities for faculty, postdocs, and students. And my favorite part is that I can advocate for the need to keep making academic science a more accessible and inclusive space.

QUEER IN ACADEMIA

Colleges and universities overall have become more open and accepting spaces for queer people, but each institution is different. Even at the same university, individual departments can foster unique cultures. It's important to take stock of whether your identities are potential assets at a particular university or they could be a liability. I have the privilege of having an invisible minority identity. I get to choose if, when, and how to come out to people I meet. As an undergraduate and in grad school, I generally kept my identity and personal life to myself. It's part of the guarded nature I learned for self-preservation as a gay teen in high school.

Something they don't mention about coming out of the closet is that it's not a one-time event. Telling key people in your life necessitates difficult moments, but you have to choose on nearly a daily basis whether you want to come out to each individual you meet. When I go into different situations, I evaluate whether my queer identity could be beneficial. Do I want to be an "out and proud" gay man as a positive example for my students? Do I want to demonstrate a personal connection to diversity, equity, and inclusion issues in a way belied by my skin color and presentation of gender? If I'm not feeling particularly confident on a given day, I may keep my mouth shut. Other days I take less direct tactics, such as wearing a t-shirt with pride colors or purposely telling an anecdote about my husband and me. (I rarely use the word "partner," unless I'm not comfortable being out in a particular situation.)

It's difficult to evaluate from the outside, but some offices are actively trying to seek and retain people from underrepresented groups. For reasons rooted in structural discrimination and unconscious bias (among other isms), many institutions still have difficulty recruiting a workforce as diverse as the population they serve. Students often ask for better representation in their academic administrators, but that's a complicated issue to resolve. There are limited ways to recruit specifically for people from groups historically excluded from academia, and applicants are disincentivized from revealing that they're from a minority group since it could evoke bias.

My past few jobs in academia have been at offices with strong commitments to promoting DEI. One of them has programs to promote scientists from underrepresented groups. As mentioned earlier, I was hesitant to out myself while interviewing for these jobs, but in hindsight, talking about my gay identity may have been an asset. I had some knowledge and skills for DEI work with students, but it was still in Q3 of my skills chart (unskilled but still like doing). However, I now think that sharing from my personal experiences would have been more of an asset to fill some of those skills gaps. Many institutions are asking more questions about how candidates engage with DEI topics, so everyone should think about how their identities, experiences, and training contribute to creating a welcoming space for all to be successful.

CONCLUSION

The idea of a linear career path is enticing but simplistic, if not actually misleading. It would be nice to have security in knowing with certainty that if you took particular steps you would end up at a desired destination. However, most careers don't work like that. Even faculty careers aren't that straightforward: you could check all of the boxes and still not land that assistant professor job or, ultimately, tenure.

In reality, most of us are wandering through the wilderness, carving our own paths. We may follow well-trodden trails for some time, and we may leave those trails when we decide they no longer help us move toward our next destination. Sometimes your path only becomes clear when you look back to see where you came from. Ten years from now, emerging professionals will ask you about your path. You can oblige them by describing the steps you took, but make sure they understand that there are many ways to get to a destination, and that your outcome wasn't "just lucky." Instead, you can tell them that you charted your skills, mapped how your values and identities fit, and gave yourself license to venture into new experiences.

REFERENCES

Bolles, Richard, and Katherine Brooks. 2021. *What Color is Your Parachute? Job-Hunter's Workbook*. Berkeley: Ten Speed Press.

McDonald, David A. 2018. "Academic Careers You May Not Have Considered." *Inside Higher Ed*. https://www.insidehighered.com/advice/2018/05/21/suggestions-alt-ac-careers-may-be-overlooked-opinion.

2

"THIS ISN'T WHAT I THOUGHT IT WOULD BE"

Building New Identities and Skills in the Academy

HEATHER DWYER AND KATHARINE P. WALSH

This chapter describes how two PhDs, one in the humanities and one in STEM, used our graduate school experience to build different skills and identities than those we had originally envisioned when electing to pursue graduate study.

We met shortly after completing our PhD programs, when we accepted positions as educational developers. As novices to the field of educational development, we spent a lot of time discussing how we ended up where we were rather than on the more traditional tenure-track path. Over time, we realized that we shared similar experiences as doctoral students, despite being from different academic disciplines and attending different institutions: we both encountered push factors driving us out of our academic departments and pull factors encouraging our participation in educational development. Heather pursued a PhD in ecology with the original goal of contributing to the field of conservation biology as a tenure-track professor. Katie pursued a PhD in European history, intending to teach history at the college level. Despite these intentions and because of our graduate school experiences, we each changed course and decided to pursue different professional roles in higher education.

Educational developers often work at university centers for teaching and learning (CTLs) and provide pedagogical support to instructors. In our current roles, we offer various programming and services to improve teaching and learning in higher education. As associate director for teaching, learning, and inclusion of a CTL at a private doctoral university, Heather is responsible for developing and facilitating faculty programs focused on diversity, equity, inclusion, and justice; offering intensive teaching institutes; and engaging in research and scholarship on educational development. Katie worked as a senior teaching consultant in a teaching center for a private doctoral university and recently accepted a position at the same institution as the associate director of learning support programs at the Student Academic Success Center. In both positions, Katie has worked to create supportive learning environments for students, whether through conducting researching on teaching and learning, helping faculty design their courses, or—most recently—managing a staff of undergraduate tutors and supplemental instruction (SI) leaders who provide peer-assisted learning in historically challenging courses.

Pursuing educational development required building new skills and shifting our perceptions of what it means to be a successful academic. As our narratives show, this process was not easy, but in the end, it was extremely valuable and rewarding. Our chapter highlights the need to effect change in the graduate curriculum and provide better support for graduate students so that future graduate students may be spared some of the struggles we experienced. We also offer suggestions for graduate students questioning their academic identities and seeking alternative career paths.

The dialogue format below allows us to explore similarities and differences in our experiences. We find the similarities remarkable given that we came from different disciplines and institutions, and given that we had contrasting motivations for attending graduate school. As such, we believe that our experiences will resonate with many of our readers.

DIALOGUE: GRADUATE SCHOOL EXPECTATIONS VERSUS REALITY

KATIE: *How did your expectations of graduate school prove to be different in reality?*
HEATHER: I don't think I had explicit expectations for grad school, but my experience was certainly not what I thought it would be. I enrolled in graduate school because it seemed like a natural next step after a positive and successful undergraduate experience. As an undergraduate, I had a supportive research mentor, a network of strong friendships, nearby family, and

familiarity with the geographic area. I excelled in my coursework, I gained some research experience, and I believed the field of conservation biology to be an urgent and worthwhile pursuit. In short, I thought my identity of "successful student" would seamlessly evolve into successful career academic. I expected that I would succeed in my coursework, that I would connect easily with my peers, and that I would pursue research questions I found interesting. Instead, I found myself unhappy and drifting in my graduate program for a long time.

KATIE: I also thought that I could translate my identity of "successful student" into future success, but my version of a successful career academic was more focused on teaching than research. I attended a small, private liberal arts college for my undergraduate education. My history department had three professors in it, and my largest class was twenty-five students. I got to know every professor personally—even those outside of my department—and I saw them regularly in the dining hall or elsewhere on campus. I loved this experience and I wanted to be just like my professors when I "grew up." I knew that graduate school would focus heavily on research and that I would need to play the research game to obtain the PhD and become a professor. But I underestimated how challenging and undesirable the game would be and how long I would have to play it.

KATIE: *You mentioned that you expected to easily connect with your peers. How were your interactions with your graduate colleagues?*

HEATHER: This was a big struggle for me; I had trouble identifying with my peers. Many of them had advantages I held as an undergrad but then lost upon entering grad school: they were familiar with the geographic area, had prior industry experience, and/or had relatives in the field. All of them seemed to have a deep passion for the subject matter which, if I had been truly honest with myself, I lacked. I also struggled with my perception that my graduate program had a preestablished cultural identity. It felt like certain social characteristics were expected, and cohort-building events reinforced those expectations. For example, our new student orientation involved a costumed dance party, which was reprised throughout the years. I felt I had to be a certain kind of gregarious extrovert to fit in. There is nothing wrong with costumed dance parties, but it seemed like enthusiastic participation in these types of events was the only way to make social connections with my peers. I could feel myself trying so hard to pretend to be someone I'm not.

I should also mention that ecology is not a very racially diverse field for graduate studies; it lags behind other STEM fields in terms of representation across racial groups and is about 90 percent white (National Science Foundation 2018; Ostriker et al. 2011). As a biracial person who often passes as white, it is hard for me to know how much this lack of racial diversity impacted my sense of belonging. Overall, much of my experience involved feeling pressure to be a certain type of person, and I am still processing the constellation of factors that may have caused me to feel this way.

HEATHER: *What was your experience with your graduate school peers?*

KATIE: I struggled with this, too. I had imagined a collective, supportive cohort who might help each other through their various ups and downs. Instead, aside from a few close friends, there was a lot of competition between myself and my fellow grad students. In a field like history, where funding opportunities are scarce, we were all vying for the same fellowships and grants, and for the attention of the graduate faculty—many of whom were influential in the awarding of fellowships and grants. When visiting scholars gave talks, faculty applauded the graduate students who attended these talks, read the scholars' work, and asked insightful questions. I found it hard to engage with these talks on top of my coursework, research, and teaching responsibilities. As a graduate student in the humanities, almost all my funding came in the form of teaching assistant positions. I loved this, but it left little time for my coursework and research. My peers didn't appear to experience the same struggles. They seemed to have read all the assigned books (spoiler alert: many of them were just reading the reviews), and they sounded confident and prepared in class discussions. Professors responded very favorably to these students.

When I asked some of my peers how they dealt with all the competing demands, their advice was to put significantly less effort into my teaching because teaching would not get me fellowships or publications, and they didn't think that it was that important for tenure-track jobs. These sorts of comments reflected their perception of teaching rather than reality. A recent study of teaching effectiveness on the academic job market found that hiring committees generally do value teaching (Walsh et al. 2022). These exchanges with my peers reinforced the idea that my version of a successful academic was different from theirs, and I started to wonder if my version existed at all. I considered leaving many times; however, I thought that if I could just keep playing the research game, then eventually I could get the tenure-track job. Plus, there were days that I really enjoyed my research, and I didn't want to look like I had quit the PhD program.

KATIE: *Did you ever think about leaving graduate school?*

HEATHER: Yes. My coursework was much more difficult than anything I had experienced in undergrad, and it seemed like everyone understood and performed with ease except me. After my second year, I started really questioning whether I was in the wrong field. To explore other options, I participated in a summer program in architecture, a profession I'd always been curious about, at another university. While I enjoyed the program, I learned that architecture wasn't right for me either. This experience was helpful for quelling my curiosity, but it didn't do much to reduce my impostor feelings, which worsened after I failed my qualifying exams the first time through. When it was time to start thinking about a dissertation project, I didn't have enough foundational knowledge to know what kinds of research questions might be appropriate to pursue, so I simply relied on my advisor's suggestions. As a result, I didn't really understand or care about the questions I was investigating. The work felt tedious and overwhelming, and like I was chasing the elusive identity of a successful academic, but I didn't know how to achieve it. Moreover, I was too embarrassed to ask for help. I thought these problems were my own fault and that I needed to resolve them on my own.

HEATHER: *Did you experience impostor syndrome, and if so, how did you deal with it?*

KATIE: Absolutely. I often wondered how I had been accepted into graduate school when my skills and interests seemed so misaligned with those of my professors and peers. I found it hard to define success, especially once I saw that the predominant view of a successful academic did not include teaching. I understand why: at a research university, faculty jobs depend (primarily) on their research. During my first experience as a teaching assistant (TA), I taught four recitation sections of twenty students each, and I graded papers and exams for all eighty students. A few weeks into the course, it became apparent that I would need to be an interpreter for my students, translating the highly academic version of history presented by the professor into more concrete knowledge. I loved teaching my recitation sections and I felt successful doing it. One day, the instructor told me, "I see that you really enjoy teaching, but don't share that too widely. People will think that you aren't focused enough on your research and may not consider you for grants and fellowships." I felt like I was getting the message from both my peers and my professors that I didn't belong. And, like you, I suffered in silence because I didn't know who I could turn to. I didn't want anyone to know that I was struggling because I didn't want to appear weak and unworthy of the money my department was investing in me. From a practical and financial standpoint, I knew that my department could easily find someone else to fill my spot if I couldn't cut it in the program.

Reflection

Clearly, our previously established identities as successful students were shaken upon entering graduate school. We felt isolated because we didn't fit what we perceived to be the desired graduate student identity. Katie's love of teaching separated her from her peers and professors; she felt pressured to performatively play the research game, in part by downplaying her identity as an educator. Heather's sense of isolation stemmed from feeling disconnected to the culture and content of her discipline. We both lacked a sense of belonging within our departments and among our colleagues. We grappled with the perception that we were the problem and it was our responsibility to fix it by conforming to our program's expectations—or quit.

Now, upon reflection, we recognize some of the structural barriers that caused each of us to have similarly negative experiences. One barrier was the absence of supportive mentorship and guidance for students like us who didn't fit the traditional academic success metric. We questioned our interest in research and expressed interest in other aspects of an academic identity (e.g., teaching) rather than subscribing to the traditional research-focused approach. Another barrier was a lack of opportunities for us to connect with other students outside of coursework and research. Class and research groups often imposed prescribed social expectations and/or fostered competition among students rather than collaboration and support. In short, we lacked a sense of belonging.

DIALOGUE: RESPONDING TO DISILLUSIONMENT

HEATHER: *What were your initial reactions to these feelings of struggle, disappointment, and disillusionment and how did you handle them?*

KATIE: I didn't know how to deal with these feelings. I talked with friends outside of grad school and with some of my undergraduate instructors. They all thought that I was doing great. They told me that graduate school was challenging, but they were confident that I would succeed. I didn't tell them I felt like an outcast or that I had seriously considered leaving the program many times. I also didn't share these feelings with any of the professors in my program for fear that they would view me as weak or unable to handle graduate school. My true ambition was to teach, but I was getting the message that the best teachers were not necessarily the best scholars. I certainly saw that in the structure of the department. Some of the instructors I admired and learned the most from were teaching-track faculty. They weren't eligible for tenure, and they didn't have many (if any) publications—likely because they had the heaviest teaching loads. Their jobs seemed appealing from a teaching standpoint, but I also saw how they were treated as second-class citizens (e.g., they couldn't vote at department meetings), and they didn't have the job security of tenure. Plus, they really valued teaching and were surrounded by colleagues who didn't share that value. I worried that if I pursued teaching-track positions, the outsider feelings I felt as a graduate student would deepen.

HEATHER: I buried my disillusionment at first. I knew deep down that things weren't working, but I didn't know what else to do. I figured it might get better, or if it didn't, at least I could teach when I graduated. In this sense, my journey was different from yours. I didn't set out to be an educator, but when I had my first TA appointment, I discovered that I really loved teaching, in part because it was so unlike my research experience. The TA coordinators (who served as mentors) were supportive, my teaching responsibilities were clear and deadline-oriented, and my fellow TAs were mostly from other departments, so I was free from the social disconnect I had developed with my own cohort. I also found the act of teaching to be gratifying, as it involved supporting students in their academic pursuits. Like you, though, I received messaging that scholars whose primary focus was teaching were not real scientists.

HEATHER: *Teaching felt like a bit of an escape to me. Did you also turn to options outside your immediate departmental research sphere?*

KATIE: Yes. I eventually started to strategically manage my disillusionment by pursuing opportunities outside of my department. I started volunteering for positions that I thought I might be good at in organizations that seemed interesting. The perpetual feeling that I wasn't good at research took a real toll, and I longed for spaces where I could feel successful. I wasn't sure how these different positions might benefit me as a tenure-track professor, but it was becoming increasingly apparent that the traditional tenure-track job probably wasn't the right fit for me anyway. I didn't know what other jobs or career paths I might pursue, but it seemed like a good idea to expand my network outside of my department and to add additional skill sets to my toolkit. First, I became active in the graduate student organization. I started organizing meetings within my department and eventually became the departmental representative to the larger, campuswide organization. This highlighted my organizational skills and my ability to collaborate with people in different academic disciplines and roles (e.g., faculty and staff). It made me aware of broader graduate student issues and it revealed other ways to engage in the higher education space. Second, I got connected with the university's CTL. Initially, I engaged as a workshop participant, but eventually I facilitated workshops at the campuswide orientation for new TAs. All of these engagements took time away from research, but they showed me that I had valuable skills and broadened my orbit by connecting me with people who weren't exclusively focused on historical research. My work with the CTL was incredibly fulfilling because it allowed me to really lean into my passion for teaching with other people who shared it. In hindsight, this strategy to pursue professional development opportunities outside of my department was a good one because it afforded me a chance to build and demonstrate professional skills such as organizing committees and working with others outside of my discipline, and ultimately, it led to a career-changing fellowship opportunity at the CTL.

HEATHER: I also pursued opportunities for professional development, but at first they all lay in the teaching realm. For a while, I entertained the idea of becoming faculty at a teaching-focused institution, and I attended teaching workshops and institutes in support of that, both within and external to my university. By about midway through my grad school career, I had gained enough experience to join the TA Consultant Program, a peer teaching consulting program for graduate students run through the university's CTL. Here I truly found belonging: the program supervisor was a caring, supportive mentor to me; my graduate student colleagues were welcoming and valued the skills I brought to the group. They were from all different disciplines, which meant they brought many different perspectives and helped me think outside the narrow box I had inhabited thus far. For example, I first learned from them the genuine importance of identity, diversity, and intersectionality in a higher education context, something that hadn't been actively addressed in my academic department. Finding this nurturing community brought me a profound sense of relief, and I spent a lot of time on my TA Consultant responsibilities. I learned foundational pedagogical principles that had not been part of my formal TA training. I practiced consulting, creating interactive workshops, managing peers, and collaboratively producing deliverables on a deadline. I also began to explore current literature on teaching and learning in higher education. Importantly, the program was structured as a community of practice, which distributed power and decision-making among the group. (The program is described in more detail by Rodriguez and Silverman in chapter 16 of this book, "Horizontal Mentoring: The Positive Impact of a Diverse Graduate Student Professional Development Community.")

HEATHER: *How was your experience with the CTL career-changing?*

KATIE: Through my involvement with the CTL, I learned about its graduate teaching fellowship, which gave graduate students the opportunity to TA for a faculty development course, to facilitate workshops on topics like providing effective feedback and designing course syllabi, and to conduct observations of graduate student instructors. I jumped at this opportunity because I needed funding and I also saw this as a chance to continue developing new skills and knowledge. Winning this fellowship was a sort of golden ticket for me, but I didn't know that at the time. When I shared my fellowship news with my department, they were not even aware that the fellowship existed, and some of them seemed unaware of the CTL itself. Unlike research fellowships, which were very much celebrated within the department, mine didn't receive recognition. There wasn't a departmental email congratulating me, and few of my peers seemed excited for me. Most of them thought that it sounded like another year of a TA position, which would ultimately detract from my research. In some ways, they were right; however, the fellowship also afforded me new opportunities, skills, and professional connections. Working at the CTL introduced me to the field of educational development—a field I didn't know existed prior to entering graduating school—and to jobs and people that aligned with my interests and skill sets.

Reflection

Our feelings of disillusionment led us to explore options outside the constraints of our departments. Some of these were intentional and strategic. For example, Heather's participation in professional development for community college instructors was in direct preparation for a potential position at a teaching-focused institution. In other cases, the gains of our explorations were not always apparent at the time, such as Katie winning the graduate teaching fellowship and working at the CTL. We did not foresee how the combination of skills we acquired through these experiences, alongside the advantages of a doctorate, might ultimately lead to new professional positions, but we pursued these opportunities anyway. And we encourage graduate students to do the same. As we somewhat aimlessly explored these various opportunities, both of us were searching for feelings of belonging and success that our previous attempts at conformity had not given us. We continued to seek them out by interacting with other communities and by building and exercising different skills. These experiences allowed us to begin to redefine academic success for ourselves.

DIALOGUE: IDENTITY SHIFTS

HEATHER: *How did your ideas about identity grow and change during graduate school?*

KATIE: As discussed, I experienced a sort of identity crisis early on because I identified not only as a historian but also as an educator; yet I didn't find much support for the educator identity among my faculty and peers. However, I didn't have other identities or career paths to explore, and no one in my department seemed to know what other options existed for PhDs in history. Most people who pursue a PhD in history plan on a career in the professoriate. There aren't obvious industry options, and even adjacent fields (e.g., museum work, archivists) have their own specialized training. Occasionally, I would hear about alumni who worked as curators or archivists or who got involved with local politics, but these examples always felt like one-offs, and "archivist" and "politician" weren't identities that I aspired to. So, a huge part of my challenge was figuring out what other potential careers existed for someone with a PhD in history. Honestly, at this stage, I was thinking more about a job and less about a career. I had been a graduate student for close to seven years, and I wanted a stable job with regular hours, ideally in an educational setting. I applied to a wide variety of positions, including director of a women's studies center, educational technologist positions at teaching centers, and teaching positions at private K–12 schools.

HEATHER: In contrast, my discipline did offer various alternatives to a traditional tenure-track position, in industry, government agencies, and nonprofits. However, I didn't seriously consider these positions because I didn't think I had the experience or expertise to obtain them. That left the more academic pathway, but I knew I would not be happy in a tenure-track faculty position at a research university. I also discovered that even at teaching-focused institutions, full-time positions are extremely competitive, and the freeway flier lifestyle of an adjunct can be taxing in many ways.

This thought process was accompanied by shifts in my own professional identity. I had to reimagine how I defined success in an academic career, which sometimes involved swallowing my pride. Academia is laden with elitism and judgment, and I was certainly not immune to that. At first, the prospect of becoming a community college instructor was difficult for me to consider. Now that I know more about students, instruction, structural inequity, and the limitations of renowned, well-resourced institutions, I appreciate the value of being a community college instructor. However, it was hard for me to see at the time.

HEATHER: *We both realized that our limited view of a successful academic career was not working and struggled to figure out other options. Was there a moment where you made an explicit decision to not pursue tenure-track jobs?*

KATIE: No, there wasn't a clear moment; the process was much more gradual.

In my final years of graduate school, I realized that there weren't a lot of jobs at small, private liberal arts colleges. In fact, there weren't a lot of jobs, period. I had witnessed several extremely successful peers struggle to get the few jobs that did exist. Many of them accepted positions they weren't especially excited about because they viewed the job as a steppingstone to another job. They moved themselves, and in some cases their families, to places where they didn't want to live because they intended to move again once they found a better job.

In my final year, there were three tenure-track positions for early modern British historians, none of which were in places I wanted to live. I was recently married, had hopes of starting a family, and after years of moving for college and graduate school, I wanted to stay in one (desirable) place for a while. I knew of several academic families who made it work with long-distance relationships, weekend visits, and so forth, but this lifestyle wasn't appealing to me. I never made an explicit decision to not apply to tenure-track jobs; there just weren't any desirable jobs for me to apply for.

However, even if there had been desirable jobs, I still questioned whether I would be happy in a tenure-track position. One pivotal moment was getting my first journal article published. After more than a year of reviews and revisions, I got the news that it would finally appear in print. I remember feeling this huge sense of relief. I called my husband to share the news and he was ecstatic—much more so than I. He asked if I was excited and I said, "Yeah, I guess. I'm just glad that I don't have to keep working on this thing anymore." I had achieved the highest marker of success for an academic—at least as defined by my faculty and peers—and I wasn't excited about it. I was just relieved that it was over. But I quickly realized that, if I wanted a tenure-track job, it wasn't really over. In fact, it was just beginning. To earn tenure at most universities, I would need to publish more articles and ultimately a book—all while teaching multiple courses and likely serving on several campus committees. And I would be doing all this while (hopefully) starting a family. It just didn't seem possible or desirable.

HEATHER: There was no singular moment for me either, but I didn't get as far as you did in terms of monitoring the job market for tenure-track positions. By the time it came to seriously thinking about applying to jobs, I only really considered positions in educational development. I had seen the impact the demands of tenure-track positions had on the personal lives of professors. For example, it was normal for some faculty to come into the lab on Sundays. It was also common that faculty would work—answering emails, grading papers, writing grants—most evenings. Their passion and satisfaction in their work may have made this sacrifice worthwhile for them, but I knew that would not be the case for me.

More importantly, I was excited about the prospect of being a full-time educational developer. I had accumulated what I'd consider deep, extended practice designing programs, managing colleagues, and consulting with university instructors on their teaching. Additionally, most CTLs are centrally located within their institutions with staff from all different disciplines. I had seen how a team with varied and diverse disciplinary perspectives could strengthen pedagogical support programming. I applied for a few openings and quickly landed a full-time position at a well-known CTL at a research university.

Reflection

Both of us faced challenges harmonizing our personal and professional identities. When most of our faculty and peers didn't share our perception of a successful academic, we felt isolated, and we questioned ourselves and our career choices. Nevertheless, we persisted! We looked to adjacent jobs and careers that seemed to be a better fit for our professional interests and identities. In doing so, we started to move away from the tenure-track identity and toward a somewhat vague professional identity. Though the uncertainty involved in this process was intimidating, it felt right. Toward the end of our graduate school career, our personal identities and values became more salient as we both questioned whether the demands of a tenure-track position were compatible with our desired way of living. These personal values helped to reshape our professional identities and views of success.

Both of us have now been in educational development and out of our respective disciplines for close to eight years, so the possibility of pursuing tenure-track jobs no longer realistically exists. This process was less about us making a deliberate choice not to be a tenure-track professor and more about a gradual process of finding fulfilling academic careers and identities in different higher education spaces. As educational developers we still use our academic training (e.g., critical thinking, research, presentation skills) every day, but apply them in different ways. Each of us feels that we have redefined what it means to be a successful academic within academia.

CONCLUSION

In closing, we'd each like to offer a takeaway of what we've learned by comparing notes.

Katie

There needs to be a broader definition for what constitutes a successful career after the PhD, whether that be within or beyond academia.

The disparity between the number of students enrolled in graduate programs and the number of available tenure-track positions is just too big. This is especially true for disciplines like history that don't have a built-in industry option. What would broadening the definition of success look like?

For graduate students, it would mean entering a PhD program with an openness to professional development rather than a laser focus on obtaining a tenure-track position. It would mean viewing your graduate school career as an opportunity to build a robust toolkit of skills. One piece of advice that I was repeatedly given when applying for jobs was to consider how I could retool my history-based knowledge and skills to fit alternative positions. For example, I could use my teaching experience to, in theory, make myself marketable for jobs at a CTL. However, what made me marketable for CTL positions was my experience working at a CTL. It wasn't a matter of retooling academic knowledge and skills; it was a matter of adding more tools to my toolkit. I encourage graduate students to adopt this mentality early on so that they have the time to build a robust toolkit. It may be hard for you to find support for this approach—as Heather and I experienced—but my hope is that, over time, departments will also broaden their definition of success to better support graduate students pursuing careers that aren't the traditional faculty path.

For graduate advisors and higher education administrators, this means realizing that there are myriad meaningful career paths for graduate students, both inside and outside of the academy. Rather than making everyone jump through the same traditional academic hoops, consider what knowledge, skills, and experiences would benefit students professionally and recognize that students likely have different career goals. In my program, all European historians were expected to have reading proficiency in two languages—regardless of research topic or career aspirations—so I spent several years taking Italian and French classes in order to pass the proficiency requirement. It was never made clear to me how or why these languages might prove useful to my professional pursuits; it felt more like checking a box than becoming multilingual. My language skills have not been primary to my work; it may have been more beneficial for me to take a course on basic programming or interpreting data, for example. Broadening the definition of success for graduate students means creating opportunities to develop nontraditional knowledge and skills and removing any stigma when they take advantage of these. It means celebrating teaching fellowships as much as research fellowships. It means connecting current graduate students with alumni in other fields, potentially allowing for the possibility of internships or other sorts of field experiences. And it means viewing these graduate students and their eventual professional choices as equally successful as those who obtained tenure-track positions.

Heather

The emotional journey that accompanies these identity shifts is ongoing.

Much of what we've discussed addresses the complex feelings we experienced as we questioned and redefined our academic identities. These feelings did not necessarily resolve upon finding a new academic home. Both of us continue to grapple with unresolved emotions as we reflect on our past and look toward the future.

My impostor feelings never fully went away. Even now, it is difficult for me to tease out the various factors that contributed to my struggles as a graduate student. Though I'm aware, in principle, of ways in which structural barriers might have made things harder for me, I still wrestle with the idea that it was *my* responsibility—to step up, study harder, be more extroverted, ask for help proactively, assert myself more. Though I don't encounter those feelings as much in my current position, the impostor phenomenon is very real in educational developers and contributes to feelings of stress and lowered self-esteem (Rudenga and Gravett 2019). The reflective process of discussing these experiences in writing this chapter has proven helpful for coming to terms with lingering emotions of self-doubt. I can now better see how individual experience is shaped by institutional factors. I encourage graduate students who experience similar emotional fallout to take the time to unpack and identify the factors that contributed to these feelings so that they may avoid lasting self-blame. I also call upon academic departments to address the fact that graduate students often struggle with identity and belonging, to acknowledge that these feelings may be the result of structural barriers, and to provide support to reduce feelings of isolation.

FINAL REFLECTION

In closing, we think it is important to recognize that the process of finding one's way continues. Unlike tenure-track positions, educational development does not ascribe to a single trajectory, so it is often unclear how early-career educational developers move up in their professions, and this ambiguity may pose ongoing emotional or logistical challenges. Though we have embraced the fact that professional identities aren't fixed, the lack of structure and perceived direction can be frustrating. Indeed, to grow professionally and personally, it is ever important to keep building our toolboxes so that we are equipped for the professional opportunities that come our way in the future. Katie's recent move from a teaching center to a student success center is an example of the kind of move one can make with a robust toolbox.

Ultimately, we hope our stories help readers recognize that if they struggle with belonging in academia or are uncertain about alternatives to traditional faculty careers, they are not alone. We encourage graduate students in particular to seek out cohorts and experiences beyond their department where they can develop new skills and knowledge, find affirmation for their personal and professional values, and pursue roles that offer growth and fulfillment on their own terms.

ACKNOWLEDGMENTS

Heather would like to thank Drs. Ann Chang and Mikaela Huntzinger for their support and encouragement as she found her professional pathway. Katie would like to thank Dr. Liann Tsoukas for being a guiding light during the challenging days of graduate school. She would also like to thank Matt Walsh and Don and Marti Phelps for their unending support and for always believing in her.

REFERENCES

National Science Foundation, National Center for Science and Engineering Statistics. 2019. *Doctorate Recipients from U.S. Universities: 2018*. Special Report NSF 20-301. Alexandria, VA: National Science Foundation. https://ncses.nsf.gov/pubs/nsf20301/report.

Ostriker, Jeremiah P., Kuh, Charlotte V., and James A. Voytuk, eds. 2011. *A Data-Based Assessment of Research Doctorate Programs in the United States*. Washington, DC: National Academies Press. Available from https://doi.org/10.17226/12994.

Rudenga, Kristin J., and Emily O. Gravett. 2019. "Impostor Phenomenon in Educational Developers." *To Improve the Academy: A Journal of Educational Development* 38, no. 1. https://doi.org/10.3998/tia.17063888.0038.107.

Walsh, Katharine, Laura Pottmeyer, Chad Hershock, and Deborah Meizlish. 2022. "How Search Committees Assess Teaching: Lessons for CTLs." *To Improve the Academy: A Journal of Educational Development* 42 (2): 3. https://doi.org/10.3998/tia.583.

3

GETTING FROM HERE TO THERE

Navigating Career Crossroads as a Black Woman Scientist

DIEDRA M. WRIGHTING

In the last year of my postdoc in diabetes research at the Broad Institute (a collaboration between Harvard and MIT), I reconnected with my master's thesis advisor and, in an unexpected flood of vulnerability, told her everything. I shared that I was struggling to balance being a wife and new mother of twin boys while maintaining a career as a productive scientist. I shared my uncertainty about being a competitive applicant for faculty jobs, given that my postdoc had not been productive. And I confided the various barriers that I was experiencing as a Black woman striving to progress within my field—for example, getting the informed mentoring I needed and navigating spaces where I was the only woman of color, which made me question whether I belonged. For over a decade leading up to this moment, I had envisioned a future as a tenure-track faculty member running my own research group. But now, I was no longer sure whether that path was viable or even desirable.

At the end of my long diatribe, my mentor made one simple yet profound statement: "It sounds like you are at a crossroads." This statement catalyzed a sense of certainty within me. Before her comment, I hadn't recognized that I had entered the terrain of a career crossroads, but once I knew where I was, I was able to set a clear goal to get through that new intersection and move more intentionally in a direction that rekindled my passion for my work in a situation I found appealing. While it felt daunting and challenging to consider heading in a new direction, at the same time, our conversation felt freeing and empowering.

This essay presents a retrospective view of how I navigated this career crossroads to ultimately arrive at a place where I am thriving and excited to go to work each day as executive director of ADVANCE Office of Faculty Development at Northeastern University. In this role, I develop and implement programming that promotes career advancement for faculty at all career stages. The office was founded by a National Science Foundation Institutional Transformation grant in 2008 to foster institutional change that promotes gender equity in STEM faculty positions. Award institutions agree to make the initiative a permanently funded part of the university once the grant ends. Thus, under my leadership, the office continues to promote diversity, equity, inclusion, and belonging and has expanded its focus to serve all faculty.

In what follows, I outline the deliberate and important steps I took to arrive here by moving in a new direction that was right for me and my family. Some of these steps included developing a vision, reconnecting with my mentors, dealing with my emotions in order to adopt a more open and flexible mindset, tapping into and expanding my professional network, and mapping my transferable skills. These actions contributed to a "career GPS" that helped me navigate the different turns that arose along my career transition journey. In writing this essay, I came to see that my decision points were clear; at the time, however, the way forward seemed murky and was fraught with emotion. Each time I deviated from my intended path, I felt a sense of loss, which has never quite healed. There are inevitably moments I circle back and wonder about the roads not taken, or all the "what ifs." At the same time, I also found fulfillment and new communities when I embarked on my new career journey. My hope is that my story will inspire professionals in academia to seek out mentors, lean into their strengths (especially those unique to their intersectional identities), and follow their passion to career satisfaction—even when it involves following a previously unknown or unimagined path.

ARRIVING AT THE CROSSROADS

In hindsight, one of the reasons I did not recognize I was poised at a career crossroads was that I was subconsciously holding on too tightly to my identity as a scientist. At the time of that conversation with my mentor, I did not realize how much of my identity revolved around being a practicing scientist. As a high school student, I was intrigued by anatomy and physiology and considered becoming a physician. In college, I was accepted into the National Institutes of Health–funded Bridges to the Baccalaureate Program (Bridges Program), a collaboration between City College of San Francisco and San Francisco State University (SFSU) designed to increase the participation of people from historically marginalized groups in STEM careers. This program not only provided me a view into the daily lives of scientists and gave me my first experience in a research lab, but also placed me in a formative relationship with a faculty member who would become a lifelong mentor. By the end of my postdoc, I had worked as an active scientist for nearly twenty years, designing and executing experiments and making discoveries on topics ranging from cancer and rare diseases of the eye to iron metabolism and diabetes, all through the use of model organisms and cell systems. The common denominator across all of my projects was the desire to understand the underlying mechanisms of disease.

My first career crossroads came toward the end of my time as an undergraduate. I was premed but found myself contemplating a career in research instead. By this point, I was excited by the idea of making discoveries in the laboratory that would help people beyond what I thought physicians could do. While I had heard of physician scientists, I thought I would be better off choosing one of those identities, not both. I chose scientist and, based on advice from my mentor from the Bridges Program, joined the master's program in cell and molecular biology at SFSU to build my résumé and compile a more compelling graduate school application. To my surprise and delight, I was accepted into the Biological and Biomedical Sciences PhD program at Harvard Medical School.

As a graduate student, my main focus was the laboratory; at the same time, I explored other activities, including teaching and promoting the professional development of undergraduate students and my graduate student peers. For example, I served as a mentor to undergraduate students in the Summer Honors Undergraduate Research Program, a ten-week summer program designed to give research experiences to promising future scientists and physicians from underrepresented groups. I also served on the leadership team for the Minority Biomedical Scientists of Harvard (MBSH). The MBSH leadership team organized opportunities for students in our graduate program to present their work, invited guest lecturers who would engage in intimate conversations about their lives as scientists with the membership, and facilitated a buddy program for incoming students to receive support from senior students. I also taught or served as a teaching fellow in several undergraduate science courses. Finally, I created a speaker series called Dinner with a Mentor. This series was an opportunity for small groups of students to meet scientists who held a variety of positions both inside and outside of academia.

During the time I hosted Dinner with a Mentor in my fifth and sixth years, I was seriously considering transitioning into a different sector. Fortunately, my institution's career services office offered a career exploration boot camp called the Career Explorations Working Group (now Career Jump Start), which helped me recognize possible career paths that could utilize my skills and play to my strengths. Ultimately, I chose to remain in academia and joined a research group as a postdoc. When my master's thesis advisor helped me realize that I was at yet another crossroads at the end of my postdoc, I drew upon what I learned in the Career Explorations Working Group to proceed methodically through that new intersection. I finally realized that while my dominant identity was that of a scientist, I was also a mentor to underrepresented minority (URM) students like me who were often navigating spaces where they were new to science and the only person, or one of few people, who looked like them in their research group, department, or program. My core belief was that they belonged in science; all they needed were the tools and the right mentors to successfully navigate the world of research. This mission was so ingrained that I did not always realize I was living it. Ultimately, I shifted from a URM scientist navigating a science career to a URM scientist who helped others navigate their careers.

MAPPING A DESTINATION

Once I realized that I was at another crossroads, my next step was to understand where I was going. I enjoyed working in the lab and making discoveries. I also enjoyed the level of respect and awe from others that came with sharing what I did for a living. Most of all, I was proud of all that I had accomplished and envisioned myself accomplishing much more. The last time I had considered a different path was when I participated in the Career Explorations Working Group. So, I reconnected with the creator of the program, who shared that the office was available to alumni, including access to the job postings database, seminars and workshops, and their resource library. She also served as a role model for me as a scientist who had transitioned into career coaching, which resonated with me as a strong possible career option. Based on my previous work mentoring undergraduates in research, I thought I would find it very rewarding to support the professional development of students from underrepresented groups.

However, I knew neither how to label these positions nor where to find them. I would later learn that these types of roles have no standardized titles; for example, they could be called program manager, coordinator, director, or assistant dean. A friend of mine had been extremely successful at finding jobs after graduate school; she shared that she regularly searched both content- and skill-based key words on the Indeed job search engine. To move forward I decided to use similar search engines to identify job descriptions that resonated with me. Rather than apply for positions, I used these sites to gain an understanding of the fields I was considering. My strategy involved cultivating field networks and leveraging my transferable skill set to market myself as a competitive candidate in these fields of interest.

I searched a variety of terms on several sites and read through hundreds of job postings, saving jobs that sparked my interest. I printed one position that excited me—a curriculum developer at Harvard Extension School—and taped it above my computer screen to serve as motivation and a reminder of my destination. Having something tangible to aspire to helped me to stay focused. Having that job description also enabled me to clearly articulate to others what I was looking for and helped me identify similar positions. It was a lot like learning a new word and suddenly hearing it everywhere; it is a matter of priming one's perception. Before long, I was finding more and more positions that fit my needs and interests. I can now see that, although it did not seem that way at the time, through the Career Explorations Working Group and much of my cocurricular work in graduate school, I had already done much of the legwork for determining all alternative paths; I just needed to identify specific positions that did that work.

Many approaches and tools exist to identify career paths that align with an individual's passions, skill sets, and vision for the future. One example is myIDP, a robust goal setting and tracking tool that provides lists of alternative careers based on interest (Hobin et al. 2012). Another example is the Ikigai self-assessment, which asks a series of questions in four areas: what you love, what you are good at, what the world needs, and what you can get paid for. Ikigai is Japanese for "reason for being" (Garlington 2022).

At this point in my career transition, I had a clear sense of the path I wanted to explore. However, I was stalled. I discovered that my uncharted emotions and limiting mindset were preventing me from moving forward. I needed strategies to attend to the emotional aspects of a career transition. In the next section, I share how adopting a positive and liberating mindset can help eliminate roadblocks.

ATTENDING TO EMOTIONS AND MINDSET

While I had a career path in mind and was excited about it, I was still not moving full speed ahead. The idea of not being a scientist anymore was very hard for me to accept. Being willing to consider other career options as a postdoc was a big deviation for me. This feeling was so strong that I pursued a parallel search for pharmaceutical and biotechnology industry positions because the idea of leaving science felt like a huge loss, like I would be leaving a part of myself behind. I also feared an impending loss of status. Who would I be if I were not a scientist? Not only was I constantly reminded of what I would be missing, I was afraid that if I did not continue along the STEM faculty member career path, I would be letting down my mentors, funding agencies, friends, and family who had supported and invested in me over the years. I would also be depriving those seeking Black women role models in STEM careers. Through conversations with others, I learned that these fears were well founded and that emotions such as sorrow, loss, fear, and doubt can put the brakes on forward progress during a job search.

During this critical transition time, I was still actively working in the laboratory, winding down and transitioning my projects and knowledge to others. One week in particular, I kept glimpsing in the rearview mirror what I imagined would have been my career. I met with a new graduate student and postdoc who were considering carrying on one of my projects. We began to brainstorm and scribbled enthusiastically on the wall-length whiteboard at the front of the room. After the meeting I sat at my desk thinking. That is what it would be like to run my own research group—invigorating exchanges among smart people with great ideas. The next day I worked with my former rotation student who had joined the lab and was struggling to isolate viable liver cells. This was a technique I had mastered as a graduate student and I was happy to share my knowledge. It was extremely rewarding to watch him learn and move his project forward. I imagined that this is what it would be like to mentor my own graduate students. At the end of the week, I was asked to show a high school student around the lab. One of my favorite things is to meet and influence young scientists. After I showed him some fluorescent cells, his eyes were wide and intrigued. I imagined that he would go on to work in a lab.

These experiences, just as much as scientific discovery, were exhilarating. How could I consider doing anything else with my life? But I felt that I did not have a choice. My postdoc had not been productive, the structure of my life had to change to accommodate both work and family, and I had promised myself that I would not do another postdoc. It was time to explore roles that would allow me to better integrate all the different aspects of my life. So I turned my attention to the road ahead, but the way forward seemed uncertain at best.

As I began to tell people of my plan to find a different path, I did not expect the range of responses I received. An elder family member confided, "I am so disappointed. I told everyone that you were going to cure diabetes." A family friend exclaimed, "It's so great that you are doing this for your family." One of my mentors pushed me to "negotiate an adjunct faculty position." A former advisor asked, "You are pursuing what you have always wanted to, right?" Each of these statements caught me off guard, triggering a flood of conflicting emotions. Was I letting everyone down? Was I just taking the easy route because I could not cut it as a scientist? Had I tried hard enough? Should I be pushing forward toward a faculty position no matter what? Would anyone even want to join my research group if I succeeded? The level of self-doubt and sense of loss were stifling. Unfortunately, my main tactic for dealing with these emotions was to suppress them. Not only was this unhealthy, it put the brakes on my career progression.

I didn't know it then, but the sadness and guilt that rose to the surface when people made comments about me leaving science has a name: disenfranchised grief. This term was coined by psychotherapist and grief counselor Kenneth Doka and refers to a loss that is "not openly acknowledged, socially mourned, or publicly supported" (Doka 1999). Examples include a pet dying, losing a job, or missing milestone events like a prom or college graduation. In a recent interview on NPR's *Life Kit*, therapist David Defoe explained that disenfranchised grief "ends our life the way we knew it. We literally have to reorient ourselves to a new way of life. There's no going back. We don't get over losses. We have to then figure out a way to move beyond them . . . navigate or create something new" (Cardoza and Schneider 2021).

My point is that a significant career transition, especially a transition out of academic research, is not a neutral time. Anyone navigating this terrain will have feelings about the process. How does one deal with these feelings? How does one answer the questions others pose? For me, the key was latching onto a larger purpose that I already cared about, one in which I could make a difference: work that was both different and yet aligned with my commitments as a scientist. In some ways, finding a workable new professional identity and life balance was even more important to me than being a scientist. Thus, I was able to justify the shift to myself and others even though those justifications never felt 100 percent right at the time. I just knew that I needed to move forward in a different direction.

I am grateful for a conversation with another one of my mentors during this period, who suggested a new mindset that helped me both recognize and navigate my grief. I had requested a meeting with her because, in the past, she asked thought-provoking questions and gave great advice. A bonus was that she was a trained scientist who had held positions inside and outside of academia that were science- and research-related while not on the tenure track: teaching and running a lab. I shared details of my situation and my main reservation for leaving a scientific career. She listened intently to my recounting of my unproductive postdoc and my inability to move forward. After listening, she expressed disappointment that my postdoc did not turn out the way I had envisioned. She recalled encouraging me during my time in graduate school when I was considering whether to take a postdoc position. Most importantly, she did not judge me. Instead, she asked me a key question: *Why do you have to stop being a scientist?* The ultimate answer—*I don't*—felt liberating.

As my limiting beliefs receded, I was able to see that the characteristics I associated with being a scientist—solving problems, learning, helping others, making discoveries, planning experiments—exist in many other fields. Going forward, I would often revisit this mentoring conversation as an anchor point, weighing new positions to see if they would enable me to continue expressing the strengths and competencies at the core of who I am. I supplemented this understanding with a workshop offered at my graduate alma mater on translating the CV, which provided helpful information on how to identify and highlight my transferable skills. From there, I felt ready to explore new paths. If you do not have access to a similar workshop, I recommend *Next Gen PhD: A Guide to Career Paths in Science* (Sinche 2018), a book that provides helpful advice for considering transferable skills and translating them to future employers. My major takeaways from this stage were twofold. First, thinking or behaving like a scientist is a part of my identity that I do not have to shed just because I am no longer doing experiments. I still think like a scientist no matter what I am doing. Second, the skills that scientists use daily are not limited to the lab bench. I realized I could use those skills in my new role.

In what follows, I share what I have learned from a combination of firsthand experience, research, and presentations I have given and heard over the years. My sincere hope is that you will find some specific advice that will help you successfully navigate your own career transition, wherever you may be on your journey.

CULTIVATING MENTORING NETWORKS

Mentoring consists of mutually beneficial interactions that "support people to manage their own learning [in order to] maximize their potential, develop their skills, improve their performance, and become the person they want to be" (Parsloe and Leedham 2009, 67). Especially as careers advance to more senior levels, mentoring is the way everyone learns the skills, attitudes, and behaviors that allow them to perform their roles. As such, mentoring is essential for success and is especially critical during career transitions. Recent studies show that effective mentoring is one of the factors that leads to persistence for women and underrepresented minorities in STEM careers (National Academies of Sciences 2019).

Unfortunately, the mentoring landscape is uneven. For a variety of reasons, mentoring experiences are not uniformly positive or effective. One barrier to receiving high-quality, consistent mentoring is the mentor's understanding of the role of mentoring and their level of proficiency with effective mentoring practices. On the flip side, effective mentoring relationships depend heavily on the mentee's ability to articulate their goals and drive the direction of the mentoring relationship. Another barrier is the belief in a one-size-fits-all mentoring model in which mentoring is delivered by one mentor without acknowledgment of unique needs in relation to the mentee's social identities and background.

To ensure that you receive the mentoring you need, I recommend a deliberate approach to identifying and cultivating such relationships. Thus far, I have shared how my mentors helped me to recognize and navigate career transitions. These mentors were well-suited role models because they had navigated similar transitions from bench scientist to academic career outside of the professoriate. While these relationships were instrumental in helping me, no single mentor could meet all of my mentoring needs at my career crossroads and beyond. The National Center for Faculty Development and Diversity (n.d.; NCFDD) provides guidance on how to deliberately identify, cultivate, and foster an effective mentoring network. Many universities provide free access to NCFDD synchronous and asynchronous workshops and materials. Specific resources include Core Curriculum Webinar #7: Cultivating Your Network of Mentors, Sponsors and Collaborators and the Monday Motivator: There Is No Guru, which provide information, exercises, and steps you can take to cultivate your own mentoring network. While these resources are targeted to junior faculty members, the underlying principles are widely applicable. Engaging in the process of deliberately cultivating a mentoring network can serve you well during a career transition and throughout your professional life.

Cultivating a strategic mentoring network during career transitions is necessary. As you consider more than one field, your job search can gain momentum through low contact or finite strategic relationships with people who can share their experience and tips to help you progress. A strategic network helps you to propel your career forward by providing specific and timely advice. One way to identify people to include in your strategic network is to ask friends, colleagues, and mentors to introduce you to people who can share their experience with different careers. To expand your network beyond those you currently know, you can also join professional associations and attend conferences. One of the best resources to meet new people at low to no cost is LinkedIn, which is also an excellent tool to market your expertise and accomplishments. LinkedIn has evolved to the point that you can use it to apply for jobs and even take professional development micro-courses. Harvard T.H. Chan School of Public Health Alumni Affairs compiled an excellent resource to learn about the tools that LinkedIn offers (Harvard T.H. Chan School of Public Health, n.d.). Here I share two LinkedIn networking strategies that can help you meet people outside of your current network who are working in fields you are considering.

Use the LinkedIn Alumni Tool. Search and go to your alma mater's LinkedIn page and click on the alumni tab. Use the filters (location, field of study, profession, etc.) to identify a list of alumni who have worked in a profession in which you are interested. By using the available filters and searches, you will generate a list of alumni with whom you could request a meeting. You can use your shared alumni status as a way to introduce yourself and explain how you identified them. You can find detailed instructions on how to use the LinkedIn Alumni Tool in the book *Linked: Conquer LinkedIn. Get Your Dream Job. Own Your Future* (Garriott and Schifeling 2022, p. 66).

Use LinkedIn's Advanced People Search. This tool helps you identify people with positions you are interested in moving into or who work at companies you are interested in working for (Garriott and Schifeling 2022, chap. 6). To connect with the people you identify, leverage how you are connected with them. For example, if you are a first- or second-degree connection, you can ask the person you know in common to introduce you. If the person you would like to connect with is further removed than first- or second-degree connections, you can use the site's "Expand Your Network" guide (LinkedIn n.d.).

As my own network expanded and I began to engage with individuals from at least two career domains, I developed a tracking sheet with multiple fields in Excel, including contact name, title, organization, contact information, date of interaction(s), meeting notes, follow-up activity, and referrals to others in their network (which kicks off a new entry in the database). I hope this example—which you can modify to best suit your needs—will help you manage your interactions with a high volume of people. Many of my new connections resulted in informational interviews, which I'll turn to next.

CONDUCTING INFORMATIONAL INTERVIEWS

Informational interviews are opportunities to meet people who hold positions that interest you. The golden rule of informational interviewing is not to ask for or assume that the interview will lead to a job. While you may get lucky and the person you interview is impressed enough to share job opportunities with you, an informational interview leading to a position is rare. So why do them? I conducted informational interviews for three main reasons, and I encourage you to do the same:

1. To gain firsthand knowledge of what a role entails and what people like and dislike about their position and organization
2. To gain advice about how to tailor my résumé and expand my knowledge in ways that can help me to land a position in a particular field
3. To stay abreast of trends and opportunities by expanding and keeping my network active

The first step is to identify potential people to interview by tapping into your network. Do you know someone, or know someone who knows someone, in a position you are interested in? If so, ask to be introduced. LinkedIn searches can be helpful for finding potential people to interview as described above. You can also search for specific companies you are interested in applying to and identify people in the role in which you are interested. It may be easier for the person to commit to a virtual meeting; however, an in-person meeting at their company would provide you the opportunity to observe the work environment.

Scheduling informational interviews is a relatively straightforward process. To set up an interview, send an email to the person you are interested in interviewing, requesting a thirty- to sixty-minute meeting. I have always been pleasantly surprised by how many people will take time out of their busy schedule to help someone learn about what they do and how they got to where they are. If a potential interviewee does not have time, they will make that clear or simply not respond to the request. Don't be afraid to ask for an interview, and don't be discouraged if you don't hear back right away. While people value helping others, they may miss your email or unintentionally forget to respond. In this case, it helps to try to send one or two follow-up emails a week or two apart. If you still do not hear back, it would be best to try someone else. Likely, you can identify and speak to other people in similar roles.

Once you have scheduled the interview, prepare, and prioritize questions to make the best use of time. It may help to send your questions ahead so that your interviewee can be prepared to answer succinctly. While your initial questions will focus on how they got their role, what skills are essential to do their role well, what an average day is like, and what they like and dislike about their role, there are three questions you should always ask:

1. *What do you read? What associations do you belong to?* If you do interview for a position in this field, reading a trade journal or an association's website could provide key information regarding the current state of the field. You can also identify insightful questions to ask during the interview. You will be more confident, feel less like a novice, and more like a colleague.
2. *Would you review my résumé and suggest what I can highlight or skills I can build to be more competitive for a position like yours?* Their insights could help your résumé stand out and make you more competitive among applicants.
3. *Can you recommend anyone who could share more information about X with me?* As you speak to the person you interview, you may find yourself wanting to know more about a specific topic you discussed. While you may ask them for another meeting, it would be great if they could introduce you to someone else who could speak to you about the topic. This tactic has the bonus of providing a different perspective while expanding your network.

On the day of the interview, wear business casual attire and plan to arrive at least fifteen minutes early to ensure that you will be on time. You should also plan to pay for any coffee or meal that you consume. Just as you plan to start on time, make sure to show that you respect their time by ending on time. If they offer a few more minutes, that is fine, but always be mindful of the time. After the interview, send a thank-you email highlighting how the conversation helped you in your job search. It is also a good idea to connect with them on LinkedIn if you have not already. Another way to show your appreciation is to give back by sharing an article or resource that may be helpful to them. When you land in your next position, let them know what you are doing and thank them again for their time investment. You will find additional advice on informational interviewing in *Building Professional Connections* (Harvard University Faculty of Arts and Sciences Office of Career Services 2021).

I conducted at least ten informational interviews during my job search after my postdoc with two groups of people: people in higher ed who had some type of curriculum development or career coaching role and scientists at companies who had roles on the business development side of pharmaceutical and biotech companies. Most of the interviews occurred because I knew the person already or a member of my network introduced me. And for the most part, the interviews went extremely well. I left the interviews feeling as if I knew more about the day-to-day tasks the person carried out, how to tailor my résumé to highlight skills that would be relevant to reviewers hiring for similar positions, and sometimes the name of an additional person I could contact for more information.

One interview stands out as the worst. Ironically, it was with the person who previously held that dream job I had stuck above my computer screen for motivation! I was already running late, and then got held up going through the building's security. By the time I arrived ten minutes late, she seemed to be fuming and our conversation never really recovered, culminating in her refusal to open her network to me and share any other names when I asked. I share this experience so you know that an informational interview can go badly and still be valuable. In this case, I felt positive about the fact that her path was similar to mine—scientist and teaching fellow turned curriculum designer—which encouraged me to keep going in that direction. So, just take these experiences in stride and with grace and keep moving along your job search journey. And of course, be on time for scheduled meetings!

While informational interviewing has its challenges—everything from a possible refusal to meet or having to carry a conversation with someone you have only just met, to a flat-out bad interview—the benefits of informational interviewing far outweigh these occasional setbacks. What I gained from informational interviewing was perspective. I realized that I would rather pursue a career in higher education than in industry. I would not have come to that conclusion without these candid conversations. They also helped me further understand what I was good at and helped me translate the skills I have into the language of a new profession.

CONCLUSION

In the end, after engaging in all these practices, I landed a position in a serendipitous yet synergistic way. For several consecutive years, the program director of the Bridges to the Baccalaureate Program at UMass Boston invited me to give a talk for the students in the program. Because I had been a Bridges

Program student myself, I like to think that meeting me was inspirational for the students, that I gave them an opportunity to believe that someone like them could pursue a career in science. Each year, the program leadership would also invite me to attend the students' final presentations. However, I had not been able to attend due to conflicts until the year I was transitioning out of my postdoc and into a new career.

During the reception that followed the talks, I spoke with a faculty member whom I had met on a previous visit. When he asked about my current work, I shared that I was searching for a position that would allow me to mentor students along their journey to becoming scientists. While I did not want to conduct daily experiments, I wanted to remain science adjacent and still write grants and papers. I braced myself for his reaction to be one of disappointment and condolences. Instead, his face lit up and he said, "You should apply for our research training core manager position. It was just posted; I will send you the link. Send me your résumé and I will share it with the directors." I did that and in a few short weeks, I was starting in the position.

In this new role, I identified and placed undergraduate students in cancer research laboratories to gain experience as researchers. I also designed programming for year-round and intensive summer programs that provided participants with the necessary knowledge to pursue and thrive in research careers. During my time in that position, I also cowrote two National Institutes of Health grants to create a course that would teach undergraduates to communicate science, navigate mentoring relationships, and understand and overcome the challenges that marginalized identities can pose while pursuing a science career; I later coauthored a paper about the course and its outcomes. I also became a certified mentor trainer and began to work closely with faculty to help them become effective mentors to developing scientists. This fulfilling and impactful work with faculty inspired me to seek roles that were faculty focused.

Today, when I stand back and examine my day-to-day work, it looks conspicuously like the life of a principal investigator. I lead a team of five smart people who design experiments and interventions that influence institutional culture and career trajectories of faculty and staff. I have cultivated a network of collaborators and mentors who help my team innovate beyond our capacity and imagination, and I get to think critically and troubleshoot problems daily.

I write and publish articles that contribute knowledge and experience to my field. I review articles for journals that influence the standard of publication in my field, and I review grants that influence the work conducted in my field. I lobby for internal funding and write external grants that help us take our work in new directions and serve more people. I give talks that disseminate our work, expand our visibility, and increase our network.

My title is not professor. I am not discovering therapeutics to treat and cure diseases as I thought I would. And part of me may always feel a pang of loss for my originally intended path as a scientist. However, I continue to move forward in my current direction, and it works for me. I help people in ways that transform their futures and ensure that they have fulfilling professional lives. More importantly, I am in my element and thriving by utilizing my strengths at work. These core skills and activities are in my professional DNA and always will be.

Everything about your search and your path should be about who *you* are: I approached my career exploration as a scientist, and that is what I remain at heart. That won't change even if my circumstances and settings do. In keeping with the main metaphor of this essay, your route, stops, and destinations may shift, but you are the stable core. Most importantly, you are the one in the driver's seat. I wish you the best on your journey.

ACKNOWLEDGMENTS

I am grateful to everyone who has provided me with helpful career advice over the years. The suggestions in this chapter are a composite gleaned from many informal conversations, books, and talks I have attended, including the influential career advice and mentorship of Jocelyn Spragg, Nancy Andrews, Victoria Love, Karen Burns White, Joan Becker, Sheila Thomas, Jane Midgley, Deborah Federico, Bruce Birren, Paul Hanson, Ting Wu, Manorack de Kok-Somviengxay, Judith Glaven, Alexia Pollak, S. Tiffany Donaldson, Lauren Celano, Frank Bayliss, Jennifer Breckler, Robert Clark, and Adán Colón-Carmona. I am especially grateful to those who provided feedback on this essay: Laura Lee Stark, Emily McMains, and James L. Sherley. Finally, Karen Cardozo's supportive insights and keen editorial skills helped take this essay from exploratory conversations into an organized reality.

REFERENCES

Cardoza, Kavitha, and Clare Marie Schneider. 2021. "The Importance of Mourning Losses (Even When They Seem Small)." *Life Kit.* NPR. June 14, 2021. https://www.npr.org/2021/06/02/1002446604/the-importance-of-mourning-losses-even-when-they-seem-small.

Doka, Kenneth J. 1999. "Disenfranchised Grief." *Bereavement Care* 18 (3): 37–39.

Garlington, Bull. 2022. "The Ikigai Diagram Will Guide You Out of This Mess." Attorney at Work, June 7, 2022. https://www.attorneyatwork.com/ikigai-career-assessment/.

Garriott, Omar, and Schifeling Jeremy. 2022. *Linked: Conquer LinkedIn. Get Your Dream Job. Own Your Future.* New York: Workman Publishing.

Harvard T.H. Chan School of Public Health. n.d. *Linkedin for Networking, Career Building & Job Search.* https://cdn1.sph.harvard.edu/wp-content/uploads/sites/36/2017/08/Published-Linkedin-Guide-SW-5-2-17.pdf.

Harvard University Faculty of Arts and Sciences Office of Career Services. 2021. *Building Professional Connections.* https://hwpi.harvard.edu/files/ocs/files/gsas-building-connections-publication.pdf.

Hobin, Jennifer A., Cynthia N. Fuhrmann, Bill Lindstaedt, and Philip S. Clifford. 2012. "You Need a Game Plan." Science, September 7, 2012. https://www.science.org/content/article/you-need-game-plan.

LinkedIn. n.d. "Expand Your Network." https://socialimpact.linkedin.com/content/dam/me/linkedinforgood/en-us/resources/youth/Expand-Your-Network-on-LinkedIn.pdf.

National Academies of Sciences, Engineering, and Medicine. 2019. *The Science of Effective Mentorship in STEMM.* Washington, DC: National Academies Press. https://doi.org/10.17226/25568.

National Center for Faculty Development and Diversity. n.d. Accessed April 27, 2023. www.facultydiversity.org.

Parsloe, Eric, and Melville Leedham. 2009. *Coaching and Mentoring: Practical Conversations to Improve Learning.* 2nd ed. London: Kogan Page.

Sinche, Melanie V. 2018. *Next Gen PhD: A Guide to Career Paths in Science.* Cambridge, MA: Harvard University Press.

4

CONTINGENCIES AND POSSIBILITIES

ALYSSA STALSBERG CANELLI

Many people believe the pathway through a PhD program is a fairly straightforward trajectory in which academic success follows a predictable logic. However, most doctoral students are also in the age bracket when life begins to "happen"—family building, caretaking obligations, health crises (of one's own or of family members), and the need for financial stability. As life unfolds, our assumptions about linear professional success start to realign into something more resembling a constellation of contingencies and possibilities. The unpredictable nature of the journey requires equal parts practical and psychological preparation for a trajectory that is inevitably shaped by a variety of personal circumstances, serendipitous opportunities, and closed doors, as well as deliberate plans.

In my current role as assistant dean of academic affairs in the Graduate School of Arts and Sciences at Brandeis University, I often advise PhD students about professional development plans. I encourage them to think within a flexible framework of contingency and opportunity—a framework that encourages agency and choice, even—and especially—when some opportunities are closed off. And as anyone who does this kind of work knows, the process of advising can and should also initiate some self-reflection on the part of the advisor. I have found myself returning to the varied meanings of contingency and how they resonate in particular for those of us who are forging our career pathways within higher education administration. In this essay I examine how the path through doctoral training is subject to many unfolding contingencies and how each of those inflection points can yield new career possibilities.

I begin with three key scenes from my own trajectory to model different ways of thinking about contingencies. From there, I outline how to explore different possibilities simultaneously, then close with some key takeaways from the essay. My hope is that this discussion will allow you to locate yourself within a constellation of possibilities and engage in decision-making that is paradoxically both more focused and flexible.

LIVING THE CONTINGENCIES: THREE SCENES

Scene 1

By the third year of my PhD program, I began to realize that there was an art to disclosing how I managed my time and how I made progress toward my milestones. I had been awarded a generous twelve-month fellowship package, with significant professional development funding and minimal teaching obligations; therefore, any activity that didn't have a direct connection to my research agenda was viewed as tangential at best. At the same time, it was common knowledge that many graduate students were picking up on-campus gigs, but it was understood that these were just things we took on to help with our cash flow and had no connection to our "real" work.

Being a first-generation college student, I was always juggling at least one, if not two or three, paid gigs in addition to my schooling since my junior year of high school, so this was nothing new. Unlike many of my peers whose parents told them that their "job" in high school and college was excelling at academics and extracurriculars, I had to work in order to pay for my life necessities, which included food, clothes, and transportation expenses, in addition to a little bit of spending money. In the PhD program, this expectation was repeated—the job that we were being paid to do through our five-year fellowship support package was to excel at our academics and research. However, most PhD stipend/fellowship packages assume that the student does not have dependents or any other significant financial responsibilities or debts. And even if this happens to be true, as it was for approximately half of my entering cohort of ten, most grad students are barely squeaking by if they are living in a major metropolitan area with a high cost of living. Ask a PhD student about whether their university requires them to pay for expenses (conference fees, research travel, cohort socials) up front and submit them for reimbursement. If they do have to go through the reimbursement process, you'll get an earful about the administrative lag and how they juggle their credit cards and bills while they wait on the university's reimbursement to come through. So at my institution, even though it was an open secret that grad students had side gigs, it was still part of the expectation that these remain secret so we could preserve the illusion that our academic success was independent of our financial resources/limitations.

In that first year, something began to shift for me, perhaps because there were options other than hourly retail or accounting, my gig mainstays before the PhD. I began to accumulate a variety of short-term project gigs: event planning assistant for a publishing conference, freelance editor for an academic editing firm, additional teaching assistant positions in other departments, learning objective assessor for the writing program, digital humanities project assistant in the Rare Books Library, to name a few. None of these affected my milestone timelines in the first four years of my program, but I soon discovered that while I didn't need to hide these from my advisor, they weren't seen as experiences worth reflecting on and incorporating into my professional identity. But I did start that reflection process, if only to secure my successful application for the next gig that came along. For instance, I discovered that while I excelled at line editing, I was excited when I was offered developmental editing projects because I liked to work with larger conceptual chunks and the structure of a long-form manuscript. I also realized that spreadsheets were the event planner's best tool, and I began to use them for my own writing projects (and wedding planning). I did not enjoy in-person or cold-calling/emailing event marketing or promoting because it felt too much outside my introverted comfort zone. I also hated the tedium of metadata entry in my digital humanities projects, but I loved the process of digitizing materials. I grew confident in my ability to teach material outside my expertise because I had developed the skill of teaching/reading/researching myself into competency two weeks ahead of the course itself. Even so, I still believed that my growing gig list had very little to do with my professional development as an academic.

Scene 2

The summer of 2014 stands out, in hindsight, as a crossroads. It signaled both the end of my fertility and the beginning of my parenting journeys, my ongoing and increasingly acute autoimmune diseases, and the closing moment of the dream I had for an academic career. I was behind in my dissertation progress; at the same time, my diagnosis of Stage 4 endometriosis at thirty-two (my first of two pelvic surgeries) kicked off our fertility journey, and I found it easier to focus on my paid gigs (teaching, editing, assessing, event planning) that went toward paying the $6K per intrauterine insemination (IUI) cycle cost (paid for out of pocket due to the lack of insurance coverage for fertility procedures for lesbian couples) instead of working on my research. For some reason, working on my own writing felt too close emotionally and metaphorically to trying to get pregnant and carry a pregnancy to term. It's not uncommon to read about the experience of "birthing" a dissertation, or experiencing the "labor pains" of the final revisions, nor is it uncommon for the structure of doctoral education to be framed as one in which advisors reproduce the discipline through their advisees who carry on the legacy.

These metaphors about birthing my dissertation were amplified to a surreally painful register because my dissertation was about narratives of race and reproduction in the white settler/supremacist nationalist contexts of nineteenth-century United States and twentieth-century South Africa. Every chapter was full of close readings of scenes of births, pregnancies, violence, assaults, grief, loss, love, hope, and trauma. For those of you unfamiliar with the methodology of close reading that we use in literary studies, it is more than just an analysis of the language/themes/literary devices in a passage. It is something much more intimate. It could be described as an erotic entanglement between the text and the scholar with the author's presence hovering just out of sight, and this entanglement gives birth to a reading that slips, moves, pulls, rejects, and holds the three together (text, author, scholar). In every aspect of my life, I was trying to give birth to something—and each of those births required all of my creative, emotional, intellectual, and physical fortitude. Which was impossible for me (for anyone) to give in all directions at once. With all of this "generativity" on the line, I felt like a failure in both pregnancy and my research.

For four years (years three to seven in my program) my wife and I underwent eleven unsuccessful IUI cycles with several early-term miscarriages. Needless to say, the emotional and physical toll of these experiences are not conducive to advancing one's academic work, particularly when the content is so saturated by the very thing that defined my body's failures. And yes, of course, I knew then and I know now that failure is not an accurate framing of what I was experiencing. But tell that to any person who desperately wants their uterus to succeed in its primary function of providing a successful implantation environment, or who is experiencing the elation of the double lines on the test followed by the grief of an early-stage miscarriage. It may not actually be failure, but it certainly feels like it when every single person in your family and network seems to achieve it so quickly and joyfully.

The fall of 2013 began the severing of the connection between me and my institution. In the summer of 2013 we decided to move to a state where insurance coverage for infertility was mandated by law. I had planned to complete my dissertation long distance, and I had won a fully funded digital humanities fellowship for the upcoming year. A month after moving to Massachusetts, during my first meeting with the faculty member who was overseeing my fellowship, he told me that I was no longer a good fit for the center because when "young women" prioritize having children, they no longer focus on the work. He wished me well, but he had too much to accomplish in this new center and he advised me to focus on the things that matter to me. I begged him to reconsider—yes, I literally begged—and I frantically listed all the ways I was not like those other young women (I was thirty-five years old, in fact). I offered to spend two weeks of every month in residence in Atlanta, regardless of the cost; I offered to work more hours for free, beyond the fellowship. As I heard myself beg and plead, blooms of shame and self-loathing blossomed in my belly. His avuncular voice shifted into condescension as he kept repeating that he had made his decision and hysterics were not going to change his mind. He ended the conversation by wishing me well in my new ventures and assuring me that this was for the best.

During the next few months, as New England's days became shorter, darker, grayer, colder, I slid into further into isolation, and the shame of academic failure continued to bloom—the only thing I was capable of birthing, it seemed. I don't think it was a coincidence that the day after I submitted the draft of my final chapter to my advisor in January 2014, I was suddenly struck by an acute case of optic neuritis. This condition is an inflammation of the optic nerve, caused by a process called demyelination. It is also a common presenting symptom of multiple sclerosis (MS). I spent the winter months undergoing a battery of tests administered by neurologists and neuro-ophthalmologists. Of course, in the middle of that, my wife and I decided we might as well go for round 2 of IVF and so we placed two embryos (instead of one, because why not, we'd failed at everything so far). And also of course, my wife became pregnant in May. With twins. She was horrifically sick during her first trimester, and we had six blissful weeks in her second trimester in which we were finally starting to feel excitement outweigh the fear of twins. And then we went for her twenty-week ultrasound anatomy scan. That experience is for a different essay, but the short version is that baby girl 2 had a congenital heart defect—an atrioventricular (AV) canal defect—which is highly associated with babies who have trisomy 21 (Down) syndrome. The next week's amniocentesis confirmed the diagnosis.

In yet another essay, I would describe the ways in which chronic childhood trauma can equip us with superpowers like compartmentalization, always seeing the way out, and intuitive decision-making. Those powers kicked into high gear as I realized that I had twins on the way, one with special needs and significant medical complications that would require proximity to a world-class children's hospital—and I had no job. I had started applying to entry-level higher ed administrative roles when I saw a position advertised at Brandeis University for an assistant director of experiential learning and teaching. I didn't think I had the experience or qualifications, so I didn't apply. However, I did have a good friend who worked at Brandeis, and we were in conversation about my job search.

In late August, she happened to run into the hiring manager and asked him about the candidates, and he said he wasn't really happy with any of them. When she asked him what he was looking for, he said someone with teaching experience who would be able to work with faculty across disciplines; someone with whom he could brainstorm, develop, and co-facilitate active learning workshops; someone who could listen to a client, ask the right questions, and propose a variety of options/solutions on the spot; someone who had strong administrative and writing skills; and someone who was adaptable and who would be willing to co-create the mission of the office with him. She told him she had the perfect person in mind. And I was offered the job ten days later, after a stellar on-campus interview experience, in which I invoked many examples from my event-planning, teaching, editing, consulting, and administrative jobs—side gigs that now turned out to be the main event. It was a low salary, but almost double the stipend rate at my doctoral institution. And most importantly, it had an excellent healthcare plan. It was a stable staff position.

It was perfect. It was serendipity. The kind that happens when you both build up a portfolio of "other" experiences *and* mention to others that you are looking for a job.

Scene 3

After three years in my first role at Brandeis (during which I did finally submit my dissertation and graduate with the PhD while also parenting twin newborns, one of whom was in the NICU for ninety-six days with an open-heart surgery—how's that for a parenthetical?), I applied for and accepted an offer to work in the Graduate School of Arts and Sciences as an assistant dean of academic affairs. This time, I was more confident in my application, in large part because I had been quite strategic about developing, managing, and completing several high-profile projects while at Brandeis. I had come to realize that I enjoyed the work of building programs and curricular structures, leading committees, and project managing the production of a university-wide report on the current state of cocurricular experiential learning experiences. I developed relationships with faculty across departments through my pedagogical consulting and report research—something that came fairly easy to me since I was fluent in the culture of an R1 institution because I had also trained in one. So when the assistant dean position opened, I applied as a strong internal candidate.

It was not lost on me that working within a graduate school was almost too on the nose in terms of how I was also working through and reclaiming my professional identity from the "tenure track or bust" ethos. During my first three years, I managed and directed the Career and Professional Development team, whose everyday truisms about career exploration, diverse career pathways, the importance of self-reflection, and the necessity of networking were ones that I was only beginning to truly understand in my own career pathway.

CONTINGENCY AT WORK

I selected these three snapshots because they collectively illustrate varied aspects of contingency.

Definition 1: A future event or circumstance that is possible but cannot be predicted with certainty. One of the foundational insights of the disability community is that able-bodiedness is transitory; disability is universal because all bodies have been and will become disabled at some point. However, many of us who are able-bodied at the time we make our professional plans assume that this condition will continue into the future. In fact, it's quite challenging to chart a future professional pathway without assuming continued health and able-bodiedness for oneself, as many people in the disability community acutely experience. Because of the long-term commitment of doctoral training (the national average time to the PhD degree ranges from six to nine years), it is very possible that disability/fertility/parenting/medical challenges will come up for doctoral students during this time—but these things cannot be predicted with certainty.

Definition 2: A provision for an unforeseen event or circumstance. Even though I did not realize it at the time, my gigs were laying a foundation of professional experiences (a contingency) that helped me excel in the interview in Scene 2. This also informs Scene 3, where I strategically leveraged my contingency of high-profile projects and deliverables when an internal opportunity arose. As I will discuss in a moment, it didn't matter that these "provisions for an unforeseen circumstance" were completely haphazard and unintentional, insofar as I only viewed them as transitory cash flow support in the moment. What did matter was that I accumulated the experiences, and I was savvy enough to draw upon them when the circumstance called for it. I was carrying a metaphorical backpack filled with the odds and ends of my gigs, provisions for the future circumstances in which a need may arise.

Definition 3: The absence of necessity; the fact of being so without having to be so. It seems banal to state the obvious truth that most of life is contingent—in the absence of both predictability and necessity—but I think we tend to forget this truth when we are deeply enculturated into academia. Traditional doctoral training requires one to deny the contingent nature of our embodied, familial, and community lives. This is why every graduate career counselor has their stories about the moment when a doctoral student starts to realize that the linear success pathway does not deliver on its promises, or when a student starts to realize that they do not want to pay the personal, family, or community cost of that pathway.

My second scene illustrates the year when I realized that the reality of my life was not compatible with the demands/conditions of playing the lottery for an academic career. My life realities included significant chronic health diseases, being married to a woman, the cost of building a queer family while dealing with infertility issues, and a daughter with significant medical and development needs that would require us to be in close proximity to world-class medical centers and schools that are at the forefront of inclusive special education practices. Chasing poorly paid visiting assistant professor positions across the country for three to five years while I published a book and eventually found a more stable position was no longer an option I was willing to consider. I began to feel the academic career door closing on me when my fellowship was revoked, but at this point, I actively pushed it shut because it was a door I was no longer willing to walk through.

When appropriate, I share parts of my story with the students I work with, because I know how important it is for the person with more hierarchical power to show their vulnerability first, which provides a foundation of trust when I start to launch into my more typical advising conversations. When I say it is okay to walk away from graduate school or from academia because you value your own health, financial stability, and family, I mean it. When I say that opportunities come at the most unexpected times in the most unexpected ways, I not only have my own life examples, but those of other students who have shared their stories with me. When I advise them to craft a strategic take on whatever gig they are doing to pay the bills, I have the data to show that these skills are the ones that get PhDs employment after graduation.

I also try to help students question their own sense of disempowerment: you can choose and make decisions about your life because it is your life, your values, and your priorities. Not your advisor's. Many first-generation graduate students hold on to the perspective of education as the way out, and when it doesn't produce that idealized resolution, the effect is often destabilizing: How do you make decisions when your guiding value is proven to be partially or wholly false? And how do you deal with all the emotions that come up: anger, betrayal, grief, shame, loss, and embarrassment? I have long since transformed my internally directed blossoms of shame into externally directed daggers of rage, but I believe that many PhD students and recent grads are tending gardens of shame blossoms within their psyches. Even if they intellectually know that their feelings of shame and failure are products of the toxic academic structure and the economic realities of the academic job market, the feelings are no less real. It is through these conversations, shared experiences, and connections that we can start to transform shame from a paralyzing internal state into something that provides us momentum to move forward. Not everyone will produce daggers of rage as I did, but at some point, the shame must start to recede into secondary and tertiary status so that other feelings like empowerment, confidence, and hope can take root.

EXPLORING MULTIPLE POSSIBILITIES

Any career counselor worth their salt will tell you that you don't need to acquire triple the number of professional experiences to apply concurrently for three different positions/roles. Rather, the same experience can be reframed in multiple ways for multiple purposes in different versions of your résumé and cover letters. True, there are some sector-specific baseline skills or experiences that may be necessary, but even so, you'd be surprised how transferable your skills and experiences truly are—if you know how to show (not tell) that transferability in your résumé and cover letter. Working with your school's career office, or hiring a career coach (of course, you should vet coaches through your network and through direct client recommendations, if possible), is one of the best things you can do to reveal how the contingencies of your life can be turned into possibilities.

If I am working with an early-stage PhD student, I advise them to be as deliberate and thoughtful as they can about plotting multiple career possibilities, and the experiences they need to acquire. It's a variation on backward design, for those of you familiar with pedagogy. What is the end point and the goal? How do I design an experience and skill development trajectory that will lead me to that goal? The most daunting (or damning) thing about PhD programs is that these trajectories are still almost always outside of full-time doctoral training in content and research, and I am still shocked by how little some programs prepare their PhDs even for the obvious tenure-track faculty trajectory in terms of the practicalities and realities of the current academic job market. Therefore, only a few early-stage PhDs are able to backward design two to three career pathways (and I certainly wasn't one of them). But those who do—not so strangely enough—find that they are also successful in the academic job trajectory. Why? Because these skills and experiences are transferable, of course.

For the vast majority of PhD students, the best strategy is to construct multiple narratives as experiences are accumulated. How does the conference planning volunteer role lead to being hired as the grad assistant who plans annual multiday professional conferences, and how can those experiences be framed within a résumé/cover letter for a nonprofit development job? How can those same experiences be leveraged for an entry-level organizational development position in a corporate HR office? Once you've done this narrative-making with your résumé materials, you can identify the critical holes in your experience for a particular kind of role, and make the plan to fill that hole. While many things about the PhD training process give us transferable skills, sometimes we need highly specific content or skill knowledge for a particular sector, and no amount of reframing will hide that hole. But you'd be surprised how easy (and fast) it can be to fill that hole in this era of proliferating low/no-cost online courses/trainings/certifications. Even a brief unpaid internship could be worth your time if it provides you exactly what you need to fill that hole in your experience.

Even if the plans/narratives are constructed in hindsight, that is perfectly okay. In some ways, I didn't ascribe meaning to some of my experiences until after I started to write this chapter. Most career development professionals talk about the chaos theory of career pathways these days: opportunities arrive, pathways are nonlinear, decisions can be intuitive, meaning can surface through time, change (contingency) is the constant we must accept.

In my second year of my current assistant dean role, the dean and I partnered on writing a grant to the Andrew W. Mellon Foundation. Our ten-year dissertation completion fellowship grant was expiring with no chance of renewal. Over the course of our conversations and collaborative writing, we created the Connected PhD, a grant that offers money to faculty for doctoral curriculum innovation and to students to fund skill-building projects and internships that equip them with concrete skills and experiences to leverage across diverse career pathways. To my mind, this was a way to transform the secret gigs of graduate students into legible and respected professional development opportunities that were highlighted, promoted, and celebrated as central to the doctoral training process. The mixed success of the Connected PhD is yet another essay, but the short version is that we have data that demonstrates the profound impact of these experiences on the career pathways and skill development of these students. As covered by *Inside Higher Ed*, the student uptake has been very high and very positive—they are finding their own opportunities and designing their skill-building experiences (Flaherty 2022).

However, as we expected and as has been extensively documented (Cassuto and Weisbuch 2021), the faculty uptake and enthusiasm has been significantly less than that of the students. Even though the grant specifically allows us to fund course release (which provides access to the holy grail of time for faculty), there has not been enough incentive for departments to make curricular and cultural change. However, we have seen success in some departments when specific (tenured) faculty members self-identify as advocates who are willing to persistently and doggedly advocate for this internal change. Examples of these changes are incorporating internship requirements into their doctoral curriculum; approving nontraditional dissertation formats; inviting recent alums to focus groups about their curricular and career experiences and taking this feedback seriously by bringing it back to inform curricular discussions; sustainable faculty/community organization partnerships that provide opportunities for PhD students to use their research/content expertise in public-facing ways; and restructuring proseminars to include recent alums and experts outside of academia. While these are the institutional takeaways, I close with some key points about what you can do as an individual navigating contingencies and possibilities.

KEY TAKEAWAYS

Set your thresholds of risk and cost and build a support network that will hold you accountable for those boundaries or help you validate a calculated risk. Only you can assess whether you have the financial/emotional/familial/physical resources to withstand multiple rounds on the academic job market. Only you can determine whether forgoing income for several months for an unpaid opportunity is worth the experience. Only you can decide whether relocating is an acceptable foundation for your life goals. But you can only clarify these things if you are absolutely clear on your values, priorities, and nonnegotiables. And only you can resolve to walk away from an opportunity that is not in alignment with these critical priorities.

I am immensely grateful to my circle of friends, both before and after and inside and outside of my graduate program. This breadth of range was so important to me. I needed people who could talk inside baseball, but I also needed people who knew me before the PhD and met me after. No single person could fill that role, and I couldn't rely on just a single perspective. For me, the commonality was that those friendships were a mutual balance of support and truth-telling.

Find/create a community of people who get it. I'm not talking about academics, although such people may be found in academia. I'm talking about the lesbians who are struggling to build their families, and the families who had a recent diagnosis of trisomy 21 (in my case). I'm talking about Black queer women communities, Latinx communities, neurodivergent communities—any community that can hold, support, and validate fundamental parts of your identity that are both present in and erased from or devalued in academia.

Question the assumption that you must go anywhere for the job. Geography has a huge impact on quality and opportunities of life as it pertains to health, family, race, gender, sexual, religious, ethnic, and other identities. It's not a coincidence that many academics who don't question this assumption are likely to identify with positions of dominant identity markers. I strongly encourage PhDs to make geography one of their nonnegotiable priorities if they have any concerns that they could live safely in a particular area.

Process your emotional struggles. I'll be honest: writing this essay brought up a lot of difficult feelings. I've done my work in therapy throughout the years, and just when I think I've moved past something, I realize that I've only just compartmentalized it. It doesn't matter the modality of your processing—whether traditional therapy, support from a spiritual leader, creating art, embodying your emotions through movement, confiding in your partner or best friend—what does matter is that you establish a practice of working it through. Shame blossoms thrive in darkness and silence: expose them to light and conversation.

CONCLUSION

The only universal piece of advice I can give is that you should plan for contingency, in all senses of the word. When you accept that there will be unpredictable twists and turns in your career and life that may reorient your initially intended pathway, then you also can be open to the multiple possibilities that may arise from such contingencies. And you can acquire a breadth of perspective that allows you to see the contingent nature of most of what we understand to be fixed and permanent. That perhaps has been one of the most profound lessons I have learned in my life—that contingency has two sides, and when things happen that are out of my control, there will be other moments when I can mobilize contingency to shift my path. Put another way: luck, coincidence, and happenstance work in both negative and positive directions. When you do some of the intellectual and mental work of exploring multiple possibilities along your career pathways, then any given change, obstacle, or setback needn't derail your capacity to find, and thrive in, a professional situation that works for you.

REFERENCES

Cassuto, Leonard, and Robert Weisbuch. 2021. *The New PhD: How to Build A Better Graduate Education.* Baltimore: Johns Hopkins University Press.

Flaherty, Colleen. 2022. "The Connected PhD." *Inside Higher Ed*, July 8, 2022.

Part 2
INTER/DISCIPLINARY TRANSFER

Most PhD programs still frame disciplinary knowledge and training as part of the tradition of academic knowledge production. This tradition emphasizes the pursuit of understanding as a goal in and of itself. The authors in part 2 weigh the pros and cons of the professorial path with its restricted focus on research, teaching, and service to the profession against what they actually love about their intellectual work. A recurring theme involves having an unrealistic concept of what faculty actually do when the authors started in their PhD programs. Realizing that their authentic goals and desires require a different path, they reject the stale notion that their PhD training has prepared them for only one thing and explore the value their disciplinary expertise and training bring when applied to seemingly unrelated areas.

The authors in part 2 find themselves with the same questions around how to open new career doors as those we heard from in part 1. They craft blended positions and forge new identities similar to the authors in part 3. They struggle to center personal values and navigate the strange class dynamics of roles where they have the same training and interests as their former peers without the same status or privileges, just like the authors in parts 4 and 5. That these themes are largely inextricable is a core theme of this book. In part 2, however, our focus is on the unique value of transferring one's disciplinary expertise and training beyond the narrow confines of the professorial path.

Many of the authors in this part draw on their experiences of working outside academia before, during, or after graduate school to reconsider their training in light of its transferable skills. Situating knowledge production as labor rather than as a higher calling and participation in the professoriate as one possible job and way to pay one's bills instead of as a consuming identity radically changes these authors' perspectives on what their training qualifies them to do and on the type of impact they want their work to make. They ask what their knowledge and experience offer to other fields that those new fields desperately need. What pain points do those domains struggle with that these authors are uniquely qualified to address and solve in an innovative way?

In "Applied Humanities at Work in STEM Graduate Education," Jessica Hutchins reflects on the value of bringing her humanities perspective and epistemology to bear on training STEM graduate students. Hutchins identified and filled gaps around communication and interpretation that industry leaders had lamented in STEM education. Through teaching, publishing, and writing grants, she became a nationally recognized expert in her new field. Hutchins shares insights into the value a humanist offers STEM fields, the importance of building broad networks as a graduate student, the permeability of faculty and staff positions when the conditions are right, the importance of your title upon entry to the new field, and the unpredictable ways in which priorities and job satisfaction are impacted by leadership changes.

In "From Humanities Tenure Track to Medical School Communications," Leigh Tillman Partington reinforces Hutchins's points about the value of humanities training to STEM, but through an entirely different trajectory and focus. Rather than focusing on graduate students, Partington shows the possibilities humanist training brings to working with faculty who graduated without Hutchins's innovations. Following the 9/11 attacks, Partington stepped away from academia to commit to full-time motherhood. Thirteen years later, she successfully pivoted her PhD training to establish a new communications position in the medical school at her PhD-granting institution. She shares her strategies for turning a temporary position into a full-time job, demonstrating her value to leadership and leveraging her experience teaching freshman composition and the personal essay to help med school faculty win tenure, promotions, and grants.

Unlike Hutchins and Partington, Stacey Wahl and Carrie Iwema started out in STEM. They share their journeys to becoming subject librarians at medical libraries in "PhDs Going Rogue: From the Bench to the Library and Beyond." Though Wahl and Iwema both hold PhDs in neuroscience and were drawn to careers in medical libraries, Iwema chose to get her master's in library science before making the transition, and Wahl focused her efforts on demonstrating the value of her transferable skills and transitioning directly into her new role. Their different entry points shaped their subsequent experiences. Wahl, in particular, relied heavily on her scientific training to identify opportunities within this new environment to pursue her broader career goals, which focused on supporting graduate students. The duo share how they each experienced collaboration, teaching, writing, and service to the profession through the lens of librarianship. Wahl notes, "I had the flexibility of a faculty job without the intense research pressures." They are forthright about the difficulties as well, noting places where their disciplinary training called for different skills and approaches than their current roles.

Sarah K. Barks closes out part 2 with their reflections in "Finding Neverland: From Chimpanzee Research to Career Services." A biological anthropologist turned career advisor for STEM students at a small liberal arts college, Barks leverages experiences as a researcher and teacher and as a postdoc granted opportunities to work in public science education. Curiosity, Barks observes, is their "greatest transferable skill" from their experience as a researcher and scientist. They have proven the unique value of their disciplinary training to their colleagues through taking over data collection and analysis tasks and establishing themselves across the college as "the keeper of knowledge about how this college prepares its graduates for the world beyond our doors." Finally, Barks discusses how applying disciplinary expertise allowed them to shape their position and title to better suit their interests.

The message these authors collectively convey is that one can love one's disciplinary training without wanting to devote oneself solely to the aspects rewarded on the tenure track. There are a range of career options within higher ed that reward teaching, research, and critical thinking and balance family and self-care. Sometimes, however, you have to create them yourself. As Barks advises, "Find people outside of academia and learn their stories. Envision yourself in a wide range of possibilities. Think about what kind of work–life balance matters to you and give yourself permission to care about it."

5

APPLIED HUMANITIES AT WORK IN STEM GRADUATE EDUCATION

JESSICA A. HUTCHINS

How many humanities PhDs imagine that their doctoral training is preparing them to work in the STEM fields? I certainly did not. As the number of tenure-track faculty jobs for humanists has dwindled in recent decades, PhD students may feel they have to choose between pursuing a faculty appointment or seeking employment outside of academia. Careers in academic administration can offer job stability and opportunities for PhDs to expand their teaching and research by applying their knowledge and skills within the context of a different field. A growing number of humanities PhDs are now finding meaningful work in the sciences by teaching communication skills and career development to augment traditional scientific training. While these careers can be intellectually engaging, academic work done by staff members inevitably occupies an ambiguous space at most universities due to traditional academic organizational structures. As a result, this work is not always recognized or rewarded equitably. This chapter describes my experience making the transition from literary research to applying humanities knowledge and skills within the context of STEM graduate education, and then transitioning again to a humanities faculty position at a different institution. It provides advice to PhDs on both the benefits and challenges of working as a staff member in academic administration. Finally, I argue that the humanities have pragmatic value for all fields of work and research; they should be incorporated thoroughly into all fields of study in undergraduate, graduate, professional, and postdoctoral education programs.

When I started my doctoral program in comparative literature, I intended to pursue a tenure-track faculty position teaching literature in an English department and was not aware that other career paths would be open to me. As I progressed in my degree program, however, I realized that the academic job market in the humanities seemed out of step with the values I had learned from my parents and my time in the working world. After earning my PhD, researching the relationships between narrative, identity, and social justice in literature of the African diaspora, I chose to work in academic administration for a biological sciences PhD program. It offered working conditions that aligned with my values, while keeping me in contact with academic life and supporting students. Although I had no training in the sciences, as a humanist, I filled several important gaps in the existing STEM education landscape by developing new courses in science communication, career development, and leadership that complemented scientific training.

In my most recent job beyond the professoriate, I worked as director of curriculum for an interdisciplinary PhD program in the biological sciences at a private medical school in the Midwest, reporting to an associate dean for graduate education and supervising two staff members. I developed curriculum for STEM PhD students and postdoctoral scholars that integrated career preparation and humanities concepts into their scientific training. While in this role, I discovered that the boundaries between faculty and staff careers are more permeable than I had believed. Although my position was classified as staff, I was doing academic work that is typically done by faculty members: I created and taught courses, conducted program assessments, wrote grants to support my projects, and disseminated original scholarship at conferences and in peer-reviewed journals. Additionally, I supervised staff who managed operations for course listings and course evaluations, noncredit career development programs and digital badges, learning management system (LMS) administration, teaching assistant assignments, and other academic affairs tasks.

After working in STEM education for six years, I gained a new understanding of the value of my humanities training and solid experience in academic administrative leadership. At the same time, the COVID-19 pandemic and Black Lives Matter uprisings led me to reevaluate my career path. I decided to move into a faculty role and wanted to work with students for whom a college education could be truly transformative, including first-generation college students, underrepresented minorities, and students from economically disadvantaged backgrounds. In 2021, I transitioned into a full-time, non-tenure-track faculty position teaching interdisciplinary humanities courses in the honors program at an access-oriented, regional public university. My academic accomplishments, administrative experience, and ability to work across disciplines all distinguished me during the hiring process. In 2022, I was promoted to interim director of the program. I hope my career journey both encourages humanities PhDs to consider the transferability of their disciplinary knowledge and teaching experiences into other realms of higher education and empowers them to apply their knowledge and skills in ways that align best with their values.

VALUES-DRIVEN DECISION-MAKING

The values that have shaped my career decision-making were heavily influenced by my parents. As first-generation college students, my parents had pursued careers that prioritized financial stability over intellectual stimulation. They both attended public universities and studied subjects that would easily translate into the working world: journalism for my mother and accounting for my father. For them, work was a way to make ends meet, and life (family, hobbies, reading books, etc.) was something that happened outside of working hours. College had enabled them to move from blue-collar backgrounds into white-collar careers, and they encouraged me to go to college from a young age. When I showed early interest and talent in the arts, my parents supported my predilections to write poetry and play music. They attended my band and choir concerts; my mother diligently drove me to piano lessons after school. They celebrated my creative publications in my high school literary magazine and a poetry award I received from a local university. Yet, alongside their encouragement of my artistic achievements, they were also quick to remind me that it can be hard to make a living as an artist. My father, the son of a professional jazz musician, knew this reality firsthand and did not want me to go through the financial instability that he had experienced as a child, which made a lasting impression on his own choice to study business and work in business fields throughout his career. When it came time for me to choose a college and declare a major, I settled on a BA in English, which kept me in contact with literature and enabled me to continue developing as a writer.

I made the decision to go to graduate school based on the encouragement of my undergraduate professors, with no real information about what it would take to earn a PhD, or what my job prospects would be like after completing the degree. During my final year as an undergraduate, I decided to pursue a PhD and become a literature professor, which seemed like a pragmatic compromise in itself; rather than taking the riskier path to become a poet or novelist, I saw the professoriate as a stable way to make a living in reading, writing, and teaching literature. Furthermore, having internalized the lesson from my parents that a college education would lead to better job opportunities, it seemed logical that earning an advanced degree would produce an even better return on my educational investment. I am the first person in my family to pursue a doctoral degree, and I am not aware that anyone in my peer group growing up had family members with PhDs. Aside from my college professors, I had no role models to help me understand what it takes to get a PhD or what the academic job market would be like. In retrospect, I had no idea what I was getting into, did not know which questions to ask of my college professors, and largely assumed (mistakenly) that their jobs consisted of what I could observe through taking their courses. Ultimately, earning a PhD was the right decision for me, but I went into it quite blindly and did not learn some of the hard truths of academic life until I was halfway through my doctoral program.

During my PhD program, I realized that early-career faculty members in the humanities are often required to make sacrifices that seemed untenable to me. Due to workloads, pressure to perform well in teaching, research, and service, and lack of work–life balance at research-intensive institutions, "tenured and tenure track faculty are at high risk for burnout" (Padilla and Thompson 2015, 555). These are the faculty that mentor PhD students and are the face of the profession. They teach us the culture and set the example for what we would expect to experience as a faculty member. And what I saw was not appealing. I knew too many people on the tenure track who were living in different cities from their partners or spouses. Too many of my newly minted PhD peers were scraping together a living through adjunct teaching at multiple local universities, living proof that "nearly half of all new faculty appointments are part-time, and three out of five new full-time appointments are off the tenure track" (Padilla and Thompson 2015, 551). In some cases, my friends who were teaching as adjuncts earned less money each year than they had as graduate students. And in both categories—those on the tenure track or in adjunct roles—I saw too many brilliant but stressed-out people burning the proverbial candle at both ends with consequences for both their physical and mental health. This did not feel right to me, and I set some pragmatic priorities for my career: I wanted to cohabitate with my spouse, achieve wellness in work–life balance, and receive fair pay for my work.

While most of my peers felt that teaching was the only job their PhD training had prepared them for, I knew we had transferrable skills and experiences that would be valued in many employment sectors. Between college and graduate school, I had worked as a store manager for a global coffee company (you know the one), and that experience allowed me to view PhD skills from the perspective of hiring managers outside of the academy. PhD training develops narrow and deep expertise in a research field; however, it also teaches us how to learn things quickly, to summarize and synthesize large amounts of information, to communicate in a variety of media and to a variety of audiences, to juggle competing priorities, to achieve objectives despite limited resources, to manage both short- and long-term projects, and to work collaboratively with people from different backgrounds. These skills are highly valued by employers because they are difficult to teach and must be developed over time. Furthermore, PhD training helps us to develop work habits that are prized by employers, including persistence, resilience, adaptability, attention to detail and nuance, and the ability to see the big picture.

Although I understood both my values and my potential value to hiring managers, it was still difficult to pursue career paths beyond the professoriate. I had developed a sense of identity as an academic that I did not want to abandon. I felt expectations from friends and family to become a professor. My paternal grandmother had told me how proud she was that we would finally have a doctor in the family, and it would be hard to explain my decision to do something other than teaching. I also felt pressure from advisors and faculty to apply for tenure-track job openings, even though I had made it clear that I wanted to pursue other paths. And my experience was not unique. I witnessed my graduate school friends and peers struggling with the tensions between chasing the tenure-track dream and desiring a career with balance and stability, while reading endless accounts of the anemic humanities academic job market. Given the commonality of this experience, it is not surprising that "graduate students are more than six times as likely to experience depression and anxiety as compared to the general population" (Evans et al. 2018, 282). It seemed to me that we were wasting the talents of highly trained, capable, and brilliant people by forcing PhD students and recent graduates into this untenable position.

I recognized that PhDs needed to be empowered to pursue fulfilling careers in any field they might choose, and I wanted to help develop solutions to the problems my peers and I were facing. While still in graduate school, working from the feminist premise that the personal is political, I started a blog to explore my own career values, opportunities, and transferable skills. I had been teaching undergraduate composition students that writing is both a process for inquiry and a product for sharing the results. I applied these tools and methods to my own career dilemma and used my blog to research career options for PhDs, to amplify the career choices of my graduate school peers, and ultimately to prepare for my own career transition. In doing so, I was hoping to change the narrative and culture surrounding PhD careers and fill gaps in PhD training that I had experienced. The blog project introduced me to the world of PhD career development and helped me understand the work that was being done in that field. Perhaps most importantly, I realized that universities were employing people to do this work and that I could be one of them.

APPLYING THE HUMANITIES TO STEM GRADUATE EDUCATION

Instead of pursuing a faculty appointment, I moved into an academic administration career that combined my desire to change the culture of PhD career education with my own pragmatic goals. From 2015 to 2021, I worked as a career and professional development (CPD) educator for PhD students in the biological sciences. In this role I developed new programs, courses, and resources on professional skills and career planning "that complement existing training delivered by faculty research mentors" with the goal of preparing graduate students "for success in exploring and pursuing diverse career paths" (Subramanian et al. 2022). I worked to build a model of graduate education that would provide explicit training for multiple career paths. My work responded to calls by national leaders in scientific education to modernize PhD training to meet the needs of a changing world and job market. The National Academies of Sciences,

Engineering, and Medicine (NASEM), for example, has called for integrating humanistic skills and knowledge into scientific education: "An emerging body of evidence suggests that integration of the arts, humanities, and STEMM fields in higher education is associated with positive learning outcomes that may help students enter the workforce, live enriched lives, and become active and informed members of a modern democracy" (NASEM 2018, 4). So, while it may seem unusual for a humanist to work in the field of science education, this cross-disciplinarity actually represents a growing trend.

The research skills in literary analysis and translation I acquired through PhD training proved valuable during my initial career transition and job search; however, greater attention to networking could have helped me avoid pitfalls further down the line. I applied my training in rhetorical textual analysis to my readings of job ads and the creation of my application materials. Analysis of job ads helped me to identify positions I would like to apply for and also helped me translate my skills and experiences into the language of academic administrators. I applied for a variety of student-facing jobs at universities and was hired into a coordinator position to develop career education courses and resources for PhD students in the biological sciences at a private Midwestern university medical school. The blog project supplemented my résumé to demonstrate my interest and knowledge in the field, as well as my ability to conceive of and independently develop PhD career development resources. After about six months, however, I felt like I had outgrown the coordinator position and wished that I had entered the organization at a higher level. If I had it to do all over again, I would have taken time during my job search to speak with people working in academic administration to learn from their experiences and to grow my network. I had served on a committee with the associate dean who led the unit where I was hired and believe that this connection played a role in landing the job. A broader network could have opened more doors and provided more options for my career transition. I also would have understood the differences between coordinator, manager, and director titles that could have helped me aim for a higher entry point.

I established my credibility as a scholar and educator in my new field through traditional academic activities, including curriculum development and assessment, publications, and by winning grants to support projects that applied humanistic skills and knowledge to STEM graduate education. One of my first assignments was to create and teach a writing course for bioscience PhD students and postdoctoral researchers. Although I was worried that the scientific community would perceive my humanistic training in a negative light, just the opposite was true. Because I had taught writing during my graduate study, I was recognized as an expert in this area. I developed an innovative and successful writing course that trained scientists to write and speak to different audiences. Although I started this project by doing a literature review to understand how writing courses for scientists were being taught at other institutions, I quickly realized that I needed to put my own stamp on the work. I drew on my experience as a writing instructor as well as my own scholarly interest in narrative theory and my knowledge of linguistics to create a humanities curriculum that was relevant to the needs of scientists. As a result, I was invited to give talks on science and storytelling at other institutions based on original scholarship that I developed for this course. I published my first peer-reviewed journal article on it as well.

I learned early on that grant writing and the ability to bring in external funding garnered both independence and prestige among scientists. One of the first projects I worked on as a CPD educator was organizing a grant-writing workshop for graduate students and postdoctoral researchers. While I performed the required functions of marketing, registration, and recruiting speakers, I also listened to what those speakers had to say, since I had not been trained to write grants during my graduate study. In the first year of my coordinator position, an opportunity presented itself to coauthor a grant with a faculty member. We applied to the National Institutes of Health (NIH) for funding to develop new courses that would integrate training for diverse careers into PhD education, and our grant was funded. It was a fast and furious learning experience, in both writing and implementing the grant. Through this experience, I learned an enormous amount about how to read and interpret funding announcements, construct a winning grant proposal, manage a grant budget and the bureaucratic processes of grant implementation, and finally, to conduct human subjects research in the space of higher education curriculum development.

I was promoted to director after two years. In this leadership role, I oversaw curriculum and education programs for over six hundred PhD students in the biological sciences. It was my job to ensure that they received high-quality training in transferable skills that would prepare them for a wide range of career outcomes. I directly supervised two staff members who managed course administration, education resource development, and education evaluation and assessment. We collaborated with faculty program leaders and course instructors in addition to partners across the university who were focused on career preparation, writing support, teaching and learning, and equity and inclusion, as well as with many other student affairs offices. A typical workday included meetings with faculty, staff, and collaborators from other institutions, teaching courses and workshops, and managing budgets and operational processes. I was responsible for hiring and promotion tasks, including writing and revising job descriptions, conducting performance reviews, establishing development plans for my staff, and participating in interviews for open positions. I also fielded emergency requests as needed and would troubleshoot all kinds of academic affairs issues for faculty and students. On other days I worked independently, reading literature to keep up in the graduate CPD field, writing grants and articles, or building new curriculum.

Over the course of six years, I received over $250,000 in grant funding, writing four successful grant applications and two unsuccessful applications. I developed two marquee training programs in science communication and leadership training with external funding from the NIH and a private foundation. These programs filled critical training gaps for graduate students and postdoctoral researchers, and they established me as a national expert in graduate career development education. These projects enabled me to travel to and present at national conferences, where I shared the results of my work. I networked with other leaders in the field of graduate career and professional development, which opened doors to additional professional opportunities and growth. For example, I was invited to serve as an external program reviewer for a bioscience PhD program on the basis of a curriculum presentation I had given at the annual meeting of the Association of American Medical Colleges Group on Research, Education, and Training. Presentations at the Graduate Career Consortium annual conference led to collaborations with other career development educators, including a peer-reviewed publication. Few of these accomplishments would have been possible—and they would not have gained national visibility—without external grant funding.

As a CPD educator, I transferred the skills and expertise I had developed during my humanities PhD training to enhance the career readiness of bioscience PhDs. In doing so, I was engaging in the applied humanities, a concept so foreign to most humanities graduate students that I was not even aware it existed until I found myself doing this work. Applied humanists "bring to bear their professional expertise on contemporary problems. Doing so may frequently require not only that they move beyond their own narrow disciplines ... but also that they address themselves to educated men and women outside of their own fields and sometimes outside of academia" (Steinberg 1974, 445). As a teacher and scholar trained in interdisciplinary and comparative methods of humanistic inquiry, with a background in business administration and a penchant for pragmatism, I found this work a great fit.

Teaching and developing programs in the field of science communication is the clearest example of my experience in the applied humanities because that work directly uses humanistic knowledge and skills to solve problems in another field, both within and beyond the academy. The ability to communicate effectively to a variety of audiences is an important skill for any scholar or professional. Educators who can teach these skills are highly valued in the sciences because few scientists receive formal training in writing and public speaking. Humanists are well positioned to teach communication because "humanities are fundamentally about representation: the representation of ideas, emotions, and cultures. By studying the most powerful imaginative forms of representation, we refine our communication skills, sharpen our critical faculties, and consider new ways of thinking" (Franke 2009, 19). In the sciences, representation is usually considered to be a transparent tool for disseminating research data. Despite the troubling rise of denial and doubt about climate science and vaccine safety in the public sphere, you will often hear scientists say, "Let the data speak for themselves" or "Listen to the data." However, humanists know that data do not speak. They are representations of human observations. They must be interpreted, organized, presented to others, and argued over. At their core, data rely on languages (both linguistic and visual). These are sign systems we participate in and that function to the extent that author and audience can reach consensus on the meaning of the representations. Humanists are not only able to teach communication skills; they can also contextualize the roles of interpretation and communication within scientific inquiry that sometimes produce unintentionally biased or unreproducible results.

ADVICE FOR PHDS EXPLORING ACADEMIC ADMINISTRATION CAREERS

There are many opportunities for PhDs to do interesting and fulfilling work in academic administrative positions. It is possible to move between fields by applying the skills and training developed during PhD study, such as learning material both deeply and quickly, and embracing learning as an ongoing part of professional life. The benefits of these roles include employment stability, work–life balance, and opportunities to develop experience in leadership and management that are widely transferrable. At the same time, the hierarchical dynamics of academic institutions can make life challenging for PhDs who are working in staff roles. Following are some of the lessons I have learned in my career so far.

Academic Hierarchies Affect Work Culture

As a staff member with a PhD who was doing academic work, I occupied an ambiguous space within the academic hierarchy. As a result, I had to navigate contradictory messages about my role within the institution. I have heard similar stories from my PhD peers working in staff roles at other universities. I often felt like a fish out of water among both the staff and the faculty I worked with. For the majority of the time I worked in STEM academic administration, I was the only staff member with a PhD in my academic unit. And because I was engaged in education and research, my work differed from that of the other staff in my unit, who were responsible for operations or student advising. In interactions with faculty members, I was praised for developing new curricula, winning grant funding, presenting at national conferences, and publishing peer-reviewed articles. However, I was also told that I sometimes spoke in a way that was "too authoritative" and that I should "defer to the faculty." Even when speaking about topics on which I have developed expertise, such as PhD career development or science communication, I was taking a risk if I presented my knowledge in a way that might question, critique, or otherwise challenge a position taken by a faculty member.

I have observed that the separation between university faculty and staff roles is reinforced through institutional and interpersonal messages.[1] In reality, however, the work of both groups is entangled and not always distinct. Jenea Cohn summarizes both the implicit and explicit messages that I received in my staff role: "As staff members, we're not 'supposed' to: teach ... do research ... develop lesson plans and curricular ideas ... give talks or presentations" (Cohn 2021). For each item on the list, Cohn also notes that staff members often perform these academic activities, either at their home institution, another institution, or both simultaneously, as I was doing. Staff members with PhDs routinely experience microaggressions that remind us of where "we fall in the institutional hierarchy.... That includes events like when faculty members and administrators do not use our proper titles or treat us like 'the help'" (Bessette 2021). In mixed meetings of faculty and staff, I would routinely be called by my first name while faculty members would be addressed as doctor or professor. Although I had been hired to augment science education, filling a gap in my academic unit precisely because I was an intellectual outsider, the message was clear: I would never be truly accepted as a scholarly equal to the scientific faculty.

Leadership Changes Can Provide Opportunities or Obstacles

If you are considering a career as an academic staff member, it is important to know that these roles are particularly vulnerable to the differing priorities that can accompany leadership changes and that those changes can come at any time. My unit went through multiple leadership changes while I was there. Each change had a drastic effect on both the work culture and the career opportunities. Under Leader A, for example, staff enjoyed a culture of esprit de corps in which we all felt valued. Our leader made it clear that everyone (both faculty and staff) had an important role to play in our mission to educate the next generation of biological scientists. Our office culture thrived on respect, trust, and transparency during this period, and it was truly a pleasure to do the work. Under Leader B, however, the hierarchy was absolute. Micromanaging was routine, decisions were made with no transparency, and the workplace became toxic. Staff job responsibilities can also change quickly as a result of leadership transitions. While Leader A facilitated my promotion from coordinator to director and encouraged me to conduct research and think creatively about my position, Leader B redefined my job to focus on operations management rather than scholarship and ultimately led me to leave the institution.

You Can Move Between Staff and Faculty Roles

Perhaps the most unexpected lesson I have learned so far in my career journey is that I enjoy teaching, doing research, and mentoring students; that is to say, I enjoy doing the work that is routinely done by faculty members. While this looked entirely unappealing during the latter half of my graduate training, my time in administration allowed me to build up my teaching and research skills slowly and without the pressure of a tenure clock. As a result, I have recently transitioned to a faculty role teaching interdisciplinary humanities courses and have reengaged with my dissertation research with the intent to publish. This transition was motivated by several factors, including a desire to spend more time teaching and working directly with students, especially students from historically marginalized backgrounds and first-generation students for whom a college education can be transformative. I also wanted to return to my research on African diaspora literature in the wake of George Floyd's murder in 2020 and the clear need to include stories of Black lives in our classrooms and in all university spaces.

The Humanities Are Pragmatic

In going to work with scientists, I wanted to earn a living while making a positive impact on graduate education. I also wanted to learn something about the humanities that I could not have learned during my own graduate training, where the intrinsic value of studying language and expression had been presumed to be its own reward. During my doctoral work, I often heard that the humanities have no practical application, as though the very existence of literature both implied and justified its academic study as a professional endeavor. Like Marjorie Garber, "I had assumed that my liberal arts training, my interest in literature, my interest, even, in criticism and scholarship were things to move past on my way to entering the world" (Garber 2008, 12). When it came time to choose a career, it seemed that by opting for pragmatism, I would naturally be distancing myself from scholarly humanistic work. Working with scientists forced me to challenge these assumptions and provided new perspectives on humanities research and education that I would probably not have gained by moving straight into a literature faculty career after graduate school.

The most important lesson I learned by working in STEM education administration is that the humanities are vital to all spheres of work and inquiry, especially if we are brave enough to apply them in unconventional areas. In fact, it is a misconception that the humanities and sciences are unconnected or exist in competition with one another. Rather, there is a need "to create a balanced development over the whole field of useful human inquiry" (Graves 1956, 1) by removing the scholarly silos that have made the humanities and sciences seem foreign to one another. The sciences have made a clear case for their application to technology, medicine, and engineering. Universities are increasingly funding STEM departments, too often by shifting resources away from the humanities. Now it is time for humanists to make an equally clear case for their value in creating a more democratic, connected, just, and equitable world.

The time that I spent working in STEM academic administration has proved to be an enhancement to my humanities graduate training and, I believe, has made me a better faculty member and academic leader than I would have been otherwise. In a teaching landscape where the majority of undergraduates are majoring in STEM fields, I have learned to make humanities content and pedagogy relevant for both humanities majors and nonmajors. I have gained valuable experience that enables me to counsel both undergraduates and graduate students on their careers and, hopefully, can help provide the support for others that was lacking during my own education. With experience in leadership and management, I can engage in university service projects that align with both my values and the strategic priorities of my institution, including program evaluation and diversity, equity, and inclusion work. Although my career journey has taken turns that I never could have predicted, each step has led me to grow as a scholar, teacher, and academic leader. My advice to PhDs exploring careers both beyond and within the professoriate is to stay curious, find the creative connections between seemingly disparate fields, and remain true to your values.

NOTE

1. Like any workplace culture, academic institutions function through a process of socialization and people receive implicit messages "about how to be, whom to 'look up to' and 'look down on,' what rules to follow, what roles to play, what assumptions to make, what to believe, and what to think" (Harro 2013, 48).

REFERENCES

Bessette, Lee Skallerup. 2021. "Stop Ignoring Microaggressions Against Your Staff." *Chronicle of Higher Education.* March 8, 2021. https://www.chronicle.com/article/stop-ignoring-microaggressions-against-your-staff.

Cohn, Jenae. 2021. "Faculty and Staff Often Don't Trust One Another. How Do We Fix That?" *Chronicle of Higher Education.* March 12, 2021. https://www.chronicle.com/article/faculty-and-staff-often-dont-trust-one-another-how-do-we-fix-that.

Evans, Teresa, Lindsay Bira, Jazmin Beltran Gastelum, L. Todd Weiss, and Nathan L. Vanderford. 2018. "Evidence for a Mental Health Crisis in Graduate Education." *Nature Biotechnology* 36 (3): 282–84. https://doi.org/10.1038/nbt.4089.

Franke, Richard J. 2009. "The Power of the Humanities & a Challenge to Humanists." *Daedalus* 138 (1): 13–23. https://www.jstor.org/stable/40543869.

Garber, Marjorie. 2008. "Good to Think With." *Profession*, 11–20. https://www.jstor.org/stable/25595877.

Graves, Mortimer. 1956. "The Humanities—Alternative to Orwell." *South Atlantic Bulletin* 21 (4): 1–5. https://www.jstor.org/stable/3197435.

Harro, Bobbie. 2013. "The Cycle of Socialization." In *Readings for Diversity and Social Justice*, 3rd ed., edited by Maurianne Adams, 45–52. New York: Routledge.

NASEM (National Academies of Sciences, Engineering, and Medicine). 2018. *The Integration of the Humanities and Arts with Sciences, Engineering, and Medicine in Higher Education: Branches from the Same Tree.* Washington, DC: National Academies Press. https://doi.org/10.17226/24988.

Padilla, Miguel A., and Julia N. Thomson. 2015. "Burning Out Faculty at Doctoral Research Universities." *Stress and Health* 32 (5): 551–58. https://doi.org/10.1002/smi.2661.

Steinberg, Erwin R. 1974. "Applied Humanities?" *College English* 35 (4): 440–50. https://www.jstor.org/stable/375571.

Subramanian, Shoba, Jessica A. Hutchins, and Natalie Lundsteen. 2022. "Bridging the Gap: Increasing Collaboration Between Research Mentors and Career Development Educators for PhD and Postdoctoral Training Success." *Molecular Biology of the Cell* 33, no. 2. https://doi.org/10.1091/mbc.E21-07-0350.

6

FROM HUMANITIES TENURE TRACK TO MEDICAL SCHOOL COMMUNICATIONS

LEIGH TILLMAN PARTINGTON

On September 11, 2001, I was a newly minted PhD and visiting assistant professor seeking a tenure-track job teaching literature—my career goal since high school. I was also pregnant with my second child. Watching the collapse of the World Trade Center twin towers on television made me ask, *Do I want to spend all day with someone else's kids or with my own?* I decided to work at raising my children full-time and I dropped out of the job search, knowing that I would never again be seen as competitive for increasingly rare tenure-track jobs.

My eventual interdisciplinary transfer from humanities PhD to communications manager for an academic department in a school of medicine marked a major transition from feeling grief and guilt for my career choices to enjoying a job that provides many of the perks of an academic faculty job, including intellectual stimulation, opportunities to collaborate with colleagues, access to university lectures and events, and a very nice tuition discount for my oldest child. My PhD, and the skills and connections I honed while completing it, have led to an unexpected and highly satisfying new career.

My work includes faculty development and support, internal and external communications, and grant writing. I've educated others about bias in writing. I have also taught effective business communication and how to build a professional identity through social media to students, faculty, and staff. My value to my colleagues is heavily based on the skills I acquired or enhanced during my years in graduate school, including close reading, digesting complex information quickly and thoroughly, excellent verbal and written communication skills, research skills, and my ability to coach reluctant faculty through writing projects (thanks to all those years of teaching freshman composition).

In 2014, I was hired by a physician friend for a temporary grant-writing position. I have since carved out a permanent position for myself in the medical school of a large, private research university. When I accepted the temporary position, I knew nothing about medical education or the practice of medicine. I was hired to write sections of a training grant and then kept on part-time to coach faculty who were writing personal statements for promotion and edit/proofread articles that the faculty were writing for submission to medical journals. My services as a writer and editor were offered to faculty who were teaching and seeing patients at a large, safety-net urban hospital in the southeastern US, particularly to help those who had fallen behind on the promotion timeline because they did not have many uninterrupted hours for writing. As the months went by, I found even more work I could volunteer to do. Draft and proofread outgoing letters for leadership? Write press releases? Create an internal newsletter? Write website copy? Organize an endowed lecture series? All of these have become part of my job, which now spans two departments. I have worked here for eight years now, and I plan to retire from this job in fifteen years. I have been promoted from writer to communications manager and have submitted paperwork for another promotion and new title. I really enjoy my job. This is not what I thought I would be doing with a PhD in English literature, specializing in British and Irish literature from 1890 to 1990. However, I have job security, work–life balance, and good benefits, and I feel valued by my colleagues and leadership.

I have the sort of work–life balance that academics rarely achieve. Until the pandemic, the stress and duties of my job stayed behind when I left the office every evening. At this time, I am still working 100 percent remotely with an increase in productivity and a decrease in commute time (from ninety-plus minutes daily to a thirty-second stroll from bedroom to office). I still leave work behind at 5:30 p.m. Being a staff member at a university where I was both a graduate student and a visiting assistant professor included a few awkward moments early on, but my former professors have been supportive, and they are happy to see me at university events. The choices that I made on this career path were not easy, but when the SARS-CoV-2 pandemic showed how little value some universities place on their faculty, I was reminded again that choosing to walk away from academia was the right choice for my mental health and the well-being of my family.

FROM TENURE TRACK TO MOMMY TRACK

When I was in third grade, one of my teachers told me I should be a writer, and I considered my career path set. In high school, my career goal became, like many of the authors in this collection, college professor. A career where I could read, write, and talk about books seemed like a dream, and I aimed for college-level teaching so that I could teach the books I loved. I imagined that I would teach literature during the academic year, write fiction during the summers, and have a great family life with lots of travel and probably some kids. My parents were both college graduates, but neither of them had any knowledge about careers in academia. They knew I was smart, and they assumed an academic career would be both stable and prestigious. I was lucky to have their support throughout my pursuit of multiple degrees.

My undergraduate degree from the College of William and Mary was a BA in English and art history. I graduated in 1988 coveting the careers of my advisors, who worked in lovely bookshelf-lined offices overlooking the Sunken Garden and took groups of students to Europe every summer. My advisor in the English Department encouraged me to go to graduate school, explaining that the Silent Generation professors like himself would start retiring about the time I finished my degree and there would be loads of tenure-track jobs. I wasn't ready to choose a specialty, so after graduation I moved north to work in publishing in Manhattan and live in (pre-gentrification) Hoboken with my best friend from college. A year later, having worked for a literary agent and realizing that I wasn't interested in working in the publishing industry, I moved back south to work in a bookstore and save money for grad school. It took two attempts to get accepted to University of Montana's creative writing program with a teaching stipend. I moved to Montana assuming I was on my way to making a living as a fiction writer, with some visiting writer gigs thrown in.

I earned both an MFA in creative writing and a master's in English literature at the University of Montana and then moved back to the south for a PhD program. The MFA program plus my year in publishing showed me the advantages of having steady work while working on my creative writing. A PhD program seemed like a good way to get back to the original dream of teaching and writing. I finished the PhD in five years. During that time, I also got married, lost my dad to cancer, and had a miscarriage and then a viable pregnancy. I turned in my dissertation and graduation paperwork in the eighth month of my pregnancy and turned down one semester of a one-year visiting professorship to stay home with my newborn daughter. I then spent two frustrating years on the job market. The "loads of tenure-track jobs" in the humanities that were supposed to open up in the 1990s–2000s never materialized due to downsizing, tenured professors not retiring, tenured positions being replaced by adjunct positions, and other unforeseen trends. I was fortunate to have no student debt, thanks to both my graduate schools offering me a tuition waiver and a small stipend in exchange for teaching freshman composition to undergraduates.

The PhD program I completed was small and traditional. I remember going to one talk by a former grad student who had begun working as a consultant for McKinsey & Company, but for the most part, we were being groomed for tenure-track jobs at research universities, despite the fact that there were fewer and fewer job postings every year. Most of the job postings for British and Irish literature in the late 1990s wanted someone who would also teach postcolonial literature and theory, specialties in which I was neither qualified nor interested. I interviewed at the Modern Language Association annual meeting with hordes of other shiny new PhDs, but I was not invited for any campus interviews. Many of my cohort did find academic positions; others took teaching positions at private high schools or moved into the private sector. Looking back, I think that a combination of exhaustion and self-doubt caused me to interview poorly. I was already suspicious that a career like that of my advisors was no longer possible. Trying to sound enthusiastic about teaching a 3/4 or 4/4 load with two to three sections of freshman comp each semester was increasingly difficult. In my role as visiting assistant professor at my degree-granting institution, I was teaching one section of comp and one section of twentieth-century British literature. Grading and class prep for two classes was already taking big chunks of my free time and leaving me with no energy to enjoy my family. Doubling that workload seemed impossible, but at that point, I saw no other career options. I was still hanging my hopes on the dream of "summers off" for family time. Now I understand that academic summers are dedicated to research and publishing, so work–life balance would have been increasingly difficult as I approached tenure review.

On the morning of September 11, 2001, I was at home, pregnant with daughter number two. The stories from that day of parents in the twin towers calling to say goodbye to their spouses and kids seemed to confirm something that I had already been thinking. I wanted to spend my days with my own kids, not someone else's. I also did not want to spend my evenings and weekends on class prep and grading. I was miserable because when I was on campus, I wanted to be at home with the baby and when I was at home, I wanted to be on campus engaging my intellect. I felt like I was shortchanging my students, my family, and myself. The only action that made sense was to step away from either parenting or teaching, and when expressed in those stark terms, there was only one choice for me. I decided to be a stay-at-home mom for a while. My husband is also a writer. He was transitioning from writing for trade magazines to corporate communications at that point, and the decision to stay home did not mean giving up an income, because I had earned nothing but stipends for teaching for the past decade.

By leaving the job market, I believed I was closing the door on academia forever. Every semester that I was at home, other ABDs and new PhDs would be presenting at conferences, publishing articles, and teaching classes. The rare jobs that opened in my specialty would be offered to scholars with more publications and teaching experience. I did not want to go through the certification process to teach public school or even apply to teach at a private school because of the burden of grading, which is time-consuming for anyone teaching a literature or writing course or even a class that fulfills a college writing requirement. I did not want to sacrifice the great family life I had established.

Over the next thirteen years, in addition to editing a memoir, a novel, a children's book, and a how-to manual written by friends, I made a few attempts to "stay relevant" in academia—presenting at a conference, attending lectures, writing a paper for a collection that would go unpublished. I tried book clubs and other ways to try to keep my brain engaged, but eventually settled for teaching a unit on Shakespeare to my Girl Scout troop and making sure my kids knew how to identify unreliable narrators and symbolism. I had to move past mourning the life of the mind and the office overlooking the quad that I had imagined. As others who have stepped away from academia know, there are ways outside the academy to pursue your research interests, including blogs and now podcasts. As Virginia Woolf wrote in *A Room of One's Own*, "There is no gate, no lock, no bolt that you can set upon the freedom of my mind" ([1929] 1976, 76). I still had library privileges at my degree-granting institution and leisure time to read. I could have written more articles and tried to get them published, but once I stepped off the entrance ramp to a publish or perish career, I found I was less interested in showing off what I knew. In 2011, a friend working for my degree-granting institution as a receptionist asked if I was interested in filling in for him a few days per month. With both my kids in school, that seemed like a good way to earn a few extra dollars and have a reason to hang out on campus again. I registered with the university's temporary employment services registry, which is a great way to get your foot in the door for higher education jobs.

FROM MOMMY TRACK TO A NEW CAREER

In spring 2014, my husband was laid off. I had been thinking about moving back into the workforce because we needed the extra income, but I immediately let my network of friends know that I needed employment ASAP, and I needed to make more than a retail job would offer. When people asked what I was looking for, I said I was willing to do anything but would love to use my writing skills in some way. A physician friend who was a division director at the medical school called me and asked if I had ever done any grant writing. He had an important training grant coming up for renewal. I had, in fact, worked on a grant for an outdoor garden for our elementary school and told him that I was sure I could help because I'm a fast learner—most PhDs have plenty of experience in preparing for a class or a presentation on the fly. He had the content expertise, but he wanted my writing skills. Because I was already in the HR system as a temp, I started the job just a few days after we talked.

As we worked together on the grant, I had the opportunity to show off my editing and close-reading skills. I worked hard to ask the right questions and get the details right. I provided status reports to my team and let them know I was available for other parts of the grant if needed. Even before we turned in the grant, my physician friend asked me to coach faculty who were writing personal statements for promotion. These statements had been returned for revisions by the department promotions and tenure committee with a tight deadline, so getting them right was critical to the promotions moving forward. I had plenty of experience in both teaching and coaching personal narratives, so that was the perfect task to begin introducing my skills to the faculty. Every faculty member I met walked away knowing I had skills in editing and writing and was there to help them. During our in-person weekly division lunches, I was soon able to ask faculty how their projects were going and to keep me in mind if they needed help with edits or a second set of eyes to proofread. I wanted to prove that although I had found the job through a friend, I was worth hiring full-time because I was bringing value to the division.

Another leader in the division asked if I could draft recommendation letters. I said yes and then Googled how to write effective recommendation letters. I also asked for samples so that I could capture the voice of the person for whom I was drafting letters. At this point, I was working pro re nata (PRN or "as needed" in this new world of medical terminology I had entered). I was already enjoying the intellectual exercise of the work and being back in an academic environment, even though I was in a faculty office building far from main campus and across the street from the hospital. I began to look for other ways to be valuable. I asked the division admins if I could proofread for them. Faculty began to stop by my cubicle or email me to see if I could proofread or reformat manuscripts for them. My response was always, "I'd be happy to help!" I asked many questions in the beginning, but I also produced top quality work quickly. I always offered to make changes if needed and I made customer service my top priority. Since I wasn't on campus full-time, I made a sign for my cubicle door with my email address and an invitation to email me to set up appointments to discuss writing needs. My reputation began to spread by word of mouth. I got shout-outs during our weekly division lunches from faculty who felt I helped them get promoted or get published. Some wrote me emails thanking me for my help, and I forwarded those to the division administrator who was my direct supervisor as well as my division director friend. Six months later, I signed an offer letter for a full-time position with benefits as a writer for the division. That was eight years and one promotion ago.

WHAT HUMANITIES PHDS AND STAY-AT-HOME PARENTS BRING TO THE TABLE

So, what does a literature PhD bring to a school of medicine? First, and importantly, you bring your ability to write, edit, and coach writing. A significant percentage of medical faculty may have English as a second or third language and need a native speaker to standardize punctuation, article use, and other quirks of English. Others may have overcome substandard educational backgrounds and appreciate having their writing reviewed by an in-house editor. Every piece of writing from application letters to grant proposals can benefit from having a second set of eyes looking for cut/paste errors, typos, and the like. I am the perfect reviewer—the intelligent, nonexpert reader. The first few times I pointed out sentences that were unclear or places where I wanted more details, impostor syndrome told me that my background in the humanities was at fault, but appreciative faculty members disagreed and told me I was making their writing stronger. My reputation grew among my division faculty and soon faculty in other divisions and other locations were asking if I was available to review their work.

I am also valued for my skills in close reading and digesting complex information quickly and thoroughly, my excellent verbal and written communication, and my research experience. Although I was initially hampered by my years at home, during which the Internet *completely* revolutionized both academic and professional communication, I have caught up. As an older Gen Xer and a humanities major, I may not be as facile with Excel and Instagram as my millennial and Gen Z colleagues, but other changes (like our university switching from Dropbox to Box to Microsoft Sharepoint as the preferred way to share documents in the past six years) affected all of us equally—we're all constantly having to learn new ways of doing things and new programs. There are plenty of free online courses covering marketing and technology, and every social media platform has training programs. Spreadsheets will never be my passion, but they are beloved by the financial analyst with whom I write annual reports every year and because we approach data, facts, and organization so differently, our reports have been praised by leadership for covering all the bases and presenting information in a way that appeals to multiple audiences. Your strengths as a PhD will always be welcome on a team.

I still work regularly on grant proposals as well. In addition to proofreading and drafting multiple letters of support that don't sound like they came from the same template, I'm often called in to cut words when the draft goes over the length requirements. When saving a proposal to PDF on the due date adds five pages to the length, I'm the one who gets a frantic phone call. Those of us who trained and taught in the humanities are experts at finding and converting passive voice, which is an excellent strategy for cutting words. Teaching and grading freshman composition makes us experts in spotting the inefficient use of language and turning it into clear, concise writing.

There are different types of writing needs at a medical school. A PhD with a science background could take a larger role in writing articles. I have a friend with a PhD in sociology who makes a very good living as a proposal and grant writer for nursing schools. However, my ability to perform a wide range of communication tasks means that I can serve a wider range of clients within my department, not just the researchers. My chair and I recently collaborated with two other writer-chair duos on a national presentation and publication about different models for academic writers in a department (Weidner et al. 2022). A department with a larger number of active researchers might need to hire a full-time proposal writer; a research center that relies on soliciting donors and fundraising might hire someone with a degree in marketing. However, I think most academic medical departments can be well-served by a PhD in the humanities. My ability to perform a wide range of communication tasks is an efficient and effective use of funding. Publications are up; our rate of successful promotions is high, and the volume of funding applications submitted has increased. In addition, the internal newsletters that I create build a sense of community, which has been important during the pandemic but was also important pre-pandemic, given that our faculty physicians are scattered across several clinical sites.

Department leaders, in addition to their research, teaching, and service obligations, have an administrative burden. They need to communicate effectively and efficiently with various audiences including faculty, staff, students, alumni, university and/or healthcare administrators, community leaders and organizations, donors, legislators, national organizations, and occasionally the media. They are asked for everything from recommendation letters to annual reports to press releases, sometimes with little warning or turnaround time. I save my departmental leadership hundreds of hours per year by drafting written communications for them and giving a final proofread once they have made their revisions. I also remove that task from the senior secretaries and administrative assistants, so they can concentrate on the other work that keeps the department running smoothly. I don't have a marketing background, but I do have colleagues in the medical school who have marketing degrees, and they've been invaluable for explaining things like what SEO is (search engine optimization) and why it's important to have the right key words in your website copy so that Google can guide viewers to your website. They have also recommended online training to help me sharpen those skills. I return the favor by giving my marketing colleagues well-written content to share on social media, in blog posts, or in their own internal and external communications. Many of them do not have backgrounds in English or journalism, and they are always happy to have content from me, knowing that it will be well-written and ready to plug in. Because I have both a thirty-thousand-foot view and a ground-level view of what is going on in the department through gathering news for the monthly internal newsletter, I've become a valuable partner in departmental strategic planning.

Because of my experience teaching freshman comp and the personal essay, I offer annual workshops on writing personal statements to fellows, residents, and medical students in one of our programs. I have presented the same workshop to faculty who are preparing a promotion dossier, although I more often work one-on-one with faculty to refine their personal statements. I make a point of educating others about bias in writing and have a personal mission to remove self-deprecating and overly humble language from the personal statements and application letters of women and underrepresented-in-medicine minority faculty. I also give presentations to colleagues and learners on effective business communication, email etiquette, and constructing a professional identity using social media. I recently gave a presentation at a national conference on effective email communication and am currently working on a team to create a staff development program for our department.

I maintain the department website and social media accounts. We use a contractor for the actual website design, but I make edits and keep the information and images fresh. Although I could have pursued specialized training in website design, my chair prefers to pay a contractor to turn my content into web pages. He values my expertise in written communications and wants me to spend the majority of my time using those skills. I use Canva to design social media posts, which satisfies my creative side. I also produce four internal newsletters. The newsletters feed the website and social media content and, again, satisfy my creative side.

The funding for communications positions can be interesting. At my research institution, many of the communications professionals are hired on the department level and most of them have marketing backgrounds. Faculty development staff are also mostly hired on the department level. The physician friend who originally hired me has a reputation for hiring outside the box—I was his second "success story" in hiring someone outside medicine who proved to be very valuable. For most of the year, he would hear kudos from people who had worked with me from all over the medical school, from the Dean's Office (promotion dossiers and annual reports) to the Office of Development (reports for donors). However, the school of medicine does not fund writers, communications specialists, or faculty development support on a division level, so when budget season rolled around, my line item in the division budget was always struck and my salary would have to be paid from discretionary funds. Initially, we looked at grant funding as a way to pay my salary, but most grants do not allow the pre-funding work of grant writers on the budget. The grant funding I have received, for website content development and curriculum development work, has been 2.5–5 percent. We also tried having other divisions and programs pay portions of my salary in return for the "loan" of my services, but as I got busier, that model threatened my work–life balance.

In 2018, I was promoted to manager, communications, and my salary line was transferred from a division within the department of medicine to the department of family and preventive medicine, a much smaller department that was now chaired by the physician who hired me. However, leadership on the division level has seen the value of investing in someone with top-notch writing and communications skills, and even though the school of medicine still won't fund it, another division within the department of medicine has just hired a writer using its discretionary funds to do the same faculty support and communications tasks that I do. A third division has announced that it will be looking to pay a contract writer for support during promotion season and to help with grant writing. Perhaps the medical school will eventually see writers as essential staff on the division level, but for now, it's enough that leadership sees our value. My next promotion will be to the level of assistant director.

I worked with our department business administrator to map out a promotion plan that reflects my increasing responsibilities, including managing an administrative assistant.

If you have taken time off to be a stay-at-home parent, don't underestimate the new skills that you are bringing back into the workplace. Your volunteer work can provide important insights into what's important to your community as well as connections to jobs. I was a Girl Scout leader for twelve years—quite a few of my early LinkedIn connections were with other troop leaders. You sharpened your multitasking skills and became more efficient with your schedule constricted by kid timetables. If you kept in contact with colleagues from your former work life, let all of them know that you are looking to transition back, even part-time or with contract work. Staying at home isn't for everyone, but I would not trade my years at home with my girls for a tenured job anywhere.

WHAT'S NEXT?

I'm still learning to navigate the class structure as a PhD outside the faculty. I am the only PhD among the staff in my department, which has inspired flares of impostor syndrome and a couple of awkward exchanges with both staff and faculty. Interestingly, one of my staff colleagues who has an MBA has been the biggest champion of calling me "Dr. Partington." She started referring to me as such both in writing and in person as soon as she found out I had a PhD. Other staff and faculty now usually refer to me as Dr. Partington in writing and in formal settings, especially when someone from outside the department is present.

I have also come back in contact with English department faculty and negotiated their expectations of a successful graduate. After the initial surprise at hearing that I work for the medical school, they've been very pleased to see me at readings and lectures. The English department is making an effort to normalize expectations around the difficulty of finding a tenure-track job and has gone as far as to invite back PhDs who are working outside academia to talk to current graduate students. Because English departments rely on graduate students to teach multiple sections of freshman composition, I doubt that the number of graduate students admitted annually will ever be limited to match job availability (nationwide, not just at my institution).

Academia will always need English professors to teach close reading, critical thinking, analytical and persuasive writing, and research skills. However, there are other arenas where those skills are equally valued, and English PhDs should not feel limited by the academic job market or defeated if they decide to step off the academic hamster wheel. Working at a medical school has given me the opportunity to support and celebrate faculty who are performing lifesaving and life-changing research. As I grow older, and as I have watched both my mother and my mother-in-law struggle with cognitive impairment, I am especially grateful to have the opportunity to hear research presentations by my colleagues who specialize in geriatric medicine and brain health. And while I'll never have the stomach to view a presentation about diabetic foot ulcers during a lunch and learn, my colleagues who work at the large, urban safety-net hospital are doing important work to address social determinants of health, health inequities, and racial justice in medicine and medical education. Supporting this work is yet another way that my job is fulfilling, both personally and intellectually.

By leaving the professor track for a staff position at a school of medicine, I have not left the life of the mind behind, even though I assumed I did when I stepped away from the tenure-track job market. Instead, I have broadened my range of interests, found satisfying ways to use my writing, research, and teaching skills, and most importantly for me, maintained a healthy work–life balance that has allowed me to be fully present and involved in the lives of my children during the crucial years of birth through high school graduation. My staff position also gave my older daughter a 75 percent tuition discount; without it, her four years at a private research institution would have been out of reach for us financially. This is not the path I thought I would follow, but it has turned out to be the right one.

ACKNOWLEDGMENTS

My family is my everything, always. The lights of my life George, Eleanor, and Audrey; my parents and sister Curtis, Margaret, and Nancy; and my in-laws John and Janet have all been my steadfast cheerleaders and soft place to land. I am so grateful for friends who have supported me along the way: Bob, Jill, David, Cathy N., Cathy S., Karen S., Jan, Mark L., Chris, Gabrielle, Penny,

Kelly, Frank, Karen P., Karen B.-W., Gavin, Beth, Terri, Kathy, Ginger, Meg, Susan J., Iris, Michelle, Susan D., Lynn, Virginia, Marian, Mary, Susan P., Brenda, and Ellen. Huge thanks to mentors/colleagues/friends old and new for never doubting, even when I doubted myself, especially Patty, Jim, Jack, Tim, Bill, Ron, Geraldine, Ted, Luke, Pat, and Jason.

REFERENCES

Weidner, Amanda, Samantha Elwood, Erin Thacker, Wendy Furst, Leigh Partington, Irfan Asif, Philip Zazove, Theodore Johnson, Kola Okuyemi, and Valerie Gilchrist. 2022. "Roles of Academic Writers in a Department: Benefits, Structures, and Funding." *Family Medicine* 54 (1): 16–23. https://doi.org/10.22454/FamMed.2022.465116.

Woolf, Virginia. (1929) 1976. *A Room of One's Own*. New York: Harvest/HBJ.

7

PHDS GOING ROGUE

From the Bench to the Library and Beyond

STACEY E. WAHL AND CARRIE L. IWEMA

Choosing to pursue a graduate degree in the basic sciences is not a decision that generally is, or should be, made lightly. While it is a better situation than some graduate programs (STEM PhDs often include tuition and a livable stipend), it is a long process with failure as your frequent companion. The process pushes you beyond your intellectual limits and can be incredibly emotional. Beyond the specific research goals, a basic science PhD teaches you how to think: brainstorming new ideas, turning ideas into practical steps, and evaluating their success. You graduate with an incredibly specific set of skills that makes you feel as if you are marketable almost nowhere beyond your current specialty (anyone looking for someone who can harvest an exceptional yield of primary oligodendrocytes?). Fortunately, you also finish with a skill set that is limited only by your imagination.

In this chapter we discuss how our research careers led to medical libraries, how we used our skills in those spaces, what challenged and frustrated us, and how that fits into each of our career journeys. We hope that our experiences will inspire you to critically examine your strengths, weaknesses, and career ambitions. As scientists, we are trained to think about the research first and how we can best answer complicated questions. We can also become laser focused on the process and the next immediate step to be successful. Sometimes we forget that we, as people, are the most fulfilled when our work leverages our strengths and challenges us, and that process is very rarely linear. Finding where you feel fulfilled, challenged, and well utilized is the hardest part, especially if you're going rogue.

Perhaps surprisingly, we found that in the library. There are tons of librarian roles within an academic library: some are focused on developing the collection, some work with the physical building and help students utilize the space, some focus on teaching undergraduates, and still others focus on graduate/professional students and faculty. The latter two groups are often called subject librarians because they work with students or faculty within a specific field. Being a subject librarian usually requires a master's degree in library or information sciences. In the last several years, there has been a shift within library culture to expand the qualifications for academic librarianship to include subject matter experts, aka people with degrees in the fields that the libraries serve. This could mean an art historian charged with serving as librarian for an arts school or, like us, scientists working as basic science librarians. We have been called "feral" librarians by some, but we prefer the term "rogue" librarians. It sounds less stray cat and more Batman. We hope our journey into going rogue inspires you to consider how you can take your career to unexpected places.

DIALOGUE: CHOOSING A CAREER PATH

CARRIE: *As undergraduates in science we were often asked, "So do you want to be a doctor?" We both quickly realized that a career in medicine was not for us, but our decisions to pursue doctoral degrees came about differently. What was your process like?*

STACEY: I loved learning, even before I could put my finger on that exact thought. In high school and college, I was drawn to the most challenging classes and fascinated by why we think what we think. I pursued a degree in neuroscience to learn more, but without any real idea of what I would do with that degree. I tried on different careers to find the right fit, including working in a physical therapy clinic, a hospital, and a sleep lab. I also did research in psychology and physical therapy. Research felt like a better fit; it was learning and discovering. I still was not sure what that meant for a career, so I took a year off to reflect and plan.

    I also taught marching band during that year and all through college. How does that fit into pursuing a neuroscience PhD? Teaching high school kids color guard (how to spin flags and throw sabers in the air) was incredibly fulfilling. The moment when you see a kid who had never been able to coordinate their body move, throw something, and catch it, all while smiling and keeping in step, is amazing. As their instructor, it was my job to get each individual student there while coordinating the group's performance with the rest of the band. It is a creative, innovative, and constantly challenging process. I wanted this challenge, and teaching in general, to be part of my career. So, what combines teaching, learning, being challenged, and science? Getting a PhD.

STACEY: *How did you get into neuroscience?*

CARRIE: My path to basic science research was more linear, but also began with an interest in psychology. I became interested in abnormal psychology while in high school, majored in psychology as an undergrad, and took a class called Physiological Psychology, aka neuroscience. I started working in labs almost immediately and became enamored with the beauty of neuroanatomy and microscopy. I completed an honors thesis in spinal cord regeneration and decided to go to grad school to continue in that area of study, but I realized that, as a psych major, I didn't have some of the hard science courses I needed to get into a good school. I took a year off and worked as a lab tech while taking chemistry classes, and then applied to several neuroscience PhD programs and chose one in a medical school setting.

But why did I choose that path in the first place? Until I became interested in psychology in my late teens, I was much more inclined toward literature and music (I played the flute). The interest in psychology came from watching the movie *Sybil* in a sophomore health class and then reading the book *When Rabbit Howls*. During my senior year psychology class, I wrote a paper on clinical lycanthropy, a psychiatric disorder in which patients believe they have been transformed into an animal. I know! My interests ran to the bizarre. Admittedly, they still do. But while I was an undergraduate, I became more interested in what I could actually see—anatomy of the brain—rather than the mysterious workings of the mind. And I was practical. A PhD program in the harder psychological track of neuroscience comes with a stipend, so I could get paid to learn. What's not to love about that? As far as what I was going to do once I had the PhD—I didn't know. That was a concern for future me. By working on my degree, I knew what I'd be doing for at least five years, and that was a reassuring thought.

DIALOGUE: MOVING AWAY FROM THE BENCH — GOING ROGUE

CARRIE: *Despite our initial enthusiasm for neuroscience, many factors came into play that led both of us in a different direction. When did you realize that you might want to go rogue and step away from bench research and a traditional tenure-track career path?*

STACEY: My training was also in a medical school, and while my lab was exceptional and well-rounded, I didn't spend much time thinking about what would happen next. I knew from my marching band days that I was passionate about teaching. I loved my research but was frustrated by the curricular organization and career guidance of my graduate program. I was so frustrated by this that I redesigned the curriculum and presented it to my program director, without being asked. This unorthodox approach to frustration should have been a signal that I would someday jump, but not yet.

STACEY: *When did you first see signs that you would not be at the bench forever?*

CARRIE: I had a very challenging experience as a grad student. I came to my program knowing who I wanted as my advisor and the area of research I wanted to focus on (spinal cord regeneration), but I had to do required rotations in a couple of other labs first. By the time I started working in my chosen lab, the primary investigator (PI) had lost funding, so I had to make the decision, one year into my training, of whether to stay there or move on to another lab. I chose the latter. My new PI had me work on a new-to-the-field technique that took a tremendous amount of time and effort to learn. During this time, my PI took a year-long sabbatical. Upon his return, there were issues with my research project (having to do with long-term animal studies and poor advice); my PI became the chair of the department, *and* the lab physically moved to a new space. I was six years into my research when the next obstacle arose—my PI was taking a position at another university, and the entire lab was moving multiple states away. As I was *almost* done, I elected to stay at my original institution to complete my bench research using another lab's equipment and occasionally commute to collaborate with my PI in the new lab. At this point I was completely disillusioned by my PhD experience, but I also recognized that it was atypical.

CARRIE: *I decided to take the safe route and give research one more shot by pursuing a traditional postdoc. What was your postdoc like?*

STACEY: I loved doing my research but already had a sense that I would not be at the bench forever, so I wanted to find a way to make a difference in STEM education as a career. This was right around the time that lots of institutions had started talking about careers "beyond the bench," and most of the advice was that you could do what you wanted (go rogue) but you needed a traditional postdoc to open doors, especially if you wanted to stay in academia. I was exploring how to affect change in graduate education as a career, so that meant pursuing a postdoc. As I was already a rogue, though, my postdoc was not traditional.

I pursued a fellowship that combined research with pedagogical training and teaching externships. I chose a new research area and a new model organism. I grew as an educator and continued to develop my career goals around student success in higher ed. I worked with undergraduates from a variety of backgrounds and learned about the different experiences in higher education for students from minoritized communities. I also learned that it wasn't *bench research* that I loved, it was *primary cell culture, oligodendrocytes, western blots, mouse work*. I loved the *environment* of my science: the community of the other students and my mentor, and the inquisitive and collaborative nature of our work.

STACEY: *What about your postdoc?*

CARRIE: I was still very interested in my research topic: development and regeneration in the rodent olfactory system. I used my postdoc to determine whether my difficulties were due to my specific unfortunate circumstances, or my career path would be more fulfilling and enjoyable away from the bench. I finished writing my dissertation and commuted to collaborate with my grad school PI while also starting in my postdoc lab. I finally defended my PhD, not quite eight years after starting it, the Friday before 9/11.

During my postdoc I worked at a prestigious Ivy League institution with great people on an interesting project. But I realized that (1) I was a capable but not particularly stellar researcher, (2) even the really outstanding researchers have a lot of difficulty getting funding and publishing papers, and (3) I wasn't particularly interested in emulating the challenging lifestyles of the "successful" researchers I knew. So ... what to do? By now, and including working in labs as an undergrad, I had spent almost fifteen years doing bench research! How could I walk away after spending all of this time and effort?

CARRIE: *How did your postdoc experience affect how you saw research as a career?*

STACEY: In every single way imaginable. In addition to my professional shifts, my personal life also saw dramatic change during my postdoc. I had two of my three kids. This massive change highlighted a feeling that had been growing in me for a couple of years. I didn't *want* to be at the bench for sixty-hour weeks, like the competitive postdocs in my field. I valued the parts of my job that did not include experiments: mentoring graduate students, advocating for postdocs, and negotiating with university units to increase support for trainees. If I became a research faculty member, these types of activities would be relegated mostly to service, only 10 percent of what most research faculty members do. I also knew that tenure-track faculty worked well beyond a forty-hour workweek until they achieved tenure and, oftentimes, well after that. That career path did not align with my interests, my passions, or the work–life balance that I needed.

DIALOGUE: JOINING THE LIBRARY

CARRIE: *When you realized that your career might take you away from the bench, how did you decide what was next?*

STACEY: Well, I was a researcher. So I began to research other careers in academia. After conducting several informational interviews and serving as a speaker for a library educational series, I discovered the concept of a liaison, or subject, librarian. This model pairs librarians with specific disciplines to give people in those disciplines dedicated support by providing individual consultations, pedagogical instruction, and program development. All the things! This was also a job open to me because I was a subject matter expert. It seemed tailor-made to leverage my expertise to serve others (I wouldn't learn about being called feral until well after I had been hired).

STACEY: *How did you get interested in being a librarian?*

CARRIE: After finally accepting that bench research was not going to be my path forward, I struggled for a bit trying to figure out how to take advantage of my years of research experience. I was weary of focusing so intently on a very tiny area (as you must do in bench research). I was open about this with my postdoc PI, who was extremely supportive. He helped me explore possibilities in scientific publishing and science policy before I decided to go rogue with medical librarianship.

Why librarianship? Multiple reasons. At the time, my best friend was in library school, so I was aware of the degree expectations. Upon exploration, I discovered subject librarians and that the library field had attracted a smattering of other basic science PhDs. I also recalled that as a child, my career goal had actually been to become a librarian! Finally, I was fortunate to live in an area with a library school, so for a year and a half I became a "post-postdoc." This meant I could continue in the lab part-time while I worked on my master of library science (MLS) degree.

CARRIE: *So I chose to get the MLS first and you went straight for the job. How was the transition directly from the bench to the library?*

STACEY: My transition to the library began during my interview. During breaks to pump milk for my two-month-old daughter (life and career moves never align perfectly!), I learned that there was a lot about librarianship I did not know. Despite this, I passionately conveyed how science could benefit from increased library interactions. A basic science librarian who has a science background can understand the research process and the mindset of the researchers, which is helpful when developing and providing services that support them.

I learned in this process of transitioning to the library that I could, and should, find ways to bring my career goals and my job responsibilities together. My training as a scientist helped me identify the spaces where I could work, hypothesize how my goals could align with those of the library, and develop a detailed plan to reach those goals. I looked at everything through the lens of how our work was supporting graduate student success, and how that could be communicated to the wider university community. This perspective helped me keep a wide-angle lens on the work I was doing and feel like I was still pursuing my career goals, in a new environment.

STACEY: *How did you transition to the new library environment?*

CARRIE: During my MLS I interned at my postdoc institution's biomedical library, where I gained real-world experience and developed professional relationships and friendships that continue to this day. Once I earned my degree, I accepted a position at the biomedical library of another prestigious institution and became a basic science librarian. I gained experience in bioinformatics, which became a through line during my library career. Unfortunately, after less than a year I had to face the fact that this particular job was not an ideal fit for me due to a regrettably toxic work environment. This led me to a position in another biomedical library at a large, well-funded research institution, where I spent almost fifteen years.

DIALOGUE: THE GOOD STUFF

CARRIE: *What have you found to be most satisfying in your library role?*

STACEY: My role was a great combination of collaborative teamwork, university-wide service, and individual project development. Despite the steep learning curve in some areas, my background allowed me to take a question, design a way to obtain an answer, and then reflect on whether or not that answer had the desired effect. This is an extremely transferable skill. I loved applying that skill in individual consultations and group training sessions.

Collaboration was a constant at the library, both within my department and within the schools I served. This was familiar territory for me, coming from research labs where everyone had different skills and being successful meant seeking out the right people to teach you what you didn't know and bringing teams of experts together to complete a project. I loved this area of my work, bringing together different university units to develop programming and working with librarians to communicate resources to diverse audiences.

I also loved how the culture fully supported continuous learning, everything from the intricacies of the library world to how to be your best self while working in it. I was able to continue learning about the library and about student success by pursuing professional development and fellowships within my university. The library supported my work in supporting student success and allowed me to take the time to learn anything that I thought could be beneficial to my work with the basic sciences.

STACEY: *What did you love about working in the library?*

CARRIE: My responsibilities changed during my time at the library but primarily included organizing bioinformatics support and training for researchers to help them access and use specialized analytical tools and databases, as well as teaching classes and providing guidance on data management plans, electronic lab notebooks, preprints, and the selection of appropriate data analysis strategies to improve research rigor. I had a secondary faculty appointment with my institution's Clinical and Translational Science Institute and created a workshop series titled How-To Talks by Postdocs, providing postdocs an opportunity to teach classes within the library. I also became a distinguished member of the Association of Health Information Professionals and a long-term member of the Medical Library Association (MLA), the premier professional society for medical librarians.

I appreciated the freedom to explore numerous areas of interest, just like you! I created a continuing education class on personal genomics and personalized medicine that I taught around the country, I cowrote a paper with you and your colleagues on the how-to series for postdocs, I attended a two-week bootcamp on coding for biologists, and I was one of the inaugural fellows for ASAPbio (Accelerating Science and Publication in Biology), a nonprofit advocacy group for preprints and open peer review. All of these experiences were outside my traditional library duties, but I was free to explore them because of the nature of working in libraries.

I was able to thrive in the MLA by serving as a co-convener of the Molecular Biology and Genomics Special Interest Group, chairing both the Awards and Continuing Education committees, helping organize an international meeting, and receiving two Presidential Awards for my work for MLA. Had I stayed with bench research, I firmly believe that I would not have had as many professional opportunities as via librarianship.

I also greatly enjoyed not feeling obligated to spend all of my waking hours thinking, conducting, or writing about my next research experiment. Instead of an 80+ hour workweek, I worked 37.5 hours unless a special project or upcoming conference required additional attention. The salary was more than adequate considering the much-reduced time commitment and therefore also reduced mental strain. Compared to the majority of traditional faculty positions, my work–life efforts were well balanced.

CARRIE: *How was your work life balance as a librarian?*
STACEY: Ah-mazing! As one of my colleagues loves to say, "There is no such thing as a library emergency." As an achiever, I still tend to think about work

more than I may need to, but I had the flexibility of a faculty job without the intense research pressures.

DIALOGUE: THE NOT-SO-GOOD STUFF

CARRIE: *So, everything was awesome? Were there any times when your background created difficulties for you in the library? Are there any drawbacks that folks considering the library as a career path should know?*

STACEY: There was a bit of culture shock moving from the bench to the library. Initially, I thought that had to do a lot with me being new. Over time, I realized that the culture in the library was much more incremental and tentative than bench research, where quality and pace are equally prioritized. In my role as a liaison, I had to shift and adapt as the departments I served shifted and adapted. As a whole, library culture is less driven by innovation and more driven by providing consistent services. Both are laudable goals, but they can be on opposite sides of a tug-of-war.

In the first year, I struggled with having to effectively communicate my ideas and plans before I did them. This is a major difference between research and research-adjacent departments at a university. Undirected discovery is an integral part of the research process; the library, like other support units, is more cautious, prioritizes feasibility and return on investment. I stretched my skills to more thoroughly explain expected outcomes and alternative approaches, which are an integral part of any scientific grant, but the slow pace at which the library allows you to try something new is a consistent drawback.

In addition to procedural slowness, there have also been some more personal hiccups (read: being treated as feral isn't fun). My institution does not require you to have a library degree to be hired as a librarian and officially supports "going rogue." This belief is not universal in librarianship, which led to professional conflicts that were hard on a personal level. I chose to view this as an opportunity to grow my communication skills and practice working through the assumptions of others. It is important to remember that no job is perfect, and that there will be people everywhere who do not get your goals or how your job fits into them.

Finally, if high compensation is a career goal, the library may not be the place for you. The salary for a librarian at an academic library is higher than at most other types of libraries, but the positions are usually not set up for upward mobility and growth, from a monetary standpoint. There are also very few leadership opportunities, so if managing people or directing a department is part of your career goals, that is something to consider when investigating a librarian career.

STACEY: *What did you struggle with in your role? Did you feel like your MLS and your PhD worked well together?*

CARRIE: Since I have a STEM PhD and a library master's, I was marginally less feral—I mean rogue—than you and was able to straddle the division between bench researchers and librarians, to a degree. Some scientists were more willing to engage with me and accept my suggestions once they realized I have a PhD. However, some library colleagues treated me as if I was an elitist and assumed I looked down on them. My PhD experience does provide me with insights into the information-seeking process of basic science researchers, and my suggestions on how to provide services for and support this population were sometimes in conflict with the typical librarian approach. Some of the more traditional concerns and areas of focus for librarians are not applicable to the population I supported, so I did occasionally feel like my time and energy weren't being used to their best advantage.

As you mentioned, the opportunities for rising up the library hierarchy are limited, even with a library degree, unless you are willing to (greatly) expand your interests beyond a focus on supporting a specific population. I considered myself a scientist first and a librarian second, so I was perhaps overly adamant that everything I did was in support of bench researchers, and if it helped anyone else then bonus. This focus can make it quite difficult to be promoted to a leadership position; take this as a word of caution for anyone embarking upon a library-based career path.

DIALOGUE: THE JOURNEY CONTINUES

CARRIE: *Whether focusing on the destination or on the journey, it's critical to have confidence in the skills, knowledge, and experience acquired on the way. We've both had to forge our own paths, and it's been a challenge not to make it any harder than it needed to be. Stacey, what's next for you?*

STACEY: My library experience was a great opportunity to learn about how a university works, collaborate with colleagues with diverse professional experience and roles, and build relationships. All of these will serve me well in my overall career plan to improve student success in STEM. Throughout my role at the library, I reflected on what that next step looked like and how to best leverage my experience to get there. A career in higher ed is often about who you know, in addition to what you know. This may be similar to other industries, but it is very different from a 100 percent research position. While it has taken some time for me to accept that, probably due to my training, where asking the right question and doing the right investigation was paramount, the library gave me the space to learn about and make connections. Overall, a career plan in academia, outside of traditional professorship, is nebulous because the roles at each university differ. That is both a drawback and a blessing. The career I want doesn't have a clear road map to achieve it. It is a bit like undirected scientific research in that way. I know what the overall goal is and am comfortable going rogue to get there.

Interestingly, during the process of writing this chapter, I was exploring opportunities available at my institution, which is something I would advise anyone interested in building their career from multiple areas to always be doing. Because of my collaborative work across the university, I was recruited to apply for a position within the School of Medicine's Faculty Affairs Office. I applied for and ultimately accepted this role. I will now be leveraging everything I learned in the library in the next phase of my journey, helping clinical and basic faculty be the best teachers they can be. This is my next contribution to student success, and I am excited to use all of the tools I have gained along the way in this new position. What's next for you?

CARRIE: I spent fifteen years as a bench scientist and fifteen years as a librarian. I'm about fifteen years away from traditional retirement age, and yes, I'm making yet another career change. This time I'm exploring user experience (UX) strategy, as I believe this discipline is the culmination of all my previous experiences. UX strategy emphasizes process and focuses on the intersection of the goals of a company/product/service with the end user's experience (meaningful, seamless, enjoyable). This tech career encompasses my research skills (PhD), my user support skills (MLS), my psychology background (BS), and my interest in aesthetics.

My intention to change careers again isn't because I think being a librarian is terrible, just as leaving the bench wasn't because I think scientific research is terrible. Rather, I'm exploring another facet of the work I most enjoy doing rather than focusing solely on my job as my identity. Not that it's been easy. When I first left the bench for librarianship, my father commented, "So you're leaving a prestigious position to go learn how to stamp books?" Gah! No, I explored other career options, still in the realm of scientific research, and that's okay. I went from intently focusing on a specific topic (olfactory sensory neuron patterning, connectivity, and regeneration) to a very broad topic (basic science research support), to the realization that I'm now more interested in something in the middle (helping biomedical researchers have an optimized experience using a government-funded diverse health database to achieve their research goals). I intend to continue to focus on biomedicine and education within or adjacent to academia. And my interests may change again with time, although probably postretirement if we go by my fifteen-year cycle!

REFLECTION: GOING ROGUE

Although getting a STEM PhD is a lot of hard work, it's worth it. At the time we began our degrees we never would have expected where they would lead, but that's the beauty of it. Getting that training prepared us to be critical, logical, and confident in our choices, no matter where they take us. In the early years it felt as if options were limited because of the singular focus of those surrounding us—research scientists seeking tenure-track positions at major universities. It's not easy to veer from expectations (Dad!). But if you've had the privilege to earn a PhD, then you also have the privilege to explore multiple career paths, as many times as you desire.

Finding jobs in biomedical libraries enabled both of us to capitalize on our previous research experiences. Librarians serve as extremely knowledgeable liaisons between biomedical researchers and the resources they need, providing research support that researchers might not even know is available. It is highly satisfying to introduce a new tool or organizational approach and see researchers light up when they realize how much time and effort it will save them. And more selfishly, it is also highly satisfying to continue to learn new skills and gather new knowledge to grow your own career, albeit in a direction you didn't necessarily anticipate when starting down this path.

    Writing this piece together has been eye-opening and affirming. While we had different processes and trajectories, we had a shared willingness to go rogue and take advantage of our research backgrounds to explore new opportunities in perhaps unexpected places. Our science PhDs individually led us to the library, a fulfilling stop on our career journeys that opened lots of doors and provided many enriching experiences. Peruse the reading list below for more information on PhDs in libraries. For anyone interested in exploring careers beyond basic science, we encourage you to talk to lots of people in jobs that look intriguing. Talk to multiple people in the *same* job in addition to different jobs. Remember that the work environment matters, and that a library job in one school may look completely different from one in another. Think about your skills and what you *want* to do, what excites you when you get to work on it, and what sounds fun (yes work can be a bit fun!). Most of all, remember that your career is only one facet of your life. It is where you spend a lot of time, so it should be meaningful and enjoyable to you. But that's the key, isn't it? *To you*. You don't need anyone's permission or approval to choose a path different from the one you began. You, too, can go rogue, into the wild of career exploration, develop your strengths in new fields like librarianship, and build your career with the positions you choose.

ACKNOWLEDGMENTS

Stacey

First and foremost, I thank my family: Dave, Ben, Amelia, and Carson. My career freedom is rooted in their love and support (and flexibility). And this chapter would not have been possible without my furry feline editors, Eli and Ruby; they were delightful distractions and mildly interested supporters.

    A career is about the work you do, but it is also about the people you interact with. I have been very blessed to interact with my people. My driven and supportive PhD and postdoc advisors Teresa Wood and Amanda Dickinson. My gracious and endlessly knowledgeable library colleagues John Cyrus, Rachel Koenig, and Emily Hurst (really, all of RED). My fellow career trailblazers Allyson Kennedy, Oscar Keyes, and Carrie Iwema. My current mentors and sponsors Sarah Golding, Jean Bailey, D Jennings, and Joyce Lloyd. My path is possible, and a joy to travel, because of them.

RECOMMENDED RESOURCES

Cataldo, Tara Tobin, Michele R. Tennant, Pamela Sherwill-Navarro, and Rae Jesano. 2006. "Subject Specialization in a Liaison Librarian Program." *Journal of the Medical Library Association* 94, no. 4 (September): 446–48. https://www.ncbi.nlm.nih.gov/pmc/articles/PMC1629419/.

Chan-Park, Christina Y. 2013. "Tips for Working with a 'Feral Science Librarian.'" Paper presented at the Texas STEM 2013 Librarians' Conference. University of Texas at Austin, July 26, 2013. https://conferences.lib.utexas.edu/sites/default/files/conferences/txstem2013/proposal/tips-working-feral-science-librarian.html.

Harp Ziegenfuss, Donna. 2021. "It's Okay to Be Feral: Exploring Librarian Identity Through Autoethnography." Paper presented at the Qualitative Report Twelfth Annual Conference, Nova Southeastern University, January 13, 2021. https://nsuworks.nova.edu/tqrc/twelfth/day2/32/.

Marcum, Deanna B. 2012. "Do Librarians Need PhDs?" *Information Outlook* 16 (5): 33–35. https://www.sla.org/IO/2012/Sept-Oct/IO-SepOct2012.pdf.

Neal, James. 2005. "Raised By Wolves: The New Generation of Feral Professionals in the Academic Library." Paper presented at the ACRL Twelfth National Conference, Minneapolis, MN, April 7–10, 2005. https://alair.ala.org/handle/11213/17073.

Oliver, Astrid, and Eric Prosser. 2018. "Academic Librarianship Without the Degree: Examining the Characteristics and Motivations of Academic Library Professionals." *Journal of Academic Librarianship* 44, no. 5 (September): 613–19. https://doi.org/10.1016/j.acalib.2018.07.006.

Ridley, Michael. 2018. "Academic Librarians and the PhD." *Partnership: The Canadian Journal of Library and Information Practice and Research* 13, no. 1 (May). https://doi.org/10.21083/partnership.v13i1.3971.

Tennant, Michele R., and Michael M. Miyamoto. 2008. "The Role of the Medical Librarian in the Basic Biological Sciences: A Case Study in Virology and Evolution." *Journal of the Medical Library Association* 96, no. 4 (October): 290–98. https://doi.org/10.3163/1536-5050.96.4.004.

Zalin, Mackenzie. 2019. "Measuring the Applications of the Subject Doctorate to

Academic Librarianship in North America." Master's paper, University of North Carolina, School of Information and Library Science. https://doi.org/10.17615/v0v9-qp23.

8

FINDING NEVERLAND

From Chimpanzee Research to Career Services

SARAH K. BARKS

Anjali is an astrophysicist. She studies the reasons galaxies stop producing new stars. Jin works in nanotechnology, developing new drug delivery methods using biomedical engineering. Levi wants to understand the impacts of climate change on marine bird populations, and Kate aims for a career in fisheries and water resource management. What they all have in common is working with me: I am their guide in their pursuit of careers in STEM.

My training and experience as a doctoral student, postdoctoral researcher, and instructor in a STEM field equipped me with extensive transferable skills to thrive in both academic and nonacademic roles beyond the professoriate. I came to my current role in career advising at a small liberal arts college seeking to make more of an impact than I found possible in research. Although my scientific research was intellectually stimulating, I was disillusioned by the small scope of the work. As an advisor to students pursuing a myriad of interests in STEM, my work touches on many more areas than had been possible on my original research track. I deploy skills developed in academia throughout my job: My research training allows me to deftly pick up and synthesize information about the problems I'm asked to help students solve. I draw on my teaching and writing experience to communicate effectively with diverse audiences. Having collaborated across labs, institutions, and countries, I am equipped to build relationships throughout my institution. With a depth of experience in scientific inquiry, I help my colleagues assess the impact of our work and refine our methods.

There are certainly trade-offs to working as staff rather than faculty in higher education. Institutional structures and policies are weighted in favor of faculty, and I am keenly aware of the difference in power that creates. However, my job security is not tied to grant funding or expectations to publish, and my evenings and weekends are my own. I find satisfaction in simply existing as an example to students of what an academic career beyond faculty can look like.

HOW I GOT HERE

As of this writing, I am the senior director of STEM career communities and analytics in the career center at a selective small liberal arts college in a small Midwestern town. I advise students and alumni on careers, internships, research opportunities, graduate and professional school, and professional development in STEM fields. In addition to my advising duties, I oversee data analytics and graduate outcomes reporting for the career center. Our center boasts just over twenty professional staff; I am one of eight career community directors. Our team is led by an assistant dean; she reports to the dean of the career center, who in turn reports to the president of the college. My role does not involve direct supervision of professional staff, although I sometimes have student interns.

Before my arrival at this institution, I had earned a doctoral degree in biological anthropology with a focus on the neural substrates of chimpanzee social cognition. I then spent a year as an adjunct instructor of anthropology at regional institutions near my graduate alma mater and completed a three-year postdoctoral research fellowship in comparative neuroanatomy. These cumulative professional and academic experiences I undertook as a graduate student and postdoctoral scientist equipped me with the skills that help me thrive in my current role.

First, in my dissertation research, I learned how to envision and execute an ambitious project, synthesize information from multiple sources, and manage massive quantities of data. I also honed my writing and presentation skills. Working with chimpanzees gave me unique lessons in patience, problem-solving, good humor, and resiliency. In my teaching experience, I learned how to organize and present information and how to explain difficult concepts. Teaching also required careful planning, strong communication, and rigorous attention to detail. Finally, in a fellowship in graduate school, I spent a year working in my university's undergraduate college administration office, where I partnered with deans and academic advisors to support students' work. There, I learned about all the pieces of the university outside the classroom that contribute to the academic experience. I gained experience working with students as a mentor and advisor and collaborated extensively across administrative departments. I learned the full scope of how a university works.

My postdoctoral research fellowship focused on the neuroanatomy of wild mountain gorillas and gave me a new suite of research skills as well as experience collaborating across labs, institutions, and countries. I proactively sought additional professional activities as a postdoc: I told my mentor I was interested in getting more teaching experience and was promptly assigned a section of the department's intro class, as well as labs. Our department collaborated frequently with scientists at the Smithsonian's National Museum of Natural History and the National Zoo, and I dove into their programs to learn about public engagement in science and informal science education. I learned how to engage diverse audiences in active learning and how to design curriculum and programming for schools, museums, zoos, and public outreach events. I was able to significantly expand my scientific and professional network through these opportunities as well.

I could not have asked for a better postdoctoral research experience. I worked on interesting projects, enjoyed the day-to-day research activities, and had the support of a good mentor. But I knew that a career spent writing manuscripts and grants was not what I wanted, for many reasons. I value security and stability, so a career dependent on grant funding terrifies me. The things that I have always enjoyed in academia are not the things that are most highly rewarded in most tenure-track positions. I love institutional service and can't say no to a committee; I find satisfaction in working to improve institutions. Given the choice between publish and perish, I'd perish.

Further, I had become disillusioned with the narrow focus of my work. I found my subfield, comparative primate neuroanatomy, fascinating. I had fallen in love with the study of primates as an undergraduate studying anthropology, and I was thrilled to find the ecological and behavioral differences between gorilla species reflected in the anatomy of their brains. I came to realize, however, that my intellectual curiosity was not enough to sustain me for the course of a long career in academia. The audience for the work I did was tiny. We often joked in my lab that just about everyone who would read a paper we put out was also a coauthor on the paper. I didn't feel that I was having the kind of impact on the world that I wanted to make, and that feeling pushed me to seek a path outside the professoriate. I had enjoyed the opportunities I had to teach and work with students, especially in a mentoring capacity. I realized that guiding talented students in their preparation for diverse careers could be the source of that greater impact I sought.

As my postdoc came to a close, I launched two parallel job searches. First, I looked for roles in what I thought of as "para-academia": not faculty, but still within the university ecosystem that I had come to know so well. On sites such as *HigherEdJobs* and the *Chronicle of Higher Education*, I searched for jobs in academic advising, mentoring, and administration. Second, inspired by my work at the Smithsonian, I applied for work focused on public engagement in science. I had conversations with colleagues in museums and zoos (many of whom had been research collaborators) and looked for roles that would let me apply my teaching and communication skills in public institutions. After interviewing for a few positions in both areas, I accepted an advisor role at a college career center. In that role, I mentored and advised students aiming for graduate school and supported their application process. A couple of years later, in a restructuring of our career center, I moved into my current position focused on STEM advising.

HOW I THRIVE HERE

Perhaps my greatest transferable skill from my life as a researcher and scientist is curiosity. My students are never boring; they come to me seeking opportunities in a myriad of fields, many of which require me to draw on my research skills in order to know how best to support their goals. I lean on my literature review savviness to compile insights and best practices and use my communication and organizational skills to present what I learn to my advisees. Of course, my own experience as a graduate student gives me insights into the process of identifying and choosing graduate programs. I counsel students to look carefully at all aspects of a potential graduate program and to talk to both faculty and current students there to get a sense of what it might be like to join that community. In particular, I advise my students to assess graduate programs' commitment to professional development: What opportunities to explore nonfaculty careers are available? How can students develop a breadth of skills beyond their own research? Are alumni doing varied work? Career advising in my own graduate program focused exclusively on pursuing faculty positions in research institutions, and I didn't realize until much later how limiting that view had been. I caution advisees applying to PhD programs that they should not count on a welcoming tenure-track market—but also encourage them to dream about opportunities outside academia as goals rather than consolation prizes.

In addition to one-on-one advising, I give frequent workshops and presentations about many aspects of launching a career in a STEM field. There, my public speaking and teaching skills come into play. My office is one small part of our college's machine, and we collaborate extensively with academic departments, other offices engaged in student support, and peer institutions. Having written manuscripts with collaborators scattered across institutions in both the US and beyond, I feel adept at managing those collaborations. Finally, I have spent enough time in diverse roles in higher education that I have cultivated extensive knowledge of institutional organization and practices. I speak the language of the university.

Within my team at the career center, my background in research and data analysis has opened up an opportunity that I had not expected when I started here. Our center is responsible for surveying every graduating class. We inquire about our graduates' next steps (employment, graduate school, postgraduate service, etc.), as well as their activities as undergraduates (particularly internships, research, and other experiential learning). These survey responses are synthesized into comprehensive reports about each class year. The information we obtain in this process is used across the institution. It is incorporated into marketing materials for prospective students and families and is used to identify student populations who would benefit from greater support from career advising staff. Faculty rely on our data to track the outcomes of graduates in their major. When I arrived here, the dean of the career center oversaw this project in collaboration with the institutional research office. He hated it. I offered to help, and the next thing I knew, the graduate survey was entirely my responsibility. It has become my baby.

First, I took a close look at our existing survey from the perspective of a social science researcher. Were we asking the right questions to learn what we wanted to know? Not always. Were there vestiges of questions that had been in the survey for years but were no longer useful? There sure were. Could I redesign the survey to yield better response rates and more specific, nuanced data? Absolutely. Fortunately, I had the full backing of my dean to do so. Over the last several years, I have made both small tweaks and major revisions to the survey itself, our data collection process, and the ensuing reports. In doing so, I have cultivated a reputation in my office and across campus as a data guru: I'm the keeper of knowledge about how this college prepares its graduates for the world beyond our doors. In the last year, I've leveraged this added value into a new role for myself, with "analytics" formally added to my job title.

My background as a scientist helps me direct efforts in my office to do our best work. My training prompts me to ask: How will we know if we are successful? What evidence will tell us that our work has the desired impact? What data can (and should) we collect to test the hypothesis that our programming effectively supports students? How do we build a system that maximizes our success? I have increased assessment efforts in our office to test assumptions. As I'm increasingly charged with tackling analytical questions of a wider scope, I've taken on an exciting leadership role in this office.

WHAT IT'S LIKE HERE

My training as an anthropologist is never far from my mind as I observe the community dynamics of my current institution. Tensions between faculty and staff are common, and these complicated power dynamics are reinforced by institutional practices. The college prides itself on its commitment to shared governance, but in practice, faculty hold nearly all the institutional power. My colleagues and I know that our innovative, exciting ideas are not likely to be implemented without faculty blessing, and that there are some pedagogical lines we simply can't cross. (Case in point: Our students aiming for careers in the health professions often have to take human anatomy at another institution, either during a summer or after they graduate while taking a gap year before starting professional school. The expertise to teach human anatomy exists among our faculty, but it's seen as "too vocational"—that is, too directly tied to a particular job or career—to fit the mission of the liberal arts.) Faculty salaries are also considerably higher than those of staff, even when staff hold identical credentials.

While faculty are recruited on a national scale and the college makes significant effort to recruit and retain diverse faculty, staff recruiting languishes and is focused primarily on the regional market (i.e., rural Midwest). I've seen too many talented staff colleagues, both in my office and elsewhere at the college, depart for better opportunities. This issue is particularly problematic when we struggle to retain BIPOC (Black, Indigenous, and People of Color) staff; the diversity of our student body is not reflected in the roster of college employees, contributing to students feeling as if they don't belong at this institution.

A doctoral degree is not required for my role, but I know that the "PhD" in my email signature is a boon in my interactions with faculty. My credentials in an academic discipline and my experience in the research world grant me legitimacy, and I have cultivated productive and collegial collaborations with faculty across the college. Professors in one department in the sciences have shared with me that they consider me a member of their team, alongside tenured faculty.

ADVICE FOR GRADUATE STUDENTS

Stay curious. Pay attention to things you do that energize you and give you a sense of satisfaction. Pay attention to things you do that drain you, that feel like a slog, that make you wonder why you're doing them at all. Cultivate your own sense of meaning and purpose, wholly separate from what academia would have you believe. In graduate school, your clearest examples of what to do in your field will come from the faculty around you. Keep in mind that they represent only one possible outcome of your training and are not necessarily representative of the professional world. Find people outside of academia and learn their stories. Envision yourself in a wide range of possibilities. Think about what kind of work–life balance matters to you and give yourself permission to care about it.

Take every public speaking opportunity that is available to you. Talk about your work to lots of different audiences, from tenured faculty to elementary school kids. If you are in a STEM or STEM-adjacent field, learn as much statistics as possible. (You really can't overdo it on stats knowledge.) If you decide that the tenure track is the right path for you, and you find success there, honor the expertise of the staff who support your work and your students.

CODA

Early in my time at my current institution, I encountered a blog post with a graphic: "What kind of faculty job do you want?" The graphic showed a triangle, with "Teaching," "Research," and "Mentoring" each at a corner. The teaching corner was labeled with "Community College," indicating that if what you value most is teaching, a community college faculty position is the right fit for you. "Research University" filled the research corner. "Elite SLAC," surrounded by "less selective SLAC," formed a bullseye in the center of the triangle; the space around them was filled by "regional comprehensive" institutions. The mentoring corner was lonely: a comparatively small bubble labeled "Neverland" (John 2014). If you value mentoring above all else, this graphic tells its reader, your dream job is a fantasy. (Later, the graph was updated, and "Neverland" became "Ranch/Farm College"—i.e., mentoring is valued over these other skills at only a tiny handful of institutions; McGlynn 2014). I realized that I was working, and loving my work, squarely in Neverland. Doing so simply required overcoming the fallacy that working in higher education necessarily means landing a faculty position.

ACKNOWLEDGMENTS

With thanks to Chet Sherwood and Mark Peltz for their mentorship, support, and general menschitude, and to Lauren Myers for absolutely everything.

REFERENCES

John. 2014. "The McGlynn Typology of Faculty Jobs." *Memoirs of a SLACer: Sociological Views on Life and the Liberal Arts* (blog). April 3, 2014. https://slac.word press.com/2014/04/03/the-mcglynn-typology-of-faculty-jobs/.

McGlynn, Terry. 2014. "What Kind of Faculty Job Do You Want?" *Small Pond Science* (blog). April 2, 2014. https://smallpondscience.com/2014/04/02/what-kind-of-faculty-job-do-you-want/.

Part 3
CRAFTING BLENDED POSITIONS AND IDENTITIES

In part 3, contributors discuss how their personal and professional identities as well as intellectual interests shifted when they took up roles beyond the faculty. In so doing, they undermine academic/nonacademic binaries and productively complicate "leaving academe" discourse, showing us how it is possible to be both in and out of academe. They reflect on how other affinities coexist alongside academic work, while also describing ways to reclaim one's intellectual identity and voice when moving into new professional situations. Collectively, part 3 models how one can grow as a person as well as a thinker, researcher, and writer while engaging in new professional responsibilities in higher education.

Contributors in this part also emphasize the energizing and healing aspects of integrating personal and professional identities through values-driven decision-making. Ultimately, while they do not shy away from the ambiguity or ambivalence of inhabiting uncharted waters and multifaceted identities, these authors show us how empowering and fulfilling it can be to cross boundaries and redefine success by prioritizing one's own needs and values for more holistic ways of living and working. Echoing part 1, these contributors remind us that career paths are not linear but informed by ongoing negotiation when trying to meet a variety of personal and professional needs in shifting circumstances.

Barbara Jacoby opens part 3 by illuminating the value of "Embracing Both/And," offering insightful "Reflections from a Boundary-Spanning Pracademic." Recounting how she moved from a grounding in French literature into student affairs and subsequently crossed additional organizational boundaries, Jacoby describes how she transferred her academic skills into a variety of subsequent domains. Now known for her contributions as a "pracademic" who merges theory and practice in the scholarship on community-based service-learning, Jacoby shows how the departure from one's original disciplinary path can lead to groundbreaking work in new areas. Since family relationships were a major factor in her decision to remain in one geographic region and at one institution for most of her career, Jacoby affirms that delimiting a job search to live with or near those you love does not preclude finding meaningful work in a fulfilling life.

In "On Our Own Terms: Becoming an Independent Researcher and Writer," Lee Skallerup Bessette describes how she found an authentic writing voice and meaningful research interests while holding a position in faculty development. Indeed, Bessette argues, changing careers may lead to a liberating shift in intellectual production: no longer beholden to the publish or perish ethos, you are free to explore and write about a variety of topics in varied modalities that better suit your chosen interests, purpose, and audience. Bessette closes with insightful tips on how to reclaim life on your own terms, including making time for rest, play, and community-building. With her inspiring contribution, Bessette describes the greater health and happiness that emerge when "decisions are driven by what you want, not what academia wants from you."

Of course, such shifts in circumstance and identity do not necessarily happen easily, and there may be losses as well as gains. Clare Forstie provides an illuminating framework for thinking about these trade-offs in "Ambivalent in a Good Way: On Both Staying In and Leaving Academia." Trained as a sociologist, Forstie offers the concept of ambivalence as a helpful way to understand career decision-making that takes into account the shifting contexts of marginalization and privilege: for example, when one lands a plum job in a geographic locale that is not safe or welcoming for those who identify with BIPOC (Black, Indigenous, and People of Color) and/or LGBTQ+ communities. Tracing a path from an administrative role to a PhD program and a teaching fellowship, and then from a tenure-track faculty position to working as a teaching consultant, Forstie unpacks the ambivalences that accompanied this journey, not least when deciding whether to relocate for greater queer community and quality of life or figuring out how to advance scholarship when no longer in a faculty role. The essay also explores the inherent tensions of "playing the game" to advance one's career while also trying to be more authentic both personally and professionally. In original and important ways, Forstie normalizes ambivalence as a common experience among those who work in higher education.

In "From Stuck to Satisfied: Creating a Joyful, Balanced Life," Kristine Lodge closes the section with intersectional and interdisciplinary reflections on an extremely multifaceted career that includes studying medieval literature, career coaching, recruiting, program administration, and customer relations in the business sector. Noting that storytelling is one of several threads connecting her diverse engagements, Lodge tells a heartwarming story of moving into greater authenticity by reclaiming her working-class origins and coming out as a queer woman after years of suppressing these aspects. For example, she is allowing her once-erased Philadelphia accent to reemerge in her speech. Lodge further describes how working at a business school and becoming an entrepreneur has finally allowed her to see and credit her mother, a hairdresser, as an entrepreneur in her own right. While acknowledging the ways that classism and heterosexism can lead to discrimination at work, Lodge suggests that embracing all aspects of who we are can lead us into more fitting work environments and more authentic ways of living that are ultimately worth the risk.

9

EMBRACING BOTH/AND

Reflections from a Boundary-Spanning Pracademic

BARBARA JACOBY

Walking faculty members through the steps of developing a service-learning course is a far cry from immersion in the plight of Madame Bovary. Or maybe not. This chapter introduces the concept of a "boundary-spanning pracademic" and applies it to my long and fulfilling career that began with a disciplinary grounding in French literature and blossomed in student affairs. I will show how these two threads never separated but became a both/and configuration, continuing to intertwine as I moved into service-learning and on to faculty development.

The second section consists of my reflections on my boundary-spanning pracademic career at a single institution and what made it satisfying to me. I recognize that some doctoral students and recent PhDs, as well as long-time faculty members, may hesitate to seek nonacademic positions for multiple reasons. Some find the prospect of "reinventing" themselves simply overwhelming; others fear their new role would not be scholarly. Still others just don't have a clue about how to start. In the final section, I offer advice for fellow PhDs seeking an alternative career path within higher education that embraces love of one's discipline and is integral to a life well lived.

FROM ACADEMIC TO PRACADEMIC

I first encountered the term "boundary spanning" in the context of university–community partnerships for service-learning in the work of Lorilee Sandmann and her colleagues (Sandmann et al. 2013). Put simply, boundary spanning is the act of crossing organizational boundaries. Within institutions of higher education, there are multiple internal boundaries. These are formal or perceived demarcations between internal subgroups, such as between academic departments, between academic and administrative units, or, in my case, between academic and student affairs. Boundary spanners are individuals who move comfortably across such boundaries to achieve goals that benefit the institution and its constituents.

First popularized by Paul L. Posner (2009), the term "pracademic" refers to an individual whose career spans the boundaries of academia and practice. Academics who embrace nonacademic careers within the university use their crossover skills to contribute to teaching and learning in a wide variety of ways. In addition, pracademics include those with significant experience in a field outside academe who bring their knowledge and insights from their practice to positions in higher education institutions. However, I knew little of these concepts when I first set out to advance my study of French literature.

I started learning French in seventh grade because I thought it was a glamorous language. By the time I graduated from high school, I had spent two years studying French literature with Mrs. Boone, a teacher I loved then and admire to this day. I was captivated by the fate of the tragic heroines we studied: Andromaque and Phèdre tortured by love in the plays of Racine, la Princesse de Clèves torn between love and duty, and, of course, Flaubert's Emma Bovary, who could never satisfy her romantic fantasies in real life. I was fascinated by them but I didn't want to be them. I wanted to be Mrs. Boone. She wasn't beautiful or exotic like them. She was actually somewhat plain, but she drew liberally on her rich scholarship and lit fires with her teaching. In addition to me, she inspired four of my best high school friends to become not only Francophones but also Francophiles, each in her own way.

As a first-generation college student from a middle-income family, I rather begrudgingly acceded to my parents' demand to matriculate at the University of Maryland, our local state institution. That decision turned out to be a fortuitous one that happily shaped my career and my life. As I pursued my three degrees in French language and literature with the intention to teach in college, I fell more and more deeply in love with my now-husband of fifty-one years. He attended law school locally and began his legal career a couple of miles down the road from UMD.

My husband's career, place-bound as he became a solo practitioner specializing in criminal defense litigation, was one of three factors that led me to seek alternative career options. Secondly, a couple of years after I received my PhD, I presented a paper at an international colloquium in Germany on the author on whom I wrote my dissertation. Twelve countries were represented, but there were only eighteen participants. I realized then and there that I needed to make a greater impact—somehow—on the well-being of the world than was possible in that extremely limited sphere. The third factor, and tipping point, was the work I did in UMD's housing office while pursuing my graduate degrees. Although my job was of the administrative assistant ilk, I worked with people who obviously relished their jobs and deeply cared about students. At the time, I had no idea that my observations of these committed colleagues were a beacon leading me toward a future career in student affairs.

As I completed my PhD, I continued to work at the housing office in increasingly more responsible positions while I applied for teaching positions anywhere within a two-hour driving radius. In the late 1970s, there was a glut of humanities doctorates and very few tenure-track or nontenure teaching positions. After receiving nothing but rejection letters for academic positions, I realized that I was ready to leave the faculty, and I also felt it was time to leave the housing office. I applied for and accepted a position with the financial aid office, which has the distinction of being the only job I ever despised. With virtually no training, I became the financial aid counselor to all UMD students whose last names began with the letters S to Z. There were thirty-eight thousand students at the time, so it is not hard to determine approximately how many students I was to advise and whose financial aid packages I had to calculate (sans computer). My office colleagues were all about the paperwork and seemed to care little about the students they were to advise and support. This was a very different, far less student-centered way of working from that of my colleagues in the housing area. I was fortunate to be teaching an introductory French course and then an honors intermediate-level course during this time. Although I knew they would not lead to the tenure track and academic job security, they enabled me to connect with students in a positive way and to stay connected to my discipline.

I went back to the housing office and spoke at length with several of the people whose care for students had impressed me. They had degrees in a field

I had never heard of: student personnel, now called student affairs. The more I learned about this field, the more interested I became. I soon gathered from them that they viewed their work as central rather than peripheral to the academic mission. In many ways, they created environments and provided support to enhance learning and enable students to succeed in college. I thought to myself, *I could see myself doing this.*

However, coming from a discipline based in primary sources, I needed to know whether this field of student affairs had a theoretical and research foundation. Here's where serendipity, or luck, came in. Down the hall from the financial aid office was the office of the vice president for student affairs, with a women's room located between them. At that time, Dr. Lee Knefelkamp, the senior faculty member in student personnel in the college of education, served as faculty associate in the vice president's office. She was there a couple of days a week, and I would run into her regularly in the women's room. We got to talking, and I would often tell her about my dissatisfaction with my work in financial aid, my growing interest in student affairs, and my concern about its primary sources. She assured me that the field was thoroughly grounded in well-researched theories of college student development and had a substantial literature of practice. I was skeptical but wanted to know more about these theories and how they were applied in practice, but there was no way I was going to seek a master's degree in college student personnel just after completing my PhD. Dr. Knefelkamp generously offered to meet with me weekly over the next several months to mentor me as an independent learner of student development theory. Each Monday afternoon we met at 4:30 when the financial aid office closed. Each week she gave me one of her personal books by leading college student development theorists, among them William Perry, Arthur Chickering, Nevitt Sanford, Lawrence Kohlberg, and David Kolb. I was sold. Student affairs at the University of Maryland was the profession for me. I never forgot what her mentoring meant to me, and I tried to pay it forward throughout my career.

I worried about what would induce an employer in one of the student affairs departments to hire me without a degree in the field. I applied without success to several positions until I landed a position as assistant director of the Office of Commuter Affairs in 1978. UMD was at that time overwhelmingly a commuter school, and this office was charged with providing a wide range of services and programs for commuter students, including running the campus shuttle bus service. Shortly after I began working there, I asked the director why she hired me. She replied, "With your literature degree, I was sure you could write." This is just one of the many ways transferable skills from my PhD have served me well in other settings. The office also housed a fledgling national organization that served as a clearinghouse of information and resources for commuter affairs professionals across the country. The clearinghouse's primary offering was a quarterly newsletter that was always wanting for articles. My first assignment in my new role was to "write something right now" to meet the looming deadline for newsletter copy. So I did. This task wasn't particularly challenging and went a long way to increase my confidence in my new role. As I grew into the position, I also became increasingly involved in the large national associations of student affairs professionals.

After serving five years as assistant director of commuter affairs and in progressively more responsible roles in the associations, I became the director and, as such, a member of the vice president for student affairs' cabinet in 1984. I found this position to be fulfilling, enjoyed supervising and mentoring graduate assistants who were in the graduate program in student affairs, and believed that our work was making a substantial positive difference in the experience of UMD's commuter students. Simultaneously I sought and was able to find opportunities to work in the academic sphere. One example was serving on the committee that developed the curriculum for the Transfer to Terp program (short for Terrapin, the University of Maryland mascot), which consisted of two credit-bearing courses designed to enable transfer students to find community and become civically engaged in a university that focused primarily on first-time students. I began doing regular conference presentations and developing articles and book chapters. In 1989, I wrote my first monograph on enhancing the educational experience of commuter students. I did not realize at the time that I had become a pracademic.

It was not until the 1990s that I was able to fully integrate my academic background with my work in student affairs, leading to the both/and of this chapter title. In 1992, I was tasked by the vice president for student affairs to develop the university's first community service program as part of the Office of Commuter Affairs. Knowing very little about this new area, I visited three local universities to learn what they were doing as far as community service. It was through these visits I realized that community service, a form of volunteerism, was fast developing into service-learning, which integrates community service into both academic courses and cocurricular experiences through the practice of critical reflection.

Here at last was the field of my dreams, which, like student affairs at one point, I didn't even know existed. I became enthralled with the possibilities for creating opportunities, inside and outside the formal academic curriculum, for students to use what they were learning to develop the motivation and agency to change the world in positive ways. As I explored these possibilities with faculty members and academic administrators, I found that the factor that enabled me to successfully raise their interest in service-learning was the fact that I had a traditional academic degree and disciplinary teaching experience. The both/and of my career became rewardingly clear.

I eventually became part of a coterie of service-learning advocates across the US and the world through related professional organizations, but primarily through writing. Although I had been in the field for only a couple of years, I realized that the scant service-learning literature offered little of the guidance I sought to develop a viable service-learning program at UMD. Since I had continued writing throughout my time with commuter affairs, I was known to the editor of the higher education series of publisher Jossey-Bass. I thought I could produce the volume of guidance I had been seeking by inviting people already well established in the field to write chapters on their particular areas of expertise. Without a formal boundary crossing, I found that I had moved into the scholarship of teaching and learning, also known as SOTL. It wasn't until later that I came to realize that a proactive aspect of an academic career is to identify gaps in the existing body of scholarship and offer to help close those gaps. After a two-hour conversation with the editor, I had a book contract on the way. This was the first of six books on service-learning and civic engagement that I edited or single authored.

In addition to writing, I engaged frequently with faculty across the US and the world about service-learning and, more broadly, community engagement, through many keynote speeches, workshops, and consultations, both in person and virtual. I later moved into a part-time position, still in student affairs, that focused solely on faculty development for service-learning and other forms of community engagement. I facilitated five service-learning faculty fellows cohorts. Based on the questions that faculty members asked me about service-learning, I authored my most recent book, *Service-Learning Essentials: Questions, Answers, and Lessons Learned* (Jossey-Bass 2015). I am gratified that faculty learning communities around the world have used the book as their text.

In addition, this part-time position based in student affairs enabled me to create and teach a service-learning course that was the capstone in the leadership studies minor. In this course, Now What? Composing a Life of Meaning and Purpose, my students were those approaching graduation who knew that they wanted to make a positive difference in the world. However, they rarely had any idea how they might go about it. Together we explored the concept and practice of social change, and the students reflected deeply on how they might be social change agents in their future professions and lives. My students personified recent research findings that tell us how today's undergraduates seek meaningful work to have social impact (Gallup and Bates College 2019).

Retirement from UMD came next with continued engagement in writing, speaking, and consulting. Although service-learning is no longer new, it is still unfamiliar, intriguing, and somewhat daunting to many faculty members. I continue to write and work with universities in Asia and the Middle East as well as domestically, both in person and virtually, on a wide range of related topics, including critical reflection and several forms of experiential learning.

At this point, you might wonder: What became of my learning and love for the French language and its literature? I have enjoyed traveling to France many times throughout the years and have found the experience to be far richer than traveling elsewhere because of my ability to speak with interesting people and learn directly about France's evolving culture. I continue to read and reread French literature in all its genres as well as a daily Paris newspaper.

REFLECTIONS ON A BOUNDARY-SPANNING CAREER

Here are some of the main insights I've gained from my trajectory.

I discovered that I could find what I loved about my discipline, my students, my university, and higher education in settings other than an academic department. When it became clear that I was not going to obtain a tenure-track or even full-time teaching position, soul searching yielded three realizations: I needed to continue scholarly research and writing, I relished the "aha" moments of facilitating student learning, and I loved being on a university campus. I came to believe strongly that the student affairs profession, once decried by an unknowing colleague as "hootenannies and jammies," is all about student learning and development, even as it is not always valued as such by narrowly focused members of the professoriate. It encompasses the areas you would expect, including housing, dining, health, counseling, career services, the student center or union, activities and recreation, and student conduct. What you might not expect is that student affairs also includes areas such as civic learning and democratic engagement; diversity, inclusion, and social justice; student success; admissions and enrollment; orientation; financial aid; academic support services; study abroad; and experiential education. Higher education has traditionally organized its activities into student affairs and academic affairs, but these distinctions are blurring and are not meaningful to students. Nor to boundary spanners.

Choosing a student affairs career does not necessitate abandoning research. Reading peer-reviewed journals and attending conference presentations reinforced that what I had learned about the field's practice was based on high-quality and extensive research. The years I spent serving on the committee that conducted a longitudinal study of UMD students enabled me to participate in research that was very different from literary analysis but equally rigorous.

I found a community that challenged, supported, and nurtured me outside my discipline. I sought to belong to a professional community, both as a recipient and provider of guidance and support. Unfortunately, I did not experience this in the French Department. I found that the student affairs profession is rich in a sense of community. I also quickly discovered that many student affairs professionals are as stimulating and intellectually curious as faculty members. The Office of Commuter Affairs shared a suite in the student union with the Campus Activities and the Office of Orientation. Staff members from the three offices regularly shared information, consulted one another, and collaborated in numerous ways to create and enhance student experiences. For this reason, Dr. Knefelkamp, the student affairs faculty member who initiated me into the world of student development theory, aptly called the suite "the fertile crescent." As an example of the support I received, a group of my student affairs colleagues surprised me with a happy hour celebration at the campus tavern and a gift of cash they collected to alleviate some of the cost of the airfare to the colloquium in Germany at which I presented a paper based on my dissertation.

I also found community in the student affairs professional associations. Their regional meetings and national conferences were completely different in tone and level of collegiality than those of the Modern Language Association. At the MLA, I read a paper and received some fairly caustic feedback from the audience. At the student affairs association conferences, I received thoughtful, constructive feedback and offers to collaborate on research and other projects.

I was able to teach and engage in scholarship outside my discipline. When I first started in commuter affairs, I hadn't yet let go of my disciplinary research. I was still doing research related to my dissertation, but I struggled to apply myself in two seemingly unrelated directions. Having realized that my literary work could have only very little potential impact, I worried that I was wasting my intellectual capacity on work that was extraneous to my new profession. With encouragement and guidance from more senior "fertile crescent" colleagues, I began to expand my student affairs conference presentations into articles for campus and national association newsletters. From there, I collaborated with colleagues to write articles for non-peer-reviewed and eventually peer-reviewed student affairs publications.

I was thus using the writing skills I developed in my academic work, but where did the boundary spanning in my scholarship really begin? As I became involved more deeply in service-learning, I found that many faculty members who were enthusiastic about it and wanted to integrate it into their courses did not know where to begin with curriculum development or locating community partners. My student affairs conference presentations gradually became fewer and my faculty development workshops more frequent. Both/and became a reality as I found that my writing became more focused on SOTL, particularly on the concept and practice of service-learning, campus–community partnerships, and educating students for civic engagement. At times I wondered whether I really knew enough to be advising others. Yet my combination of disciplinary background, teaching experience, and knowledge of service-learning eventually led me to confidently broaden my SOTL work to include experiential learning, civic and community engagement, critical reflection, curriculum development and backward design, and assessment. Simultaneously I continued to contribute to student affairs scholarship and the advancement of the student affairs profession; at one point I was selected to become a senior scholar in one of the professional associations.

My boundary-spanning career would not have been as satisfying or my SOTL as successful had I not found a way to teach throughout my career. While teaching courses here and there in my discipline was helpful to my work in faculty development, my most gratifying teaching experience was the Now What? course that was part of the leadership studies minor, formally part of the college of education. However, the minor is managed by Leadership and Community Service-Learning in Student Affairs, where my final position at UMD was housed.

I discovered what I liked to do and what I was good at. I thought deeply about what skills and knowledge I particularly enjoyed using and how they may be transferable to other arenas. I reflected on what energized me about my discipline and my work. Studying French literature plus completing a dissertation developed readily transferable skills in oral communication, writing, reliance on original sources, and successfully completing a complex project. I also realized that I could learn as much about myself from determining what is not meaningful to me as from what I found fulfilling. From teaching French 101 ("je m'appelle, tu t'appelles, il s'appelle"), I learned that this level of teaching did not provide enough intellectual stimulation for me. Likewise, my work in the financial aid office made it clear that focusing on numbers rather than students in a non-collegial environment made me miserable.

Here are a few pieces of advice and encouragement for those of you considering working beyond the professoriate.

Be broad minded about how you can contribute to student learning. Choosing another career path is no reason to stop teaching. Presuming you enjoy it, I recommend you continue to do so. There are many non-disciplinary credit-bearing courses. At UMD these include UNIV 100 (The Student in the University), UNIV 104 (Reading and Writing at the College Level), UNIV 218 (Connecting Across Cultures), and UNIV 362 (Designing Your Life After College), among many others. Most institutions are always looking internally for people to teach English composition 101, sometimes called introduction to academic writing. Community colleges are often seeking part-time instructors, as are departments that offer evening courses through an extension program. In addition, there are programs on many campuses, including study abroad and co-curricular service-learning, with curricula taught by pracademics. For those of you who are still in graduate school, I recommend that you consider a graduate assistant position outside your academic department. Student affairs departments regularly hire graduate students outside the college of education. Such positions offer insights and experiences that could lead to a career in student affairs. Other areas that offer graduate assistant positions useful for professional development include centers for teaching and learning, academic advising, career counseling, disability support services, and math and writing centers.

Find your path to engage in scholarship by recognizing what you know and can contribute. From my work in commuter affairs, I learned from students about the challenges they faced, including transportation and housing issues, financial problems, caring for family members, working at sometimes more than one job, and lacking a sense of belonging on campus. I realized that faculty members may not be aware of these challenges and how they can support their commuter students. Sharing this information with faculty in multiple ways became the beginning of my work in faculty development.

How do you create a path to scholarship outside your discipline? I suggest beginning by offering to give workshops through the center for teaching, panel or solo presentations at regional teaching conferences, and eventually presentations at national conferences. I got my start doing a series of well-paid webinars for a private faculty development provider because one of their staff members attended one of my national student affairs conference presentations. Once you have done a conference presentation, it is not difficult to turn it into an article. Articles become book chapters, and chapters become books.

There are also multiple ways to begin writing for academic and broader audiences through the *Chronicle of Higher Education* and *Inside Higher Ed*, both of which publish opinion pieces, advice, and blogs. In addition to peer-reviewed research journals, the student affairs profession has a bimonthly magazine, *About Campus*, which contains articles on how to make the campus environment an effective place for students to learn and has a broad audience of administrators, faculty, staff, and policymakers in higher education. For those of us who crave the autonomy faculty members cherish, there is great satisfaction in writing about whatever we please for publication. It is also a delight to write with no concern about professional advancement or peer review.

Don't dismiss a long boundary-spanning career in a single institution. Do you love not only being on a university campus but particularly being on *your* campus? There are distinct advantages to staying with a single institution. You can more readily identify institutional strategic priorities to which you can contribute, such as recruitment, retention, diversity/inclusion/social justice, global citizenship, sustainability, and civic engagement. Many institutions are seeking ways to integrate the high-impact educational practices promoted by the Association of American Colleges and Universities. These include first-year seminars, common intellectual experiences, learning communities, writing-intensive courses, service-learning, collaborative projects, e-portfolios, internships, and capstone courses. Institutional focus on these priorities has spawned careers beyond the faculty both within and outside academic departments. For example, the Women's Studies Department at UMD has long had a senior internship requirement and has a former faculty member on staff as internship coordinator to locate internship opportunities for students and support them in the process of applying for and completing them.

Within a single institution, it is easier to gather word-of-mouth leads and to ask colleagues to look out for opportunities that might interest you in areas that you might not think of. Other careers exist in areas such as academic affairs/provost office, libraries, admissions, registrar, institutional research, community engagement, alumni programs, educational technology, university relations, research administration, graduate school, and the ombuds office. You are more likely to be favorably considered for such positions if you are familiar with the workings and idiosyncrasies of the institution.

Network, network, network. Universities abound in ways to meet and learn with academic and nonacademic colleagues. The campus daily email lists workshops, seminars, and opportunities to join various learning communities. I regularly attended workshops offered by the teaching center and sought paths of meaningful interaction with faculty and academic administrators. I alluded earlier to the role regional and national professional associations play in providing opportunities for attending and presenting sessions on various professional topics. Here I add that these associations offer multiple ways to meet informally with colleagues whose work you admire and who have had interesting career paths. I have found that people generally enjoy sharing their passions and pathways.

Campus-based faith communities offer other perhaps unexpected opportunities for interchange with academic and nonacademic colleagues. I joined the board of directors of the campus Hillel. My fellow board members were an interesting and well-connected range of faculty, administrators, and community members. Through a monthly Jewish faculty lunch and learn that I started as a board project, I developed collegial relationships as well as helpful connections to other faculty members across campus.

I recommend that you seek advice from a broad range of people and develop a multifaceted team of mentors. Your formal academic advisor can be helpful but is not always so. Dr. Knefelkamp was the mentor who introduced me to the theoretical grounding of student affairs and encouraged me to join the profession. As I transitioned from student affairs to service-learning, I sought the guidance of the director of the teaching center as a boundary spanner who had moved from his discipline of cell biology to head the center as well as teach a course for doctoral students who sought to enter the professoriate. He invited me to do several workshops in his center's series on service-learning, experiential learning, and community engagement. He recognized me as a boundary spanner and encouraged me to be the first student affairs professional to apply to become a Lilly Teaching Fellow and also a fellow of the Academy for Excellence in Teaching and Learning. I was the first nonacademic to be accepted, and both opportunities offered rich interactions and led to substantial contributions to teaching student success.

CONCLUSION

Academic or pracademic, a career is not a life. But it is a core part of our being, how we think, what we love, and who we are. I remain a lifelong Francophile. French language and literature became my avocation. France remains my favorite travel destination. I relish its cuisine, its urban and pastoral beauty, all aspects of its culture, and its joie de vivre. I'll never know whether I revel in all things French less or more than I would have had it remained my full-time academic focus. My point is: we do not have to fall out of love with our discipline to engage in another long-term, loving relationship with a boundary-spanning pracademic career. A disciplinary identity will remain fundamental as it brings credibility to our profession and scholarship, albeit outside the bounds of traditional academe. It will always add richness to our work and our lives. We will always experience the world through its lens. We will always embrace a lively life of the mind.

Finally, love of my discipline and profession complement the other loves in my life. I made the decision to work beyond the faculty and to remain at UMD in the context of the love of my husband and my pride in his flourishing, place-based legal career. Staying in place enabled us to enjoy intimate relationships with my aging parents and young nieces. No one lies on their deathbed wishing they did more work. As much as we value our disciplines, we all hold values that supersede them. Although we know intellectually that career success is but one element of a fulfilling life, sometimes we struggle to put it in perspective. So my final piece of advice is: let love of family and friends, spirituality, absorbing interests, even leisure activities bring as much or more purpose and value to life as work. In the words of Phyllis Mable, a dear departed pracademic colleague, "Live, love, leave a legacy."

ACKNOWLEDGMENTS

I am blessed to have worked with three extraordinary mentors. The first is Dr. Ann Demaitre, who guided me through three degrees in French literature and gave me the opportunity to teach the honors intermediate French class that was her own. The second is Dr. Lee Knefelkamp, who so generously engaged with me in a weekly tutorial that enabled me to learn student development theory and to determine that student affairs was the career path for me. The third is Dr. William L. "Bud" Thomas, Jr., who hired me as director of the Office of Commuter Affairs and subsequently provided me with the opportunity to launch the university's community service-learning program. It is service-learning and community engagement that continue to be the focus of my consultancy, scholarship, and faculty development work. And there's one more: my husband of fifty-two years, Steve Jacoby. He always was and always will be my greatest fan.

REFERENCES

Gallup and Bates College. 2019. *Forging Pathways to Purposeful Work: The Role of Higher Education.* Gallup. https://www.gallup.com/education/248222/gallup-bates-purposeful-work-2019.aspx.

Posner, Paul L. 2009. "The Pracademic: An Agenda for Re-engaging Practitioners and Academics." *Public Budgeting & Finance* 29, no. 1 (Spring): 12–26. https://doi.org/10.1111/j.1540-5850.2009.00921.x.

Sandmann, Lorilee R., Jenny W. Jordan, Casey D. Mull, Victoria D. David, and Kristi Farner. 2013. "What Is It, Really?" Theory and Measurement of Boundary Spanning." Paper presented at International Association for Research on Service-Learning and Community Engagement Conference, Omaha, NE, November 6–8, 2013.

10
ON OUR OWN TERMS
Becoming an Independent Researcher and Writer

LEE SKALLERUP BESSETTE

In this essay I share my journey toward finding my authentic writing voice and meaningful research interests while holding a position in faculty development. Indeed, changing careers can lead to a liberating shift in your mentality around productivity and writing: no longer beholden to the publish or perish ethos, you are free to explore and write about topics in modalities that better suit your interests and purpose.

As a contingent faculty member for many years, I wrote about pedagogy and technology both on my blog at *Inside Higher Ed* and on *Prof Hacker*. As such, the move into faculty development and academic technology made a lot of sense for me and my career. When I first moved into faculty development, I explained to my kids that my new job was to help faculty be better teachers and use technology effectively in their teaching. Currently, I am assistant director for digital learning in the Center for New Designs for Learning and Scholarship (CNDLS) at Georgetown University. My job involves developing and delivering programming around pedagogy and technology, working with faculty to design courses and digital assignments, and collaborating with my colleagues to promote inclusive teaching practices across the campus. I also have the opportunity to teach in the master's program in learning, design, and technology. The work is incredibly rewarding, varied, and intellectually stimulating; I get to work with dedicated faculty teaching all manner of interesting topics, as well as teach future generations of learning designers. The job is never the same. The technologies and circumstances change and so we have to change and adapt accordingly, learning new skills and techniques along the way.

One of the most common questions I get when offering informational interviews is whether I still have time to do research. This isn't surprising. Most of us did a PhD not only because we were passionate about a subject, but because we wanted to immerse ourselves in and learn more about it through research. In my case, it was studying Canadian and Québécois literature through my PhD in comparative literature. What gets conflated in this question is not only the doing of the research but also the output of said research: Will we have the interest or time to write academic, peer-reviewed journal articles or single-authored scholarly monographs? While many of us chose to do a PhD because we loved our subject and possibly also research, I'm less sure how many of us equally love the academic genres we are expected to write in.

My answer, then, is yes—you'll have time to do research, and if you make time to write, you will have time to write. But I also answer with another question: Are you sure you want to do strictly academic writing, or write only about your current research areas? For me, one of the most freeing parts of my work is that I don't have the pressure of hiring, tenure, and promotion driving my scholarly output or worrying whether I am publishing in the "right" journals or with the "right" publisher. Moreover, I am no longer limited in what I research; instead of a narrow field of expertise, I am free to explore whatever subjects interest me and thus shape my research profile according to my own values, rather than the values that academia imposes. While research and writing are still a part of my professional work, what I write about and where I publish are now much more varied. And even though writing and research are a part of my work, it isn't a publish or perish situation; one of the main reasons that writing in particular is part of my current job is because I am good at writing, and I choose to do it.

That freedom has made research and writing fun again. And because I'm enjoying the process, I'm writing and publishing more than I ever have before. This is in no small part because I no longer have class prep or grading to do on top of answering endless student emails. But just having more time doesn't automatically translate into more writing time. For me, it was the freedom to explore my interests in a variety of ways, instead of how academia narrowly defines research, that reignited my passion for new inquiries. I am also fortunate that part of what I am interested in researching and writing about is directly related to my work, so it is both for work and for pleasure. But even in exploring other areas that are less related to my job, any other writing I do is my own because it isn't by the demand of an academic position. In this chapter, I outline my own evolution as a researcher and writer while not in a faculty position, followed by advice on how you, too, can rediscover your passion and set your own agenda for research and writing.

LOSING AND REDISCOVERING MY VOICE

As a contingent faculty member, I worked hard to maintain my research profile and productivity, even though, as I was constantly reminded, I didn't "have" to, as it was not required, nor was I compensated for that labor in any way. I still clung to the hope of eventually winning a tenure-track position, but I also loved the work I was doing. I had a deep "affective investment" in my work (Melonçon 2019), particularly my research and traditional forms of scholarly output, the feelings that cause so many adjuncts to stay in contingent roles despite poor pay and working conditions. I pursued a PhD in comparative literature because it allowed me to do the three things I enjoyed the most: reading, writing, and teaching. I also enjoyed the intellectual stimulation research and scholarly outputs provided (as well as the positive affirmation). But being part of a dual academic couple, parenting two small children, plus being in a thankless role as a contingent faculty member wore me down.

I tried, in vain, to revise my dissertation and start a second book project while waiting endlessly for word on essays I had submitted years earlier. I tried to remember what it was that I loved about writing and research, but I found very little of the enthusiasm I once had when embarking upon graduate school. I also felt constrained by the limitations of the scholarly article. I never quite figured out the right tone for the essays I submitted to journals and collected volumes, the right angle on a topic, or the right journal or publication. Despite my best efforts, my scholarly writing never quite fit anywhere, and my writing voice was not a good fit for scholarly writing. I had been writing for as long as I could remember, and I had always been a good writer, but academia was making me seriously question my writing ability. I wanted to be challenged to become a better writer, not beaten down by Reviewer 2 and dismissive feedback that contradicted itself. This is not necessarily the fault of the genre, but of those gatekeeping the genre. Once you are in academia, the two become impossibly intertwined, in the same way that research and scholarly article or writing and scholarly article become conflated.

My undergraduate degree had been in professional writing, and my original career goal was to become a journalist. But literature spoke to me in a way that the writing courses never did, and so I continued my studies in literature while still keeping a foot in the world of professional writing, which was quickly expanding due to the rapid growth of the Internet. I had the good fortune of having one of my instructors teach us how to hand code in HTML in 1996, and from then on, I was writing on the Web whenever I could, particularly for a friend's zine; essentially, I was blogging before blogging existed. When I started my PhD, I was told that if I ever wanted to be taken seriously as a scholar or accepted as an academic, I had to give up writing on the Internet, so I foolishly and naively took their advice and gave up any writing that wasn't academic or scholarly.

That was the last time that writing had brought me joy, in those spaces on the nascent Web. A decade after giving up writing on the Web, my scholarly writing crisis occurred just as social media and other Web 2.0 tools were becoming more prominent and more popular. I started a blog. I got on Twitter. Yet again I was told repeatedly that blogging and tweeting were not legitimate forms of scholarship or writing, but I was finally finding joy in writing again, not to mention finding a community of colleagues and friends who felt as I did about academic writing and publishing, contingency, pedagogy, and technology. As I have written elsewhere, I got my first faculty development job because of Twitter (Fruscione and Baker 2018), but what social media/blogging provided for me was not only a path out of contingency to a new professional role, but also a path toward new and more fulfilling forms of scholarly engagement and research activities.

It wasn't until I was in my current position in faculty development and had fully freed myself from the expectation of traditional scholarly output that I was able to flourish as a researcher and a writer, this time on my own terms. No longer having the pressure to produce traditional scholarly outputs freed me to explore new forms of engagement, writing, research, and opportunities. I was able to write more and more freely about the things that mattered to me: pedagogy, technology, affect, parenting, disability. I was also able to move across genres and media: book, essay, memoir, podcast. Most importantly, I could be much more discerning about who I wrote for; I vowed to contribute academic writing only to friends' collections and calls, as well as publications where I knew that the peer-review or editorial process was generous, generative, and supportive.

I now have a podcast on living with ADHD, an edited volume on affect and careers beyond the professoriate at a university press, two memoir manuscripts, and other nontraditional, but no less scholarly, outputs. Each of these nontraditional outputs have led to new and exciting opportunities and collaborations, along with more traditional academic opportunities, such as contributing to an edited volume or special issue of a journal, participating on a panel at a conference, or even being invited as a guest speaker. While these activities are not directly related to my job, they hone the skills I do practice every day: writing, editing, listening, empathizing, communicating. Above all, these activities are fun. And, because the job demands less of my time outside of the usual working hours than teaching contingently ever did, I actually have more time for scholarship than I ever had before.

Ironically, because of my public-facing writing and the community I formed through it, I find myself doing academic work in what I was actually trained to do. Given my academic trajectory, I never assumed that I would ever be called upon to lend my expertise on Québécois literature and culture, as well as translation, other than to be the person who annoyingly overexplains Quebec at gatherings or on Twitter. But first, I was asked to write about Quebec for a new (at the time) online publication. Then I was asked to teach an online class about Quebec. Later on, I was invited to become a part of the Data-Sitters Club when they came across three different French translations of the Baby-Sitters Club series and needed someone who could help understand and explain the differences and why three translations would even be necessary (*Data-Sitters Club* n.d.).

In other words, I am perhaps more of an academic now than I was before I moved into faculty development; this identity just doesn't look the same as it did when I only had a narrow definition of what research and scholarship could be!

REFRAMING LIFE AND WORK ON YOUR OWN TERMS

In what follows, I offer several tips for reigniting your passion for writing and making it your own. But first, a few caveats.

I must acknowledge that I have benefitted from a great deal of privilege and a number of instances of unplanned good timing, the most important of which is that my move into faculty development coincided with my kids aging into a period where I was not needed as much, and so the demands on my time were reduced twofold. My husband has always had stable and well (enough) paying employment, with benefits, that eased some of the pressure on me to work in order to just survive. But regardless of your circumstances, if you are pursuing a career path beyond the professoriate, there are still a number of things you can do to rediscover your passion for your writing and research.

I also understand that my writing and work is very public, which isn't an option, or even desirable, for everyone. Your positionality certainly has to be taken into consideration when deciding what you want to do next in terms of research, writing, and scholarly output. I am fortunate that my employer and supervisors have largely been supportive of my public-facing work, but this isn't the case for everyone in a contingent or staff position in academia. Another challenge is that not all public-facing work is received equally: visible minorities (particularly women of color), members of the LGBTQ+ community, and those with visible disabilities are unequally and often viciously targeted online. These are all considerations when trying to decide what's next for your scholarly work. None of the steps I outline below require a large, public-facing presence for these reasons. Writing and sharing your research widely (rather than within the smaller academic community of your discipline or subject) is a choice to be made in the later stages, if at all.

The first and probably most difficult step is to let go. I mean it. Let go of the pressure, the expectation, the internalized definition of what research or scholarly output means. When I started blogging in 2009, I rediscovered my voice, even while being told, repeatedly, that I was wasting my time and what I was doing wasn't real scholarship and didn't count. Although I knew that my writing online was having more of an impact than any peer-reviewed journal article or book chapter I had previously published, I kept trying to write and publish scholarly work in no small part because that was what "counted." It wasn't until I let go of the need to "have" to publish in peer-reviewed journals that I found the time, energy, and capacity to devote to exploring a myriad of topics and writing about them however I wanted to. Aspiring applicants often ask whether publications matter when applying for faculty development–types of positions. What employers are looking for is whether you can write and engage deeply with a subject, and while scholarly publications are one way to show that, they certainly aren't the only way. While the work you have done previously is in no way wasted because of the skills you have gained, you are relieved from the metric of your worth being measured by the number of publication lines you have on your CV. You are also relieved of the pressures or prescriptions of *how* to produce that work.

The next step is to rest and reflect. You might not be writing or researching right now because you are burned out but are still trying to force yourself to "be productive." Stop. Make a choice not to write, not to do research, not to do anything scholarly. I am in that phase, again, right now. I was extraordinarily productive during the pandemic because of the urgency of the moment, writing op-eds, guesting on podcasts, joining panels. I wrote so much over the past two and a half years, but circumstances have stopped me and forced me to reevaluate my research and writing priorities. Lately I have turned down and withdrawn from some projects. And I am okay with this. In our society writ large, and academia in particular, our worth and even our identities are based on our productivity. Doing little or nothing is hard and can feel really uncomfortable. But it is important to take the time to reassess what it is you want for yourself. I don't know at the end of this period of rest what I will be researching and writing. Maybe nothing! And that's okay, too. After all, I do already have a full-time job.

In my current process of resting and reflecting, I took stock of what I have accomplished in my writing career thus far and feel good about what I have produced and the impact that it has had. While writing is a large part of my identity, it isn't all I am nor all I have to offer. I want to make sure that I am writing for reasons that are right for me. So . . . Read for pleasure. Start a journal. Play mindless mobile games on your phone. Binge watch your favorite sitcom. Find a new podcast to listen to or catch up on old favorites. Rediscover a hobby you have given up because it took time away from research and writing. Use the time to start reflecting on and redefining who you are without the title researcher or scholar or academic. It's not that you stop being those things when you move into a new role; rather, those labels no longer need to be your central or only identity anymore. It is time to take your narrative and your identity back from academia and begin to live life on your own terms.

Now, you can really start to explore and play. Certainly, that work began with letting go, but now you're relearning how to be curious about something for curiosity's sake, instead of for the metric of research output. For example, during the pandemic, I took up sewing, which was as surprising to me as to anyone.

I hadn't contemplated sewing since eighth-grade home economics class. But I gave myself time and space to play and explore sewing my own clothes. It gave me a fresh perspective on learning as a novice, on persistence, on failure, on creativity, and it gave me a whole new arena to write about. It also has exploded my wardrobe and brought me a tremendous sense of joy and satisfaction. Another way to put this step is to engage in meaningful play. Most of us become interested in our subject through a sense of wonder, and we need to rediscover that feeling of wonder, wherever that feeling takes us, even away from the thing that we have invested our professional lives working on. That's okay, too. It's part of letting go. And if nothing catches or holds your attention, just keep exploring. There's no timetable, no clock, no hard-and-fast deadline anymore when it comes to your research and writing.

When you find something that sparks your curiosity, start to research, but not in the way you've been trained. Peer-reviewed journal articles and monographs published by academic presses are just one way to research a topic or subject. Start looking at online publications, podcasts, communities on social media; you are not limited by what is in the university library holdings. What does your local public library have on the subject? Freewrite about what you find, wherever it takes you. Just have fun with it.

What if you run into a dead end, or find that the topic isn't as interesting as you first thought? That's okay. Just go back to exploring. I have ADHD, so I am well-acquainted with starting a lot of projects and then not following through on any of them. I would beat myself up for not being persistent enough or dedicated enough or even good enough, but now I am able to admit that something looked interesting but once I tried it, it wasn't for me, and that's okay! Beating myself up kept me from doing the one or two things that I was interested in or was good at, because I didn't have any energy left over after all of the self-loathing. Reflect on why you lost interest or hit a dead end, and use that information to explore areas that might be more aligned with your genuine interests. Keep repeating the exploring and researching steps until you find something that really clicks or that you can't let go of. Maybe you'll rediscover a passion for some area of your prior research. Maybe you'll find new topics based on your new career. Maybe it will have nothing to do with either of them, and that's okay too. Maybe instead you will take up an unexpected new hobby or activity (like sewing for me!). The important point is: do something for you in service of you.

Now you get to decide what you want to do with your newfound interest and knowledge. Join or start a local community or an online community. My own ADHD diagnosis led me to research and write about neurodivergence, but also to create a podcast with a friend and colleague, which connected us with communities of fellow neurodivergent people in higher education (*All the Things ADHD* n.d.). I've also joined a number of sewing groups online and have connected with an incredible community of plus-size sewists, where it's not just about sewing, but also about confronting fatphobia. I am learning so much from them, in places and spaces where I wouldn't be if I were to limit myself to just traditional academic circles.

So, create a blog or podcast. Pitch essay ideas involving your newfound knowledge to various publications. Edit a volume of essays. Offer a webinar or workshop. Present at an academic conference. Write a peer-reviewed journal article. Or any combination thereof. The point is: there is no longer any pressure to do anything in only one way. Do what makes sense to you and is what you want to do, when you want to do it.

Another advantage of this approach versus a more traditional academic mode is that you get to be in community with people who share your interests, rather than in competition. Gone is the scarcity mindset that leads to the worst tendencies of (some) academics who would hoard their research, or only engage with others who could service their career ambitions. Instead, you are free to associate with anyone you like, in whatever ways work best for you, with the goal of just nerding out. It is also incredibly empowering and reassuring to realize that you are not, in fact, alone during this process. These kinds of collaborations have led to some of the most impactful and fulfilling work of my career. The best example might be my involvement in the aforementioned Data-Sitters Club, a group of (mostly) female-identifying academics in various roles who all are interested in digital humanities and the Baby-Sitters Club series—popular young adult (YA) books primarily for girls published during the 1980s and 1990s by Ann M. Martin (*Data-Sitters Club* n.d.). We are writing books on digital humanities approaches to literature as applied to this large corpus of writing that has been largely ignored and marginalized in the academy: YA for girls. We work together to come up with topics, troubleshoot issues, and write the books themselves. We've spoken at conferences, contributed to a book on the Baby-Sitters Club series, won awards, and our books are being used as teaching tools. I even had the opportunity to supervise a paid internship for a student who worked in the Ann M. Martin archives! But that isn't the only collaborative experience I have had: others include writing for *ProfHacker*, editing a book on affective labor, and even collaboratively writing an essay with my colleagues at work. Particularly in the humanities, we have for too long valued the lone scholar model—the single-authored book or article as the gold standard for research. We don't need to write and research alone anymore.

Like any research or writing, what I have described is an iterative process; it isn't linear. As I mentioned, I am currently on my own writing hiatus to reset my goals and priorities after a period of extraordinary (and extraordinarily fulfilling!) productivity. Know that there will be setbacks and missteps and abandoned projects along the way. But that's okay. You are reshaping your identity to be something *other* than a productive researcher and scholar in the narrow traditional sense. We talk a lot in academia about impact, engagement, and dialogue, but more often than not, our traditional scholarly outputs tend to be monographs or monologues for only a select few. Why not take all of your experience and expertise and passion and channel it into more productive and meaningful activities? A crucial part of finding your voice as a writer is letting go of what academia expects of you and finding subjects and modalities that work best for you. Another great way to help you find your voice is to join or form a local writing group. It's a low-stakes way to get feedback on your writing from people who are there to be helpful and to get help in return, which is often a completely different experience from academic feedback.

To help you through this process, it is critical to set aside dedicated time for this work. I'm not necessarily saying that you should write daily as much as guard time for yourself to engage in this process, whatever step you are on. It may only be for an hour on a weekend, but make that date with yourself and keep it. Start with something small and manageable, then you can build on it and devote more time as you grow more confident in the process, and more confident in your voice and in your work.

CONCLUSION

Ultimately, the scariest and most exciting part of moving into a new career is getting to ask yourself, *What's next?* With the financial and professional security that a job beyond the faculty can provide, you become free to use that energy that was spent worrying for imagining and visioning. What would you do differently if you found work–life balance and your major anxieties around the job market and paying the bills were all but gone?

Maybe, the answer is nothing. And that's okay. Most of us have spent the majority of our adult and professional lives single-mindedly focused on one goal that the current state of academia makes it just about impossible to achieve. It's exhausting and draining and, in some cases, debilitating. If you take away anything from this chapter, it's that you need to be okay with *not* being productive. I didn't write this chapter to help you be more productive; I wrote it to help you find joy again. Ultimately, that's what doing it on your own terms is all about—finding the place where you are happy and healthy and can make decisions that are driven by what you want, not what academia wants from you.

Reclaiming my voice as a writer and a researcher happened when I started writing and researching for myself again. If I am as productive or even more productive than I was before I moved into my new role, it's because I *enjoy* the work I'm doing. Because it makes me happy, I want to do it, make time to do it, even look forward to doing it. But it isn't my entire life, either. I coach swimming. I've taken up sewing. I read more. I spend more time with my family and friends. All of these activities are more pleasurable now because I don't feel guilty about doing them, constantly thinking about how I should be writing/researching instead.

And I even still teach, albeit much less than the 5/4 course load I had when working contingently. I have been fortunate enough to also be able to teach one course a semester at Georgetown, almost always on subjects that I am passionate about. Currently, I am teaching a graduate-level design studio course on digital identity, but I've previously taught literature courses, writing courses, and digital studies courses. I have also had the opportunity to teach online. These courses are usually extra, and not a part of my job duties (although many faculty development positions include guaranteed teaching in the contract/job description), but I think it is important since I work in the area of teaching and learning that I keep an active connection to the classroom. The difference is that now teaching is no longer a slog, working from someone else's syllabus and taking up every moment of my life; instead, it is one of many scholarly activities that complement one another and my varied interests. As mentioned, through my public scholarship, I was even able to get back to my doctoral specialization: Québécois literature. This was something I had given up hope of ever being able to do again, but here I am, once a year, teaching an online course to students about the history and culture of Quebec.

Circling back to the question that opened this chapter: Will I still have time to write and do research in my new career? If you are asking that question because you're hoping to remain a "serious scholar" or "academic" in the eyes of your tenured colleagues, it won't work. Those who are willing to dismiss higher education professionals as academics because they are not in a faculty position (or working in contingent roles) won't be impressed by your maintenance of a robust research agenda. And that pressure of having to produce will still be there, sapping the joy out of the work.

It is a hard habit to break, looking for validation from the academy for our academic work and research. But when you finally kick the habit, you learn that there are so many different and better forms of validation out there for you to experience. I have had so many unexpected and wonderful opportunities since I let go of the narrow ideas about what scholarship should look like that I had internalized from academic socialization. I hope sharing my story helps you find your way to generating writing and research on your own terms: because you want to, not because you have to.

REFERENCES

All the Things ADHD. n.d. Podcast. https://allthethingsadhd.com/.
The Data-Sitters Club, The. n.d. https://datasittersclub.github.io/site/.
Fruscione, Joseph, and Kelly J. Baker. 2018. *Succeeding Outside the Academy: Career Paths Beyond the Humanities, Social Sciences, and STEM.* Lawrence: University Press of Kansas.
Melançon, Lisa. 2019. "Affective Investment." Last modified June 13, 2019. http://tek-ritr.com/affective-investment/.

11

AMBIVALENT IN A GOOD WAY

On Both Staying In and Leaving Academia

CLARE FORSTIE

My path through academia might best be understood as an ambivalent one, often marked by strong, opposing feelings. As an undergraduate student, I was not certain that the tenure-track faculty path was the right fit for me, even as I saw myself as a future teacher and scholar. As a graduate student, I felt that I should make choices that felt authentic to my interests and values while also knowing that I needed to "play the game" to be employed, eventually. I worked in institutions and lived in communities where I was both hypervisible and invisible and felt both valued and devalued for my focus on students and teaching.

In this chapter, I describe my path in higher education, from my administrative role to my PhD program to a significant teaching fellowship, a tenure-track faculty position, and, finally, my current work as a teaching consultant. Along the way, I name and unpack the ambivalences that are central to our work, and I identify the specific strategies I used to navigate unresolved experiences. I share an ambivalent framework for decision-making in higher education and acknowledge the contexts of marginalization and privilege that affected how I have been able to make those decisions. My aims are to normalize ambivalence as a common experience among those who work in higher education, to remind us that career paths are not linear, and to highlight the centrality of our personal and community contexts in our decision-making process.

SOCIAL CONTEXTS OF AN AMBIVALENT ACADEMIC CAREER

My graduate school journey started while I was working full-time in higher education administrative as a grants manager in a school of public service. While the work itself was manageable enough, I really loved my colleagues, whose own commitments to making the world better were transparent in the ways they approached their work and their colleagues. One of the benefits of that job was a tuition waiver, for up to two courses per semester, which allowed me to experiment with graduate classes in an adjacent field before deciding to take the leap to a full-time PhD program. My first master's degree in American and New England studies, in other words, was nearly free. My experiences in that program sparked my interest in research and teaching, and I began to explore the possibility of pursuing a PhD.

At that point in my late twenties, when I contemplated a possible future in the professoriate, I felt consistently quite ambivalent. On the one hand, I wanted to engage in what one of my graduate school professors described, eyes sparkling, as the "life of the mind" enabled by an academic (implicitly, tenure-track faculty) position. I wanted to do this kind of thinking work in community, primarily through teaching, in conversation with undergraduate students. I wanted to think critically about the world around me, specifically my own queer communities, and share that thinking with others through research. I needed this kind of engagement so badly that I contemplated leaving a well-paying administrative job, also in higher ed, and moving my family to an as yet undetermined state, far from our families and communities.

On the other hand, I had been warned by previous mentors who helped frame this ambivalence by giving me "real talk" about what this life of the mind requires: willingness to work endless hours, live in communities potentially hostile to my existence, and endure intense competition for jobs that might allow me and my family to survive. I learned, quickly, that academia is not a meritocracy, and that success (meaning a tenure-track job specifically) is neither guaranteed nor particularly likely. I wasn't sure that my values and interests in equity, humility, and ongoing critical approaches to research and pedagogy would align with those present in academia, with its deep investments in white supremacy (Ahmed 2012; Smith 2019; Tuck and Yang 2018) and commitments to preserving hierarchies and power differentials.

In my research I argue that ambivalence as a sociological, rather than individual, psychological phenomenon, is highly undervalued. According to sociologist Neil Smelser, "The nature of ambivalence is to hold *opposing affective orientations* toward the same person, object, or symbol.... Ambivalence tends to be unstable, expressing itself in different and sometimes contradictory ways as actors attempt to cope with it" (1998, 5). Insights from sociological research on ambivalence emphasize its ubiquity (particularly in families, which I feel deeply now as a parent, and in immigrant communities) and its contextualization (ambivalence comes from social contexts, in other words). Both of these themes connect to my advice for those still in graduate school as well as those considering, or currently in, tenure-track faculty positions.

Sometimes I find that narratives about academia are too binary, too simplistic, and too linear. Primarily, it's important to be skeptical of binary thinking of all kinds, and ambivalence offers a both/and approach. Ambivalence allowed me to balance a sense of authenticity with a sense of strategy about next steps, and as with life, there was grief and joy along the way. Making these norms visible and identifying their benefits and drawbacks allows for more clear-eyed decision-making and might present you with unexpected opportunities to explore positions within academia that could more closely meet your needs and desires for a fulfilling life. A first step in moving toward these opportunities is the decision to apply to a new kind of position.

Even given my ambivalence about whether to become a professor, I found myself enacting the advice I find myself giving so often: I applied to PhD programs and would decide what to do next depending on acceptances, if any. These days, I tell others that you lose little by submitting an application (well, aside from the time and potentially money spent on the application process). You make the decision that's in front of you, taking the next small step given the contexts in which that step is embedded: community, family, economics, inequities, survival. For me, it's much easier to understand the scope of just that next decision, so that is where I focus, even now. Perhaps not coincidentally, as this essay collection indicates, just-in-time decision-making is becoming more of a norm in a disruptive global economy.

It's important to me to name the contexts that enabled me to experiment with, then undertake fully, graduate school. As an undergraduate, my white, middle-class family supported me in my elite, small liberal arts education, and although my student aid required campus employment, my hours were minimal and allowed me to engage in the kind of intellectual and social experimentation that's considered, unquestioningly, part of the "normal" college experience. My racial identity facilitated a sense of belonging in many of my courses and student organization spaces, which I heard from my BIPOC friends (and now know from extensive research) was not always possible or supported in our predominantly white institution. I met my partner while in college, and we began to build a life together before I even graduated, which enabled us to pool our resources in ways that are more challenging for single college graduates. My break-time employment in a fascinating array of temporary office jobs helped me develop a résumé and skills for me to transition into an administrative job following graduation, a reminder to broaden our scope when it comes to skill development. Finally, I graduated with a double major in sociology and what was then called women's studies, along with student debt, but not the crushing kind that saddles many of my peers and, increasingly, college students today.

All of these factors facilitated my try before you buy approach to graduate school, and I truly loved my first master's program. There, I began to explore ideas that persist through my research today. In fact, my frustration with simple narratives of community (and especially queer community) progress led to my first research project as a graduate student interviewing patrons of a closed lesbian bar. I later used the word "bittersweet" to describe the reactions of those patrons, many of whom felt a sense of ambivalence about both the bar's existence and its closing. To some patrons, the bar's closing represented a loss of a sense of community, even a sense of family. Others were actively excluded from the bar while it was open and felt a sense of loss of community even while it existed. Most were ambivalent about the bar: sad to lose a community space but also recognizing that some had lost that space already. This research prompted me to think concretely about how ambivalence shapes and is shaped by our experiences, lives, and social contexts. As I began to wrap this research, and my first master's degree, in conversation with my partner and a faculty mentor, I decided to apply to sociology PhD programs.

Following my mentor's wise advice, I started thinking about the job market immediately. I wanted to teach, and the strongest route to a sustainable teaching position in higher ed is a disciplinary PhD, for better *and* worse. Given that I wanted to teach and was interested in research on gender and sexualities, an undergraduate mentor shared with me that a PhD from a long-established discipline (like sociology) would give me greater access to a broader range of positions and was more likely to be recognized as legitimate by hiring committees when compared with, for example, a gender studies PhD. While this was painful to learn, it was one example of strategic thinking I would not have known had my advisor not shared it. I also knew enough to be strategic about where I applied, and where I considered accepting. Given my ambivalence about tenure-track faculty positions as a future career path, and given the stressors of graduate school, I only applied to programs I had heard had a good culture, meaning a sense of collegiality rather than competition. I also applied mainly to elite institutions, both because I knew I should be funded for this work and also because they would position me well-ish once I arrived on the job market. As I told my friends and family, and as I made my final decision about where to attend, this elitism made me feel gross, even as I recognized its necessity as a strategic approach. Clearly, ambivalence is strongly threaded throughout my thinking about academia, and each decision required a careful balancing of the contexts of academia (power, inequality, and job prospects), my skills and interests (I wanted to teach and think), and my values (I strongly resist reinforcing false narratives of meritocracy).

I could afford to apply to eleven PhD programs, which cost me around $700 at the time. I was accepted to two of those programs, visited both, and decided to attend my PhD-granting institution in part due to its elite status, in addition to the engaging scholars and possible cohort-mates I met during my visit. I thought it would best position me to get that coveted tenure-track position. Perhaps, in the end, it did. And still, I feel gross about the elitist elements of that decision. For me, feeling ambivalent about decisions like these is an important signal about whether and how I put my values into practice. Decision made, my partner and I packed up our much-loved home, dog, and cats; said goodbye to our friends, family, and community; and moved to a very strange, and very large, city. I celebrated my thirtieth birthday just before we moved, which made me one of the older members of my graduate cohort.

GRADUATE SCHOOL STRATEGIES: BEING AUTHENTIC WHILE PLAYING THE GAME

In my PhD program I found myself surrounded by a close cohort, many of whom also became lifelong friends. These relationships sustained me and continue to do so. I was plopped into the middle of cross-disciplinary conversations, exactly what I was hoping to find in graduate school, and supported by many kindly critical mentors, the faculty I aspired to be. And still, the struggles were many. As my partner struggled with her health and found it nearly impossible to make connections in our new city, I struggled with anxiety, workload, and fears that I had made a tremendous mistake. Here, too, we were privileged: my partner's full-time job didn't quite make up for the more than 60 percent salary cut I had taken to pursue a PhD, but we were able to live comfortably. We had good health insurance, good therapists and healthcare providers, and we could live in relative safety. Amidst this ambivalent experience of graduate school, I began working toward my future in academia.

It is important for me to name what we mean when we're thinking, talking, and writing about academia or higher ed. So often, when we report leaving academia, what we mean, implicitly, is that we're leaving a tenure-track faculty position, or the possibility of such a position. Often implicit in these words is an assumption about the best kinds of tenure-track faculty positions. At least at my institution, former grad students hired at R1 institutions were the most celebrated as the stars of the department, among faculty and grad students alike. Assumptions about what constitutes academia (or, perhaps, the most valued academic positions) have real consequences for us as individuals, for resource allocation, for teaching, and, importantly, for undergraduate and graduate students. As I knew before I applied to PhD programs, academia is incredibly diverse, and what we often imagine as the standard is actually quite rare.

Over 90 percent of four-year institutions in the US are not R1s (Carnegie Classification of Institutions of Higher Education n.d.), suggesting that most higher ed institutions are focused on teaching as their primary function, although research, and of course service, may also be valued. Few of the graduate students I work with now (at an R1 university system) understand the array of types of institutions beyond predominantly white R1s: tribal colleges, small liberal arts colleges, R2s, community colleges, and specialized institutions focused on particular fields (Carnegie Classification of Institutions of Higher Education n.d.). Very few graduate students are also aware of the array of diverse institutions within these groups—for example, HBCUs (historically Black colleges and universities) and HSIs (Hispanic-serving institutions) alongside PWIs (predominantly white institutions). Institutional classifications also create their own hierarchies, with doctoral institutions generally listed first despite not being the most common kind of institution.

Within each of these institutions is an equally diverse array of positions, some student-facing (student affairs, admissions, financial aid, health, non-tenure-track teaching, and athletics, to name a few), some supporting students less directly but no less importantly (facilities, food service, faculty service offices like teaching centers), and some supporting research primarily (research center staff and grants and contracts offices, for example). Some more centralized roles may include administrative leadership, policy- and compliance-oriented offices like human resources, and positions focused on systematic approaches to diversity, equity, and inclusion across the institution.

One question I've considered along my path is: What does it mean to join academia, or leave academia? By what processes do we learn to ignore, or forget, the rest of academia? If you are still teaching in a college or university, or if you work in a contract or non-tenure-track position, have you left academia? Do you need to? When I started my PhD program, I had some preliminary sense of the range of institutions, having by then worked at and attended two different types, and a bit about the ranges of positions, because people in these positions were my colleagues and friends. As time went on, I began to realize the ways that graduate students learn to focus almost exclusively on research-oriented tenure-track positions, effectively erasing the rest of academia.

I can't remember the exact moment when I really understood that teaching, or that anything other than a position at an R1, was taboo as a career choice at my institution. Perhaps it was the glazed eyes of faculty if anyone dared mention an interest in teaching. Perhaps it was the discourse about teaching—for example, the ways teaching was devalued, or the ways it was described as a chore alongside the more exciting work of research, both on the part of faculty and graduate students who were learning the norms of academia along the way. Perhaps it was the institutional signaling about how teaching is materially valued: interface with students (and associated emotion work) assigned primarily to grad student teaching assistants; or instructors who primarily teach described as not being real faculty and not compensated as such; or research assistantships coveted and privileged over teaching assistantships; or fewer courses offered to support teaching skill development than research skill development. Perhaps it was the way we all talked about the aforementioned stars in our field, powerful researchers whose ideas were just so compelling that they landed that coveted R1 job.

In my winding path through graduate school, I aimed for an ambivalent middle road between authenticity (my commitment to teaching and to complex narratives) and strategic decision-making for survival. I sought funding to present at any and every conference I possibly could, both to develop my presentation skills and to build networks with new colleagues, many of whom were (and remain) generous with their time and resources. When I saw a call for papers even vaguely related to my research and interests, I would often think, *Why not?* You lose nothing by submitting an abstract. This practice yielded a strong publication record by the time I graduated. I insisted that I be treated as a potential future colleague by faculty, and many did treat me this way. I actively distanced myself from those who did not, building a diverse network of supportive faculty around me instead of a single mentor (although my primary mentor treated me as a colleague from the moment I arrived on campus). From my previous administrative role, I already knew what it felt like to be treated with respect as someone with knowledge and skills, an experience graduate school challenged me to remember.

Most importantly, I knew I wanted to teach, and I knew my department would not adequately train me to do so. I became involved with my institution's teaching center, to start. I completed a graduate teaching certificate program and eventually earned an assistantship through the center, building an ongoing mentorship relationship along the way. I talked with colleagues about teaching praxis and eventually cofounded a committee for sociology graduate students interested in teaching. I kept my radar up for opportunities to think and write about teaching and actually teach, beyond teaching assistantships. I eventually co-taught a course with one of my mentors, which allowed me to flex my teaching muscles in new ways. And when I discovered a diversity fellowship for queer graduate students at a distant public institution posted in a listserv, I saw that the position required teaching and jumped at the chance to apply. The position would enable me to develop my teaching skills teaching one class per semester, in addition to working as an affiliate of a campus gender and sexuality center, while also preserving 50 percent of my time to complete my dissertation. I saw this fellowship as a way to practice being what I had planned to be: an out, queer faculty member focused on supporting students.

ALMOST-FACULTY: IN/VISIBILITY IN THE RURAL MIDWEST

I admit that I had to Google the location of the fellowship institution, and, even now, when I explain where it is, I use my hands to form the neighboring states. I point to an area above my wrist to show where it's located, close to two neighboring states. I applied to and was awarded this competitive fellowship, after participating in a job application process that resembled that of a tenure-track faculty position. *This is what it feels like to apply for professor positions*, I thought as I laced up my purple Doc Martens and fretted about my blue hair. My faculty mentors at my PhD-granting institution expressed some skepticism that this step would further my career. But I applied anyway, keeping my eye on the proverbial prize of a teaching-focused tenure-track position. Yet again, my partner and I packed up our home and our pets and moved, this time to the small town in which this institution was located, then to a nearby small city. The much lower cost of living alongside the reality that my partner and I were both employed in higher education meant that the stress of financial survival was minimized, at least in the short term. Strangely, we found it both easier and harder to connect with queer and progressive communities, another ambivalent process I explore more fully in my research. On one hand, in the small college town in which I worked, and even around the small city where we lived, I often felt like an object of curiosity, both due to my and my partner's visible queerness and, perhaps more importantly, the fact that we weren't *from* there. And yet, our whiteness and middle-class lives allowed us to be objects of curiosity, rather than hostility. On the other hand, we found queer and progressive communities that welcomed us warmly, even as outsiders, as many of those community members were also outsiders themselves in similar ways.

Within my fellowship institution, I was surprised to find that my new colleagues treated me as an early-career faculty member, someone whose knowledge and expertise was valuable to them as individuals and to the institution as a whole. That was not my experience as a graduate student; being treated this way made me realize the value of being seen as an asset, rather than a potential liability or distraction. Sometimes, being seen as an asset was uncomfortable, as I suddenly became an expert on all things queer in a way that felt, at times, a mite tokenizing. But overall, my colleagues saw me, and they trusted me to do good work. A subsequent guiding theme in my higher ed career decision-making process is to recognize the contexts in which our knowledge and experiences are valued, rather than ignored, tolerated, or actively dismissed. While this theme has been present throughout my career in higher education, I felt it most acutely during this fellowship. Sometimes this realization has appeared initially as a gut feeling, and I feel it in my posture, and, ultimately, the quieting of impostor syndrome (so common among academics). For me, this feeling has a lot to do with the social contexts we are in, as academics. I've felt it at conferences, where participants expressed enthusiasm about my research, for example, or asked thoughtful questions that engaged with my ideas, rather than performed the asker's knowledge. At my fellowship institution, my student services role was clearly needed, and students often visited my office to share their experiences and seek support. And my new faculty colleagues asked me to speak to their departments and to their classes, sharing my research and perspectives on how best to support LGBTQ+ students. Our bodies' signals matter in our decisions, too. For example, I know when I feel able to breathe, take up the physical space to which I'm entitled, and when my shoulders relax that I am headed in the right direction.

I also began to work more directly with students, both in teaching my own courses and in supporting the recently rebranded gender and sexuality center on campus. I facilitated programming, partnered with colleagues from across the institution and beyond, helped hire a fantastic director, responded to various campus crises, and spent many hours chatting with students both in the newly designed center and in my neighboring office, where a comfy couch drew students, staff, and faculty alike. I was firmly enmeshed in student affairs even as I was teaching my own courses for the first time and conducting my dissertation research. Although I was offered the possibility of a permanent position within the institution, one that would continue the student affairs/faculty role I held in my fellowship, I felt the pull of the larger tenure-track job market.

I still feel ambivalent about the decision to decline that hybrid faculty and student affairs position. On the one hand, I sense that it would have been fulfilling in a way subsequent positions were not, and I think I would have been able to do really good work in the role. On the other hand, given the political climate in that region, it would have been difficult for my family to sustain a life in the longer term, even given the relationships we formed when we lived in the area, many of which we maintain. Also during this time, my partner and I took initial steps down the path of becoming parents, a process about which ambivalences abound (Connidis 2015). After investing time, money, and many intense emotions, my partner gave birth to our kiddo in our small, Midwestern, Catholic city. And in this process, I began thinking through yet another layer of community: *What does it mean to raise a child in this community, compared to another?* The decision-making math became immediately more complicated. Community climate now mattered both for my partner and me, and also for our kiddo's future.

I had already had one "soft" year on the job market in the second year of my fellowship, and the third year of my fellowship was my "hard" job market year. Here, too, I was strategic about where I applied: I wanted a place that explicitly valued teaching in a community that wouldn't be too hostile to my family. And, still, I knew that wherever we went, being a middle-class family with two parents and a child afforded us some level of legibility, some protection not available to many of my peers. After that year of constant application revision and submission, hoping and dreaming about possible positions and places, I landed exactly one on-campus interview and one job offer for the coveted tenure-track position at a teaching-focused institution.

LIVING THE DREAM: FACULTY AND TEACHING AMBIVALENCES

I remember the thrill of receiving the phone call when I got that job offer. I had made it! I was about to accept a tenure-track position at an institution with excellent colleagues, with a 4/4 teaching load, and with the freedom to pursue my research as I wanted. I could see a clear path to tenure, to the life of the mind I had wanted for nearly a decade. I earned that position partly due to privilege, I'm sure. I had been accepted to an elite institution for my PhD, and I had the capacity and resources to move somewhere rural to develop my teaching career. I felt safe *enough* in these places, safe enough to conduct my research, and to do the work my fellowship required. Prior to receiving the call,

I had prepared my response, asked for one or two course releases in the fall to accommodate my move from the Midwest and newborn child (which the provost refused), and ultimately accepted the position with a tiny bit more money. Once again, my partner and I packed up our expanding lives, our two-week-old baby, and our pets and moved to a town with a much higher cost of living. We hoped we would not be moving again for some time. We hoped this would be a place where we could finally embed ourselves in communities for the longer term. And, we thought, how bad could it be? We were moving to a coastal town in a progressive state.

Even now, I feel ambivalent writing about this position. I feel ambivalence about these higher education professional narratives even as I feel ambivalence about living within them. Many of my colleagues who are part of the current "great [academic] resignation," particularly among adjunct faculty, truly face horrific, even abusive, working conditions. A small, elite core of faculty lead busy, stressful lives but have the resources to build academic communities that are inaccessible to most. And still, I feel strongly that academia is uniquely but no more and no less hostile, unequal, and hierarchical than any other field. There are many ways in which academia preserves inequality; some would argue that this is its primary function (Baldwin 2021). And other types of institutions, other fields of work, do the same. For me, higher education remains a field of possibility, one in which we can engage in questions of liberation (hooks 1994) in ways that are unique and, perhaps, uniquely transformative. And as with any institution within any field, context matters, and no job is perfect.

There were aspects of this faculty position that I truly loved. My colleagues were wonderfully supportive, and fully human, and allowed me to ask novice questions and stay humble about my work. It is too simple to say I loved teaching. I did, but teaching a 4/4 most semesters meant that I could not engage in the well-researched effective teaching practices I truly wanted to implement, the ones I thought might actually be transformative for my students. I experimented with some strategies that worked, and others that were utter failures. My students both sustained and drained me. My favorite moments were those in which I learned from them, and, along the way, we just happened to explore relevant sociological concepts and their everyday applications. And even as students resisted thinking and talking about concepts like racial inequalities, I'm sure I received less pushback than my BIPOC colleagues, especially adjunct colleagues. My research moved forward, achingly slowly, but the achievable tenure requirements meant that I was relatively free to pursue research that mattered to me. I sought and was awarded a book contract for my dissertation work from a prestigious university press.

And yet, all institutions are socially located. My institution was in a region of the country that, I quickly learned, was among the most segregated, and overtly and unabashedly racist to boot. What shocked me most was the belief among my students that they were living in one of the best places in the country. My queer and trans students shared their experiences of exclusion in their families and communities with a shrug, as though these circumstances were the best they could expect. Despite our efforts attending local events (baby in tow), we could not make inroads in local queer communities. For some reason, it was harder to connect to a sense of community here than it was in our previous, rural Midwestern home. My privilege was most definitely showing, and, with an eye toward my family, my partner and I began making plans to leave following our first year. We could not envision raising our child in a community so hostile to difference, to outsiders, and so unwilling to see and accept us as we are. Given the incredibly tight job market, I had an inkling that a change in career path would be necessary to live the quality of life we wanted. I launched another soft year on the academic job market but expanded to positions outside of tenure-track faculty ones. I more actively kept an eye on administrative and non-tenure-track teaching positions, and I had a couple of bites, but no concrete offers. One day, a position was posted to a faculty development listserv that seemed like the perfect match: a position at a teaching center back in the Midwest, close to my family and queer-friendly communities that, we thought, might better align with our values. Taking my own advice that you lose nothing by applying, and I submitted my cover letter and CV. And I waited.

LOSSES AND GAINS: JUMPING OFF THE TENURE-TRACK TREADMILL

Leaving a tenure-track position is a Big Deal. Suddenly, colleagues who previously spoke to you as an equal aren't sure what to do with you. You become illegible as an academic—that is, the very particular kind of academic encapsulated by the tenure-track faculty position. Conversations with former colleagues can become awkward, as many aren't aware of the other kinds of positions within academia, even as they work alongside these positions every day (and some disdain them). In reality, it is also true that conversations are awkward if you don't achieve the coveted R1 tenure-track position. Your mentors ask you at conferences, *Now, where are you again?* They mispronounce your institution. They don't send celebratory emails across the department when you get that job. And yet, a stumbling leap off the tenure track and onto other ground really separates the community wheat from the chaff. Those who cared about me as a human being, outside of my research productivity, continue to stay connected, and some make special efforts to do so because they feel enriched by this relationship. I, too, choose which relationships I want to continue, and those that remain hyper-focused on research productivity have fallen by the wayside. Such is life, and friendship, across the life course.

I felt incredibly ambivalent leaving a tenure-track job. I felt, on the one hand, a loss of community, and a loss of intellectual engagement in my field. I continue to grieve this loss, especially as I wish for the time and energy to continue to live the life of the mind I wanted, and even as my dissertation book is about to be launched. That life feels less and less possible, as a parent of a young child during the ongoing COVID-19 pandemic. And yet, I yearn for it. I also felt a tremendous sense of relief, as the work of my job felt manageable within a reasonable work week for the first time in a decade. Suddenly, I had my evenings and weekends back. My family moved into a home in a community where houses sport rainbow flags, and where my child reads at least as many books about families like his during family week as he does books with moms and dads. My child has queer teachers, and friends whose parents are queer, and for the first time since we left our home in the Northeast US, it's not a big deal. And, simultaneously, racial inequities are especially acute where we live, where our city is yet again among the most segregated in the nation. We live a half-mile from George Floyd Square, itself a site of tremendous ambivalence, one where a Black man was brutally murdered by police and also where creative experiments in community have grown, been repressed by the state, and continue to grow and grow and grow. Anyone who lives here knows that simplistic narratives of progress (or lack of progress) cannot possibly capture the simultaneous pain and joy of GFS.

Ambivalent thinking remains useful in my current job, too; I am a teaching consultant at a university system-wide teaching center. I am reminded again about the importance of colleagues, of community, and the relationships I'm forming in my current work will both sustain me and, I imagine, allow me to engage the hopes I have about academia as a field. As my current colleagues know, I remain clear-eyed about the immediate possibilities for change, and I maintain that relationships, not institutions or the organizations within them, are the primary foundation of social change (Palmer 1992). In my role as a teaching consultant, I have my radar up for the kinds of relationships that might foster critical social change, along the lines of revolution and abolition (Love 2019), even as I know there are institutional roadblocks to these kinds of change. And I have been reminding myself that my job and my identity are two separate things, something I had forgotten along the way through graduate school and into a faculty position. Especially during the pandemic, narratives of self-sacrifice for students, for institutions, and for equity have run rampant, and burnout has become a cliché, if a deeply felt one. Disconnecting my identity from my job has become critical for my survival in these times.

WHAT'S NEXT? AN AMBIVALENT FRAMEWORK FOR DECISION-MAKING

I often share with grad students that I feel quite allergic to giving advice, as the context of the person giving the advice is so essential to its interpretation. Even so, given my context, readers can make an assessment about whether to implement the threads of my advice. Above, I've shared the following advice: (1) focus on the next small step; (2) be strategically authentic in your decision-making; (3) learn about the range of possible institutions and positions that constitute academia (and unpack your own thinking about which of these positions is most valuable); and (4) go where you're valued, where you can find your communities. Here, I'll share three additional bits of advice, grounded in the sociological approach to ambivalence described in the introduction to this chapter.

First, ambivalence is a normal part of our experience of our work. I am not sure whether academia as a field is more or less ambivalent than other fields, but the kinds of ambivalences I experienced in academia include how much time to allocate toward teaching compared to research; how to value our work while having a life outside of our academic identity; how to support students' mental health needs while protecting our own; managing flexibility alongside clear boundaries; and being our authentic selves along our sometimes narrow career paths. I have felt ambivalence in all of these dimensions of my academic life, and I have made decisions about where to dedicate my time and energy accordingly, in alignment with my values. My advice is to take note of ambivalence in your current work, and in your potential future work. In some ways perhaps, ambivalence, or at least noticing our ambivalence, is healthy. So few of us in academia, and in life, get to work in our dream job, and what happens when our dream job sours, anyway? Keeping our eyes open for job opportunities can be one way to think through those ambivalences along the way, even if we decide not to apply to those opportunities, or we decline them if we are offered them. Even exploring other positions can help us think through whether we should stay in our current job or continue on the path to tenure-track faculty. This was true for me as I contemplated the job offer at my fellowship institution.

Second, the contexts of our lives matter. We get to decide if the prestige and possible life of the mind afforded by a tenure-track position is truly worth it, given the array of sacrifices we and our families make. There are no clear, concrete right or wrong answers, except perhaps when we feel them in our gut. I transitioned into my new position just before the pandemic changed everything in academia—for me, especially teaching. My transition to online teaching (and consulting about online teaching) felt stressful but manageably so, and I am not sure I would have felt the same had I stayed in my previous role. I feel tremendous relief that we live close to my family, which operated as a de facto bubble after vaccines became available. I also feel relieved that I live in a city in a state where basic science is not routinely dismissed, where vaccine rates are relatively high, and where community-mindedness (if imperfect) is more normalized than individuality. Community has always been central to my decision-making processes, about my research topics, about my and my family's career moves, and about how we live our everyday lives. We are always asking: What communities do we want to create? Participate in? Where do we hope to make change? In my gut, I feel that this work in community is more possible here than it would have been in other positions, other places, other times.

Finally, foster ambivalence about narratives of higher ed, especially what's considered normal, or expected, or valued. This comes both out of theories of ambivalence and out of my field, sociology. In fact, it was one of the first ideas sociology offered that drew me to the field. I often share that it's important to be skeptical of binary thinking of all kinds, and ambivalence offers a both/and approach. Ambivalence allowed me to balance a sense of authenticity with a sense of strategy about next steps, and as with life, there was grief *and* joy along the way. Making these norms visible and identifying their benefits and drawbacks allows for more clear-eyed decision-making, and might present unexpected opportunities to explore positions within academia that could more closely meet your needs and desires for a fulfilling life. Maintaining a sense of ambivalence alongside excitement for new positions, keeping your eyes open for opportunities (even if you don't think you need them), and recognizing opportunities when they arise may lead to a circuitous path through academia and beyond. But that, I'm coming to believe, is also quite normal.

To close, a story: I met with my undergraduate mentor at a conference in the pre-pandemic days, likely my last disciplinary conference ever. We grabbed a quick breakfast in one of the conference hotels, and I somewhat shamefacedly told her that I was leaving my tenure-track position for one at a teaching center at a university closer to my family. I was just beginning to realize and work through the grief of leaving my tenure-track position, and I still felt embedded, strongly, in the hierarchies of academia. I'm not sure how my mentor always seems to know exactly what I need to hear, but she shared in that moment that one of the things that impressed her about me is the way I always seem to choose the path that works best for me, and how I remain true to myself, expectations be damned. I felt prouder about my decision in that moment, and I think about it often, as I settle into my current position and contemplate how I might reengage with intellectual communities working toward equity and change. This work will always be incomplete for me, and, yes, highly ambivalent, but I am in a space now where it feels more possible than ever to engage in work that sustains me *and* create the families and communities we need to support social change.

REFERENCES

Ahmed, Sara. 2012. *On Being Included: Racism and Diversity in Institutional Life.* Durham, NC: Duke University Press.

Baldwin, Davarian L. 2021. *In the Shadow of the Ivory Tower: How Universities Are Plundering Our Cities.* New York: Bold Type Books.

Carnegie Classification of Institutions of Higher Education. n.d. "Basic Classification." Accessed December 21, 2021. https://carnegieclassifications.acenet.edu/carnegie-classification/classification-methodology/basic-classification/.

Connidis, Ingrid Arnet. 2015. "Exploring Ambivalence in Family Ties: Progress and Prospects." *Journal of Marriage and Family* 77 (1): 77–95. https://doi.org/10.1111/jomf.12150.

hooks, bell. 1994. *Teaching to Transgress: Education as the Practice of Freedom.* New York: Routledge.

Love, Bettina L. 2019. *We Want to Do More Than Survive: Abolitionist Teaching and the Pursuit of Educational Freedom.* Boston: Beacon Press.

Palmer, Parker J. 1992. "Divided No More: A Movement Approach to Educational Reform." *Change: The Magazine of Higher Learning* 24 (2): 10–17. https://doi.org/10.1080/00091383.1992.9937103.

Smelser, Neil J. 1998. "The Rational and the Ambivalent in the Social Sciences: 1997 Presidential Address." *American Sociological Review* 63 (1): 1–16. https://doi.org/10.2307/2657473.

Smith, Christi M. 2019. "Race and Higher Education: Fields, Organizations, and Expertise." In *Race, Organizations, and the Organizing Process*, edited by Melissa E. Wooten, 25–48. United Kingdom: Emerald Publishing.

Tuck, Eve, and K. Wayne Yang, eds. 2018. *Toward What Justice? Describing Diverse Dreams of Justice in Education.* New York: Routledge.

12

FROM STUCK TO SATISFIED

Creating a Joyful, Balanced Life

KRISTINE LODGE

I started a new job recently. The chief operating officer welcomed me on LinkedIn and said she was excited that I would bring my unique background and skill set to the job. I am more used to people pausing when they hear about my work experience and skills. They are curious about why I have a PhD but work in a job outside academia. "How did you get here?" is a question I'm used to answering. But this company leader was intrigued by my previous work in academia. Her excitement was a change from previous jobs where I felt I had to minimize my PhD degree and experience to fit in. Finding an organizational culture where I am celebrated has been the culmination of a journey away from stuffing myself into boxes that did not fit and toward accepting that all of my personal and professional experiences and values matter and allow me to be my best, most creative self both at home and at work.

In this essay, I explore the impacts of my family's working-class background and my orientation as a lesbian on my career. I discuss the assumptions that led me to pursue a career in academia, which was ultimately a very poor fit for my values, interests, and skills. And I describe what happened once I began to take the advice I give my coaching clients who feel stuck and afraid to move forward: know yourself; know your values; find the communities (work and personal) that champion you. Through reflecting on my trajectory, I show how my career has been a process of integrating my multiple identities and values into a coherent whole, and that spanning boundaries can be a positive and joyful way to live both personally and professionally.

It is not easy to explain what I do because my career path has not been linear: while writing my dissertation, I took a full-time job at my university's career center, where I taught career classes, coached students, collaborated with faculty, and redeveloped an internship program. After this job, I worked in recruiting, program development and management for a graduate program, and now, customer success. For the last five years, I have held my full-time jobs while starting and growing my own business.

Currently, I have a combination of jobs: I am a full-time senior partner success manager for an organization that provides customer service, IT, and other services to a variety of companies. In this role, I manage relationships between my company's internal teams and our partners. I solve problems and drive strategies. I am also a self-employed career coach, helping academics land jobs in other industries that are aligned with their values and skills. Both jobs require the ability to build and maintain relationships, persuade others, ideate, plan, and execute. I love both jobs; they are the right career fit for me at this point in my life.

My jobs have spanned boundaries and industries. What connects them all are my values and interests: my drive to be creative, my desire to help others, and my strong tendency to leap in and get things accomplished. I also have a love for stories. As a doctoral student, I studied stories: what they meant to medieval cultures, what their authors may have meant, and how they influenced Anglo-Saxon society. As a recruiter, I analyzed stories in résumés and interview answers to help find good candidates. I help people create stories about their interests, values, skills, and experience as a career coach. Stories have been central to my professional life.

This essay tells another story: how my career has also been a process of integrating my personal and professional identities into a coherent whole, especially those parts that I have been socialized to keep separate. For most of my life, bifurcation has been at the center of my personal and professional life. I spent a significant part of my adult life trying to live as a straight woman, coming out as queer/lesbian in my late thirties. I am also the product of a primarily working-class upbringing, which I went to great lengths to hide, both from myself and from colleagues, until I recently began to reclaim and celebrate it.

Consider this essay, then, as a sort of academic bildungsroman in which I went from a closeted, working-class upbringing to being an openly queer person with a PhD in English literature, a wife, two kids, a large, loud cat, and a job as a strategist and manager as well as a flourishing business providing career coaching to academics. I will explore how, despite my early determination to leave my working-class values, ways of speaking, and acting behind, I have come to celebrate and cultivate my working-class accent, my directness, and everything I have learned from my mother, the hairdresser. In closing, I will also give advice and tips on career pivots based on my own experience.

YOU CAN GO HOME AGAIN

I am the daughter of a hairdresser and an IT professional. One grandfather was a machinist; the other was a doctor. As a child, I spent most of my time with my mother's family, so I most strongly identify with growing up as a working-class child. I grew up in a suburb where many of my classmates' parents held professional jobs and most of my classmates expected to go to college after high school. I learned, early on, how to code switch between accents, mannerisms, attire, and conversation topics. As I moved into college and graduate school, I internalized messages that I should not volunteer what my mother or my maternal aunts and uncles did for a living. I smoothed out my accent. I hid (including, sadly, from myself) the knowledge that I am queer. I stifled the skills that make me a successful entrepreneur (drive, willingness to take risks, asking tough questions to make the next iteration better) to fit into academia's values.

The attempts to erase or transform my life were heavily influenced by my mother's expectations. I am both the oldest child and oldest daughter, one of three children. My place in the family as well as my gender helped shape my understanding that I was responsible for helping make my mother's dreams for a middle-class lifestyle come true. If she could not climb the class ladder herself, then I would. I made many of my personal and professional choices to satisfy this intergenerational desire. In the pursuit of an "acceptable" middle-class career and identity, I rejected my identity as a queer person as well as my family's class markers. My mother's occupation, hairdresser, was shameful to me. I lost sight of the story of "my mother the small business owner" in my attempts to erase the story of "my mother the hairdresser." But ultimately, my mother's career became an inspiration to me. It was not academia who gave me the example of a woman who was a subject matter expert, who managed others, who made change: that would be my mother. In closing this essay, I will discuss how I have come to embrace this view of my mother as an entrepreneur through my own entrepreneurial experiences.

Despite my attempts to validate and nurture only part of my identity, I have survived and come to the knowledge that it was not possible to discard the assumptions, habits, mindsets, and accent that influenced my childhood and young adulthood. Just as I tell my clients who come to me feeling stifled and frustrated by academic positions that do not fit well with who they are, my life is better, richer, more fulfilled when I stop attempting to hide from half of my identity and use all my skills and experience. As I contemplate my life in my forties, I see how my mother's work ethic and perseverance shaped me in positive ways and has helped me to succeed.

The seeds for this essay were planted in 2019, when I traveled to the East Coast with my then-fiancée and two kids to see my family. It was the first time I had been back East to visit since I came out as a lesbian in 2014. Before the trip, I spent a lot of time worrying about what it would be like to see family who had only known me as a supposed straight person. I worried: Would anyone say anything? What would I do if they did?

I was waiting for homophobia. So it took me by surprise, midway through our trip, when my eight-year-old son casually asked, "Mom, why are you talking funny?" I did not expect my accent to be an issue, although it should not have surprised me. My son, the native Oregonian, did not hesitate to call out my pronunciation of "forest" at age four: "Mommy, it's FOURest not FARest!" To my son, hearing me speak with my Philadelphia accent during that trip was different, strange, "funny." To me, speaking with my native accent felt easy, effortless. I realized then how much energy I put into suppressing it in my daily life. Although I had spent a great deal of time and money in therapy untangling and healing the internalized homophobia caused by my upbringing, my son's question held up a mirror to the ways in which I still downplayed my working-class roots and sought distance from them.

My accent is another place where bifurcation has played out in my life. Philadelphia is unique in having a variety of accents in one small geographic region. If you want a pop culture window into the intense regionalism of the area's various accents, read Meredith Blake's (2021) article about how Kate Winslet learned to speak with a Delco (Delaware County) accent for *Mare of*

Easttown. Yes, as anyone local to Philadelphia and its suburbs will tell you, there is a difference between how someone in Delco speaks from someone who grew up in South Philly. But geographic location is only one factor in the region's accents. Age, race, and class play large roles in accents as well, as Labov et al.'s (2016) study on the influence of schools and speech patterns shows. I have a West Philadelphia working-class accent. Although I grew up in the suburbs, I speak like my mother's working-class family whose roots are in West Philly. I grew up saying the stereotypical things people assume that you say if you are from the region: "wudder" for water; "youse" for the plural "you." I also think "attitude" is best pronounced "attytude."

However, my accent is not universal within my nuclear family. My father's side of the family, who hail from upper-middle-class Northwest Philly and nearby towns Manayunk and Germantown, do not say either "wudder" or "youse," as my paternal grandmother often reminded me during visits to her house. My father's accent, although similar to mine, is not the same. These differences are alive and well in my family of origin. After my parents divorced, there was a division between what and how I spoke in my mother's house—my primary residence—versus how I spoke at my father's. I learned to code switch between accents, because I learned, early on, how much language matters, and the accent you use to say it is as important as the message you want to convey.

The differences between my parents' and my grandparents' accents were signs of class to which my paternal family was very attuned. My grandmother, in particular, was concerned with how my two siblings and I spoke. When we were with her, we were expected to use the accent and speech patterns of her upper-middle-class life. And, as I have moved further from home both geographically (I live on the West Coast) and in class status (my education has allowed me to secure jobs that place me in the middle class), I have further embraced language and speech patterns that signal my middle-class membership to others. Which is why, if you listen to me speak in my daily life now, you will not hear me say "wudder," "attytude," or "dis/dem." I have learned to enunciate vowels rather than swallow them. I do not reflexively, unless talking with my family, refer to strangers as "Hun." It is not simply that my accent would sound very strange to others where I live now. Having a strong, regional accent marks me as "different" and causes people to make assumptions about me that have implications for my life and career. Stephen Colbert is a native of Charleston,

South Carolina. But you would not know that listening to him speak. Colbert told *60 Minutes* in a 2006 interview that assumptions about Southern accents were a reason to get rid of his drawl. Colbert describes his current accent as a "boring baritone" (Safer 2006). In my own experience, people have assumed me to be "intense," "talking too fast," or "intimidating" when they hear me speak with my native accent. However, if I lived in the Philadelphia area, it would be seen as working class.

Accents do not simply impact others' perceptions of whether I am smart/stupid or intense/easygoing. My accent could literally cost me money. Jeffrey Grogger published a paper on the perception of speech in whites and African Americans living in the Southeast. Grogger (2019) found that those who speak with "racially and regionally distinctive speech patterns" (948) earned lower wages than those who speak with mainstream speech patterns. In US society, we place high value on having a mainstream accent or not having a discernible regional accent. As academics, we experience pressure to conform to values that the industry (yes, academia/higher education is an industry) holds. In my experience, that includes values around regional accents. Can you think of someone in your department or program who speaks with a strong regional accent? What position does that person hold? If you hear someone introduce themselves as being from a part of the country that is known for a distinctive accent, but the person speaks in General American English without a strong accent, they likely have altered their accent and speech to advance their careers. That is what I did.

My accent was one of several things I attempted to jettison to climb the career and class ladder. But the trip to Philadelphia in 2019 served as a catalyst for me. I did not want my children to hear my Philly accent and label it as weird or strange. I wanted my children to see my accent as an intrinsic part of me, not something I only used when speaking with relatives back East. And I was shocked by the amount of energy I was spending to speak differently than the way I did growing up. Since that trip, I have made an effort to speak more in my native accent. I still don't say "wudder" either at home or at work, but I'm more likely to speak quickly and to swallow my vowels. I am no longer worried about fitting into a mainstream accent and using it to hide my origins. My working-class accent is a part of who I am.

MIDDLE CLASS AND QUEER WITH BENEFITS

Another important strand of my personal and professional life is my queer identity. I have only acknowledged my identity personally and publicly in the last ten years. Prior to this, I lived (very unhappily) as a straight, cis woman in a (seemingly) heterosexual marriage. I clung to this identity, although it was painful and not authentic, in part because of the expectations of my family, especially my mother, to achieve the comforts of a middle-class life. Being openly queer places potential obstacles in my path due to the ongoing potential for discrimination. As a white, cis woman with a terminal degree and an understanding of middle-class language and norms, I'm incredibly privileged and able to navigate bureaucracies and other systems of power. Yet, since coming out, I've been aware of ways in which being queer carries risk. Whether it is my wife and I not presenting as a couple in rural Oregon, or having to come out at work, which I've done with three different employers, I have regular reminders of how being a queer person can be at odds with other aspects of my identity.

One way this impacts me is through benefits provided by my employer. I have what my mother would call a "sit-down" job that brings me benefits my mother did not have access to during her career: health benefits, a 401(k) with employer match, and generous paid time off. Because I've had consistent access to healthcare and PTO through my employment, I have not had to go to work while ill because I had no PTO to cover the gap. Prior to 2020, I went to work while sick because of pressure to be present for students, but that's very different from choosing between working while ill or not getting paid; I saw my mother make this choice repeatedly throughout my childhood. Discussions about the impact of the pandemic on frontline workers have brought up many memories of watching my mother calculate whether she could afford to stay home for a day to rest and take care of herself. Coming from a working-class background has meant that I do not take the health and financial benefits of my jobs for granted. My desire as a young adult for the kind of job security I have found as a middle-class adult kept me closeted far longer than I might have been otherwise.

However, my identity as a queer woman potentially impacts my work and access to benefits. Because health and financial benefits are largely accessed through public and private employers in the United States, being unemployed can be risky. Being openly gay in the US can result in loss of employer-sponsored benefits: half of people who identify as LGBTQ+ experience employment discrimination in their lifetime (Sears and Mallory 2011). Further, Brittany Charlton's (2018) study of people ages eighteen to thirty-two revealed that "sexual minority women and men were about twice as likely as their respective heterosexual counterparts to have been unemployed and uninsured" (1). I am fortunate that working in higher education for much of my career gave me access to good benefits but also provided me a safer space to be openly queer than other industries.

Queerness is a part of my life that's both intrinsic as well as a newer identity I'm still exploring. Being closeted for eighteen years of my adult life meant that I had access to a lot of the privileges that many cis, straight folks take for granted. I am still unpacking what it means to work as an openly queer person in a work setting where most of my colleagues identify as straight.

THE ACCIDENTAL CAREER COACH

When people hear that I have a PhD in English literature and that I originally planned to be a medievalist, they are curious about why I am working outside of academia. When I was new to my job at the college of business, my subject specialization was one of the first things new colleagues would mention. "Oh, you're that medievalist!" they would exclaim. "I heard about you! How did you get *here*?"

In coaching roles, I frequently hear what I call the "accidental banker" story. One of my colleagues coined this term after we took our graduate students to visit to a bank. Each person who spoke started their story with, "I never planned to be a banker but . . ." My accidental banker story is that I never planned to be a career coach. When I was in the fifth year of my doctoral program, I was very stuck on my dissertation. My funding was running out, and I wasn't sure what to do next. A friend referred me to someone she knew who worked at the university Career Center for an informational interview. The Career Center planned to hire someone to teach their career classes. I interviewed for the role, was offered it, and fell in love with career coaching.

How I connected the dots between Anglo-Saxon hagiography and career coaching is both simple and complicated: I love a good story. And I use my experience studying and analyzing stories as a doctoral student in my current job helping people to get excited about their story learn how to tell it. Loving stories—reading them, analyzing them, and helping people create structures for theirs—has been the focal point of my career. However, there's a dark side to stories as well that placed unexpected barriers to my career path.

I love career stories in particular. I love coaching clients on how they want to frame their story, and I love hearing people tell them. As someone with a literature PhD, I can tell you that career stories are underappreciated as a genre: they are ubiquitous (most of us can't escape having to respond to "Tell me about yourself" in an interview) and intimidating to learn to tell. But stories about how someone became a [fill in the blank] are some of the most memorable I've heard. The career advising/coaching/counseling space is a dynamic one where you get to see the students' or clients' story evolve. As a career coach, I get to help students imagine and work toward their future lives. Being a witness to them shaping their stories is one of the best parts of my job.

When I began college, I had no clear idea of what I wanted to do. I knew what I did not want to be: a hairdresser, a truck driver, a postal service employee. Those were all jobs held by my mother, uncles, and aunts. I knew that they involved long hours, not great pay, and no benefits. They also were not high on the list of "acceptable" occupations either. I did some career exploration in high school through a career exploration program that was state-funded. In retrospect, it was my first introduction to my future career. I remember having long conversations with the program coordinator about the program and his work. Had he found a way for me to do some career coaching or program development, I suspect my professional life might have looked different. However, based on my love of reading and writing, I was placed with a fifth-grade class at a local elementary school, not the first time someone would assume that an English major or interest in the subject best aligns with classroom teaching as a career. I found aspects of my volunteer work fun, but I could not see myself teaching full-time in a K–12 classroom. As an undergraduate at a small, liberal arts, historic women's college, though, I fell in love with higher education and medieval literature. I had small, discussion-based seminar classes and a college with a strong community. What could be better, twenty-something me thought, than to be a faculty member at a small liberal arts college where I would get to lead discussions about Chaucer at the head of a seminar table, just like my English professors? Being a faculty member seemed to be all that I could desire: I could continue to learn, I could teach, and I could talk about medieval literature. And I would be paid for this!

It is not surprising that working-class college students, many of whom are first-generation students, are drawn to academia. One study suggests that first-generation students make up 30 percent of doctoral degree recipients (Roksa, Feldon, and Maher 2018, 728). The apparent guarantee of lifetime employment that tenure still evokes seems incredibly stable if you have grown up with parents who have held lots of different jobs or moved in and out of the workforce. Also, if your understanding of what it means to work or have a career is shaped by jobs that your family do to earn a paycheck but don't enjoy, jobs that may be low-paying and involve a lot of customer contact, as in the case of my mother's work, then you might, as I did, have a hard time seeing beyond a consistent paycheck, health and retirement benefits, and the promise of a job where you do not spend all your time on your feet.

Interestingly, I did have an example of middle-class occupations in my immediate family. My father was an IT professional who, by the time I was a college student, managed the IT department for a local community hospital. My paternal grandfather and aunt were anesthesiologists. However, although I understood basically what those professions were, they had limited impact on my life as a child both socially and monetarily. I was not close to my dad; my mother and her family are the ones who raised me and shaped my views of what it means to work, to earn money, to have a career. My dad's career was like a story in a different language to me.

When I fell in love with academia as a student, I was falling in love with the apparent lifestyle of academia rather than the actual job. I liked what I saw as a student and made my decisions based on that experience, rather than on a more thorough or objective understanding of what doing the job actually entailed. Much like students I have coached who want to work for Nike or Lululemon because they know the brand, I made the decision to apply to PhD programs because I loved Academia: The Brand. Like my students who base their career interests on their experiences as a customer, I chose to pursue a PhD in English literature because I loved what I did as a student. Like many other PhD students, I had little insight into what it was like to be a professor, especially at an R1 university, the type of university most likely to hire a medievalist. This was work I should have done as an undergraduate student considering PhD programs in English literature. I should, at least, have considered other options in passing. However, I was in love with the idea of continuing to learn and talk about medieval literature, and graduate school seemed like the best next step for me. And my maternal family was not in a position to advise me. They had no experience of working in middle-class occupations. The idea of exploring careers did not exist for them; they had jobs. I did not receive much pushback on my decision from my father's side of the family, either. While this seems surprising in retrospect, my father's family had several members with terminal professional degrees. A daughter and granddaughter with a PhD may have seemed perfectly reasonable given the trajectory of many family members.

Ultimately, I fell out of love with academia during my doctoral program. I came to feel stifled and frustrated by what, years later, I recognized as a hatred for the ways in which academics must write in order to succeed in the academy. And, while my dislike of academic writing made an academic career a very poor fit, that is not the only way in which an academic career became less desirable for me. I was twenty-two when I began graduate school in a terminal master's program, and twenty-six when I began my doctoral studies. By the time I was thirty, I wanted different things than I had at either age twenty-two or twenty-six: the ability to live where I wanted, to buy a house, to have a job with stability and benefits instead of a small stipend. This growth and change is something that we need to honor and celebrate in students and colleagues rather than assume that they are willing to do anything for a tenure-track job or that what they want won't change over time.

HOW I MET MY MOTHER . . . AT THE BUSINESS SCHOOL

The last piece of my identity that I want to share with you is my identity as an entrepreneur, something that I now understand both through owning my own business and through having coached students in a college of business, many of whom are interested in entrepreneurship or have come from families who owned small businesses. In my own coaching business, Incipit Career

LLC, I support academics and PhDs who want to leave academia to work in other industries. I offer individual and group coaching; create content, including marketing content; and write blog posts and newsletters for my subscribers. In addition, as an entrepreneur, I have learned how to do sales and marketing, how to set up workflows in customer relationship management systems (CRMs), and how to do basic website design and setup. In the hours before or after my full-time job, I meet with clients from all over the world individually and in small groups over Zoom. Through my business, I've been published in the Muse and Fast Company, have spoken at various universities, and been featured in publications on leaving academia. I love my business and helping my clients succeed in their career pivots.

I began my business to earn extra income and to be able to work more closely with clients with PhDs than I could previously. However, my business is much more than a source of income. It is a way for me to channel my drive to take risks, develop programs, run projects, and own the process from start to finish. It fulfills some of the interests I'm unable to fill in my day job. I say, and I'm not kidding, that owning my own business makes me a better employee. I founded my business in 2017 not long after my divorce when I had two small kids, a parallel to my mother's experience that I observed after the fact. I am very proud of the work I do as a small business owner who is also a queer, cis woman. Becoming an entrepreneur has been an exciting journey that's forced me to travel far out of my comfort zone and has helped me reclaim a connection to my family of origin and further heal the bifurcations in my life. My business also helps me align with values of entrepreneurship and risk-taking that have not been present in my full-time jobs.

My mother's path to entrepreneurship has both similarities and differences to mine. When I was very young, my mother owned her own hair salon. She rented a space in a local building, provided a range of hair services, and employed three stylists. My mother was a small business owner who had to manage income, expenses, bills, and payroll, and I sometimes wonder what it would have meant for both her identity and mine if she had been able to maintain this business. My parents' divorce when I was six, however, meant that she lost the business and was never able to recover the capital to launch a new one. She gained her main source of income by working at various salons throughout my childhood. However, she was not content to give up being her own boss completely. With her father's help, she transformed half of our house's garage into a full-fledged salon with a separate entrance, a shampoo bowl, a helmet dryer, and a professional-grade chair. She saw customers on evenings and weekends when she wasn't working, many of them from her old business.

Growing up, and earlier in my career, I understood this story as one of desperation. We needed the extra money so badly that my mother needed to "do hair" at home. It was something I felt ashamed of when my peers in high school all seemed to have parents who worked outside the home without needing a side gig to survive. But now I see it as more than just a powerful dedication to her family and work ethic. I see my mother as an entrepreneur who continued to hold onto that piece of her identity. Although she no longer owned a salon that employed others, she maintained her own professional space and status as small business owner. When I started working as a career coach at the business school, I did not expect to find pride and satisfaction in my identity as a daughter of an entrepreneur. In fact, I had not connected my mother's identity as an entrepreneur with my own. I still saw my mother's act of doing hair at home to be the shameful secret thing she needed to do for our family to survive. But working in an atmosphere where building your own business, and the often messy creation process, is valued and celebrated as a goal, I was able to reframe this story as one of risk-taking and success. Now, I am proud to be the daughter of a small business owner and entrepreneur who is carrying on my own version of entrepreneurship.

TAKEAWAYS FROM A CAREER COACH

As someone who has made multiple career pivots, what follows are the insights I believe are most transferable to readers across the disciplines and at all career stages.

Be honest with yourself about who you are. Many of my career and personal struggles came from my desire to fit myself within others' expectations, whether it was to try to be straight, to speak in a certain way, or to pursue a career as a tenured professor. You are the one who is in charge of your life and career. Your advisor, your principal investigator, or your partner are all people who might have opinions, but you are the one who ultimately decides what you do for work.

Know, and accept, your interests and values. There is tremendous pressure in academia to conform to a specific set of values to be successful. These values may not be your own. In my own experience, I found that I loved collaborating with others in my work. Being a tenured professor would have been too lonely for me. I need a balance where I can be an independent contributor as well as have the opportunity to work with others to plan and carry out projects. My current job as a partner success manager is ideal for me because I often work as the project manager, making sure that my company's clients have what they need. But I need to collaborate with my colleagues to ensure that our projects are completed. You also have a set of interests and values that drive your career choices. When you can acknowledge what you like to do, you are better able to explore options and make plans for your career.

Be curious about what other people do, especially if it is work you are interested in doing. It is standard practice in other industries to ask for informational interviews. You can find PhD alumni through LinkedIn research or by asking your institution. When you find someone who has a job you're interested in, ask for twenty to thirty minutes of their time to learn more about what they do. If you're intimidated by LinkedIn, there are many resources available to help you create your profile and learn how to use the platform to connect with others. Diedra Wrighting's essay in this volume reviews many of them.

Accept that your career will be nonlinear and involve change. The traditional view of academia is fairly static. Ideally, you accept a tenure-track role at one university and, if you're promoted to tenure, you'll stay at that institution or perhaps make one or two moves during the rest of your career. This type of longevity is not the norm in other industries. Since I accepted my first full-time job while in graduate school, I've worked as a career coach, a recruiter, a career coach again, and now as a partner success manager. Since 2017, I've been a small business owner concurrently with my full-time jobs. Job and career changes will also happen naturally as your values and interests change over time. My most recent career change was sparked by many factors: a desire to work remotely for better work–life balance, to learn a new skill set, and to be better compensated for my work. These are different motivations than ones I had in my early thirties. If you wonder, *What's wrong with me?* because you are no longer motivated by interests and goals from earlier in your career, don't worry. Priorities change, and that's perfectly normal.

CONCLUSION

I spent the first half of my life fleeing my working-class upbringing and values to embrace middle-class norms. My desire to conform to the values of academia as a graduate student and aspiring professor both reinforced and reflected my desire to stamp out evidence of my working-class accent and background in my personal life to conform to the norms of upper-middle-class, white, straight, cis life. My assumed identity was not one I wore well, and it came with a great deal of personal turmoil. As I reflect on my experience of moving into and through academia, then into staff positions in higher education, and now working in industry and as an entrepreneur, I realize how much I've learned to let go of others' expectations to conform, to minimize my instinct to code switch and conform, and to learn to speak in a way that suits and pleases me rather than others. My career has been about embracing the seeming contradictions of my personal and professional selves. I am not any single job title or descriptor. My life and work now mesh together beautifully into a joyful, messy, and energetic whole.

REFERENCES

Blake, Meredith. 2021. "How Kate Winslet Mastered the Near-Impossible Accent TV Fans Can't Stop Talking About." *Los Angeles Times*, April 29, 2021. https://www.latimes.com/entertainment-arts/tv/story/2021-04-29/mare-of-easttown-hbo-kate-winslet-accent-dialect-coach.

Charlton, Brittany M., Allegra R. Gordon, Sari L. Reisner, Vishnudas Sarda, Mihail Samnaliev, and S. Bryn Austin. 2018. "Sexual Orientation-Related Disparities in Employment, Health Insurance, Healthcare Access and Health-Related Quality of Life: A Cohort Study of US Male and Female Adolescents and Young Adults." *BMJ Open* 8:e020418. https://doi.org/10.1136/bmjopen-2017-020418.

Grogger, Jeffrey. 2019. "Speech and Wages." *Journal of Human Resources* 54, no. 4 (Fall): 926–52. muse.jhu.edu/article/738203.

Labov, William, Sabriya Fisher, Duna Gylfadottír, Anita Henderson, and Betsy Sneller. 2016. "Competing Systems in Philadelphia Phonology." *Language Variation and Change* 28 (3), 273–305. https://doi.org/10.1017/S0954394516000132.

Roksa, Josipa, David F. Feldon, and Michelle Maher. 2018. "First-Generation Students in Pursuit of the PhD: Comparing Socialization Experiences and Outcomes to Continuing-Generation Peers." *Journal of Higher Education* 89 (5): 728–52. https://doi.org/10.1080/00221546.2018.1435134.

Safer, Morley. 2006. "*60 Minutes: The Colbert Report.*" CBS News. April 27, 2006. https://www.cbsnews.com/news/the-colbert-report.

Sears, Brad, and Christy Mallory. 2011. "Documented Evidence of Employment Discrimination & Its Effects on LGBT People." UCLA: The Williams Institute. https://escholarship.org/uc/item/03m1g5sg.

Part 4

CENTERING PERSONAL VALUES, CULTIVATING WORK–LIFE FULFILLMENT

The authors in part 4 help readers think about career decisions through explorations of integrity, alignment, and authenticity, sharing how their inner voices as graduate students revealed cognitive dissonance between what dominant others say they should be and how they honestly felt. The graduate student chapters of their stories mirror Martha Beck's (2021) "dark woods" moments of feeling "lost, exhausted, troubled, and unsure." Many of their experiences are illustrations of the stressors of graduate student life being addressed by national initiatives such as the Graduate Student Mental Health and Well-Being project (CGS 2021). As our authors navigated competing personal and professional commitments as well as moments of misalignment, they let us in on their process of role refinement.

In addition, their choices reflect life design principles (Burnett and Evans 2016), including sociocultural experiences; priorities of work, family, leisure, and rest; and alignment of their values, commitments, and intentions about a life that serves. These experiences of discernment led each contributor to their current employment, respectively, in a career center, a graduate student recruitment office, and a teaching center. They recount experiences and interactions with mentors who offered affirmation and who revealed new, unseen avenues. As our authors developed new skills and changed roles, they found integrity in roles aligned with their values. Rather than try to squeeze their skills and experiences into cookie-cutter molds of faculty roles, authors in this part pursued employment where they could apply and nurture the skills, interests, and values they already have. Their roles give them a sense of purpose and fulfillment and bring value to their communities, what Pamela Slim (2013) refers to as their "body of work."

At the same time, contributors convey the challenges, burdens, and tensions along their journeys, including the effects of the burden shift in DEI work toward minority groups. We hear how they are in the process of healing from fragmentation and integrating their personal and professional selves. Part of their self-recovery involves their current work with and in academic systems to help others do similar inner restorative work.

Alexis Boyer opens part 4 with "Finding Your Place, Finding Your Voice," in which she tells us about the unresolvable tensions she perceived between pursuing a faculty life and having a family. She says out loud what many of us keep to ourselves: "I came to resent that this work demanded so much of me and left so little time for anything else." During a meeting with a career advisor, she realized that advising was a path that was viable and appealing to her; further conversations with other career advisors and internships affirmed that conclusion. She also shares how, once she became self-affirming and acted with integrity, many of the stuck places she was experiencing in finishing her PhD were now flowing. The aspect of career advising that is most affirming to Boyer is "creating space for students to recognize their strengths and empowering them to take their values into account."

Kristine Sikora then shares similar wisdom in "Well-Being as a Guiding Light Toward a Fulfilling Career." Sikora recounts early struggles to fulfill parental expectations of success as well as academic experiences that left her feeling inferior, unsatisfied, and unhappy. During graduate school, she observed and nurtured her strengths in communication, student mentoring, and project management. She also engaged in hobbies where she practiced creative and technical skills in graphic illustration, photography, and website design. In finding and expressing her voice, Sikora currently puts these skills to use in advising and recruiting prospective graduate students. In her workshops, she shares the wisdom she lives in her own life: "I urge them to ask themselves why they want to pursue a certain career path and whether that path will allow them to live the life they want for themselves."

In the final chapter of part 4, "Embracing Uncertainty: Following My Values Toward a Career in Faculty Development," Ryan Rideau shares his commitments to both being a good parent and supporting marginalized students in higher education. He also relates moments of feeling shaken, discouraged, constrained, and unsure about how to have a meaningful impact on racial justice efforts on his campus. Knowing that the success of marginalized students is tied to the success of marginalized faculty, he joined a center for teaching and learning as a specialist in instructional and professional development through an equity and justice lens. The work allows him to "dream with others about new possibilities" while contributing to classroom climate through daily interactions with faculty across fields and disciplines.

REFERENCES

Beck, Martha. 2021. *The Way of Integrity: Finding the Path to Your True Self*. New York: The Open Field.

Burnett, Bill, and Dave Evans. 2016. *Designing Your Life: How to Build a Well-Lived, Joyful Life*. New York: Knopf.

CGS (Council of Graduate Schools). 2021. *Supporting Graduate Student Mental Health and Well-Being: Evidence-Informed Recommendations for the Graduate Community*. https://cgsnet.org/wp-content/uploads/2022/01/CGS_JED_GradStudentMentalHealthReport.pdf.

Slim, Pamela. 2013. *Body of Work: Finding the Thread That Ties Your Story Together*. New York: Portfolio/Penguin.

13

FINDING YOUR PLACE, FINDING YOUR VOICE

ALEXIS BOYER

After I finished my PhD in January 2018, I did a lot of things I'd always promised myself I would. I moved, got married, adopted a dog, and started thinking about having a baby. I'd put my personal life on hold for a long time as I finished my degree, and everything felt like it was moving at warp speed. While things in my personal life sped up, my academic life slowed down. I applied for faculty positions and a couple of postdocs, but I never heard back. The academic career I'd been preparing for and putting off so much for never panned out. Every humanist's nightmare played out for me in real time, and I struggled to figure out what to do with myself. This is not a unique or even interesting story; see, for example, McKenna's (2016) article in the *Atlantic*, "The Ever-Tightening Job Market for PhDs." I've heard it so many times as told to me by doctoral students who are in the process of living through one frame or another. Sure, the details are always a little different, but the core issue remains—many doctoral students put off or delay elements of their lives in order to train for and finish degrees that will qualify them for academic careers that might never work out for them.

While I don't regret getting my PhD or waiting to start my family, I wish I'd been encouraged to consider both pursuits simultaneously. I must acknowledge that there are many ways to have/start a family, not all of which involve marriage and childbearing. I'm narrating my experiences and my personal choices, and I do not intend to negate or malign those who choose to do things differently. Of course, no one ever told me explicitly not to start a family while still in graduate school, but so much in terms of expectation is left unspoken in academia. While I may have been able to take a leave of absence had I chosen to start a family in graduate school, I would not have been able to afford to pay for the childcare that would have allowed me to come back to work. These economic concerns influenced my decisions and are consistent with many graduate students' experiences (Woolston 2022a, 2022b). I also knew intrinsically that if I wanted to be taken seriously as a scholar, I'd need to buckle down and focus.

I focused long enough to finish my degree, but I was never able to give everything I had and was to my academic life and career. In the final year, I blamed my lack of confidence and difficulties writing on my flagging commitment as I came to resent that this work demanded so much of me and left so little time for anything else. In what follows, I'll share the story of how I found my way to a career that has allowed me to pursue the life I wanted while giving me the opportunity to use the skills I developed while pursuing my PhD. My experiences and the work I do now as a career advisor have laid bare the ways our higher education systems fail to acknowledge trainees holistically. If we are going to reimagine doctoral education as a space that allows for diversity, equity, and inclusion, we need to find a way for trainees to remain whole as they pursue their degrees, and we need to recognize and embrace a multitude of career possibilities postgraduation.

LOSING MY VOICE

Unfortunately for me, I never felt like a particularly good academic. I never felt as though I was devoting enough of myself to my studies and my work. I struggled with the isolation of writing and research, which translated directly into difficulty connecting with other scholars in my field. I didn't have much of a connection with the small group of people who were interested in the same things I was, and that made it difficult for me to imagine that anyone would want to hear or read anything I had to say or write. More than anything else, I struggled to find my professional, scholarly voice—the one that would enable me to write convincingly and with authority about the subjects I knew best. I picked up languages, read endlessly, taught, tutored, supervised, and more. But speaking and writing with confidence and conviction eluded me.

Cultivating this scholarly voice is one of the countless difficult and unnamed tasks many graduate students face as they move through their programs, and various factors including gender, race, and socioeconomic status influence each student's speed and success. It's the voice one uses when writing for publication, speaking at a conference, or giving a lecture, and it conveys both authority from years of study and genuine curiosity that comes from knowing there is always more to learn. There's no real timeline for this process, but my best guess is that it should happen sometime between coursework and qualifying exams. Looking back on the final years of my PhD, I can see a little more clearly why I was having such a hard time writing and speaking with any semblance of confidence and authority even after so many years of study. I imagined that I was struggling with the material—that my chosen field of study was too difficult for me—but really I was facing a more inward struggle. I couldn't embody the academic persona and take on the voice of a skilled master because that wasn't what I wanted. My identity had become so wrapped up in the academic I was working to become that I didn't realize I'd lost my sense of purpose. Cultivating my voice meant doing some work reflecting on who I was, what I was good at, and what I wanted.

I knew who I was when I entered my PhD program. I was a ready and willing educator excited to teach and break open the world of biblical history to interested students. I loved digging deeply into historical contexts, into the meanings of words, and exposing the many layers of cultural bias that we unconsciously impose on ancient texts. My doctoral thesis addressed images of pregnancy and childbirth in apocalyptic literature, and I was well aware of the fact that my interest in the subject matter came from my own maternal aspirations. I craved the kind of balance and stability that would support my maternal ambitions, yet those were not the values I saw playing out in the lives of my mentors. I wanted to get married and have a family, and I had waited until I finished my degree, thinking that what came next might offer time to pursue those things. What came next, however, was the ultracompetitive tenure-track job search, and I quickly realized my personal goals were at odds with the go anywhere, publish or perish mentality I would need to pursue it successfully. I worked hard for years for my PhD so I could become a professor, but I had wanted to be a wife and mother for as long as I could remember.

The hardest part of my decision to stop applying for academic jobs and abandon the faculty job search was getting to know myself apart from the scholarly identity I'd been trying desperately to embody. The more time I took to understand myself and ask myself what I wanted and what motivated me, the more confident I became in making choices and decisions that were different from the ones I'd planned. My identity was wrapped up in two personas, professor and wife/mother, that I had planned to embody simultaneously, and all of a sudden I felt as though I had to choose between them. I couldn't see myself continuing to struggle as hard as I was to maintain my professional identity while navigating wedding plans, pregnancy, and new motherhood. It had never occurred to me that I should take these personal goals into account when looking for a job. I believed that I was training for one job and there were no other options for which I was suited.

WHISPERING

I started working with a therapist, which I'd highly recommend to anyone and everyone. Most institutions have mental health resources readily available for students. I also reached out to a career advisor I'd met during my graduate work. I hated the idea of networking, but that's what my career advisor told me I needed to do. I'm a bookish introvert and spent so much time alone in my library carrel that I joked with friends that I had forgotten how to interact with other human beings. It was a badge of honor that demonstrated how hard I was working! Moreover, I didn't want to talk to people and tell them about my perceived failure as an academic, even if my new quest for fulfilling employment outside the professoriate felt right. As a trained researcher, I recognized that I needed information about different jobs, and networking connections would surely be a strong source of that information.

My career advisor probably didn't realize it at the time, but he was actually my first networking connection. He shared his story about pursuing a graduate degree in philosophy and deciding midway he didn't want to finish. He told me about how he got into career advising. He explained that he enjoyed working with students, teaching, and advising and told me about all the ways his experience in the classroom lent itself to his work in career advising. I enjoyed the same things. I enjoyed them so much that I took on as much student-facing work as I could while I was pursuing my degree. I was a teaching fellow, a writing fellow, a graduate resident assistant, and even the instructor of record for one class. These were the experiences I enjoyed most. They got me through my degree, but I never connected the value of communicating on different levels, presenting information, facilitating discussion, close reading, and writing to any context other than a college-level class in biblical studies. As I began to see advising as a viable career trajectory, I started speaking to all kinds of student advisors, learning how to communicate the value of my skills and experiences, and imagining myself in their fields. The more I spoke to others, the more I realized I wasn't alone. These connections rallied around to support me and connect me; they became my friends and colleagues.

One of my most influential connections came from my thesis advisor, who introduced me to her friend and former student. She was an academic who had no qualms about leaving her field and finding an interesting position in administration at a law school that she loved. I met her just once, but in the twenty minutes she spent with me, she became my hero and role model. She had a family and a job she loved in an academic setting, but she wasn't a professor. She gave me permission to stop apologizing and told me that my skills were valuable and essential. I was enthralled by the fact that she was still involved with our professional organization even without a faculty position. She was leading workshops about careers outside the professoriate from inside the academy! She told me that I could still write, work with students, and publish in my field or maybe in a different field. I could still use all of my teaching skills, and I could still work at a university. I just needed to find out where I fit best, and what fit me best. Her example showed me how to reframe and see value in the skills I'd learned and developed within academia, which in turn helped me come to terms with who I was becoming.

SPEAKING SOFTLY

After meeting a few different kinds of college-level student advisors, I started to apply to advising jobs, and I found that writing became easier. As I wrote cover letters trying to convince academic institutions that I had enough experience to guide their undergraduate and graduate students through their academic or post-academic experiences, I convinced myself that it was true. Remembering my first networking experience in my career office, I applied for an internship in career advising. I had never done career advising before, and I recognized that I needed training. This internship offered training and mentorship, and a safe, time-bound space to try something new. I wasn't a typical internship candidate having recently finished a PhD, but I told them my story in interviews and landed the job. In that role, I had the opportunity to talk with students every day. We weren't talking about biblical history anymore, but that didn't matter to me. My supervisors invested in me and taught me. I learned a lot, and they helped me realize that I had a lot to offer. I could relate to the student experience, and I knew what it was like to engage in academic research. My students respected me and my experiences and trusted my suggestions. I was still teaching, my students were learning new skills, and I felt my impact so acutely as students emailed to tell me they appreciated my help and guidance or that the résumé I reviewed helped them get an interview.

In a lot of ways, I felt like I was doing the job I was trained to do; it was just a little different. Instead of organizing a trip to the museum to view and discuss ancient artifacts, I organized a trip to an agri-tech start-up so trainees could see what a lab in industry looked like and meet some employees with interesting jobs. Instead of organizing guest speakers and lectures, I organized company presentations and workshops. The role was a natural fit for me, and I thrived in it. As I transitioned into this new role, I finished writing a book chapter in biblical studies, which was later published. The confidence I developed from learning and excelling in a new field helped me find the confidence I was lacking in academia. In my new role, I was praised and valued for contributions as an advisor and facilitator. In this role, I also had time for a few other things; I got married and adopted a dog.

ASSERTING MYSELF

That first internship was a steppingstone toward my next job as a full-time graduate student advisor. That role gave me the opportunity to help graduate students find their voices, or at least offer them a moment to reflect and consider what might be standing in their way. We talked about the fact that there is no such thing as a linear career trajectory, or even so much as a right way to do things. I worked to empower graduate students to make whatever choices felt right to them and offered strategies to help them reflect and evaluate different scenarios. My supervisor called me an advocate for graduate students, and I was proud of that title. At the same time, I continued to pursue my personal goals. My full-time job offered generous maternity leave according to standards in the US, and the most wonderful team of colleagues and friends celebrated with me, remotely, as my husband and I welcomed our daughter into the world in the midst of the COVID-19 pandemic.

In the summer of 2021, I took on a career advising position at a different school. It wasn't a wholly new position for me—I'd worked as an intern in the same office for several months after I finished my PhD—but everything felt new. After becoming a mom during the COVID-19 pandemic, I felt the potential challenges of transitioning back to in-person work looming over me like storm clouds. When we went back to the office, I cried every day as I pulled out of my driveway, leaving my heart at home with my husband and our little girl. It was hard (and it still is sometimes), but it wasn't as hard as I knew it could have been if I'd had a different job in a different place. I wanted this job and this career, and I enjoyed the work.

I still enjoy the work I do as a career advisor for graduate students. I love meeting with my students one-on-one and hearing their stories. It is fun to sit with them and dream up courses of action that would move them toward their goals. I like creating resources and workshops to help students learn the skills they will need to pursue various careers in technology, government, nonprofit, and even academia. My experience in my own academic program, while vastly different from that of my students, offers a unique understanding of the academic system and its power dynamics. I know the yearly cycles of coursework, academic job postings, and industry recruiting, and I get to apply that knowledge in a variety of different situations. No day, week, or month is ever the same, and I'm encouraged to try new things, make mistakes, and learn from them. The best part of this job, however, is creating space for students to recognize their strengths and empowering them to take their values into account as they look for opportunities to make an impact.

CONCLUSION

The 2021 fall semester ramped up tentatively with a mixture of in-person and virtual meetings and events. My colleagues had become very creative and adept at leading engaging and participatory virtual sessions with various online tools. In one such session, the facilitator asked students to post one potential job title they would like to pursue after they finish their degree. Among the answers one might expect like principal investigator, senior scientist, and Googler, one of my students posted "dad." It made me smile as it simultaneously broke my heart. It reminded me of the decisions I'd made for myself that brought me to that moment and the challenges that my students still face.

I had convinced myself that any delay in the development of my personal life caused by graduate school would be worth it in the long run, and I was not the first nor will I be the last to make that choice. Some of my students choose to wait to pursue personal goals while they are navigating their PhD programs. Other students with young families tell me about how they struggle to manage the lives and needs of their people while performing time-sensitive lab work and participating in all facets of academic life. They miss spending time with their families as they attend the elective lectures, conferences, and departmental service opportunities that are unstated requirements for those who wish to pursue tenure-track careers. Feeling behind in life or spreading yourself thin between academic life and family life are both deeply stressful. Graduate students with young families find themselves forced to make choices about which types of stress they wish to take on for themselves in addition to the inherent stress of academic inquiry.

Institutions continue to mint new PhDs, while ignoring the fact that most of their students do not find employment as faculty at academic institutions. This leaves entire cohorts of PhDs ready to move forward without any clear direction in which to go. There is pain and bitterness that comes from working long and hard for something that never works out. Some even experience feelings of helplessness as they graduate with no idea how to put their degrees to use in contexts outside the professoriate. It doesn't have to be this way. You can find ways to explore opportunities outside the professoriate while you're in your doctoral program through networking connections, project work, or even formal internships. You can find a problem that you're passionate about, that aligns with your values, and pursue ways to contribute to a solution. I've found that within my role as a graduate career advisor. I can use my newfound voice to talk about my experience with anyone who wants to listen. I can meet graduate students who find themselves at this complicated juncture and walk alongside them as they do the necessary work to distill meaning from their experiences, find their voices, and forge their own ways forward.

REFERENCES

McKenna, Laura. 2016. "The Ever-Tightening Job Market for PhDs: Why Do So Many People Continue to Pursue Doctorates?" *Atlantic*. https://www.theatlantic.com/education/archive/2016/04/bad-job-market-phds/479205/.

Woolston, Chris. 2022a. "'Not Even Enough Money for Food': Graduate Students Face Cash Crunch." *Nature: International Weekly Journal of Science* 611:189–91. https://doi.org/10.1038/d41586-022-03478-x.

Woolston, Chris. 2022b. "Stress and Uncertainty Drag Down Graduate Students' Satisfaction." *Nature: International Weekly Journal of Science* 610:805–8. https://doi.org/10.1038/d41586-022-03394-0.

14

WELL-BEING AS A GUIDING LIGHT TOWARD A FULFILLING CAREER

KRISTINE M. SIKORA

As a first-generation Chickasaw/Japanese woman from a remote region of Hawai`i, I lacked the privileged support system one was assumed to have when making decisions about their education and career. Succumbing to the weight of familial obligation, I followed a path toward a medical career that was ultimately unfulfilling. However, eventually I found the courage to pursue new opportunities and discovered a love for research. I am now an associate dean at a large research institution and am thriving in an administrative role, applying transferrable skills I developed during my PhD training. My journey to a nonprofessorial career in higher education via a biomedical PhD was nonlinear and messy, but it taught me to approach difficult career decisions through an unbiased lens with well-being as a guiding principle. Identifying what brought me happiness and fulfillment ultimately had positive downstream effects on my professional journey toward a fulfilling career. To individuals exploring nonprofessorial career paths by way of a PhD, I offer the story of how I found my joy through self-reflection, how I recognized and developed my personal and professional strengths, how I found the voice to advocate for myself and overcome impostor fears, how I found my stride as I molded my ideal job, and how I established and continue to maintain a healthy balance between my personal and professional lives.

"What do you want to be when you grow up?" I toss the rhetorical question to the audience and pause to survey the nonverbal responses from the attendees. On this day, my participants are a mixture of current undergraduates and recent graduates from institutions throughout the country who are participating in one of our many summer programs at the university. As part of a professional development series, my seminar summarizes the basics of considering and applying to graduate or professional programs. As usual, my question elicits a mixture of chuckles, knowing smirks, dismissive head shakes, and panic-stricken wide eyes. After a moment, I continue by revealing my own hopes and dreams: "I want to be someone who finds happiness in each day, who is present for their family, and who is respected by those in their personal and professional circles." The looks of amusement turn into ones of concern while panicked faces relax and turn contemplative. "I want to be someone with a stable job that earns enough money to give their family what they need but also allows for a healthy work–life balance," I continue. "I want to be someone with the power, confidence, and tools to make a difference in the lives of those who need it most." The room is silent, and I am the only one left smiling as my audience considers what they want for themselves beyond their job and whether their current career plans are in direct alignment with their personal values and well-being.

I give this seminar multiple times a year, usually at the request of student groups, faculty, or colleagues at colleges and universities with undergraduates who are considering graduate or professional school. While I change the title and specific content to fit the audience and their interests, the essence of the presentation focuses on why and how one would pursue a degree beyond a bachelor's. As an associate dean and director of graduate recruitment at a large, very high research, STEM-dominant public doctoral university, a significant part of my job involves speaking with prospective students about our advanced degree programs. However, as someone who has faced adversity and stumbled up the winding path to a nonprofessorial career in academia, I always preface my presentations with a question that prompts the audience to keep their values and identities at the forefront of their minds when making decisions that affect their lives and careers. I urge them to ask themselves *why* they want to pursue a certain career path and whether that path will allow them to live the life they want for themselves. I encourage them to start by identifying values that are important to them as individuals and then highlight how this simple exercise can have positive downstream effects on their professional journey toward a fulfilling career.

By first recognizing and naming what brings them joy, they can be free to consider various educational and career paths through a lens unbiased by false assumptions or obligations such as "a PhD is better than a master's" or "I need to be a lawyer to make my family happy." After identifying potential paths, they are then able to evaluate their strengths and pinpoint which skills they need to develop to be a competitive candidate for those next steps. Once they are prepared to step into a professional role, I warn them that the most difficult part of the journey is finding the right words to advocate for themselves and fight for the jobs that most closely align with their dream careers. Job descriptions can be intimidating, and the best candidates for a position are often those who may not meet the preferred qualifications but who can demonstrate that they are a versatile and valuable asset. Each job and promotion they secure not only enables them to apply and expand their skill set, but also opens doors to a new world of opportunities. By keeping their own well-being as a top priority, they can discover a healthy balance between their professional and personal lives.

FINDING MY JOY

I had a difficult time understanding my own career options when I was a college junior, faced with the choice of whether to stray from the path that was laid out for me by my family or pave my own. I grew up under a weight of expectations to fulfill the family duty of taking care of my parents and younger siblings, have a family of my own, and become successful, specifically a wealthy and renowned medical doctor. My early life was lived according to my parents' values, which I unquestioningly adopted as my own: family comes first, hard work will be rewarded, and failure is unacceptable. I was a naturally creative child and aspired to be an illustrator or creative writer but was constantly reminded by my family that "art is a hobby, not a career." Living in a remote town on a remote island in the Pacific Ocean with parents who had not graduated from college, I lacked the privileged support system one was assumed to have when navigating higher education and choosing a career path. With my parents as my only career advisors, I deferred to them to help me determine my next steps. As a result, I stayed close to home for college and attended the University of Hawai`i at Mānoa, where I majored in biology with the intent to eventually apply to medical school. I worked hard and tried to fit in among the other premeds but always felt awkward and out of place. At the time, I was unaware of my lack of privilege and blamed myself for not achieving as much as my peers had by that stage in my undergraduate career. Compared to their lives, which seemed so linear and well-planned, my life felt messy and unorganized. I was embarrassed by the gaping social and economic chasm that existed between myself and those who were supposed to be my equals and searched for any and all opportunities to fill that gap and overcome my feelings of inferiority.

As I entered my third year of college, I applied for and was accepted into an undergraduate research program for students from underrepresented backgrounds who wanted to pursue a research career. I entered the program for all the wrong reasons, but mainly so I could take advantage of the included tuition benefit and stipend and gain research experience to improve my chance of getting into medical school. What I did not expect was that I would fall in love with research and find a home among scientists. I had been so paralyzed by my fear of disappointing my family that I never allowed myself to explore a career outside of medicine. As I spent more time in the lab and with peers in my program, I began to open doors to opportunities I had never considered, which was both daunting and exhilarating. The other program scholars whose economic, social, and ethnic backgrounds mirrored my own understood my anxiety about fulfilling familial obligation and encouraged me to be brave and lean on them for support. I developed new skills and found that I had good hands for bench work, I tackled unique challenges that required creativity and the ability to see the big picture, and I discovered my love of seeing new cities as I traveled and presented at conferences. Most importantly, I met inspiring academics whose career paths were full of adventure and fulfillment *because* they were nonlinear and messy. Hearing their stories made me envious of their grit and motivated me to approach new challenges with courage. To my surprise, I found joy in every moment and opportunity I took for myself. I finally asked myself *why* I had been rushing down a path that did not bring me satisfaction when happiness was so easy to find if I only slowed down and opened myself up to discovering it.

This revelation brought out the best in me, both academically and personally, which became apparent to my family as I began to openly discuss my new career options and my next steps. They were disappointed about my change in career path and anxious about whether one could be successful in a research profession. However, they were curious to learn more and even began to ask questions about my experiences in the lab. They were shocked to learn about the importance of scientists in the advancement of health and medicine, and after learning that graduate school was fully funded, they began to enthusiastically push for me to become a wealthy and renowned scientist instead of a medical doctor in debt. We were finally on the same page, and it renewed my resolve as I devoted myself completely to becoming a competitive applicant for graduate school. Gaining the support of my parents was a small but very important personal victory that made me realize that the well-being of myself and my family were not mutually exclusive. I decided from that moment on that I would always push myself to be brave and follow my joy when making difficult life choices.

FINDING MY STRENGTHS

I followed this new guiding principle to graduate school and saw myself becoming a professor at a large academic medical institution, running my own lab as a principal investigator, and teaching and mentoring students. It was during my third year in my PhD program at the University of Michigan when I was again faced with the question of whether this career path would bring me joy. The thought of running my own lab and mentoring students was appealing, but after learning more about the challenges that faculty faced, I knew that the constant pressure to publish papers and secure grants would cause me overwhelming anxiety and eventually overshadow my love for research. Already as a graduate student my fear of failure often led to me sacrificing self-care just to push my research forward and meet the expectations of my mentor. I still loved science, but I wanted a career with financial security and the freedom to create my own schedule so that I could maintain a healthy work–life balance, especially if (or when) I decided to start a family.

At the time, my institution offered limited support to graduate students who wanted to explore nonprofessorial careers, so I sought hands-on experiences that would hone skills that could be marketable in other academic career paths: leadership, teaching, and mentoring. I served as a graduate teaching assistant for an upper-level undergraduate lab course, volunteered as an instructor and eventually became the director of a summer science academy, and mentored undergraduates and master's students in my PhD advisor's lab. I became adept at communication and found that I was proficient at public speaking and presenting complex topics in a way that was accessible to various levels of learners. Especially rewarding was teaching and mentoring high school and college students, specifically those who came from underrepresented backgrounds and lacked resources and guidance, as I had at that stage. I was able to identify with the issues they faced and provide suggestions for how to find resources and navigate the next steps in their educational careers.

I made a significant impact on students' lives by simply listening, empathizing, and giving them what they needed to either keep moving forward or pivot toward a different path. I enjoyed sharing my story and envisioned myself happy in a career that involved the advocacy for, and development of, programs that would benefit undergraduates seeking professional hands-on opportunities such as undergraduate research and career shadowing. Not only did the work feel natural and give me a sense of purpose, but I was good at it, which boosted my confidence to a level I had not yet experienced during my PhD training. In pursuing opportunities that brought me joy, I discovered I had strengths in communication, student mentoring, and project management and began to intentionally dedicate effort toward building and strengthening those skills by continuing and expanding my communication and outreach efforts. As I wrapped up my degree, I charged myself with a mission to leverage my strengths and new credentials to pursue pathways that would lead toward a career in higher education. My goal was to find an academic or administrative position where I had the power and influence to effectively create opportunities and advocate for high school or college students.

FINDING MY VOICE

Over the next four years, I continued to conduct research and teach, expanding my professional skill set and network. I also experienced personal growth as I got married, started a family, and dedicated time to exploring the creative outlets I had always enjoyed, such as drawing and creative writing. What started out as hobbies eventually developed into a comprehensive set of technical skills that included graphic illustration, photography and videography, and website design. I even tried my hand at creating a Web comic and published twice-a-week strips for a year. In the summer of 2016, not long after moving to Colorado, I was exploring job opportunities at nearby universities and found myself sitting in a small conference room with the dean of the Graduate School at the University of Colorado Denver. Serendipitously, he had been a faculty member at the University of Michigan when I was a graduate student, and while we had not interacted much directly, he recognized me. He had heard through the campus grapevine that I was looking for teaching or administrative positions in the Denver area and invited me to chat about a position he had been trying to develop for the past year: a recruitment director whose charge was to increase the number of applications for the university's graduate programs. A full-time student recruitment position was unique in the higher education community as these responsibilities were often taken on by an admissions officer or as part-time work by a senior faculty member. In searching for student-facing positions, I had never come across a job posting such as this, let alone considered a job that did not specifically include student advising or teaching in the description. My initial reaction was to retreat. I worried that jumping into this type of recruitment work would lead me down the path to becoming a human resources professional and close the door on opportunities to develop programs, teach, or mentor. Self-doubt overwhelmed me and I was certain that I was not only unqualified but that I would never be happy doing this type of work.

However, my concerns and impostor fears gradually faded as he explained that this individual would hold a leadership position in the Graduate School and would be expected to travel, attend conferences, build a national recruitment network, advise prospective students, and build marketing resources for graduate programs. When he added that this individual would also be charged with increasing student diversity within the programs, I was hooked and refused to let fear stand in the way of a job that was so clearly perfect for me. The thought of traveling again made me remember how much I had enjoyed visiting new cities during my undergraduate career and how few opportunities I had had to travel and attend conferences beyond graduate school. I immediately began to internally brainstorm where I would go, and from which states I should prioritize recruiting students. I was elated by the idea of leveraging and expanding my professional network and remembered a number of colleagues from Hawai`i and Michigan who would be excellent allies in helping me connect with students from underrepresented backgrounds. Finally, as I thought more about advising prospective students, it occurred to me that I would need to make intimate connections with undergraduate research programs. When it dawned on me that this would open opportunities for me to become involved in program development and student support, I began to understand how this position could be a launching point into the career in higher education for which I had been searching and preparing.

Upon relaying my interest in formally applying for the position, I was again struck with an overwhelming sense of anxiety as I realized that this was a completely new experience for me. The Graduate School team was looking for a director-level candidate with professional experience in leadership, marketing, and recruitment. Not only was this job outside the academic paths I had been exploring, but I did not meet the desired qualifications for the position. For the first time in my professional life, I had to openly advocate for myself and find the right words to describe the value of my skill set. I articulated my strengths and clearly outlined how my experiences, while not exactly matching the qualifications of an ideal candidate, were unique and would make up for any perceived deficiencies on my résumé. I specifically highlighted the transferable skills I had developed during and after my PhD training such as data analysis, communication, mentoring, networking, project management, organization, time management, public speaking, and graphic and Web design. As someone who had found opportunity and success in academia—a system and culture that discriminates against those with less privilege, such as myself—I had clear and concrete ideas for how to develop and integrate strategies for enhancing equity and diversity into key recruitment initiatives. I laid out plans for building out the recruitment strategy from the ground up and leveraging existing resources, such as my own growing professional network and skill set, allowing me to operate within a small budget. My excitement and ambition were palpable throughout the interview process as I overcame my impostor fears and found my voice. It did not take long for the dean to reach out with an offer.

FINDING MY STRIDE

Since taking on this new role, my job has evolved and expanded beyond simply increasing the number of graduate applications. Many of these changes are the direct result of my efforts to shape the job so that it utilizes my strengths, aligns with my personal interests, and fulfills my need to help others. Because this was a new position, I was able to establish a foundation based on what I had identified as key needs and goals for our programs and campuses. From there, I envisioned how various projects would fit together to create a comprehensive marketing plan that also allowed for customization based on each program's needs. The individual skills I had been developing over the years were instrumental as I created and tailored the specific tools that I would need to carry out this plan. I was able to quickly build out a diverse set of marketing assets and services because I had become adept at marshaling resources and did not have to outsource tasks such as database management, data collection and analysis, website creation, and graphic design.

I credit my initial success to being able to find my voice and effectively communicate with my colleagues and stakeholders. This was especially important since I was a team of one managing multiple projects simultaneously. Being able to clearly articulate my plan and goals has served as the most valuable tool in my professional toolbox. Ironically, this is the most difficult skill for me to implement. I find that good communication can be complicated and emotionally draining as it is not restricted to the words you say, but also includes nonverbal cues, mannerisms, and tone. In my experience, however, a good communicator is able to confidently present well-formed ideas and thoughts, and also display a higher level of empathy and emotional intelligence. I found that I was able to earn respect from colleagues and program heads by first establishing a sense of trust and showing them that I was genuinely invested in putting their needs before my own agenda. During my first year, I spent most of my time listening and assessing our existing resources, which allowed me to find institutional allies, determine what made our campuses and our programs unique, and understand how to best connect with our target audiences.

Unlike other higher education administrators who work in communication, enrollment, or marketing, I lacked formal training in business administration, public relations, or advertising and did not measure my success by how much money I brought to the university. Rather, I was invested in the success of our prospective students and knew that approaching my work with authenticity and honesty was the most effective way to build a strong network. As a result, instead of garnering a national reputation as a recruiter, I established myself as a trusted resource for faculty, student advisors, program administrators, and those looking for advice about whether to pursue an advanced degree. My personal background and experiences facilitated effortless connections with individuals who shared one or more of my identities, allowing me to enrich my network with contacts from minority-serving institutions. I leveraged these connections to advocate for policy and process changes that reduced or eliminated barriers for those who want to apply to our graduate and professional programs. Notable changes include the implementation of equitable admissions processes, the elimination of the GRE requirement, increased application fee waiver accessibility, and greater transparency around the application process.

I had found my stride with this new position as I fully utilized my strengths and skill set to create a job that brought me immense joy and fulfillment. It was a wonderful feeling to look forward to each day and tackle new challenges or conceptualize new projects. My dedication and strict work ethic did not go unnoticed and I was promoted to assistant dean, and eventually associate dean, when it became apparent that my title needed to reflect my growing responsibilities and impact. With each promotion, my new title also enabled me to further expand my network throughout academia, earning me a spot at the table with senior faculty, deans, provosts, and chancellors. Because my work also involved networking and making connections with industry and higher education partners, I made a conscious decision to also retain my director title, which is more relevant than assistant or associate dean outside of academia. With each move forward, I became empowered to tackle larger challenges and pursue opportunities that would enable me to make a significant impact on campus culture and student success.

FINDING MY BALANCE

Today, I am recognized as a leader and key representative in the higher education recruitment, marketing, admissions, communication, and DEI spaces at my institution. As a unit of one, I am a member of the Graduate School leadership team and report directly to the Graduate School dean, who gives me the flexibility to independently craft my project portfolio and weekly schedule. Our office is relatively small, and I collaborate closely with my counterparts in the Graduate School who oversee their own units of student progress and career development. Together, we primarily serve the campus in an administrative capacity, providing support services for our graduate programs and students, implementing and maintaining graduate-level policies, working closely with university leadership to advocate for graduate students and research trainees, and conferring doctoral and master's degrees. My primary role is to maintain the recruitment machine I have built by adapting, expanding, or eliminating various elements to keep up with changing consumer demands and program goals. I also serve as the Graduate School representative on campus-wide committees related to recruitment, information technology, admissions, communications, and DEI. Recruitment occurs year-round, but individual projects are cyclical and revolve around university schedules and program application deadlines. After years of building out my operation and gaining a better sense of the annual academic rhythm, I have reached a point where I can breathe a little easier and establish a healthy balance between my work and personal life.

Fall is the busiest time of year. I spend most of the days between August and December in meetings with colleagues, traveling to conferences and events, speaking with prospective students, updating marketing materials and websites, and running advertising and email campaigns. When travel is not possible, I create virtual opportunities where our programs can interface with prospective students and college advisors. While the workload is sometimes daunting, I have the flexibility to create my own hours and take time off when I need a break. The well-being of myself and family is still a priority, and I often take family obligations, such as school concerts, birthdays, doctor's appointments, and vacations, into account when I plan how and when to launch new initiatives at work.

As the year ends, the semester winds down and I am able to devote my full attention to celebrating the holiday season with my family and making the most of my winter break. The new year is always full of excitement for the start of the spring semester as students return to campus. This is the time of year when I focus my attention on planning larger projects I will finalize in the summer and implement in time for fall recruitment. There are fewer events in the spring but an increase in requests from student groups from other universities and colleges to visit our campuses for tours and information sessions, which I organize in collaboration with our programs. I also dedicate a large portion of my time to service by coordinating administrative support for our student organizations, promoting our pipeline and summer research programs, judging student posters at undergraduate research symposiums, and serving as a reviewer on undergraduate research program grant review committees.

Spring is also the time when the dean conducts my annual performance review and I am asked to reflect on my accomplishments, whether I met the goals I set for myself, what challenges I encountered, and which targets I want to set for the next year. I summarize my list of projects and provide data on how my efforts have impacted the number of prospective students in our database, applications, and enrollment rates, especially of students from underrepresented backgrounds. We discuss issues I faced and strategies for how to overcome future obstacles as well as which initiatives I felt were not worth the time or financial investment. Because my position lacks a preset path for upward mobility, I also use this opportunity to discuss career advancement and how to strategically prepare myself for promotion within my institution to positions such as assistant vice chancellor or executive director.

Summer is my favorite time of the year. During these few months, I reflect on where I came from, how I got to where I am, and why I use joy and well-being as my guiding principles. My schedule is full of speaking engagements, often to scholars in summer, undergraduate, and postbaccalaureate research programs. However, unlike during the school year, the tone of my seminars is more personal and less geared toward the marketing of our programs. Colleagues and friends who have gotten to know me and my story invite me to speak with their students who also come from backgrounds underrepresented in STEM fields. I see myself in their determined faces, and together we commiserate on our struggles and celebrate all that we have achieved despite systemic barriers. Rather than touting myself as a role model or source of inspiration for these budding scientists, I instead offer myself as an empathetic ally and advisor. I use my story as a frame of reference so I can impress upon them the importance of making decisions for the right reasons and encourage them to never undervalue that which brings them happiness. "What do you want to be when you grow up?" I ask them.

MAINTAINING MY MOMENTUM

I chose a difficult career path and often struggle with maintaining my momentum, especially now with public institutions of higher education collectively experiencing the stress of declining enrollment, increasing student attrition, inadequate state funding, and student, faculty, and staff burnout. The demand to increase and expand recruitment and enrollment efforts is becoming overwhelming and the lack of financial and staff support is demoralizing. While I am able to reflect on my past experiences with relative clarity and pride, my career path has not been linear nor well-paved, and I am already encountering new challenges as I move through higher education, searching for a step upward. I remain mindful of the possibility that at some point, higher education may no longer bring me joy and I will be faced with the difficult decision of pivoting to a new path or reshaping my current role. I find comfort in recalling that my past experiences in making these types of decisions have been overall positive, especially when I keep my own well-being as a priority. There is also something empowering about utilizing skills I developed during my PhD training in my current role, despite not being formally trained for this career path. While my next step might not be clear, the skills I have gained thus far can be transferred and leveraged in any job, and every new opportunity I embrace will allow me to continue to grow and mature as a professional.

To those who are exploring nonprofessorial career paths via a PhD or beyond a doctoral degree, I offer empathy and encouragement. You are not alone in your search for a meaningful and rewarding career and will likely find failure before success. There will be times when your resolve will waver, and you will question whether your hard work will pay off as you fight through barriers that seem insurmountable. I implore you to take the time to identify and name the things that are important to you and bring you joy. Follow those values and view opportunities through an unbiased lens, allowing yourself to make decisions that will bring you closer to your goals. With every step you take, embrace every chance to test your skills and discover your strengths and areas for growth. Intentionally develop the strengths that will give you a competitive edge as you pursue your next step. Often the hardest skill to master, especially if you are experiencing impostor fears as I did, is the ability to advocate for yourself. Finding your voice and articulating how your strengths, skill set, and experiences can be an asset for the institution or company will be instrumental in securing the position you want. Your time to shine will come as you settle into your new job and find your stride. Showcase the numerous ways in which your doctoral training can be leveraged as you shape the job to align with your interests and specific abilities. Resist the urge to compare yourself to your coworkers and those who have been specifically trained for their profession, and instead find the courage to be innovative and approach tasks and challenges with a perspective only you can offer. Finally, I encourage you to remain willing to adjust your personal and professional lives to maintain a healthy balance between the two. This may require a significant amount of effort as you constantly shuffle ever-evolving and often conflicting priorities. However, retaining the integrity of your well-being will ensure that it is strong enough to support and guide you through your next big career step.

15

EMBRACING UNCERTAINTY

Following My Values Toward a Career in Faculty Development

RYAN RIDEAU

My commitments to racial justice and family have served as foundational values in navigating my career journey. In this reflective essay, I discuss key decisions that led me to a career in faculty development, a career I have now worked in for over five years. I share how this work has been consistent with my values and interests. However, I also discuss the ways I have experienced racial battle fatigue and how I continue to negotiate these feelings. It is my hope that this essay will provide insights for current graduate students and early-career BIPOC professionals who seek to do racial justice work in higher education.

I remember sitting in front of my computer anxiously waiting for the clock to strike 10:00 a.m. I was about to lead a new workshop for faculty members at my institution on anti-racist teaching practices. I had done countless workshops on similar topics to much success. But the stakes seemed higher this time around. This was the summer of 2020, at the height of global racial justice protests following the murders of unarmed Black individuals George Floyd, Ahmaud Arbery, and Breonna Taylor. These protests led many faculty members to form new commitments to racial justice work, and as such, I anticipated that this would be one of the largest workshops I had ever led. I was anxious because I wanted to encourage faculty members to continue anti-racism work; I recognized this as an important opportunity to build upon their current interest and motivation. But I was also anxious because I was struggling to make sense of this racial moment as a Black male and how I would lead this workshop in front of a majority white audience. As I opened the Zoom room to nearly a hundred people, those feelings of anxiety dissipated. I was at ease, facilitating and managing conversations about decentering whiteness, abolitionist teaching, and fighting for racial justice (Love 2019). My knowledge of these topics and confidence allowed me to share important information, but also to push back on problematic assumptions and comments. Ultimately, participants were better prepared to integrate anti-racist teaching practices into their instruction. It was one of those days where I believed that I was doing meaningful and fulfilling work.

I had not always possessed such clarity about my career. Much of the previous decade was full of uncertainty about my professional journey. To get to this point felt like a big achievement. In 2009, I decided to leave my PhD program in African American studies as well as my pursuit of a faculty career. Until then, becoming a faculty member was a career I thought I should do. I was attracted to the idea of being a professor, contributing to scholarly knowledge, and having an impact on young people. When I did not pass my qualifying exam, my confidence was shaken. While I had supportive and encouraging faculty mentors, I found myself questioning the meaning and significance of my work, and whether I truly enjoyed it. This ultimately took a toll on my mental health. I decided to leave this program and embraced the uncertainty of my future career.

MY FOUNDATION AND VALUES

While I had no idea what my plan would be moving forward, I needed to stay true to my own personal values. I was taught in my close-knit family that my success was in part due to the groundwork of individuals before me. I had loving parents, grandparents, aunts, and uncles who have supported and sacrificed for me. I learned that family must play a central role in my life.

I also have a strong commitment to working toward racial justice. As a kid, I remember immersing myself in narratives of segregation, racism, and struggles for freedom and liberation. I heard stories from my grandparents about their experiences with violent racism and segregation in Louisiana; ultimately, they moved to California for expanded opportunities like so many Black people during the Great Migration. Growing up in Los Angeles in the 1990s, I vividly remember watching video footage of the beating of Rodney King by four white police officers, and their subsequent acquittal. Although I was young, I learned early that racism was pervasive and knew that I wanted to play a role in uprooting it. Whatever career I pursued, I needed it to allow me to prioritize my family needs and make meaningful change toward racial justice.

KEY DECISIONS TO NAVIGATE CAREER UNCERTAINTY

My path from deciding to drop out of my initial PhD program in African American studies to my current role as a faculty developer was defined by several key decisions that were guided by my values. The first decision was determining what to do following my departure from my PhD program. I knew I wanted to work on issues of racial justice but needed to think about where I wanted to do this work. I began reflecting on my time as an undergraduate. I was reminded of the times I experienced microaggressions and feelings of marginalization and inadequacy due in part to the low numbers of BIPOC students at my university. As a result, I became a student leader in organizations that fought to increase the racial diversity on my campus. I was passionate about this work, which taught me about the inner workings of higher education and coalition-building toward racial justice. In reflecting on this time, I also realized I would not have made it through my time as an undergraduate without the support of a mentor who was a staff member. This person was someone who listened and shared advice with me about academics, responding to racism, and broader activism work. He mentored me and so many other BIPOC students. I realized how higher education professionals like him who were not faculty members can play an important role in supporting students at institutions of higher education. This realization allowed me to envision a career in higher education outside of a faculty role in which I could support BIPOC students.

To pursue a career in higher education, I knew that I would need to go back to school. This led me to pursue a master's in higher education at the University of Virginia. I subsequently worked in student-facing positions, starting as an intern in the Office of African-American Affairs at the University of Virginia, where I organized an initiative to support Black male students, mentored Black student leaders, and developed cultural programming. After earning my master's degree, I worked as the director of undergraduate diversity initiatives for the College of Liberal Arts and Human Sciences at Virginia Tech. In this role, I created a new academic minor, Diversity and Community Engagement. I also mentored student leaders and provided research opportunities for students in the humanities, social sciences, and arts. In each of these roles, I worked closely with students from minoritized identities and developed programming that I believed could address the harm they experienced. I was able to see the impact of my work on many students. But ultimately, I began to realize how my work was constrained by structural barriers. For example, I was concerned about the institutional culture and systems that led the students I worked with to feel isolated and marginalized and to seek me out as a source of support. I felt my role was only serving as a Band-Aid to much larger problems. Given the limitations of my role as a mid-level professional within the hierarchical structure of higher education, I knew I could not address these larger structural problems.

I understood that without a PhD, I would not be able to work in a position in higher education that would allow me to create systemic and structural change. I needed to consider whether I was ready to pursue a PhD for the second time. I remembered the feelings of anxiety I had in my initial PhD program and the toll it took on my mental health. I was concerned about experiencing those feelings again. With my first child on the way, I was worried that the work and stress of pursuing a PhD would impact my ability to be a good parent. In consultation with my partner, we decided I should apply for the PhD program in higher education at Virginia Tech on a part-time basis. I started out as a part-time student while retaining my position as the director of undergraduate diversity initiatives. I enjoyed my coursework and found supportive faculty members who were invested in my success. Continuing my studies provided me with frameworks and theories to better understand what I was experiencing in my work in higher education. Ultimately, the toll of juggling a full-time job, part-time school, and raising a family proved to be too much. I decided to leave my job and enroll as a full-time student. Doing so would allow me to finish my degree earlier and be more active in raising my child. This appeared to be the right choice for us as a family.

As I progressed through my PhD program, I found myself unsure about what area I wanted to work in, in higher education. To that point, I had only considered student-facing roles. As I learned more about the ways institutions worked, I became open to new possibilities. In my coursework, I learned the extent to which colleges and universities, and predominantly white institutions

(PWIs), were inhospitable places for BIPOC faculty members. My partner was just beginning as a faculty member, and many of the issues she experienced—being challenged in the classroom by white students, having the value of her research questioned, and additional service burdens—have been trends in the literature about BIPOC faculty members for decades. I began to understand how institutions had ignored these long-standing problems. While I had a commitment to advocating for BIPOC students, I learned how the success of these students was tied to the success of BIPOC faculty members. I found myself interested in working in spaces to address these and other related problems. It was in this vein that I sought to learn more about the field of faculty development. I began as a graduate intern on the faculty affairs team in the Office of the Executive Vice President and Provost at Virginia Tech while I was a graduate student. In that role, I worked on our Future Faculty Development Program, helped to organize data around faculty equity, and was privy to conversations about policies that impacted faculty life. I enjoyed this work and saw it as a space to make meaningful changes that could impact the lives of faculty members.

These various roles were critical to my professional journey and solidified my interest in a faculty-facing role. In reflecting about this path, I realized the extent to which my values informed key decisions. No matter what decision I made, I knew that I had to play a role in advancing racial equity. But I also centered my family life in all these decisions and thinking about the best choice for us as a unit. These grounding principles guided me through uncertainty and are what ultimately led me to work in faculty development.

SOLIDIFYING MY ROLE IN FACULTY DEVELOPMENT

I was nearing the completion of my PhD when my second child was born. My partner secured a faculty position at another college in the Boston area. This was an exciting professional change and an opportunity to be closer to her family. But this move also increased my sense of urgency to secure work given our move to a significantly more expensive area of the country and the birth of our second child.

I began to look for a position in faculty development where I could bring an equity and racial justice lens to this work. Initially, I found very few job openings in these areas. I started to expand my search, but my heart was not with many of these positions. As my frustration mounted, one of my dissertation advisors suggested I look at positions at centers for teaching and learning. While I was familiar with CTLs and even collaborated with the staff from the office at Virginia Tech, I did not fully understand their roles. As I explored the field of faculty development and CTLs more broadly, I learned just how important these centers could be to advancing racial justice efforts at a university. No serious effort to advance racial justice at an institution of higher education can ignore its teaching mission. In fact, this must be a core part of these efforts. CTLs can play a role in advancing institutional racial justice efforts and support the creation of a supportive and empowering learning environment for the most marginalized students.

After my advisor made this suggestion, I then saw the job announcement for the position of associate director for teaching, learning, and inclusion at the Center for the Enhancement of Learning and Teaching (CELT) at Tufts University. This was a position that aligned with my interest and values. I applied and was excited to be offered this position and begin a career in faculty development. It was a position that I held until recently. My main responsibility was to support faculty members in their instructional and professional development through a lens of equity and justice. There were several aspects of this position and working as a faculty developer that I enjoyed. First, I appreciated the opportunity to have a position where I could create and design relevant workshops, institutes, and long-term programming to support the needs of faculty members. I interacted with faculty members who wanted to learn how they could support students and improve their teaching. I also supported the development of faculty members who were new to racial justice work. In these ways, I had an opportunity to play an important role in shaping the pedagogical culture at Tufts.

Second, while I am trained in the field of education, I appreciated the opportunity to interact with individuals from a range of fields and disciplines. Earning my PhD provided me with knowledge about the fundamentals of research and a better understanding of the work of a faculty member. While I enjoyed learning from faculty members from disparate disciplines, sometimes these interactions were intimidating and challenging, particularly when I entered a space where I had little to no knowledge of the content or context. For example, I was trained in qualitative research. I felt intimidated when faculty members discussed their research in a formal lab-based context. I was less familiar with this type of research and work environment, and as a result, I struggled to relate to some of their challenges. Despite these occasional feelings of intimidation, I found it enjoyable to interact with faculty members in diverse disciplines and fields. Whether this was listening to computer scientists talk about machine learning, or veterinarians speaking about the intersection of race and veterinarian practices, I enjoyed collaborating with colleagues about how the work of inclusion, equity, and justice informs their practice.

Third, I enjoyed being able to continue to produce research. I was able to engage in scholarship relevant to my background and position, such as a project I worked on with colleagues about the experiences of BIPOC doctoral students enrolled in higher education programs at PWIs. This research informed the types of programming I offered and provided me with greater knowledge to perform my work. I will admit that finding time for research was difficult with the day-to-day demands of faculty development. But nonetheless, I was fortunate to work in a space where research was encouraged and seen as relevant to enhancing my career.

Fourth, I was able to contribute to meaningful racial justice work across the campus. The CTL where I worked is located under the purview of the Office of the Provost and Senior Vice President, and as such, I worked across the university. In my role, I served on a working group about the evaluation of teaching for the Schools of Arts and Sciences, and Engineering. The goal of the group was to design a more holistic and equitable process to evaluate teaching effectiveness. In my role, I shared best practices about how to infuse equity into the evaluation process. I am optimistic that my work on this committee had and will continue to have a lasting impact on the faculty, particularly those most harmed by the current system of teaching evaluation. Another example of my broad impact was that I supported the Friedman School of Nutrition as a member of the Antiracism, Equity, and Inclusion Subcommittee. On this committee, I collaborated with others on a school-wide syllabus template and discussed ways to center equity in the curriculum. While I enjoyed individual work with faculty members, committee work allowed me to impact a broader constituency by addressing institutional inequities and policies.

Finally, I enjoyed the flexibility of this role. The work of a faculty developer is demanding and can require putting in extra hours. However, I worked in an office where I could prioritize raising my two children, with an understanding that I would get my work done. For example, my supervisors set up a system that allowed me to continue to work remotely most days of the week so that I did not have to commute and could spend more time with my children. And when my oldest son was out of school with an injury for several weeks, my supervisors were flexible with me about work obligations to ensure that I was able to attend his medical appointments. I appreciated their trust in me to get my work done. I would not have been able to work in this space without this flexibility or trust. In these ways, working in this role aligned with my values and personal priorities.

RACIAL BATTLE FATIGUE AND THE LIMITATIONS OF RACIAL JUSTICE WORK

There have been many benefits to my work in faculty development; however, as a Black male, I have experienced burnout in this work—more specifically, racial battle fatigue (Smith, Allen, and Danley 2007). Racial justice work is deeply personal. Although I am passionate about this work, I find it exhausting and painful when I am facilitating a session with faculty members and participants are uninterested in doing this work. It is all too common for individuals to make problematic comments or to verbalize microaggressions. In these moments, there is a personal element of anger inside of me that wants to address the situation with rage, but my role requires me to call out the comment in a supportive manner. This latter response often requires suppressing my initial instinct and emotions, something I have never felt comfortable doing.

One of the big challenges for me of engaging in this work came during the summer of 2020 when many faculty members had a renewed focus on racial justice. At my institution, there were few resources for faculty to turn to, to help them understand how to integrate racial justice into their work, so I was frequently called upon to support these individuals. Some days, I was able to do this work well, as I described at the beginning of this essay. On other days, navigating my own emotions was difficult. While I was grateful for faculty members wanting to do racial justice work, I was still processing what was happening and often did not feel in the right mental and emotional state to support others who were still understanding their identities. I wanted to provide people with the opportunity to engage in this material and encourage them to do more work around these topics, but it was difficult as I managed my own emotional responses.

To address this, I tried to find those areas of work that brought me joy. Those have been the spaces and programs where I could interact with other BIPOC faculty members, staff, and students. Two programs that served this purpose for me were the Mutual Mentoring Program for faculty members of color and our Pedagogical Partnership Program. In the Mutual Mentoring Program, I was surrounded by a group of faculty members where we shared a common language and similarities in experiences. We offered real support and advice to each other in a space built from an ethic of care. This was a great system of support for me, even though I facilitated the program. In the Pedagogical Partnership Program, I worked with majority BIPOC students in a program that matched individual students with a faculty member to provide feedback regarding their pedagogical choices. I enjoyed serving as an informal mentor for the students, as well as learning from them and hearing about their experiences on campus. In both spaces, the Mutual Mentoring Program and the Pedagogical Partnership Program, I felt a sense of comfort and joy. I was fortunate to have supervisors and colleagues that made space for me to pursue these important efforts. They were conscious of the emotional burden and labor placed upon me doing racial justice work in a predominantly white space. I was comfortable communicating my feelings with them about doing this work, and we collectively determined how to proceed in a way that was best for my sustained growth and well-being. I cannot understate how much of a privilege this was for me.

Another challenge of this work was to remain hopeful that systemic change was possible. Following Derrick Bell's concept of racial realism, I understand racism to be permanent (Bell 1992). And in studying the legacy of racism in the United States and institutions of higher education, I am not optimistic about substantial change occurring at either institutions of higher education or society writ large soon. As such, I am constantly grappling with the question of the significance of my efforts. But it is important that I remain hopeful and work to be a part of positive change. One of the ways I tried to make sense of this in my work was to be realistic about what I can accomplish. I know that my workshops influenced the individuals who are interested in improving their teaching from an equity standpoint. Because of institutional reward systems, however, many people who are the biggest roadblocks toward creating a more equitable and just institution have little incentive to do this work. I knew that I would never be able to reach these people and often didn't want to waste my energy on them. This was partially a way to protect myself, and also to keep momentum going forward rather than being bogged down with people resistant to change. These interactions helped me to be realistic about my work, and to acknowledge the small victories with those making important changes.

Even as I try to be realistic, I also try to dream about alternative systems. In *Becoming Abolitionist: Police, Protests, and the Pursuit of Freedom*, Derecka Purnell (2021) brings in the Black feminist radical tradition of dreaming and envisioning structures and systems that may not seem possible. Fighting for big societal change requires us to continue to think and dream with others about new possibilities. We may not have all the answers, and that is okay. But as I think about the challenges of racial justice work in higher education, reading Purnell's work is a reminder of the importance of continuing to dream about new racially just systems and structures, even if they seem impossible. Thinking and dreaming about new higher education structures excites and motivates me to continue to move forward, even if the work seems insurmountable.

CONCLUSION

Despite feeling uncertain at times, I have enjoyed working in faculty development and am committed to this work. Recently, I was promoted to the position of assistant provost for faculty development at Tufts University. In this role, I am building upon my previous work, including continuing the Mutual Mentoring Program and the evaluation of teaching project. The role also allows me to work on a larger structural level. This includes designing mentoring and leadership development programming for faculty members through a lens of racial justice and working with faculty members to design more equitable hiring and promotion guidelines. While I was sad to leave my work colleagues in my previous role, I believe this position will give me an opportunity to have a bigger impact on the university. Before taking the position, I spoke to my supervisor about the ways I valued my family. He expressed similar ideas and was supportive of this flexibility in my work. The opportunity to pursue bigger structural changes and to be able to continue to work in a space where I could prioritize my family helped me to accept the position. I am only a few months into this role, but I am excited about the possibilities and the opportunity to continue a career in faculty development.

As I reflect upon my journey, I am reminded of a recent experience. I was facilitating a meeting for our Mutual Mentoring Program. At this meeting, I had two previous participants who were recently promoted to the rank of associate professor speak to junior faculty members. I asked the two faculty members to offer any advice they wish someone would have shared with them as an assistant professor. I distinctly remember one of them saying, "Be careful of people who give you advice." He went on to talk about all the faculty members who shared advice with him about getting tenure and how much of what they shared conflicted. He realized that they shared what worked for them. This really stuck with me. As I share my story, it is important to remember that I did what I felt was best for me. I made decisions based on my own values, what was best for my family, and that allowed me to pursue racial justice work. My path was filled with, and continues to be full of, uncertainty. From this essay, I hope to inspire others to follow the path that works for them, a path and journey that is grounded in their own values and is fulfilling professionally and personally.

ACKNOWLEDGMENTS

I would like to thank my previous supervisors Annie Soisson and Dana Grossman Leeman for their unwavering support and genuine care for my success and well-being. Thank you to Adrian and Rafael for reminding me to live for the moment. And finally, to Petra for your partnership, love, and support throughout the ups and downs of this uncertain journey.

REFERENCES

Bell, Derrick. 1992. "Racial Realism." *Connecticut Law Review* 24 (2): 363.

Love, Bettina L. 2019. *We Want to Do More Than Survive: Abolitionist Teaching and the Pursuit of Educational Freedom*. Boston: Beacon Press.

Purnell, Derecka. 2021. *Becoming Abolitionists: Police, Protests, and the Pursuit of Freedom*. New York: Astra Publishing House.

Smith, William A., Walter R. Allen, and Lynette L. Danley. 2007. "'Assume the Position . . . You Fit the Description': Psychosocial Experiences and Racial Battle Fatigue Among African American Male College Students." *American Behavioral Scientist* 51 (4): 551–78. https://doi.org/10.1177/0002764207307742.

Part 5
NAVIGATING INSTITUTIONAL STRUCTURES AND CULTURES

Contributors to part 5 share their experiences doing advocacy work within the ecosystem of higher education. Writing about their roles in centers for teaching and learning, diversity, equity, and inclusion offices, postdoctoral scholar offices, and LGBTQ+ centers, the authors give us windows into improving conditions for marginalized others, creating spaces of belonging and traumatic recovery, and disrupting normative, oppressive practices. They show how institutions both enable equity work and function as a barrier to change, themes explored by Sara Ahmed in *Complaint!* (2021) and *On Being Included: Racism and Diversity in Institutional Life* (2012).

Each of our contributors in this part speaks to their own experiences of not belonging and the ways they self-advocate for space and boundaries. As they navigate institutional priorities and project decisions, they also maintain awareness of their physical, emotional, and spiritual well-being at the forefront. Values and alignment with purpose are common themes across the essays. The authors show us the importance of self- and community-defined measures of success because their horizons of observable, systemic change in advocacy work can be distant. In addition, our contributors describe their strong interpersonal foundations—family, peers, mentors, and interoffice and interinstitutional colleagues. These microstructures help them combat depression, anxiety, isolation, burnout, and vicarious trauma—mental health challenges particularly prevalent among people in helping professions (Kolomitro, Kenny, and Sheffield 2020; Lipsky and Burk 2009).

In the first chapter of part 5, "Horizontal Mentoring: The Positive Impact of a Diverse Graduate Student Professional Development Community," Marisella Rodriguez and Sarah Silverman describe early experiences of exclusion in their disciplinary PhD programs, especially related to racial identity, first-generation graduate student status, and neurodiversity. Facilitated discussions in the Teaching Assistant Consultant (TAC) Program, a cross-campus community of practice for graduate students through their teaching center, engaged them in conversations that were essential for "surviving the PhD," as they write. They have applied principles from the TAC to create a peer mentor community for educational developers to "surface shared values and diverse experiences related to teaching and learning."

In the ensuing chapter, "When One Door Closes, Another Door... Also Closes: The Rewards and Challenges of Work in Diversity, Equity, and Inclusion," Jacob McWilliams describes how his academic journey as a trans man drew him to work that would "make room for transgender and nonbinary folks like me" in higher education. He provides a detailed description of typical responsibilities and tasks of DEI professionals to help readers with PhDs decide whether they are prepared for the work. We can sense his feelings of fulfillment and joy through examples of when his office could help students meet material needs and flourish. In contrast, McWilliams also paints a realistic picture of the challenges, disappointments, conflicts, contradictions, and non-negotiables that led him to choose a career outside of higher education and DEI work.

Next, in "Cultivating Community as an Administrator," Sarah Hokanson illustrates the integration of her roles as researcher, practitioner of postdoctoral professional development, and parent to twins. Through stories of her advocacy for postdoc employment conditions, supportive mentoring, and professional development, we see how she is "a more successful administrator, advocate, supervisor, mentor, and mother" because she has allowed herself "to be human at work." Hokanson describes how she applies her chemistry PhD research skills to designing her postdoctoral scholar programs. At public events for postdocs, she creates the welcoming, family-inclusive space that she values for herself and her young boys, who join her at these events. Throughout her chapter, Hokanson explores the punishing, externally driven but internalized cultural messages about excellence and overwork that she and other female academic staff professionals navigate.

We end this part on Navigating Institutional Structures and Cultures with "Queering Careers: LGBTQ+ Advocacy on Campus and Beyond" by Kimberly

Creasap and Dorian Rhea Debussy. They describe their paths from advanced academic degrees in sociology and political science respectively into work in an LGBTQ+ center. Creasap and Debussy invite readers with PhDs to apply queer praxis to thinking about academic careers—"an active refusal of the competitive, linear, exclusive belief systems embedded in academic career pathways"—and to "blaze collaborative, challenging, nonlinear paths that prioritize community, collaboration, and belonging." Debussy relates experiences with transmisogyny that led to a role outside academia that enabled them to make a greater impact on behalf of trans people through health care advocacy and policy expertise. The chapter ends with recommendations for "queering your career," advice that applies to any person with a PhD considering a career in higher education beyond the professoriate.

REFERENCES

Ahmed, Sara. 2021. *Complaint!* Durham, NC: Duke University Press.

Ahmed, Sara. 2012. *On Being Included: Racism and Diversity in Institutional Life.* Durham, NC: Duke University Press.

Kolomitro, Klodiana, Natasha Kenny, and Suzanne Le-May Sheffield. 2020. "A Call to Action: Exploring and Responding to Educational Developers' Workplace Burnout and Well-Being in Higher Education." *International Journal for Academic Development* 25 (1): 5–18. https://doi.org/10.1080/1360144X.2019.1705303.

Lipsky, Laura van Dernoot, and Connie Burk. 2009. *Trauma Stewardship: An Everyday Guide for Caring for Self While Caring for Others.* San Francisco: Berrett-Koehler.

16

HORIZONTAL MENTORING

The Positive Impact of a Diverse Graduate Student Professional Development Community

MARISELLA RODRIGUEZ AND SARAH SILVERMAN

In this essay, we advocate for graduate students to be positioned at the center of defining their own success. This recommendation is motivated by our respective journeys in political science and entomology graduate programs and discovery of educational development as an academic career path. When we were first-year graduate students, our shared understanding was that the tasks required to be successful as academics were largely traditional: teach, research, publish. Yet, taking these steps in practice felt isolating and oftentimes overwhelming. Graduate student training is challenging for each person and takes a toll on mental health and well-being, especially for students of color and those from other historically underrepresented groups (Phelps-Ward 2021). We are grateful to have carved out spaces of safety with support from a unique mentorship structure during our time as graduate students in the Teaching Assistant Consultant (TAC) Program at the University of California, Davis. Housed in the Center for Educational Effectiveness, the TAC Program enhances graduate students' skills as educators and provides consultation training for peer instruction.

Through the peer-led structure of the TAC Program, we were immersed in horizontal mentorship, an approach to supporting and guiding peers in achieving their professional and personal goals in a manner that transcends vertical power structures (VanHaitsma and Ceraso 2017). The TAC Program is peer-led by fellows who design and facilitate professional development trainings for both peer instructors *and* members of the TAC fellowship cohort.

Fellows play a key role in shaping the program's goals by instilling new values and areas of focus based on the interests and skills of the fellowship cohort. Invigorated by the collaborative and inclusive approach to program design, we served as both fellows and program coordinators. This mentorship structure provided a unique form of supportive on-the-job training and, more importantly, served as a model for equitable collaboration and decision-making in higher education. We attribute the lasting impacts of these experiences to the diverse group of fellows, representing multiple disciplines, socioeconomic backgrounds, ethnic/racial communities, and ways of teaching and learning. Our experience of horizontal mentorship in such a diverse and inclusive community uniquely prepared us for the collaboration and relationship-building that underlies so much of the work educational developers do.

In this essay, we draw on our shared experiences to provide friendly advice to graduate students who are struggling with the culture of their program or the decision of whether to leave their disciplinary research track. Inspired by the methods of collaborative ethnography (Roy and Uekusa 2020), we view our collaborative storytelling as a form of research intended to empower.

WHERE SHOULD WE BEGIN?

Therapist and author Esther Perel named her podcast *Where Should We Begin?* She opens counseling sessions with this question, prompting the client to set the direction of the conversation. In a similar vein, the questions we, as fellows, would ask instructors at the start of a consultation include *Why do you teach?* and *What do you think your students might be going through this semester? How do you think they might be feeling?*

These questions have stayed with us from our days as novice consultants participating in a community of practice, through a total of four jobs over five combined years of post-PhD work consulting with other instructors. These questions focus less on the expertise that we as consultants bring to the table and more on the lived experiences of the instructors and their own teaching goals. They demonstrate our shared understanding that reflection on instructors' experiences rather than our formal expertise can most effectively guide us and our clients to success in teaching and professional success more broadly.

For many disciplines, graduate student success is defined by three broad measures. The first measure is that of expertise. Graduate students commit themselves to years of coursework and dissertation preparation until their disciplinary skill set becomes second nature. The second measure is the practice of research. Failure to produce what a discipline identifies as credible research—keeping in mind that a single project may take years to refine—suggests an inability to succeed. The third measure is attaining a tenure-track faculty position at the end of a graduate career. This final measure is the most fraught. Survey research suggests that graduate student enrollment vastly outnumbered faculty positions in social science and STEM fields in recent years (Carey 2020; Dickey 2019). While many graduate students are successful, they lack agency in many of these areas, oftentimes at the whim of stipend funding, peer reviewers, and limited faculty job opportunities. In this essay, we describe how we learned to define success for ourselves, and how you can too—at any stage of the journey.

IT'S NOT ME, IT'S YOU

Marisella

I breathed a sigh of relief. After months of back-and-forth communications and revisions, I finally had the approval to proceed with my dissertation plans. This outcome had been hard earned; it involved a rotating list of names to fill co-chair and committee seats, several unanswered emails requesting feedback, and countless hours trying to see the connection between my research and the different methods proposed by each would-be committee member (based on their own expertise, of course). It felt like I was going in circles. Is it normal to receive such contrasting feedback on my dissertation? *Yes*, I was assured by friends, *it was the same for us too*.

I was so grateful to have this experience behind me that I hardly knew how to answer the question posed by my advisor (and dissertation co-chair) when it was just us remaining in the room: "So how does it feel?"

"I'm glad to be done. I can't believe how complicated this all was." If only I had looked up from gathering my things, perhaps I would have noticed that this was a trap.

My advisor proceeded to inform me that I should have known better: "You should have reached out earlier. Why do you need co-chairs, anyway? We work together just fine. Why are you still deciding which method to use? You will not be able to complete this plan in time for the job market. Why not wait another year?"

I had answers for each question, replies that would throw it back on the program's lack of transparency surrounding each step in the degree-earning process. But this line of questioning felt personal. Perhaps it was that after four years of an advisee–advisor relationship, everything started to feel personal. Or maybe it was that the other faculty member in attendance had simply offered, *See you next week!* and left. Instead of defending the quality of the proposal sitting in front of us, I found myself defending my credibility as a PhD candidate.

"I've never done this before," I replied in a shaky voice, internally begging myself not to cry. "I didn't know the first thing about starting a dissertation other than what you've told me, what other students have told me. I'm the first in my family to get this far . . . I don't have anyone else's experiences to rely on other than my own."

"I don't see how that's related to any of this," I was told.

Sarah

The department chair and the graduate advisor sat in an empty classroom that had been repurposed for our meeting, which had been called to discuss my various failures in the program. I had not passed my first-year exam. I had registered for the wrong class and not gotten a good enough grade. Most importantly, and most confusingly to me, I had not done enough to integrate socially into the department. *Why don't you attend graduate student happy hour? Why don't you study with the other students in your cohort? Why don't we see you around in the hallways?* I understood that I would need to pass my exams on a second attempt in order to stay in the program, but I didn't understand why I needed to make the department the center of my social life to do so.

I came to graduate school to keep learning, but like Marisella, I found that learning was secondary to figuring out the arcane details of how to navigate my graduate program. After an inspiring research experience, the realities of life as a graduate student were a disappointment: research was constrained by funding and support from advisors, and program requirements were so undefined that I found myself poring over the graduate student handbook just to get some idea of what I was supposed to be doing from day to day. Undiagnosed as autistic at the time, I misinterpreted many directions and requirements in the program, which always seemed to be phrased in the most confusing ways. Students were encouraged to "study together" and "network" with professors and other students at departmental events, but I never felt that I got anything out of these things, even though advisors always said they were extremely important. When I struggled on my first-year exams, advisors were quick to note that I wasn't an active participant in departmental life, a possible explanation for my failure. They were right that I wasn't very socially integrated into the department, but I couldn't help but wonder why there weren't more clear guidelines for how to succeed beyond "talk to professors" or "hang out with other students."

COMMUNITY OF PRACTICE AS A TOOLKIT FOR SURVIVING THE PHD

Marisella

I entered the TAC Program in my fourth year as a graduate student. In our first meeting as a cohort, we spoke about what it meant to learn and to teach. *What are you doing when you teach? What are students doing when they learn? How do you know when students are learning?* These conversations on defining teaching effectiveness—with graduate students who looked like me, with different experiences and a shared commitment to helping all students learn—sparked my intellectual curiosity and motivation in a way that I had been waiting to feel in my own graduate courses. *Finally*, I thought, *a space where I can learn, be heard, and be seen all at once.*

Months later, David posed a question to the group: "Why is our work important to you?" In David's hands was a ball of yarn. He unraveled enough yarn to hold onto one end and spoke about teaching as a tool to decenter power. Teaching can shift power from instructors to students, and sharing in the wealth of knowledge empowers all of us to be agents of change. Afterward, he rolled the ball of yarn across the table and over to me.

"Learning means admitting there's something you don't know yet," I said. "When learning to teach, you demonstrate that vulnerability to students. Our work helps people feel confidence in these moments." After speaking, I held onto a bit of yarn and rolled the ball to the next person. By the time everyone at the table had responded, there was a spider's web of yarn across the table symbolizing shared values in our work.

This activity was one of many exercises that encouraged our community to reflect on the value of teaching and the importance of our work as teaching consultants. I was struck by the peer-centric approach to every element of the program. It is designed, implemented, and refined by graduate students in the service of graduate students. Fellows are selected with the goal of creating a diverse, interdisciplinary team that represents the needs and interests of graduate student instructors. During peer-led meetings, discussions on teaching spanned topics ranging from classroom accessibility to the consequences for graduate students and adjunct instructors when they serve as low-cost labor for universities. Through these discussions, we collectively nurtured a community of practice. I leaned on this community of peer mentors for advice about teaching, guidance on navigating interpersonal challenges in my graduate program, and, ultimately, career advice when applying for educational developer positions.

Sarah

My experience in the TAC Program also provided a model of collegiality and collaboration that felt qualitatively different than that of disciplinary environments. A far cry from the amorphous expectations in my program that I "network" and "spend time with" other students, in the TAC Program we got to know each other through intentional discussions, taking the time to introduce ourselves, talk about our pasts, our backgrounds, and our identities. The obvious implication of this structure was that it is difficult to support one another in community without knowing anything about what motivates the other people and why they teach in the first place. To this day in my work as an instructional designer, if I am having difficulty connecting with a new client, I fall back on this question from TAC meetings: *Why do you teach?* Before the TAC Program, I thought that most of academic collegiality looked like departmental happy hours and awkward lunch meetings at conferences. The TAC Program empowered me to continue seeking out the kind of intentional collaborative relationships that worked for me and in which I felt like I could effectively show up for others.

SHAPING OUR OWN SPACES IN HIGHER EDUCATION

Marisella

I pursued a PhD to, quite literally, stay in the classroom. The classroom had always been a space for me to learn about myself—my history, my positioning in the world—and gather the language to contextualize my feelings and experiences. I learned to speak about my Mexican American identity and compare my lived experiences with those who held different minority and privileged positions from me. I learned about the experiences of women and people of color—people with limited agency who did the unthinkable by taking up space for themselves. The classroom was where I felt valued and seen. I dreamed of sharing this gift of knowledge and acceptance with students like me.

Sarah

My teaching appointment turned out to be a bright spot in the otherwise frustrating day-to-day of graduate student life. Teaching was an area where I felt I could provide support to students in ways I wasn't being supported in my program. Before I had the language of backward design, universal design for learning, or transparent teaching, I found that I could set students up for success by clearly laying out the purpose of each activity, specifying the criteria for success, and giving multiple options for how to complete assignments. I found I could help them feel valued and respected by offering flexibility when they were struggling. While I was nowhere near an expert in teaching at this time, I found myself able to support students based on my own negative experiences and intuition about how the learning environment could be improved.

My participation in the TAC Program followed a similar trajectory, with two key differences: I was still relying on my own past classroom experiences and intuition, but this time I was supporting other instructors rather than students, and this time I also had the peer mentorship of other TACs (both experienced consultants and fellow beginners). I recall that during the first several meetings the program leader and peer coordinators assured new consultants that we did not need to be experts on pedagogy or consulting in order to effectively help other instructors. "Fall back on your experience as a teacher and as a learner," we were told in moments of uncertainty. However, the lack of emphasis on formal expertise wasn't an indication of lack of structure. The TAC community itself was run within a warm and inviting structure, creating an environment of predictability and support that my grad program lacked. Expectations, to-dos, and important dates were laid out in a comprehensive weekly email. Meetings began and ended at the established times and included breaks. Interactive group work was punctuated by individual reflection. Through our structured professional development exercises, the TAC Program taught me how to extend the recognition of lived experience in teaching to others. A frequent job of TACs was to guide other instructors in drafting a statement of teaching philosophy for the purpose of individual reflection or job applications. Through this exercise, I began to truly see lived experience as a form of scholarship, as my clients drew on evidence from their classrooms to demonstrate their own effectiveness as teachers.

SAYING NO MEANS SAYING YES TO A NEW KIND OF SUCCESS
Marisella

The community of practice that grew from my time in the TAC Program gave me the support and resilience to survive my PhD career. I was nearly resigned to the idea that some barriers to success are immovable for certain communities, in certain contexts. Fortunately, my peer mentors modeled how to stand firmly by one's values and encouraged me to define success for myself. Once I realized the pull of education as a career path, my mentors helped me understand and communicate the need and urgency of this role in higher education. My position as an educational developer is to help educators design and implement meaningful learning experiences that are accessible to all students. If I can enhance learning for one or more students, then I consider myself a successful educator and academic.

On my last day as a traditional academic, I declined a job offer as an adjunct lecturer, emptied my desk of old journal articles, and walked past faculty and graduate student offices with their doors closed. I rode the elevator down from the sixth floor and thought about the classroom research I might help with at my new job, reminded myself to reply to a new colleague's email welcoming me to the team, and wondered whether she would be interested in co-presenting at an upcoming conference. I walked home, away from my graduate building, the publish or die mentality, and an academic culture that is content to see another scholar of color exit the field.

Sarah

Like Marisella, my experience in my graduate program and the TAC Program helped me to reconceptualize success and failure. Because success is so narrowly defined in graduate programs (publications and tenure-track jobs), I believed I would not be successful in academia because I could not see myself in a tenure-track job. The TAC Program was an opportunity to understand failure not as an absolute personal failing but as a stop on the journey of learning how I could be successful without having to stuff myself into a very specific box. For me, there was so much joy in finding educational development as a career path, both because the work brings me joy and because I was elated to move on from the traditional academic path that felt suffocating.

I held on to that personal feeling of joy at the moment I had to tell my thesis advisor that I would be taking a job in educational development rather than pursuing a postdoc in the hopes of eventually securing a tenure-track position. Ultimately, he was supportive of my decision, although not all advisors will be of all students.

LESSONS LEARNED FROM TWO PEER MENTORS

Through our experiences in the TAC Program, we cultivated a community of peer mentors that practices key skills from our time as fellows: skills of active listening, including asking questions and thinking through points of view that may feel challenging for the other person to engage with on their own. We role-play difficult conversations with academic advisors, discuss strategies for navigating changing career paths, practice negotiating pay and promotion, and, more recently, supported each other during the stress of the COVID-19 pandemic. Our community happens to be a collection of educational developers that found career inspiration in the TAC Program. However, our mentorship is more than a career resource; we use it as a support structure to set our own standards for success and gather the confidence to meaningfully move toward those standards, in and out of the classroom.

As graduate students, we experienced feelings of isolation and exclusion. For others navigating graduate degrees and seeking a professional home, we encourage you to explore alternative ideas of community. Our community of practice did not appear overnight. We nurtured it through prompted discussions designed to surface shared values and diverse experiences related to teaching and learning. While the TAC community was in many ways career-oriented, several of our TAC colleagues successfully pursued careers outside of educational development. What might you encounter and gain from diverse communities if you search for them?

For folks navigating their own PhD journeys, we leave you with the following lessons:

- Find communities that welcome and support diverse bodies and ways of knowing. To do so, you may need to engage with peers outside of your department cohort, academic department, and even discipline. Be aware: you may face the disappointment of further exclusion from your department colleagues and culture. But in our experience, it's worth it.
- There are many community spaces to explore, both on and off a university campus, if you simply search for them. Examples include career- or industry-focused groups, affinity groups based on ethnicity or shared background, recreational teams, and professional development gatherings to help bolster key skills.
- It is okay to say no to the academic career pipeline your graduate program is likely preparing you to enter. Or, say yes. *The decision lies with you.* Our TAC training as educational developers was a career pipeline that worked for us. However, it was also an opportunity to engage with a diverse community of colleagues and practice new skills.
- Reflect on and identify the values that are important to you, recognizing that these will likely change and evolve over time. Use this self-knowledge and awareness to drive your personal and professional goals.

Our community is a space for us to redefine success for ourselves. Just as values evolve, career directions and life goals shift. We are both in the process of navigating such a shift: We have veered away from educational development since writing the first draft of this essay. Sarah is focused on teaching courses in disability studies, while Marisella's role is shifting toward management and mentorship. For us, saying no to traditional ideas of success led to finding community and embracing unexpected opportunities. What success looks like for you is for you, *and only you*, to decide.

REFERENCES

Carey, Kevin. 2020. "The Bleak Job Landscape of Adjunctopia for PhDs." *New York Times*. March 5, 2020. https://www.nytimes.com/2020/03/05/upshot/academic-job-crisis-phd.html.

Dickey, Colin. 2019. "The Academic Job Market Is a Nightmare. Here's One Way to Fix It." *Washington Post*. April 15, 2019. https://www.washingtonpost.com/outlook/2019/04/15/job-market-academics-is-nightmare-heres-one-way-fix-it/.

Phelps-Ward, Robin. 2021. "Pictures of Health: Examining Well-Being and Resistance of Graduate Students of Color." *Journal of Student Affairs Research and Practice* 59 (4): 355–70. https://doi.org/10.1080/19496591.2021.1943416.

Roy, Rituparna, and Shinya Uekusa. 2020. "Collaborative Autoethnography: 'Self-Reflection' as a Timely Alternative Research Approach During the Global Pandemic." *Qualitative Research Journal* 20 (4): 383–92. https://doi.org/10.1108/QRJ-06-2020-0054.

VanHaitsma, Pamela, and Steph Ceraso. 2017. "'Making It' in the Academy Through Horizontal Mentoring." *Peitho Journal*: 210–23. https://cfshrc.org/article/making-it-in-the-academy-through-horizontal-mentoring/.

17

WHEN ONE DOOR CLOSES, ANOTHER DOOR ... ALSO CLOSES

The Rewards and Challenges of Work in Diversity, Equity, and Inclusion

JACOB MCWILLIAMS

In this chapter, I highlight both the rewards and the challenges of pursuing diversity, equity, and inclusion work in higher education as an alternative to the professoriate. I describe how PhD programs can help folks develop skills that are needed and desired in DEI work, and I shed some light on the specific work that DEI professionals in higher education can expect to do. I also present some of the challenges of doing DEI work in institutions whose leaders are either unqualified for or uninterested in enacting transformational change on their campuses. And I talk about my decision to leave higher education, after nearly twenty years working in college and university settings, and to move toward something that higher education couldn't offer me. I end with a brief discussion of what I've learned through my exit from academia and into work in service of another public-serving institution: public libraries.

The institution of higher education is inherently conservative. I use the word "conservative" not to describe any particular political leaning but to highlight the university's orientation toward the people and societies it serves: drawn to stability, resistant to change, and nostalgic for a mythical idyllic past (Oakeshott 1956; Rauch 2008). As a conservative institution, higher education is designed to shore up the interests of those who profit the most from the injustices baked into society's status quo. It's also designed to align with the interests of white supremacy and, by extension, the interests of misogyny and classism and xenophobia and fatphobia and ableism and transphobia. This explains why campus diversity and inclusion efforts so commonly fail, and why even when they succeed, they rarely result in any significant shifts in policy or practice. Tenure and promotion practices overwhelmingly favor the most privileged (white, nondisabled, Ivy League–educated, and financially secure) faculty members (Carter and Craig 2022). Admissions policies continue to favor applicants who come from privileged backgrounds, and universities have exacerbated this problem by maintaining a spending gap between supports offered to white students and those offered to BIPOC students (Garcia 2018). The problem goes all the way to the top, in stubborn intransigence in who gets tapped to lead universities toward the more socially just future they often promise potential students and faculty. University presidents are still predominantly white, straight, cisgender men (Gagliardi et al. 2017), and executive leaders almost never arrive at their position with any meaningful or direct experience with DEI initiatives.

At the same time, many higher education institutions have by choice or by force found themselves grappling with the challenge of enacting deep and sustained change in how they approach DEI work. Some campuses are dragged to the conversation by students, staff, and faculty who refuse to accept business as usual and who demand institutional change. Other campuses have been led to the conversation by their boards or their chief diversity officers or their presidents, or by a growing awareness of the impact DEI initiatives can have on admissions numbers and revenue streams. As DEI becomes more central to the work of higher education, campus leaders are increasingly looking for professionals who can guide them in building more systemic, strategic, and sustainable DEI approaches (Ballard et al. 2020). They are increasingly seeking professionals who bring the skills many PhD holders carry: training in research design and evaluation, experience working with students in formal or informal learning contexts, and an ability to convert theories and policies into practice.

I was drawn to DEI work in higher education by both the prospect of using my doctoral training for social justice purposes and the enticing promise that I would be able to bring about meaningful change for students, faculty, and staff. In 2017, I left a postdoctoral research and teaching position to run the Women & Gender Center at the University of Colorado Denver. I was thrilled to take on this new role, and I got to work enacting a mission of providing education, advocacy, and support on issues related to gender diversity, gender equity, and gender-based inclusion. Three years later, I was demoralized, disillusioned, and furious at the ways campus leaders undermined, both actively and passively, the work of the university's DEI professionals. At the end of 2020, at the height of the COVID-19 pandemic, I made the decision to leave my position and higher education altogether. I had no job lined up, no idea what I might do next, and no doubts that I had no choice but to turn my back on academia and move toward something—anything—else.

CAREER IN DEI: HOW I GOT HERE (BUT FIRST, MY PATH INTO A PHD)

In the early 2000s, I earned an MFA in creative writing and quickly learned that although I didn't like writing poetry very much, I very much loved teaching writing to others. I loved designing courses, loved trying out new teaching strategies, and loved working with undergraduates—particularly the undergraduates who never really expected to find themselves in a college writing class. I cobbled together a full course load as an adjunct instructor at a handful of colleges across Massachusetts. As everyone who's tried adjuncting knows, it's a career path that's paved in shit and bordered by shards of glass, rusty nails, and detour signs that point to nowhere. I careened across that particular road and into a university staff position as a curriculum designer and research coordinator—and learned just how much more I wanted and needed to learn about teaching and learning. I encountered the field of the learning sciences, a subdiscipline of education focused on building what scholars in the field have described as "a new science of learning" (Sawyer 2006). As someone who taught mainly from intuition (Raskin [1994] invites us to consider the possibility that when we say "intuitive," we usually mean "familiar") with minimal training in pedagogy, I was intrigued by a key premise within the learning sciences: that "the schools we have today were designed around commonsense assumptions that have never been tested scientifically" (Sawyer 2006, 1). In 2009, I started doctoral work in Indiana University's learning sciences program.

At its best, the learning sciences produces academics who can approach teaching and learning from a commitment to access and social justice; academics who can reveal forms of learning that schools weren't designed to recognize or value; academics who can celebrate and advocate on behalf of learners and teachers; academics who can critique failures within educational systems and propose alternatives. At its worst, the discipline is no different from any other area of academia: it can produce arrogant, opportunistic fools who know just enough to weaponize their knowledge and bend learners, educators, and policymakers to their will. Most learning sciences programs produce new PhDs who are mostly somewhere in the middle. Learning scientists do like a good bell curve.

Learning scientists are interested in the concept of *communities of practice* (Lave and Wenger 1991). A community of practice is, briefly, a group of people united around a shared interest or passion. Communities of practice have shared norms, expectations, language, behaviors, and formal and informal strategies for apprenticing new members. It's through apprenticeship—what Lave and Wenger call "legitimate peripheral participation"—that people learn what it means to be a member of that group. In my doctoral program, new students were apprenticed into the discipline using the communities of practice model. We were trained to do things like transcribe audio or video data, conduct focus groups or interviews with research participants, and analyze datasets using SPSS or similar tools. These are *legitimate* activities in the sense that they are authentically part of what all learning scientists do, and it's through practicing these kinds of activities that graduate students learn how to also do the work that's at the center of the discipline. That central work could be described, if I'm being generous, as building new theories and practices of learning. If I'm being more cynical, I might describe the central work of the field as publishing papers in the right journals in order to get the grants that support tenure and promotion. Both are, of course, central to sustaining a career in the learning sciences.

In life, as in theory, it's sometimes communities of practice all the way down. At the same time as I was apprenticing into a new professional community of practice, I was also figuring out how to navigate a shifting identity within the LGBTQ+ community. I had started exploring questions related to my gender identity: Was I really female, as I had been designated at birth? Or were there other words that described my gender more accurately? What would it mean to let go of my identity as a queer woman and to embrace a new identity as a queer transgender man? Who would I be, and what communities would I belong to, if I continued a path toward transition? This messy identity work was challenging on its own, but it was even more so because I had to look far outside of my professional community for support and mentorship. My home program had no faculty members who looked like me or who had any direct experience with transgender folks. My classmates didn't share my identities. I believe I was the first openly queer and the first openly transgender student in my program. The faculty didn't share my identities either. To my knowledge, my program is still batting .00 in this area—it has yet to hire its first transgender or nonbinary faculty member.

As any learning scientist well knows, representation matters (Darling-Hammond et al. 2020; Nasir et al. 2006). It matters in tiny ways and it matters in really big ways. I argued, hard, for an all-gender restroom option in the area of the building where I worked and taught. I pushed, hard, for a broader core curriculum that included queer perspectives alongside canonical scholarship. I didn't get it. (I've heard that some faculty within my program are now using one of my publications on queer approaches to learning to do exactly the work I wished someone else would do. That's . . . a win? I guess?) My dissertation data included video of me interacting with kids. I tried once to explain to a member of my committee how much I hated analyzing that video, listening to my pre-transition voice and seeing my pre-transition body. The committee member waved a hand dismissively. "Everybody hates how their voice sounds on recordings," they said.

And through it all, I kept coming back to something important, and very painful: the learning sciences community of practice—and the academic community more broadly—did not have a whole lot of room for people like me. With the exception of gender studies programs, it's exceedingly, excruciatingly rare to find a transgender or nonbinary person anywhere in academia. As uncommon as it is to find a trans or nonbinary faculty member in the disciplines that mattered most to me, it's disappearingly rare to find a trans or nonbinary person in a leadership role *anywhere* on *any* campus. There may be a transgender or nonbinary dean or provost somewhere; the world of higher education is very large, after all. But I didn't know of any during my time as a doctoral student or in the two years I spent in a postdoctoral research position immediately following my PhD. No openly transgender or nonbinary person has, to my knowledge, been appointed to serve as a university president or chancellor anywhere in the United States.

I wanted two things at once. First, I wanted to change higher education, to force it to expand a little bit and make room for transgender and nonbinary folks like me. And second, I wanted to do that in a way that felt a little less isolating, a little less marginalizing, than my experiences within academia had felt so far. I started talking to folks on my campus who worked in staff positions in DEI. They helped me think about the skills I had to offer, helped me reformulate my application materials, and helped me make the decision to leave the professoriate behind in favor of work as a DEI professional.

In 2017, I successfully convinced a hiring committee that the skills I had developed in my PhD program and in a postdoctoral research and teaching position qualified me for a staff role running the Women & Gender Center at the University of Colorado Denver. I worked in this role for four years and it was both the most fulfilling higher education work I've ever done and the most challenging, frustrating, and heartbreaking professional experience I've ever had.

WHAT IS DEI IN HIGHER EDUCATION?

The purpose of DEI-focused campus centers is to help make the campus a more welcoming place through a combination of education, advocacy, and support. A DEI role is most commonly situated within Student Affairs, although Jones and Kee (2021) describe a range of other departments where DEI work can be funded and supported through staff roles. Diversity-focused offices typically emphasize a key identity or community and carry names such as Black Student Services, Latinx or Latine Student Services, or LGBTQ+ Resource Center. Funding for these centers comes from a variety of places; some are funded through student fees, others through grants or endowments, and others through special funds set aside by executive leadership.

The fact that DEI offices are most commonly within Student Affairs is important. It demonstrates what, and who, higher education believes DEI is for: it's for students—but for students in all areas *outside of* the classroom. A DEI office under Student Affairs is an office focused on student programming and community-building. The reach of these offices doesn't extend to, for example, redesign of academic content or support for reshaping the faculty search and promotion process. However, DEI professionals increasingly bring with them the academic credentials that make them well suited to taking on the kinds of complex DEI issues that thread through all aspects of an academic environment.

Because DEI professionals are often called on as diversity "sensemakers" for the institution, the work they do largely falls into the "other duties as required" area of a job description. Today's DEI professional might do some combination of the following:

- Develop programs for students who share one or more marginalized identities.
- Design and implement a fundraising program for scholarships or to support or sustain DEI projects.
- Deliver trainings to campus stakeholders on issues related to DEI and supporting staff, students, and faculty who belong to historically marginalized communities.
- Draw on qualitative experience working directly with marginalized communities to inform discussions about changes to campus policies and practices.
- Write grant proposals and grant reports.
- Conduct research, analyze data, and publish findings internally or in scholarly articles or book chapters.
- Participate in admissions, recruitment, and/or hiring panels as the "diversity perspective."
- Advise undergraduate and graduate students on projects and theses and serve on dissertation and thesis defense committees.
- Teach courses in their area of expertise.
- Design, implement, and analyze program and campus-wide surveys or evaluation plans.

The skills required of DEI staff are similar in some ways to the skills required of faculty. One major difference is that DEI professionals tend to focus on the wide variety of learning experiences that students can have as they progress toward their degree. Another difference—one I hadn't expected when I moved into my staff position—is that staff are typically not covered by policies related to academic freedom. Although DEI professionals are called on to support and advocate on behalf of marginalized communities, they may face professional consequences up to and including termination if they actively support policies that do the same or actively oppose policies or practices that cause harm.

I think PhD work in any discipline is helpful preparation for DEI work, and the major challenge is figuring out how to demonstrate the connection between the skills you've developed and the work you are prepared to take on in support of DEI. Most faculty mentors are ill-equipped to help PhD students in this respect. They mostly haven't ever worked in staff roles, and they may even have internalized a belief that university staff positions are lower-skilled, lower-impact roles than faculty positions are. In my case, the best advice I received about how to present my skills, passion, and expertise came from people working in DEI-focused staff roles. I peppered them with questions about what their work entailed and what skills they found most useful; I asked for help converting my multipage curriculum vitae into a briefer, more skills-focused résumé; I worked with them to prepare a presentation for my interview; and I learned from them how to talk about what kinds of DEI programs and projects I would be prepared to take on. Of course, this is a good process to follow for any career transition, not merely into DEI work.

In a lot of ways, my time as first the coordinator and then the director of the Women & Gender Center was more fulfilling than I imagined it could be. My favorite part by far was the relationships I got to build with students, and the ways I was able to help empower them to develop projects, theories, or career pathways that mattered to them. I also had chances to drive or support campus-wide change, like when I advised my university on integrating gender pronouns into student records or when I helped to develop a lactation policy to support students who were parenting. The university's DEI leader, who also served as a member of the chancellor's cabinet, was dedicated to ensuring that decisions about marginalized communities also included members of those communities, so I was fortunate to have regular opportunities to advocate directly with my campus decision-makers. I was particularly proud of my ability to build an office that centered the needs of queer and trans/nonbinary students of color. When COVID-19 hit in 2020 and our campus shut down, I worked with my team of students to expand services into the community surrounding the campus. One student established a community fridge project to ensure access to fresh, healthy food; another focused on arts activism and worked with local arts organizations to establish public conversations about Black women in the arts.

At the same time as I was watching my students flourish, I was also watching campus leaders consistently act in opposition to their own stated commitments to DEI. Campus leaders had decided to not only join the DEI community of practice but to place themselves at the center of it without any meaningful apprenticeship into the shared values and commitments of the community. They knew the right words to say but hadn't grasped the nuanced meaning of those words. They learned a small number of DEI behaviors to perform in public but had little awareness of why those behaviors carried value and resonance. My university hired a new system president who struggled to remember the order of letters in the LGBTQ+ acronym and who instructed staff to submit to his office for approval any public statement dealing with "sensitive" topics—including COVID-19 science, issues related to race or racial equity, climate change, or freedoms granted in the First Amendment (Hernandez 2020). When my campus's widely respected vice chancellor of diversity and inclusion retired, executive leaders installed interim replacements without input from staff, faculty, or students. More importantly, those replacements were puzzling choices—they lacked any substantive skills or expertise in DEI work. Some faculty on my campus made their own puzzling choices. In summer 2020 they released statements in support of Black lives, then dusted off the exact same exclusionary syllabi and required readings they had been assigning for their entire careers. In July 2020, I worked with a Black student who was devastated to learn that her introductory criminology course, a graduation requirement for her major, played respectability politics with its subject. Police and prisons, according to the required texts, were civilizing forces and an essential bulwark against thuggery.

All of this is to say that DEI work in higher education isn't all that different from *any* work in university settings. Higher education has designed itself as a workplace in which institutional actors, even those who are working for institutional change, ultimately reinforce conservative, change-averse, and unjust value systems (Ahmed 2007; Phipps 2020; Rhodes, Wright, and Pullen 2018). What we want is to participate in an authentic reckoning over how universities have reinforced white supremacist values. Instead, we're participating in conversations about whether Breonna Taylor's name should come before or after George Floyd's in the press release.

The ship was sinking and I was rearranging deck chairs.

I hated it. I came to dread every part of my job that didn't involve working directly with students—and as the pandemic expanded across the world, even my interactions with students felt more and more challenging. I spent hours a day checking in with students over Zoom, trying to help them feel connected to another human, any human. Nobody at my university was doing the same for me. I was constantly furious, constantly sad. I was struggling with depression and deep anxiety. I was burned out, but still felt determined to find a way to stay in higher education, my professional and scholarly home for two decades. It was clear, though, that my identities and my DEI work had placed me inside of a kind of glass silo: I could see leadership roles elsewhere in my institution and in higher education, but I understood that I would not be seriously considered as candidates for any of them. This is partly because DEI professionals aren't valued as highly as professionals working in other areas of higher education, and partly because the people who hire folks into leadership roles very rarely bring direct experience with or understanding or appreciation for DEI work, and partly (maybe mostly) because effective DEI work requires people to fight against institutional momentum. I believe that there's no way to make meaningful change inside of conservative institutions without also making meaningful enemies.

"Enemies" isn't the right word, exactly. I have pushed back hard against some leaders in my institutions, and still managed to maintain positive and mutually respectful relationships with them. But even so, my job was to make it harder for them to take the easy path. This is an important role that DEI professionals fill—and it's also a very, very reasonable explanation for why DEI professionals rarely move into leadership roles outside of the DEI department.

I reached my limit in the waning months of 2020, after several terrible sleepless nights where I wondered who I would be if I wasn't a higher education professional. In the end, I decided all I could do was try to find out: I decided to not only leave my position but to also leave higher education altogether. My last day of work was January 6, 2021. I spent most of that day thinking less about my final actions as a DEI professional in higher education than I did watching media coverage of that day's violent attack on our democratic systems.

I remember feeling simultaneously devastated by the January 6 insurrection and also unbelievably relieved that I would not have to spend a single minute wordsmithing yet another perfectly crafted statement that would make grand and meaningless promises of "We are better than this, and we are committed to upholding democratic values."

I now work in a public library system as a learning and development specialist, another role for which my PhD made me highly qualified. In order to make this career shift, I had to do at least three things: first, I needed to actively reject the messages I had received about my worth and the value I add to an organization. Universities operate on a scarcity model that contributes to what Renn (2020) describes as "ungenerous thinking." When faculty and staff believe their positions are precarious, they may feel pressure to prove their worth by demeaning or degrading the value of others. They become susceptible to suggestions that they are easily replaced, and they find themselves willing to accept lower pay, less recognition, and poorer working conditions as a result. I left higher education feeling stupid, worthless, and broken. I needed time, my family and friends, and a lot of active self-reflection to return to a place where I saw my value enough to be able to communicate it to potential employers.

Second, I needed to once again return to my skill set and figure out how to show that the skills I developed in my doctoral program and work in higher education were applicable to nonacademic environments. This process was similar to the one I used when moving into a nonfaculty role in a university setting: I talked with people working in the fields I wanted to enter and they helped me find the language to clearly describe the value I could add to an organization. I learned, for example, to talk about my work experience as reflecting my lifelong commitment to public service within public institutions—a commitment that I've put to new use in my work within a public library system.

Third, I had to acknowledge my grief and let it in. The grief wasn't just about having to leave higher education behind. My DEI work wasn't just about advocating for others; it was also about advocating for myself. I had spent countless hours attending meetings where I had to argue for the basic humanity of transgender people, making those arguments to folks who had no problem with openly disagreeing. I fought against hiring or promoting folks who had actively caused harm to the LGBTQ+ community and who weren't all that sorry about the harm they had caused. I lost those fights again and again and again. I spent my time working on projects that were supposed to make higher education more welcoming to trans and nonbinary folks—but this work didn't make much of a difference for me as I was transitioning socially, medically, and legally. For example, several months after taking on my role as the director of the Women & Gender Center, I received notice that my legal name change petition had been approved. I was excited to finally be able to request a new email address that aligned with the first name I had been using for years. Here's how my phone call with the campus IT department went:

Me: I'm calling because I've changed my name and I need to request a new email address.

IT: You women need to stop getting married and divorced so much. Hahaha! What's your new last name?

If I had been calling on behalf of another student, I would have intervened in that moment to first explain that it's important not to make assumptions about someone's gender based on the sound of their voice. After that, I would have explained that there are lots of reasons why people would change their legal name and it's not appropriate to make assumptions or jokes about name changes. And I would have ended by clarifying that the appropriate way to respond to this request is to simply ask what the caller's new legal name is and what they would like to see reflected in their new email address. But in that moment, I had no response—I was too flooded with the shame and embarrassment that I regularly told students they had a right not to ever feel.

Moving to a new position in a new field didn't magically make all of my struggles disappear. I still encounter fear, discomfort, and confusion. I continue to face transphobic policies or practices that impact my daily work life. And truthfully, public libraries are dealing with many of the same issues that public universities face. Library leaders often struggle to put equity commitments into practice. They can be eloquent and timely in releasing public statements of solidarity while failing to take meaningful action on equity and inclusion. They can hide behind the mealymouthed assertion that libraries, like public universities, are supposed to be apolitical. In fact, libraries—like public universities—are by their nature deeply political. Deciding who can sign up for a library card, and with what documentation: a political decision. Deciding which books and periodicals to display, and where to display them: a political decision. What programs to offer, what accommodations to make for unhoused patrons, what to do when someone complains about the library's social justice book club or Young Republicans meeting: all political decisions. Some political decisions are just more palatable, more popular, more comfortable, and more socially accepted. (By "intuitive," we sometimes mean "familiar." When we say "apolitical," we might also mean "familiar.") Library leaders have the same tendency toward conservatism that I've experienced in higher education, and even those leaders who are most committed to social justice may not be able to resist an unending pressure to slow down, to scale back, to put their focus on more comfortable priorities, to let things go.

Also, in library land I still don't see too many leaders who look like me. I don't yet know why this is, but I suspect the reasons are similar to those that limit trans visibility and representation in higher education.

All of this is to say that I'm trying hard not to fool myself here. In making the transition to work in public libraries, I carried with me the lessons I learned from my work in higher education and DEI: that all cultural institutions are designed to conserve and protect social inequities. Libraries are not exempt from this indictment (Hudson 2018; McMenemy 2009; Nataraj et al. 2020). For all my criticism of the institutions that employ me, I am not exempt either. I've made my choice to try to do work I can be proud of inside of systems—universities first, and now public libraries—that have caused generational harm and that continue to visit harm on vulnerable communities. I want to believe that I have done more good than harm, that I've been a force for positive change within my institutions, but even if that's true there's no question that I *have* caused harm. I've resisted change and leaned into the status quo. I've drawn on power systems that benefit me because of my whiteness, because of my education, and because of my maleness.

I have no words of wisdom or sage self-reflection to share here. Doing work that's meaningful, that's valuable, that enables us to spend our lives learning and growing into the people we want to become ... that requires us to lean as hard as we can into the conflicts and contradictions of the choices we've made and will continue to make. Let's try to confront our past mistakes in order to better understand them, and try to make better mistakes tomorrow.

REFERENCES

Ahmed, Sara. 2007. "The Language of Diversity." *Ethnic and Racial Studies* 30 (2): 235–56. https://doi.org/10.1080/01419870601143927.

Ballard, Dawna, Brenda Allen, Karen Ashcraft, Shiv Ganesh, Poppy McLeod, and Heather Zoller. 2020. "When Words Do Not Matter: Identifying Actions to Effect Diversity, Equity, and Inclusion in the Academy." *Management Communication Quarterly* 34 (4): 590–616. https://doi.org/10.1177/0893318920951643.

Carter, TaLisa J., and Miltonette O. Craig. 2022. "It Could Be Us: Black Faculty as 'Threats' on the Path to Tenure." *Race and Justice* 12 (3): 569–87. https://doi.org/10.1177/21533687221087366.

Darling-Hammond, Linda, Lisa Flook, Channa Cook-Harvey, Brigid Barron, and David Osher. 2020. "Implications for Educational Practice of the Science of Learning and Development." *Applied Developmental Science* 24 (2): 97–140. https://doi.org/10.1080/10888691.2018.1537791.

Gagliardi, Jonathan S., Lorelle L. Espinosa, Jonathan M. Turk, and Morgan Taylor. 2017. *American College President Study 2017*. American Council on Education. https://www.acenet.edu/Documents/American-College-President-VIII-2017.pdf.

Garcia, Sara. 2018. *Gaps in College Spending Shortchange Students of Color*. Center for American Progress. https://cdn.americanprogress.org/content/uploads/2018/04/03090823/Gaps-in-College-Spending-brief.pdf.

Hernandez, E. 2020. "Campus Statements on 'Sensitive Topics' Like Race, Climate Change Must Be Run Past President's Office First, CU Says." *Denver Post*, August 25, 2020. https://www.denverpost.com/2020/08/25/cu-free-speech-race-covid-university-of-colorado-sensitive-topics/.

Hudson, M. 2018. "Community-Building vs. Customer-Driven Librarianship: Countering Neoliberal Ideology in Public Libraries." *Progressive Librarian* (46): 146–49.

Jones, S. M., and C. Kee. 2021. "The Invisible Labor of Diversity Educators in Higher Education." *SoJo Journal: Educational Foundations and Social Justice Education* 7 (1): 35–50.

Lave, Jean, and Etienne Wenger. 1991. *Situated Learning: Legitimate Peripheral Participation*. Cambridge: Cambridge University Press.

Lehr, Amanda, and Tatiana McInnis. 2020. "We Condemn All Institutional Racism Except Our Own." McSweeneys. June 24, 2020. https://www.mcsweeneys.net/articles/we-condemn-all-institutional-racism-except-our-own.

McMenemy, David. 2009. "Rise and Demise of Neoliberalism: Time to Reassess the Impact on Public Libraries." *Library Review* 58 (6): 400–404. https://doi.org/10.1108/00242530910969758.

Nasir, Na'ilah Suad, Ann S. Rosebery, Beth Warren, and Carol D. Lee. 2006. "Learning as a Cultural Process: Achieving Equity Through Diversity." In *The Cambridge Handbook of the Learning Sciences*, edited by R. Keith Sawyer, 686–706. Cambridge: Cambridge University Press.

Nataraj, Lalitha, Holly Hampton, Talitha R. Matlin, and Yvonne Nalani Meulemans. 2020. "'Nice White Meetings': Unpacking Absurd Library Bureaucracy Through a Critical Race Theory Lens." *Canadian Journal of Academic Librarianship/Revue canadienne de bibliothéconomie universitaire* 6 (December): 1–15. https://doi.org/10.33137/cjal-rcbu.v6.34340.

Oakeshott, M. 1956. "On Being Conservative." In *Rationalism in Politics and Other Essays*, 407–37. London: Methuen.

Phipps, Alison. 2020. "Reckoning Up: Sexual Harassment and Violence in the Neoliberal University." *Gender and Education* 32 (2): 227–43. https://doi.org/10.1080/09540253.2018.1482413.

Raskin, Jef. 1994. "Viewpoint: Intuitive Equals Familiar." *Communications of the ACM* 37 (9): 17–18. https://doi.org/10.1145/182987.584629.

Rauch, Jonathan. 2008. "Not Whether but How: Gay Marriage and the Revival of Burkean Conservatism." *South Texas Law Review* 50, no. 1.

Renn, Kristen A. 2020. "Reimagining the Study of Higher Education: Generous Thinking, Chaos, and Order in a Low Consensus Field." *Review of Higher Education* 43 (4): 917–34.

Rhodes, Carl, Christopher Wright, and Alison Pullen. 2018. "Changing the World? The Politics of Activism and Impact in the Neoliberal University." *Organization* 25 (1): 139–47. https://doi.org/10.1177/1350508417726546.

Sawyer, R. Keith 2006. "The New Science of Learning." *The Cambridge Handbook of the Learning Sciences*, edited by R. Keith Sawyer, 1–18. Cambridge: Cambridge University Press.

18

CULTIVATING COMMUNITY AS AN ADMINISTRATOR

SARAH CHOBOT HOKANSON

F eeling a sense of belonging within academia did not come readily to me. I didn't always identify with what I was trained to think of as a successful person. That person often didn't feel authentic or well-aligned with my identities, most especially my responsibilities as a single mom. During my work as a PhD student and postdoctoral administrator, I began to figure out where I belonged and the work I was meant to do, setting aside my own doubts and barriers. I have found renewed purpose in creating the community I had always hoped I'd find, and that I hope will be supportive and inclusive for our PhD students, postdocs, and faculty too.

ABOUT ME

I wear many hats at work. Primarily, I am the assistant provost and assistant vice president for research development and PhD and postdoctoral affairs at Boston University (BU), where I have worked since 2015. I am also the principal investigator of several National Institutes of Health and National Science Foundation educational research awards focused broadly on professional development and creating inclusive learning and training environments in academia. My professional ambition is to contribute to such sweeping changes in higher education that my current job as constructed is no longer necessary. Thirty years from now, I want graduate students and postdocs to wonder how it could be that the strong mentoring practices, internships, professional development, competency-based education, and other innovations I have yet to create were not always integral parts of how faculty and departments operate.

I am also a divorced, single mom of rambunctious twin sons, Finn and Erik. I am an avid runner and passionate Steelers fan. I asked Finn and Erik what my strengths are, and they said I have skills in chocolate chip cookie baking (best ever, I am told), throwing football pass routes (400+ yards on warm evenings at our local football field), and being kind.

SNAPSHOT OF A NEW ADMINISTRATOR

Finn and Erik, age four, ran at full speed down the hallway between my office suite and the space we had reserved for the first annual postdoc holiday party. I could hear their chatter in the distance as I made my way down the corridor of decadent red and gold carpet and opulent chandeliers. *MOMMY! This room is . . . AWESOME. We can see the city from here! The CITGO sign is so BIG.* They were right. The room is awesome, impressive, intimidating, with wooden paneled bookshelves next to floor-to-ceiling windows overlooking the Boston city lights and Fenway Park.

I walked steps behind them, in slow motion, my heart pounding and my anxiety building. Bringing my children to this event had not been part of the original plan. In fact, bringing my children to this event violated nearly every piece of mentoring advice I had received during my academic training. But, as a single mom whose babysitter was unavailable on the only evening the event space was available, I had to improvise. I tried to save face, writing to the postdocs emphasizing the importance of including family and friends within our community. But personally, I didn't believe my own bullshit. *No one is going to take me seriously as a leader of anything*, I thought, as I watched Erik attempt to smush an entire cupcake in his mouth in one bite.

I stood in the center of the room and watched as groups of postdocs walked down the hallway. Before my office was established, the fancy places on campus weren't exactly welcoming postdocs regularly. Nor did the university really know who all the postdocs were before my office existed; it had been my job to figure that out. I took a deep breath, stepped through the open doors to the hallway, and welcomed them in. *Here we go, just two hours left.* Behind me, the catering staff had given Finn a rather full cup of orange juice I was certain would end up on the red wool carpets.

But a funny thing happened during those two hours. I may not have believed my own bullshit, but the postdocs did. They brought their partners, roommates, and for a few families, their small children. Several women thanked me for being a role model, normalizing that it was possible to be accomplished professionally and still make space for family.

Finn and Erik made a friend, a nine-year-old girl. That little girl came to our party every year that her mother was a postdoc, happily coloring or playing with the twins each time. Her mother had never been able to attend social events as a PhD student parent, and her excitement lit up the room that evening as she moved table to table introducing herself. Several years later, that postdoc wrote to me that the social networks she found at the party changed the course of her academic experiences—she found colleagues to write with and talk to and a childcare share with another postdoc mom. She thanked me for making BU feel like home and gave me a dinosaur coloring book to offer to the kids who attended future parties.

Our holiday party continues to be one of the greatest joys of my job, a two-hour celebration of the ways our office helps ensure PhD students and postdocs at BU are not in isolation, but part of a community.

LIFE BEFORE BU

My early academic career followed a traditional linear pathway in STEM, from my undergraduate studies in chemistry at BU, to a PhD in biochemistry and molecular biophysics at the University of Pennsylvania, to completing a postdoctoral fellowship in chemistry and chemical biology at Cornell University. I tried on many subdisciplines during my training, including electrochemist (undergrad), enzymologist and protein designer (PhD), and structural biologist (postdoc). Though timing played the biggest role in why I didn't pursue a tenure-line faculty position—my then husband became unemployed right as I gave birth to our twins, and so getting a "real job" became more urgent—the truth is, I now see the serendipity of my circumstances. I didn't find the research areas I am passionate about until I began my scholarship in an administrator capacity.

I did exactly what I tell our BU PhDs and postdocs *not* to do and applied to any job I was qualified for without a strategy. In fact, my only goals were to get a job that paid higher than my postdoc fellowship as quickly as possible. Through this search process, I saw a position posted in *Nature* for a science policy and diplomacy position at the British Consulate General, Boston.

When I reflect on my role at the British Consulate General, Boston, it almost feels like I am recalling a movie or television show plotline rather than my own professional life. I was a "SINner" (part of the UK Science and Innovation Network), and our team was responsible for building UK–US scientific partnerships, such as collaborative funding calls or fostering academic collaborations. I was also part of teams that arranged and hosted diplomatic visits, from scientific ministers to government officials, and even a few royals. It truly was as glamorous as it sounds, and what I liked most about the position was its lack of routine. But a lack of routine coupled with extensive required travel and evening hours didn't allow me to be present as a mother in the ways I wanted to. And so, I said goodbye to my expenses-reimbursed trips to the UK, stored my cocktail dresses in a closet, and started a new path as an academic administrator.

WHAT I DO ALL DAY

I was hired at BU in February 2015 to establish and direct a university-wide office called Professional Development & Postdoctoral Affairs (PDPA), the first office at BU exclusively focused on supporting postdocs. There was no institutional prescription for what the postdoc office had to be or do—the page was blank, and I held the pen. This is notable for two reasons: first, the challenges and creativity associated with building an office from scratch increased my interest in the role; second, it demonstrated not only a trust in my leadership from day one, but a real willingness on the part of our institutional leaders to allow me to think in unconstrained ways about what was possible, rather than what existed in other places.

My role at BU has grown substantially over time, from director (2015) to assistant provost (2019), and my responsibilities have grown to include director of Responsible Conduct of Research (2020) and Research Development (2022). A common pathway for staff promotions in higher education is through accepting a new role that is a higher grade and salary, either internally or externally. My academic career pathway, though not completely atypical, is unusual. I got promoted by expanding my role, taking on more work and leadership in ways that made my job bigger and bigger. This reflects my own entrepreneurialism, work ethic, drive to solve problems, and extraordinary success. It also reflects the way I was mentored and supported in the Office of the Provost. My growth was matched by a growth in our institutional and grant-funded resources—I was a team of one, then two, and then four. Now PDPA has eight staff members.

At a high level, my office and our initiatives provide four main support structures for postdoc affairs: data, professional development, resources and services, and policy development. For PhD students, we primarily offer a centralized professional development curriculum, though more recently we have begun to contribute to other parts of PhD-related academic affairs. Finally, recognizing that mentoring relationships are the foundation of graduate and postdoc training, we now provide resources for faculty research development.

Underpinning and bubbling up from those workstreams is a substantial amount of what I informally call "case work." I vowed upon my arrival that my door would always be open for postdocs (and now PhD students and faculty) to have conversations about anything and everything they were experiencing at the university. Despite my substantially heavier workload these days, it is a principle I refuse to compromise.

Though we are a go-to office, and my role has an especially significant amount of power and influence over how postdoc affairs is handled at BU, every aspect of our work is highly collaborative with colleagues in the Office of the Provost and outside of it in departments, research centers, and schools/colleges. Our policies and practices must align with the existing structures that are managed by offices like Human Resources, Disability and Access Services, and the International Students & Scholars Office. We lean heavily on the clinicians in our faculty staff assistance office and our ombudsperson to help in difficult moments. And most importantly, we collaborate with the students and postdocs themselves, and they are co-creators of many of our initiatives.

At the same time, no one at BU does what I do all day. My job is so many things all at once that I have not really found a person locally who has an equivalent role. That can sometimes make the work that I do seem isolating, even if I am doing many of the pieces of my job collaboratively. Beyond BU, I have found the graduate education and postdoc affairs professional communities to be full of supportive and warm collaborators. Since these roles require trust and community-building to be successful, it is not surprising that those skills would also translate into helping colleagues. Whether it is a quick phone call to learn how an institution is approaching a challenge I am facing, or deeper collaborations focused on building content and establishing national programs, I have found my people. It is lovely to have connections that show acceptance for me as a professional–mother and gratitude for my honesty in navigating those roles.

NAVIGATING IDENTITY IN THE WORKPLACE: UNPACKING MY OWN BAGGAGE

When I started at BU, I often welcomed postdocs to our floor with a smile and a joke—*Welcome to Professional Development & Postdoctoral Affairs, located in the upstairs of Downton Abbey*—a reference both to the show that was popular in American pop culture at the time and to the opulent appearance of my workspace. For PhD students and postdocs in distress, stepping on to the ninth floor of Silber Way almost always carries with it a jolt; the way the space looks perfectly captures both the immense power differentials they are in and the potential ramifications of invoking the power and advocacy they seek from me. But the truth is, that joke (which I have now discontinued) was always more for me than it was for them, a manifestation of my own initial discomfort in the space.

Years before I joined the Office of the Provost, I was a low-income BU undergraduate from western Pennsylvania. I held two on-campus jobs, one work study job entering athletics payroll data and a teaching fellow job in the Chemistry Department. They interfered with my studies but were the only way I could afford to live in Boston and keep pursuing them. If my friends noticed our differences, they never acknowledged them. They were used to walking to our destinations in the city rather than taking the subway, my habit of ordering soup in restaurants, and me occasionally borrowing their computers to complete assignments to avoid finishing my work in the dark and dusty basement computer lab.

I noticed our differences, though, and wherever I could, I tried to mask them. My own actions were further justified by the academic advice I was given. An English professor my freshman year gently told me that I was an excellent writer, but that no one would take me seriously academically unless I gave up my "hick" (native to western Pennsylvania) accent and turns of phrase. I practiced for a semester and now speak with a nondescript Midwestern accent no one can place. My PhD thesis committee advised me against changing my name when I married to avoid signaling that I was no longer committed to my science and had suddenly taken up homemaking. (Since I'm now divorced, perhaps I should have considered that completely inappropriate professional advice?!) In big and small ways, I was taught repeatedly during the early phases of my career to conceal any part of me that could reveal that I didn't belong, that I wasn't enough. I had so much potential, each person said—all it took to realize all of it was to be less of myself.

That emotional baggage followed me around everywhere I went on campus. Even now, there is sometimes a suitcase full of feelings that trails behind me as I walk to meetings on Commonwealth Avenue. But I knew it was central to my job to advocate for and help to shape an environment where PhD students and postdocs felt a sense of belonging. I wanted them to have the training experiences I didn't, where they could choose to integrate their social identities and background into their work in ways that supported their success and mental health. So, initially I compartmentalized—I embarked on a path to becoming an advocate for DEI for the trainees' sakes, all while holding myself privately to antiquated and unreachable standards.

CHANGING PERSPECTIVES

Three things shifted my perspective over time. First, my experiences within the Office of the Provost at BU have largely been inclusive. I feel valued and accepted by my supervisors. Their support for me isn't contingent on fitting a particular mold and leads to my growth rather than to tearing parts of me down. I am sought after by colleagues for the person I am, the unique perspectives I hold, and the experiences and expertise that I bring. And they also see me as a full human being. When I got divorced and had to start my life over, my boss brought in items from her home she was not using. Her lamps are on my bedside tables and her food processor is in my kitchen cabinet, both reminding me that I am not alone. She has shown me that leaders can be successful and still be vulnerable at the same time. These supportive interactions have, layer by layer, allowed me to become more comfortable being open about parts of me that were once closed.

The second is the work I have done to become a social justice–trained facilitator. To be successful in that work, there is no hiding. In my case, that means on a regular basis examining, acknowledging, and being willing to leverage my own privileges, rather than being held back and consumed by the few areas where I have been disadvantaged. I have learned through those professional development opportunities that though my past and present will always be connected, they are also distinct and different. I am not a low-income undergraduate on a scholarship anymore and no one sees me that way; I am a white cisgender female middle-class assistant provost and assistant vice president with a robust Starbucks habit and a Peloton bike. Changing the lens through which I view myself has increased my own sense of belonging in Silber Way—I am in fact "one of them"—and has intensified the responsibility I feel from the position I have and the privileges I hold to champion our institution's DEI efforts.

Third, is there really any aspect of life that hasn't been impacted by COVID-19? Almost overnight, COVID-19 threw the compartments of my life together and mixed them into total chaos. Any notion of what "professional" was supposed to look like was challenged or discarded during the pandemic, and slowly I am reimagining how the pieces fit back together. During the pandemic I did things I never did before because they were no longer choices, they were part of my sanity and survival. I learned how to say no to things, take time away from work, and ask for help or flexibility when I can't juggle my parental responsibilities with my professional ones. It has surprised me how routinely I now do this, without apology and with confidence. The grace and support I have been given by my supervisors and colleagues also prompted me to increase the grace I give in return.

EARNING TRUST REQUIRES TRANSPARENCY

When I worked in government, having information and being in control of the narrative were two of the most valuable forms of professional power. I do not find academia to be entirely dissimilar, though administrators are generating information through data gathering and making decisions as much as we are chasing it. Every aspect of my current role requires strategic communication skills in some form or another, but successful policymaking in a university setting depends on doing it well.

I was invited by the Boston-wide postdoc association to serve as a panelist alongside four nationally recognized and seasoned postdoc office leaders across the Boston area. Hundreds of postdocs filed into the auditorium, and they were invited to write questions on cards for the moderator to read. As they were writing, one of my colleagues from another institution leaned in and whispered to the rest of us, "So before we start, what did your institutions approve you to answer tonight?" As the other leaders began to answer, my mind began to race. It had not occurred to me to clear topics or answers with anyone in the Office of the Provost; a postdoc panel didn't feel like a speaking engagement that required oversight or media training. There was no time to process or develop a different plan, and I decided that if I got fired because of something the attendees tweeted, at least I couldn't be fired for lack of honesty.

The panel was hosted at BU and a large percentage of the audience was our postdocs. Their questions were pointed and critical, and they shared stories that were raw and vulnerable. The panelists next to me shifted with discomfort, grateful that for the most part I was in the hot seat. Each time, I took a deep breath, made eye contact, and answered every single query. I took ownership of where we were as an institution, promised the actions that I thought I could reasonably take, and shared real data in response to their concerns where I could. The panel lasted well beyond the two hours it was scheduled for and past the delivery of the post-event pizza, which turned cold in the lobby.

As PhD students and postdocs become more involved in advocacy and activism, there seems to be a temptation in academic administration to further restrict their access to information. From my perspective, it is those moments that are most important for holding dialogue. When their experiences are so affected by an issue that they are willing to overcome power dynamics to say so, we need to hear our students and postdocs and engage them more, not less. After all, we can't be trusted to be acting in their interests if we haven't heard directly what those interests are.

Also, sometimes what students and postdocs perceive as inaction can be clearly explained in terms of real limitations that are not visible from their vantage point. Often, I find that PhD students and postdocs just do not understand how slowly things change in the academy. I get it, though. I don't always understand why either. I view it as part of my job to challenge the pace whenever I can.

MY PHD SHOULD HAVE BEEN IN SOCIAL WORK

I am often asked about the relationship between my job at the British Consulate General and my current role at BU, as it is not the linear career progression many people expect. I usually give a version of the answers I gave in my interview, focusing on the great many skills that overlap between the two jobs. From the beginning I approached this job as if I were a politician and the postdocs were my constituents. Though it is true that they do not elect me, if I cannot convince the postdocs, PhD students, and faculty that I am trustworthy and that our resources are valuable, the office will no longer exist.

Since arriving at BU in February 2015, through June 2022 I have met one-on-one with 546 postdocs and PhD students—546. It is a staggering number of interactions, especially considering that each case is usually made up of several meetings and emails rather than one. It is by far the most rewarding part of my job, but it is also emotionally draining in ways that are hard to describe.

Though I have sought out substantial training on the job, I walked into this aspect largely unprepared. I quickly realized that to process and act on the large volume of requests, I needed a system to classify what I was dealing with. The first tool I created was a triage rubric, modified from medical rubrics I had found online. This rubric, through a color-coded framework, described each type of case and the general actions I needed to take. This helped me mentally sort through my next steps, so I was responding proactively rather than reactively. I keep a running spreadsheet that tracks my appointments, serving as a dashboard that I can use to both watch for trends and describe my own impact.

Finn and Erik can sense when I am preoccupied with difficult cases. My entire mood changes and my body language at home is different when those workdays end. Now that they are older, I can be more specific about the problems I am solving and even make small parallels to the types of problems they might have experienced or observed at school. But when they were younger, it took a while to figure out how to titrate the information appropriately. To this day they can describe the story of how I "helped a postdoc find a job."

One December 27, I received an email from a postdoc with the subject line "HELP! Urgent plz read" that described how their faculty mentor had just delivered the news that their funding had unexpectedly run out and their job would be ending in four days, on December 31. This would be a point of panic for anyone, but for an international postdoc, this was particularly serious because the monthlong clock on their visa expiration would begin ticking immediately following that termination date. Given the timeline, I did not have the luxury of waiting until after break to address this concern.

This was not a conversation to be had by phone and was prior to Zoom as a ubiquitous substitute for in-person interactions, so I packed a bin full of toys and took the kids to campus to meet this postdoc. My borrowed office on the

Medical Campus had a waiting area with couches and tables and I set the kids up there to play while I spoke to the postdoc "privately," written in quotations because that office is enclosed in glass.

The kids could see the entire interaction from their couches in the waiting space. They watched, riveted, as the postdoc sobbed in raised voices and begged me to find them a place to work. On the car ride home, the twins pressed me for answers about why the postdoc was crying and why I was the person who had to help. And most importantly, they wanted to know how exactly I was going to find the postdoc a job!

This situation was more complex than the loss of funding (they usually are), and the mentoring relationship was fraught. I bought time with bridge funding from the department chair to extend the appointment while I scrambled to find a more permanent placement. For several weeks I met with the postdoc to revise their job materials and to identify BU research groups that might be a match for their expertise, but those groups did not have vacancies or current funding for a postdoc.

These sorts of placements without a dedicated bridge funding program often take both magic and good timing rather than skill, and I was running low on both. Finn and Erik were concerned, and checked in often:

FINN: Mommy, did you find that postdoc a job?

ME: Not yet, Finn.

ERIK: Is she still sad?

ME: Yes, she probably still is sad. I am meeting with her next week.

FINN: Maybe by the next time you pick us up from school, you will have it fixed.

ERIK: She could be the weather watcher [a job in their kindergarten classroom]. Tom [a classmate] is out sick this week.

In the end, the postdoc found a position outside of BU. Permanent visa crisis averted, but it did not feel like a win. I moved on to other work and other cases, and to some extent didn't recognize that what the twins had observed was influential; to me it was another day in the office. Months passed without talking about it and I assumed it was left behind.

Later that year, the twins and I used my office parking lot for a doctor's office visit nearby, and our appearance upstairs was motivated by the office candy jar. While we were there, a postdoc I knew well stopped by the front desk to pick up their business cards that the office had ordered. As I made conversation about upcoming events and where they would be using the cards, the twins suddenly interjected:

FINN: Are you sad?

POSTDOC: [nervous laughter] No, why do you ask?

FINN: All postdocs are sad.

POSTDOC: [more nervous laughter] I guess some of them are!

ERIK: Mommy will help you if you are sad. She gives postdocs hugs and finds them jobs.

POSTDOC: That's good to know! [even more nervous laughter] See you later, Sarah.

I was mortified, to say the least.

At home that evening, in the way that only kids in kindergarten can, the twins specifically and directly described their perceptions of my job and the toll it was taking on our family. Sometimes, they said, Mommy has a headache because the postdocs are sad. On those days, Mommy gives fewer hugs because she gave so many hugs to the postdocs. We give you more hugs that day since you ran out of them, they said proudly. The hug I then received to close the discussion was more like a punch to the stomach. It is my understanding that every parent is humbled by their own limitations on a regular basis. That moment was a strong call to action to manage my own stress, if not for my own sake, then at least for theirs. I was forced to examine my inability to manage the weight.

I do not have many forward-facing colleagues to compare notes with inside the Office of the Provost, but this type of stress and burnout is a common phenomenon for student affairs administrators (Lederman 2022). The pandemic has exacerbated this for all of us by intensifying our demands at home and at work. I am still learning what works for me, but I have developed some basic practices that have made a difference, particularly in the transition from work to home. Many of my personal shifts are small, like getting up and moving around between meetings or meditating before leaving the office for home. I also ask for and accept help more often, whether through using the ombudsman or Faculty Staff Assistance to talk through my own challenges or through connecting with a colleague.

Frequently postdoc offices and graduate schools are staffed by prior PhDs/postdocs like me and not social workers. I'm not sure my training in biochemistry and molecular biophysics is of much use to the people I work with unless someone stops by to troubleshoot an enzymatic assay! Practice may not have made me perfect at this aspect of my work, but it has made me a better resource over time. The emails and cards from postdocs I receive on a frequent basis are as good of a metric as any that most of their stories come to positive resolution, and that I made an impact to help get them to a good place.

DON'T LET PERFECT BE THE ENEMY OF THE GOOD

Though the role I hold now is most often described as a practitioner role, I did not leave behind my identity as a researcher when I moved from the bench into policy and then into administration. I conceptualized my office in the model of a research–practice partnership, explicitly tying those two parts of my professional self together. Our research and scholarship directly inform the work that we do. But research–practice partnerships by design are grounded in continuous improvement, which also can exacerbate my own perfectionist tendencies. I often over-rely on self-criticism as a primary form of evaluation.

I am not sure what a reasonable definition of "excellence" as an administrator is, or even what a reasonable expectation is for the impact I should achieve over the lifetime of my career. Not having a clear roadmap for the answer has tended to mean in the past that my default was a combination of pushing myself to achieve more—aim higher, work harder, get outcomes faster. I am still learning how to resist the overwork culture I was trained within. The best advice I can give to other administrators is to find the self-talk and mantras that work for them, that balance the tensions that lie between dreaming big and getting through their workdays. Every day does not have to be an extraordinary day to achieve extraordinary outcomes; there can be ordinary days mixed in, or days where things outside of work need to take priority. When I have to cancel a meeting to take a call with my son's school, or my facilitation wasn't as impressive in a workshop as I know it can be, instead of my inner voice saying, *No one is going to take me seriously as a leader of anything*, it now says, *You gave what you had today and that is enough, even if you gave more yesterday or can give more tomorrow. You are enough.*

CREATING A SENSE OF BELONGING FOR OTHERS

A month ago, our Graduate Student Advisory Board meeting was rescheduled into the evening, a time usually reserved for spending time with Finn and Erik. The agenda was hearing concerns from PhD students—I knew I should attend. But the last-minute timing meant childcare would be complicated, and so I brought the twins along instead. This time, I didn't think twice about it.

The meeting was being held in the same multipurpose ballroom we use for the postdoc holiday party. The twins bolted ahead down the same hallway, this time with full ownership of the space. By the time I reached the room, they had set up their own meeting within the meeting. The administrators and staff complimented the twins' good (silent) behavior and commended my role modeling of how to manage the daily juggle that is academic parenting. I thanked them and said it was my pleasure, and this time, it wasn't bullshit. Because I belonged there at that meeting—and more importantly because I *knew* that I did—the twins belonged there with me when I needed them to. It was as simple as that all along.

As I think about my next chapter, I know that I can't settle for role modeling what inclusion or authenticity can look and feel like in one moment and call that creating community. I am a more successful administrator, advocate, supervisor, mentor, and mother because I have allowed myself to be human at work. But that's the easy part. My experience and comfort can't be enough, even if it makes other people feel comfortable. The harder part is the work that I do with departments and programs toward disrupting the culture and practices that were in place long before I ever learned them. Entire careers have developed and been dependent on adhering to these norms for decades. Even now, the metrics for long-term success in the academy remain largely unchanged. It's a big ask of faculty to take a leap as individuals that our institutions haven't paved a clear path for. It's my job to translate our institutional values into policies and initiatives to help them get there.

ACKNOWLEDGMENTS

My gratitude to Gloria Waters for providing the mentorship and support that allows me to reach for exciting career heights as my full authentic self, and for the grace given to me in moments when I need to pause and regroup. And many thanks to Bennett Goldberg, who opened doors to new collaborations (and friendships!) that have challenged me to be better, and have shaped who I am and how I lead.

REFERENCE

Lederman, Doug (Host). 2022. "Turnover, Burnout and Demoralization in Higher Ed" (No. 77), May 4, 2022. In *The Key with* Inside Higher Ed. Podcast. https://www.insidehighered.com/audio/2022/04/14/ep77-turnover-burnout-and-demoralization-higher-ed.

19

QUEERING CAREERS

LGBTQ+ Advocacy on Campus and Beyond

KIMBERLY CREASAP AND DORIAN RHEA DEBUSSY

In this chapter, we use *queer praxis* as a framework to challenge expectations of what a successful career in the academy looks like. By "queer," we mean challenging (hetero)normative pathways in our careers, and by "praxis," we mean the combination of reflection and action. We discuss the power and pitfalls of putting queer theory into practice in one's professional life. By sharing our personal narratives, we encourage readers to think about how they can "queer" their career trajectories, while emphasizing that there are multiple pathways into this work. This chapter situates the advice within both a broader queer praxis and the lived experiences of the authors. Our focus in this chapter is primarily on the work of LGBTQ+ affairs in higher education, but the broader point applies to all readers: there is personal and professional value in challenging normative career pathways that can lead to meaningful work, no matter your field.

In *The Queer Art of Failure*, queer theorist Jack Halberstam challenges us to rethink the very notion of failure, arguing that our concept of success is a heteronormative one, tied to advancement and conformity (2011, 11, 89). In this sense, heteronormativity extends beyond gender and sexuality, instead referring to how social norms are (re)produced in all sectors of society. We apply this to our thinking about careers—not only in a literal sense (in LGBTQ+ centers), but as a way of thinking expansively about career development. Rather than thinking of failure in terms of shame or loss, Halberstam suggests failure can be an act of resistance in a corrupt structure or "a refusal of mastery" or nonconformity. Similarly, faculty roles often embody notions about excellence that are constructed in a white, patriarchal, ableist, and Eurocentric system, which exclude those of us from nondominant groups. Historically marginalized faculty and staff are more likely to do unrewarded community-engaged scholarship, mentorship, student advising, and work toward institutional diversity goals. This absorbs the amount of time that white, straight, cisgender scholars devote to research and teaching, which is then rewarded in the form of grant funding, research assistance, salary increases, tenure, and/or promotion.

We seek to build careers—and lives—that refuse these norms and, instead, support and advocate for the faculty, staff, and students who are marginalized on college campuses and beyond. We who choose career pathways beyond the professoriate are not "losers" forced into a "Plan B." We employ *queer praxis*—an active refusal of the competitive, linear, exclusive belief systems embedded in academic career pathways—and blaze collaborative, challenging, nonlinear paths that prioritize community, collaboration, and belonging.

We first met as colleagues through Five Colleges of Ohio, a consortium of Ohio liberal arts colleges. We both worked in LGBTQ+ affairs on our respective campuses and earned doctorates in social sciences (sociology and political science, respectively), but we had pursued different paths to our positions. Kim had moved from faculty positions in sociology and gender studies into being the director of a gender and sexuality center. Conversely, Rhea aimed her energy toward this career path prior to finishing her doctorate; throughout graduate school, she held volunteer, intern, and part-time positions at the university's LGBTQ+ center, while also maintaining her involvement with several community organizations. Our experiences show that there is no single way to queer your career.

TRANSITIONING TO QUEER CAREERS

Queer praxis enables us to think beyond the linearity of a career ladder or the tenure track in order to envision creative approaches to career development and transition. Both authors have worked in the field of LGBTQ+ student and academic affairs, and we each pursued different paths to our positions. One of us (Kim) made the transition from faculty to academic affairs and the other (Rhea) prepared for a career in LGBTQ+ student affairs during graduate school.

Kim's Path from "Just Visiting" to Academic Affairs

I decided to pursue a PhD in sociology after becoming an activist. As an undergraduate student majoring in international studies, my career aspiration was to become an American diplomat abroad. But less than a month after I graduated from college, the terrorist attacks on September 11, 2001, rocked the world and drastically shifted American foreign policy priorities. The democracy promotion programs of the 1990s were replaced by the War on Terror—invasions of Iraq and Afghanistan, CIA detention programs, broad military authority—which soured my interest in representing America abroad.

In the wake of robust social movement responses to these policies, my interests drifted toward understanding how everyday people change their communities. I marched in anti-war demonstrations in Washington, DC. I volunteered at an abortion clinic to oppose restrictions on women's healthcare. I worked with a local women's group to try to save a free clinic. Sociology offered methods, tools, and language that helped me understand social movement tactics, strategies, and community-building in greater depth than experience alone.

I started my doctoral program in sociology in 2006 and assumed that one day I would become a tenured professor at a liberal arts college. I enjoy the rigors of puzzling over social theory and doing research, like many academics, but I equally enjoy teaching small seminars, mentoring students, and building connections between my classes and the community. As it turns out, I do work in a liberal arts college and my job *does* involve doing all of those activities, just not as a tenured professor.

My first job after earning my PhD in sociology at the University of Pittsburgh was as a visiting assistant professor of sociology at an elite liberal arts college in the Northeast. I worked with wonderful colleagues and bright students, and I was well paid for the first time in my adult life, earning more than both of my parents combined. But I had always lived in college towns or major cities; moving from Pittsburgh, a vibrant urban center, to a small town in a rural setting gave me total culture shock. Where were the artists, poets, queers, punks, activists, and weirdos I had loved my whole life?

After one year of rural life, I accepted a $20,000 salary decrease (still much more than I had made as a grad student, I reasoned) and moved on to another visiting assistant professor position at a liberal arts college in North Carolina.

I loved my colleagues, my students, and the city, and I was close to friends and family. Except I was "just visiting," and given the international research agenda I was struggling to keep alive, I decided that stable, meaningful work was more important to me than a job title. The crumbling tenure system did not necessarily hold the promise of stability that it once did.

This was the moment at which I decided to queer my career. I was sick of teaching Introduction to Sociology. I was tired of moving from state to state for temporary gigs. I was fed up with the competitive jockeying for tenure-track positions. I decided to prioritize one nonnegotiable: I wanted to live near family. So, I threw strategy to the wind and applied to every job—academic, research, nonprofit, government—within my geographic parameters. Simultaneously, I found people with doctorates who were leading diverse types of centers on campus. The women's and LGBTQ+ center directors were instrumental in shaping my job search. They helped me understand how my skills as a sociologist of gender and sexuality could transfer into jobs like theirs. They provided me with language and insider information to use in my application materials (much of which we pass on to you at the end of this chapter). Hearing about their work energized me, something I had not felt in the slog of preparing for classes and receiving rejection emails for job after job.

Serendipitously, a job as director of gender and sexuality became available at a liberal arts college one hour away from my family. Armed with my newly acquired insider knowledge from the center directors on my campus, I was hired to lead a department and co-direct a new student center with colleagues in multicultural student affairs. Though the university had a long history of LGBTQ+ affairs (courses, student support, etc.), I was the first person to officially have LGBTQ+ student support in my job description. This came with a huge responsibility and opportunity to institutionalize policies that would help meet the needs of queer students—and, as it would turn out, faculty and staff, too.

All this experience has led me up, down, and across the proverbial career jungle gym—not up a ladder—to where I am now, which is leading a civic engagement center at a liberal arts college in Southwest Ohio. I am more at home in academic affairs, where teaching is optional and I can help shape the curriculum. I still grapple with theories of social change, engage in research projects that benefit the community, and teach small seminars. I also serve on our campus LGBTQ+ Task Force and work with local nonprofits that serve queer communities. I work with faculty, students, and community partners to address local and global challenges and gain a deeper understanding of how to build communities—all reasons I became a sociologist in the first place.

Rhea's Path from Higher Education to Healthcare Advocacy

As a first-generation college student, I genuinely had no idea of what I wanted to study when I began college. By the beginning of my second year, I had, however, found myself involved in several activist spaces: protesting the surge of troops in Afghanistan in 2009, organizing fellow students to rally against budget cuts that would eliminate jobs for custodial staff on campuses across Georgia, and much more. It was also during this time that I came out—initially as a gay man.

My coming out experience was less than ideal, and as someone who lived at "home" and attended a largely commuter college, this meant that I also had to engage with my biological family regularly. Shortly after coming out, I found myself directly encountering anti-LGBTQ+ bias in my biological family's home and then dealing with housing insecurity, as many LGBTQ+ youth and young adults have and unfortunately still do. I often don't speak about this experience publicly, as there are still many painful memories associated with that time of my life. However, this would eventually shape the career path that I envisioned for myself.

By the end of my undergraduate career, I had completed two terms abroad at the University of Oxford, which helped me undergo a great deal of intellectual and personal growth. Following that program, I knew that I wanted to pursue a graduate degree in political science, and I found myself at the University of Connecticut shortly thereafter. When I began graduate school, I presumed that I would eventually enter a very traditional career path—a tenure-track job that involved teaching political science to a new generation of students. Simultaneously during this time, I also found myself getting involved at the campus LGBTQ+ center, which is where I found mentorship, community, and chosen family in Connecticut.

Before I was even halfway finished with my program, I realized that I wanted something different for my career. I had found so much joy in the various volunteer and leadership roles that I'd taken with the campus LGBTQ+ center, and I soon realized that I also wanted to directly support the LGBTQ+ community via my work. In short, I wanted to solve the problems that had faced me during my undergraduate career, while also working to address the much larger systemic issues that were continuing to affect the success and well-being of LGBTQ+ students both at my university and beyond. Shortly thereafter, I worked with my mentors to adjust my career trajectories, and when finishing my last two years of graduate school, I positioned myself to enter the student affairs/DEI job market, rather than the tenure-track market.

Within a month of earning my doctorate, I had accepted an offer for a new LGBTQ+ focused role at a small liberal arts college in Ohio, and after entering that role, I let both my experience and the needs that the students were so clearly communicating guide my work across campus. In addition to that, I worked to collaborate in a genuine and meaningful way with community partners throughout the state. Within a year, the campus went from a 3.5 out of 5 on the Campus Pride Index (i.e., the leading LGBTQ+ campus climate assessment tool) to a 4.5 out of 5. By my second year on campus, the score had reached a 5 out of 5, which fewer than fifty schools across the country had achieved in that particular year.

By my fourth and final year on campus, I found that I was drawing more and more national attention—along with more and more transmisogyny—for my advocacy, particularly in relation to transgender rights in athletics. Ironically, that transmisogyny, which was intended to threaten, demean, and silence me, resulted in me wanting to find a larger platform to do this work, especially given the increased legislative attacks on the rights of gender-diverse people. Several people had encouraged me to apply for my current role with Equitas Health, given my policy expertise, long history of healthcare advocacy, and reputation for being a collaborator who could get the work done. Ultimately, I did apply for that job, and just over a month later, I then knew that I'd be leaving my decade-long career in higher education for a new one in healthcare advocacy.

A DAY IN THE LIFE: WHERE IS YOUR LGBTQ+ CENTER SITUATED?

Queer praxis is also situated in our daily work lives. We have provided support for LGBTQ+ students, shaped institutional policies to make them more inclusive to diverse genders and sexualities, and engaged community partners and nonprofit organizations to facilitate equity-based work beyond our respective campuses. This diverse set of activities allows us to make decisions about how we engage in teaching, mentorship, research, and community engagement.

The first thing you should know about a day in the life of an LGBTQ+ affairs professional is that there is no standard day. In any given week, you might spend a whole day helping students in crisis and the next working with colleagues to draft gender-inclusive housing policies. Here is a brief list of the kinds of work you might do as an LGBTQ+ affairs professional:

- Support and mentor LGBTQ+ faculty, staff, or students (and sometimes their parents!) as they explore their gender identities, gender expressions, sexualities, and/or romantic orientations.
- Meet with staff or faculty who need a knowing person to vent to about sexism, cissexism, or gender-based inequality. (Reporting this officially goes through Title IX, but sometimes people just need a sounding board that Title IX officers are not able to provide due to the constraints of their job.)
- Support student organizations who are doing intersectional social justice work related to the LGBTQ+ community, the BIPOC community, and more.
- Cultivate relationships with LGBTQ+ alumni to assist with fundraising, connecting with students to talk about careers or life, and supporting reunion events on campus.
- Write or revise policies around name and pronoun usage, residential life, and bias reporting and response.
- Start or participate in an LGBTQ+ employee resource group.
- Educate and train faculty/staff/community on LGBTQ+ topics that help them improve their work with students.
- Lead faculty development workshops on LGBTQ+ inclusive classrooms.
- Work with the campus wellness center to ensure access to LGBTQ+ inclusive healthcare resources both on campus and beyond.
- Visit classrooms and speak to students about the campus resources available to LGBTQ+ faculty, staff, and students.
- Develop curricular and/or cocurricular programs that address various aspects of gender and sexuality.
- Teach a course in your field or a gender and sexuality studies program.
- Communicate best practices for a transgender- and intersex-inclusive

health insurance policy to your campus human resources department.
- Work with a local community group who needs help with a community survey of LGBTQ+ populations in your area. You may help directly, depending on your field, or you may play matchmaker with faculty and/or students.

The second thing you should know is that the scope of day-to-day work generally depends on where an LGBTQ+ center or office is located in a university structure. LGBTQ+ centers can reside in academic affairs, student affairs, or diversity and inclusion divisions. If you enjoy working closely with students as a mentor and enjoy cocurricular programming, student affairs may be where you look for jobs. If you hope to maintain the ability to teach in a classroom or have a hand in curricular matters, academic affairs would be a better fit. In practice, the work will overlap occasionally. For example, if you are the primary person on campus working with queer populations, *everyone* will seek you out no matter where your office is structurally located. Even if your job is in student affairs, a queer staff member might come to you to talk about bias they experience or about how to teach the rest of their colleagues about gender and sexuality.

While this can be a heartwarming testament to your ability to connect with people, it is also a testament to the lack of resources for LGBTQ+ people on campus. A lack of resources can often put you in the uncomfortable position of becoming a spokesperson for all queer people. This can be tricky if you—like many LGBTQ+ professionals in higher education—are a white, gay, middle-class, cisgender man. You may be called upon to represent a racially, ethnically, and economically diverse set of people, including those with different identities within the broader label of LGBTQ+. Is this problematic? Yes. Is this also the reality of economically challenged universities? Yes.

Having a PhD may also benefit you in ways that you find uncomfortable. For example, faculty colleagues will likely find you more credible than your colleagues who do not share their training and expertise. While working in student affairs, Kim observed that she was invited to faculty meetings to which her student affairs colleagues were not. She was able to influence academic affairs colleagues on policies related to gender because she has *academic* expertise in gender studies. Lived or professional experience of those who do not have a PhD in an academic subject can be discounted by academic colleagues.

Sometimes this means advocating for colleagues who are equally deserving of respect, even though they may not always receive it. To queer your career means being willing to question, prod, and use your academic privilege to create more collaborative ways of working.

PRACTICAL TIPS AND ADVICE ON QUEERING YOUR CAREER

To queer your career, you must be prepared to reject traditional academic pathways and hierarchies, build relationships across many divisions of the university, and respond quickly and decisively in a rapidly changing environment. But where does one begin? In this section, we share some tips for anyone interested in queering their career.

Tip 1: Seek out people who have a PhD and are working "beyond the professoriate." Just like queer people, "we are everywhere" applies to people on campus working beyond the professoriate. When you get out of your home department and start searching for people in nonfaculty roles, you will likely find many. Look around your own campus for PhDs in nonfaculty roles or seek them out in professional organizations. For example, the American Sociological Association has a section for sociologists in practice settings that includes people working in higher education. Conduct an informational interview or informal coffee meeting to learn about their work. Building relationships with these folks can be crucial for gaining insider knowledge about the day-to-day responsibilities of the job or latest trends in their fields. Notice how you feel when they talk about their work. What makes you feel excited and energized?

Tip 2: Research your "dream job" for an LGBTQ+ focused role in higher education and identify what potential steps you may need to take to get there. One of the best pieces of advice given to Rhea was to find several job ads for positions that were dream jobs and to search for commonalities among their minimum and preferred qualifications. When searching through these postings, it is helpful to keep track of what skills and experiences you currently have, but it's even more useful to identify the skills and experiences that you currently lack, since this will help you create a professional development road map. And finally, it is also important to understand the progression of LGBTQ+ focused career paths in higher education. Depending upon your skills and experiences, you may not be readily qualified to serve as a director of a LGBTQ+ center, and you may need to search for other jobs, such as those for associate/assistant director in those particular spaces, too.

Tip 3: Highlight your transferable skills, while paying close attention to the gaps in your current application materials. You have several transferable skills. Pause and let that sink in. You have transferable skills and many of these can be directly useful to a queer career—both inside and outside of higher education. In many graduate programs, we are socialized to think in terms of the tenure trifecta: teaching, research, and service. Break any one of those apart and you find dozens—if not hundreds—of transferable skills. For a position in LGBTQ+ student affairs you might highlight mentoring queer students; planning symposia or events that will transfer to program planning; public speaking and presentation; workshop facilitation around potentially sticky subjects like gender and sexuality; data collection and analysis (as it transfers to assessment); and how you design learning outcomes and assess your courses.

Tip 4: Learn how to talk about your nontraditional path to this work with confidence. An important skill that is hard to develop is the ability to speak confidently about yourself and your experiences. For so many reasons, this can be challenging, and when thinking about issues of impostor syndrome, it can be downright daunting. Of course, there are additional complexities for queer women, LGBTQ+ people of color, gender-diverse folks, LGBTQ+ people with disabilities, and so many others who hold multiple marginalized identities. The information here is not meant to presume that this step is easy. In fact, this is a common but difficult challenge to overcome. However, it is important to find a way—within or just outside of your comfort zone—to speak about your experience with confidence. As you're likely aware, graduate students and early-career faculty spend years feeling like they have to prove or qualify themselves ("I know I haven't read everything about this, but . . ."). This is a habit you will need to actively challenge during the job search.

Tip 5: Be prepared to demonstrate your ability to work across identities. Finally, a queer career often means that you directly work across many identities within the broader LGBTQ+ community, and you'll likely serve a portion of the community that does not share a specific identity with you. Even so, it's crucial to demonstrate that you can successfully work across identities in a culturally humble and effective manner. As with many of the tips above, there is no one correct way to demonstrate this, but if you are lacking significant and meaningful experiences serving LGBTQ+ people of color, gender-diverse folks, identities within the plus of the LGBTQ+ community, and others, then this may pose a serious challenge to your desire to pivot into a queer career outside of the professoriate. In short, you absolutely must be prepared to demonstrate your ability in this capacity, as it is often a basic expectation of employers, rather than simply a preference.

CONCLUSION

While you may not end up working in LGBTQ+ affairs, we hope this chapter inspires you to think about how you can queer your career in any field. Queer praxis offers a way of thinking about career development that restores agency for job seekers who can often feel subject to the whims of a volatile job market. Our experiences show how refusing normative pathways can lead to new challenges, networks and kinship, and meaningful work that employs our skills and talents. This is particularly true, given both of our recent transitions into roles outside of LGBTQ+ affairs. Simply put, queer praxis can give you the tools and agency to identify paths to rewarding new opportunities, and we hope that the tips and insights from our experiences can help you on your own queer career journey.

REFERENCE

Halberstam, J. 2011. *The Queer Art of Failure*. Durham, NC: Duke University Press.

AFTERWORD

Fostering Career Versatility in PhD Education

TREVOR M. VERROT

As a graduate career coach at a large Midwestern research institution, an important part of my mission is to help PhD students maintain agency over their future careers. Often, it can seem as though the programmatic aspects of pursuing a PhD (do this, then this, then this ...) lead inexorably toward the career outcomes modeled by faculty advisors, committees, and alumni. Any deviation or wavering from these anticipated goals often draws negative judgment from faculty or graduate students themselves; most likely, it arises from a diffuse culture of expectations within the academy. The very language used to discuss multiple career pathways for a PhD candidate can reinforce this hierarchical judgment of outcomes. For this reason, the editors of this volume have encouraged contributors to avoid the term "alt-ac careers" because this formulation implies that "ac" was the goal, the pinnacle, or the paragon and any alternative constitutes deviation—a second-best plan B.[1]

Amidst this culture of expectations, PhDs can and must seize the narrative of their own development and choice-making, transcending the expectations of advisors and peers, and perhaps even their own preconceived notions, to regain affirmative agency over their present and future careers.[2] The narratives in this collection do just that, revealing the thought processes and the struggles of PhDs who have found work in higher education outside of traditional tenure-track roles. These narratives serve as invaluable exempla that build an awareness of possibilities, demonstrate methods for engaging in a personalized career development process, and provide a strong collective argument for changing the ways the academy approaches graduate training.

THE BIG PICTURE

While it would be incorrect to say that PhDs find broad support to explore multiple career outcomes, the academy today is less antagonistic to the prospect of PhDs pursuing diverse career pathways than it was in generations past. The idea that a PhD, as a highly trained subject matter specialist, should only value working within the professoriate was perhaps most true in the second half of the twentieth century amidst a historically anomalous explosion of access to higher education and the rapid expansion of colleges and universities to meet the needs of a burgeoning undergraduate population. Many faculty advising and producing new PhDs today were trained in this era and developed their approach to graduate education within that milieu.

Since the 2010s, however, the conversation has changed considerably. Leonard Cassuto and Robert Weisbuch (2021), in their recent volume, *The New PhD*, summarize this evolution and argue for a model used in liberal arts undergraduate education—that a degree does not equal a job, but is rather versatile training with broad applicability. An English major, for example, does not get a job "doing English," but rather gains valuable skills in research, analysis, and expression that transfer across virtually limitless industry sectors. The challenge lies in construing those broad skill sets into defined nonacademic job roles. Knowing that undergraduates need to develop strategies for representing themselves on the job market in light of this challenge, liberal arts institutions have emphasized the importance of internships, networking, specialized career development programming, and alumni relationships to train and support students in career development. Likewise, the graduate training conversation now tends to revolve around how we can best impart these career development tools and resources rather than debate about whether we should offer such support at all.

Demonstrating the sea change in attitudes toward diverse careers among PhD students, academic and professional organizations have produced initiatives and resources in explicit support of diversified training for multiple career outcomes. The Association of American Universities, for example, launched the AAU PhD Education Initiative in 2019 with the stated purpose of making "PhD career pathways visible, valued, and viable for all students" (AAU n.d.). This initiative involves a landscape analysis of institutional approaches to diverse careers in PhD education, an active sharing of data regarding PhD outcomes to make the true range of careers readily transparent, and an active promotion and sharing of effective strategies for promoting diverse career interests among graduate students for use by granting bodies, institutions, and disciplinary societies.

In addition, supported by funding from the National Science Foundation, the Andrew W. Mellon Foundation, and the Alfred P. Sloan Foundation, the Council of Graduate School's PhD Career Pathways Project further contributes to PhD career initiatives through data collection and resource development and sharing (CGS n.d.b). Likely responding to expressed needs among graduate students over the past decade or so, many disciplinary societies have already embraced career preparation as a concern. Through a grant from the Andrew W. Mellon Foundation, for example, the Modern Language Association launched the project Connected Academics: Preparing Doctoral Students of Language and Literature for a Variety of Careers, which engaged multiple partner institutions, compiled data, and created numerous resources in the form of workshops, toolkits, and mentoring activities (MLA Commons n.d.). Further, many universities have extended their career development services to graduate students, connecting PhDs with the same entities that share internship opportunities, networking strategies, and career coaching support for undergraduates.[3]

At a theoretical and perhaps even structural level, it is clear that higher education as a whole no longer takes the default position that a PhD ought to be a professor. The cultural shift in attitudes toward PhD outcomes, however, has not yet fully taken place. Individual faculty may still not be supportive of graduate students pursuing diverse career outcomes. Some faculty who trained under different circumstances may simply be ignorant of the realities of the current academic job market or unwilling to adjust to these realities. In some disciplines, faculty may be incentivized to produce PhDs who carry on their own legacy of research and scholarship, or, more immediately, may rely on their graduate students to perform their research: if a graduate student were to entertain the idea of a summer internship in another field, for example, this loss of labor may compromise faculty research and even jeopardize grant funding. Despite the new encouragement of career exploration and championing of diverse outcomes in various quarters, there remain practical barriers that often result in individual faculty being unsupportive, and this often plays out in how departments structure and manage PhD programs.

While outright institutional discouragement of exploring career pathways beyond the professoriate may be diminishing, graduate training in the main still lacks intentionality in how career development support is provided to PhD students. To return to the issue of a diffuse culture of expectations: even if program faculty and advisors are supportive of their students seeking multiple career pathways, the absence of expressed affirmation of that pursuit and explicit training toward that end is often perceived as discouragement and hostility. For example, in a study involving forty-five interviews of PhDs in a wide range of disciplines in diverse career fields at US higher education institutions, Brandy Simula (2019) observes that only a small number reported that their advisors encouraged them to explore multiple career options and were supportive of careers beyond the professoriate. The majority reported hostility toward diverse careers or that no possibilities beyond faculty path were mentioned. To not acknowledge varied opportunities is to discourage exploration of those opportunities; it is advising by omission.

Anecdotally, I often find that faculty are not against graduate career exploration. However, since these possibilities represent roads not taken by them personally, it falls outside their area of expertise, and so they tend to be silent on the subject. Whether intended or not, doctoral system advisees perceive those silences as disapproval. Acknowledging that many alumni from the program have found gainful, satisfying work in numerous ways; actively sharing department, campus, and disciplinary resources; and being open and honest about knowledge gaps and their own decision-making processes can go a long way toward enabling faculty to affirm graduate students in their efforts to discern myriad opportunities and plan for the future.

The narratives in this volume illustrate many facets of the dynamics outlined above. Readers will notice the ways in which the authors found (or did not find) institutional support, faculty guidance, or training that allowed them to explore opportunities, gain supplementary skill sets, and achieve awareness of multiple pathways, allowing for an informed choice among possible work options. As a career coach, my goal for the PhD students I work with one-on-one is that they will gain sufficient insight into the ways in which their training is more broadly applicable and learn what it will take to (re)present themselves to hiring managers and committees outside of a faculty search. This knowledge frees students to make affirmative choices in how to spend their time and energies and provides a powerful affirmation that things will, indeed, be okay, based on actual observation of outcomes.

Here, the COVID-19 pandemic has further emphasized an extremely important theme in graduate education: concerns about mental health. While it is no substitute for proper mental healthcare and active steps taken at all levels of the academy to support graduate student mental health and well-being, beneficial career development support can bolster mental health by alleviating the stress of an uncertain future and providing increased situational context to PhD training over the long course of a career (Charles, Karnaze, and Leslie 2021; Redekopp and Huston 2020).

In what follows, I point out common coaching techniques, questions, and challenges faced by PhDs in the career development process, referencing particular sections of this collection as illustrative of these dynamics.

PURSUING CAREER DEVELOPMENT ON YOUR OWN TERMS

Graduate students and postdocs seek career coaching for different reasons. Some students reach out to me when they are feeling anxious about a difficult academic job market in their field, others when they have lost excitement or motivation for their program, and still others when they fully intend to stay laser-focused on pursuing a traditional tenure-track job, but wish to learn more about other opportunities "just in case." In all of these situations, I ask the student to tell me (or in some cases, develop) a life narrative leading up to the present moment that clarifies why the student made some past decisions, how they have viewed themselves as an active agent in their life choices, and what their past expectations have been. In other words, this is an attempt to answer the basic question *Who am I and what do I want from life?*

This type of agency and internal direction is only more important in disruptive economies where external factors can be so unstable. As the essays in part 1, "Creating, Finding, and Opening Career Doors," illustrate, undoing the single-track model of the PhD journey requires considerable self-reflection to contextualize the graduate school experience as but one part of a multidimensional life that often must reconcile changes in life conditions and economic demands with traditionally narrow expectations for career progression.

Know Yourself

There is tremendous value in describing one's own professional development in writing, as it provides structure to the series of events and forces the writer to choose nuanced words to express feelings and moments that, at the time, and perhaps even in recurring memory, seem ill-formed and inchoate. The narratives provided in this collection offer just the kinds of positive affirmation that counteract the strong negative forces the lack of career training can have in closing down life opportunities for PhDs.

What normally follows the personal narrative exercise is an inquiry into values, interests, personality, and skills—or VIPS, for short. The rationale behind articulating these things is to develop rigorous criteria for evaluating choices. In many cases, career and professional development can become a fundamentally reactive process: When I see what jobs are available, I will decide what to pursue. Or, if the right opportunity comes along, I will know it when I see it. Or, I'll put some search terms into the jobs site, and apply to those I like. In all of these cases, candidates are responding to things over which they have little or no control, which involves a reactive process that puts primacy on an external source of opportunity. In contrast, by articulating one's VIPS, the PhD student can proactively set criteria—limits to what they will and will not do—based on a deeply self-reflective examination, and then pursue options accordingly.

The personal life narrative can reveal ways in which the PhD candidate may or may not have thought about effective decision-making in prior stages. To illustrate, I will share one common story I hear frequently: As an undergraduate, Jane took an introductory history course to fulfill a general education requirement. She did well in the course, performing at the top of the class, and the professor suggested she continue on to advanced courses in the subject. Three semesters later, Jane's sustained impressive performance prompts another professor to suggest she major in history and write a senior thesis in the professor's area of expertise. Flattered, and perhaps even enjoying the research that will go into the project, Jane agrees. Her thesis earns top honors, and several faculty members recommend she go on to graduate school to advance her research.

Lacking other job opportunities, and perhaps unaware of other ways she might apply her liberal arts training, this seems like the best option.

Now, Jane is four years into a PhD program, having done well on coursework, qualifying exams, and dissertation work, but never having truly affirmed that a faculty role is ultimately what she would like to do for the rest of her career. Years of academic progress have been justified solely by the positive feedback of external teachers, mentors, and advisors, on whom Jane has modeled her own professional choices, never affirming them through a rigorous process of self-assessment. Such an insight is an example of what can emerge through the personal narrative. In this case, a systematic self-assessment and discernment approach may help Jane confirm her current career path toward the professoriate, which would be inherently valuable in itself, but it may also provide specific reflections that could justify a change of pathway. Part 3, "Crafting Blended Positions and Identities," and part 4, "Centering Personal Values, Cultivating Work–Life Fulfillment," offer models of how self-assessment and values clarification can lead to changes in self-perception as well as professional and personal roles or lifestyles.

Part 4 in particular shares the deeply personal ways contributors have negotiated personal values, demands, and challenges with professional priorities. These essays can inspire PhDs to acknowledge and validate the elements impacting their own career development and to strategically engage supplementary support to complement their PhD training.

Use Self-Knowledge to Guide Inquiry

Once graduate students begin a rigorous process of self-reflection, I direct them to apply this newly articulated self-knowledge to guide exploration of local support structures. PhD students often neglect to take full advantage of the array of resources their institutions have to offer. Especially in large, R1 institutions and statewide systems where the sheer size of the organization, with myriad offices, centers, departments, and schools, one is challenged to develop functional knowledge of how universities work, let alone how skills gained in a PhD program may transfer across multiple domains in higher education and beyond. So, if you are still in graduate training, now is the time to map your institutional landscape for resources to aid in your career discernment, professional development, and well-being at department, division, and university-wide levels. These may include advising, workshops, or programs offered by your own faculty; centers for teaching and learning; and career centers, alumni networking events, and a variety of therapeutic resources through the health center or student affairs. Once you have identified those resources, it's time to actively use them! Part 5, "Navigating Institutional Structures and Cultures," may be particularly useful here as you consider where and how to find affinity-driven communities of support.

Ideally, sharing VIPS reflections in a career coaching context can yield several kinds of information. Values are the sorts of qualities one would like to find in a job: is the role mission-based or profit-oriented? Will it have clear boundaries to facilitate work–life balance? Will the job involve teamwork or isolated efforts? What sort of compensation am I willing to accept? Interests are preferences that can be incorporated into work, or in fact protected from work. Interests should not be limited to academic foci (though those are important, too), but include hobbies and additional domains of affinity as well. For example, I may be interested in both editing and cooking. Should I necessarily pursue a role as cookbook editor? Perhaps, but if cooking is an important balance to work, a stress-relieving escape, it may be better to protect this interest from work life rather than incorporate it into a future career.

With regard to personality, graduate students are often tempted to engage with personality tests or empirical-seeming evaluations to gain insight into facets of themselves. More often than not, however, I discourage the use of such inventories, as I find that the results become self-fulfilling: the test said I am an extrovert, therefore I shall be extroverted. Rather, most graduate students can independently think about the ways they prefer to take in new information, solve problems, and interact with others in the workplace. I use these observations in coaching appointments because they are uniquely based on the graduate student's personal experience and can yield workable parameters for assessing what kind of organizational culture the student finds appealing.

Apart from values, interests, and personality, many graduate students are challenged most when encouraged to think about the skills gained in their training in new ways, largely because of how the academy thinks of its own output. Among faculty and university administrators, academic activity is generally conceived as one of three things: research, teaching, or service. Indeed, for many tenure cases, these are the categories through which output is organized.

Sensing this conceptual framework, PhD candidates naturally think these are the skills they are acquiring through their PhD training. Reducing graduate training to this categorical framework, however, creates a myopic view that obscures the true and deeper value of what graduate students are learning, because this frankly idiosyncratic tripartite structure aggregating many disparate skills does not easily map onto nonfaculty roles within the academy, let alone outside higher education.

If PhDs think of themselves as skilled teachers, based on the fact that they spent so much time in graduate school doing it, they may believe teaching is the only other thing they can do, apart from capitalizing on their subject matter expertise in a faculty position. Furthermore, it is not uncommon for a student to tell me, "I like research, but I hate teaching" (or the opposite). When I question this, it often turns out that the student does not care for some aspect of teaching, rather than the whole enterprise, and this reveals a fundamental lesson that research, teaching, and service are not skills in themselves but rather clusters of activities, many of which are imminently transferable, and which, chances are, the PhD student approaches with varying degrees of enthusiasm.

Teaching, for example, involves the articulation of learning objectives, the design of instruments of evaluation to measure learning objectives, lecturing, discussion leading, recordkeeping ... the list goes on. Similarly, research can be broken down into long lists of activities that include analytical methods, presentation skills, study design, programming languages, and so on. Service includes activities such as serving on a committee, organizing a symposium, presenting at a colloquium, or mentoring early-stage graduate students in the program. As much as possible, I encourage PhD candidates to break down their activities in a granular fashion in order to separate out which activities appeal to them most.

Reflection on skills requires a slightly different approach than reflection on values, interests, and personality because it is so tied up in the frameworks of graduate training that do not immediately lend themselves to application in other contexts beyond academic work. However, deliberate deconstruction of these frameworks elevates individual tasks that, in themselves, may have seemed insignificant, but nonetheless are imminently transferable to other contexts both within and beyond higher education; however, they must be properly recontextualized according to the expectations of another role or industry framework. Part 2, "Inter/Disciplinary Transfer," highlights the many ways people have applied the skills honed by doctoral training in varied professional roles, including applying humanities expertise in STEM contexts.

Self-reflection not only aids in decision-making and navigation of local resources, but also serves as a valuable source of language for self-representation and new identity formation. If for so long a PhD candidate has thought of themselves as an aspiring professor, to destabilize that assumed future self leaves a void that can be accompanied by feelings of anxiety and grief surrounding a perceived loss of self. Filling this void with language from a systematic self-reflection process reassures a doctoral student that they are still very much in control. For example, "I am a person who values mission-driven work, is committed to environmental sustainability, who enjoys working collaboratively with creative professionals, and using advanced skills in interviewing gained through a PhD program in sociology." This shows how elements of the reflection can be combined and recombined in ways that allow the graduate student to envision different futures while staying true to self.

Explore Opportunities in Community

Following a period of self-assessment and resource gathering, I encourage PhD students to use their reflections as a starting point to learn more about possible career pathways. This requires networking, which I prefer to reframe as community-building, finding allies, or even making friends—all valuable outcomes beyond immediate instrumental needs. While building a professional community is important at all stages, those closer to finishing their programs should step up the networking and really begin to identify others in their orbit who can help them discern whether particular positions or organizations represent a positive work platform. Part 1 in particular emphasizes the importance and value of networking. Essays in this part offer many concrete examples of how to broaden your professional communities, while also highlighting the need for skills and strengths assessment, as well as the professional development required to gain some of the capacities you may need for desired roles in and beyond the professoriate.

Social circles tend to narrow in graduate school; it takes intentional effort to look outside what can become an echo chamber within a program, department, or discipline. Alumni are a great place to start. Many departments disseminate lists of alumni who represent a range of career pathways and who have volunteered their availability to current graduate students. Social media platforms, such as LinkedIn, can also serve this purpose. Most educational institutional pages on LinkedIn, for example, include a search tool that allows one to search for alumni broken down by what they studied, where they work, and what they do. Using the language developed in reflection, reaching out to alumni (and even complete strangers!) in disparate careers, but with whom one shares an abiding interest, can go a long way toward landing an informational interview and learning more about what it would take to pursue that career path.

In addition to alumni, the local landscape of expertise close at hand is another often fruitful place to build community. For example, if PhD candidates find great joy in statistical analysis itself, but assuming the burden of generating their own research interests does not excite them, they could explore ways of applying their advanced training to helping others in developing the statistical components of their own projects. For this, they could reach out to on-campus offices of institutional research, research support labs, grant development services—whatever analogous units exist at their institution—to take full advantage of local resources before broadening their networking efforts. There is much to be learned about how a PhD can work within higher education beyond the professoriate, especially from the many colleagues currently working around the institution itself.

One point of resistance to community building is the feeling that, if PhDs are not investing 100 percent of their time and energy into their program, they are somehow wasting effort or compromising the quality of their research or dissertation. In response, I describe ways in which reaching out and holding conversations, especially via social media, can take place in a few minutes a day, for example, while enjoying a morning coffee break. Networking need not derail one's academic work or be an hours-long slog to which one dedicates significant off-hours time. Slow and steady wins the race, and keeping the effort humming along several intentional minutes every day or week keeps professional exploration moving forward.

Further, concerns about not spending time writing or in the lab in order to conduct informational interviews, training, or even internships can be minimized through open and honest conversations with advisors and mentors, whenever possible. Additionally, if one were to miss a few hours of writing time, or even a few weeks over a summer, to pursue a professional development opportunity, for example, would footnote 4 of chapter 2 of the dissertation really be any weaker? Thinking practically about time spent, rather than letting anxieties overshadow the thought process, can help to rationalize sustained networking efforts.

From Exploration to Defined Next Steps

Building community in a defined career pathway will answer many of the practical questions that often arise along the way. *Do I need an internship to get this job? Do I have the skills they actually want? I have never worked outside academia before—Will I like it? Do I need to apply for entry-level positions or do my years of graduate school qualify me for something more? Should I apply with a CV or a résumé? What do résumés look like in this field?* The nuances of pursuing particular roles at specific organizations in well-defined, nonacademic industries can vary so much that prework to answer such questions via networking is essential to navigate the process effectively. The mere fact of having a PhD will not speak for itself; rather, the candidate must learn new expectations and different cultures of self-representation. Each informational interview, each narrative that an exploring PhD student encounters (like those in this volume) should constitute a data point from which to extrapolate a personalized development plan, and the more information the change-seeking candidate has, the smoother the transition will be.

To conclude, I will first summarize a series of steps or phases that a PhD candidate might go through to chart a career development plan, and then close with some thoughts about working in and around the academy. The first phase is clearly self-assessment—know thyself, as the Greek aphorism goes. Resist the urge to externalize the forces determining your future and tell your story clearly, in a way that contextualizes graduate training for what it is: not as an end in itself, but rather as the beginning of something new. Next, gather resources and explore opportunities. Third, learn from those who already navigated the terrain—program alumni and other individuals in the world who are living aspects of a life you admire—and convert that exploration into research to make a professional growth plan. What will you need to do to be a compelling candidate for your next job? Is there any additional training or experience you could pursue before actively applying? How might you need to adapt your application documents? Fourth, execute your plan—with help!

You are not alone in this process. Seek out resources and expertise at your institution in the form of career coaching, volumes like this, and the network you cultivated, to sustain you through the transition. Fifth and, importantly, *repeat*. Indeed, the process does not end. As difficult as this realization may seem for a PhD candidate, the first, second, or even third job post-PhD will, in all likelihood, not be the last one. Remember, job changes do not occur only for "negative" reasons such as job loss or precarity but also organically due to positive growth, such as advancement through promotion or being drawn to new opportunities and interests. In an ongoing cycle, these professional development phases repeat throughout one's working career. Being aware of what stage you find yourself in at any given moment in your career can prove both reassuring and clarifying.

In closing, this volume highlights narratives of PhDs working outside traditional faculty roles, which is a subset of all PhDs who have found meaningful work beyond the professoriate in higher education. This is a much-needed emphasis because it is often an intellectual leap for a PhD to imagine a rewarding existence beyond the faculty, even if an academic appointment is identified as personally untenable or was never desired in the first place. *Higher Education Careers Beyond the Professoriate* exposes as false the notion that, if a PhD candidate steps away from an academic trajectory, they are fundamentally cast out of the ivory tower. As part 3 in particular demonstrates, living an academic life is not a simple in-or-out binary: one can remain fully embedded in a university community and enjoy a vibrant culture of intellectual inquiry without pursuing a tenure-track role. The narratives in this volume serve as encouraging evidence that embracing diverse career pathways can lead to a range of fulfilling work within higher education in the larger context of a meaningful life aligned with one's inclinations, interests, and values.

NOTES

1. In the same vein, the Council of Graduate Schools has published the document "Shaping New Narratives About PhD Careers: A Communications Resource to Advocate for Career Diversity" (CGS n.d.a), which outlines additional language to avoid assumptions and loaded terms when discussing PhD careers.
2. This approach is drawn from the work of Marcia B. Baxter Magolda. See, for example, "Three Elements of Self-Authorship" (Magolda 2008).

3. My own role at Indiana University, the first of its kind in the College of Arts and Sciences expressly dedicated to serving graduate students, was created in 2019. Similar administrative and career services roles for graduate students have been developed at other institutions. As noted by Natalie Lundsteen in the foreword to this book, the growth of the Graduate Career Consortium is indicative of this new extension of career services to graduate students.

REFERENCES

AAU (Association of American Universities). n.d. "AAU PhD Education Initiative." Accessed August 4, 2022. https://www.aau.edu/sites/default/files/AAU-Images/Graduate-Education/One-Pager.pdf.

Cassuto, Leonard, and Robert Weisbuch. 2021. "Career Diversity: A Liberal Arts Approach to the PhD." In *The New PhD: How to Build a Better Graduate Education*, 113–43. Baltimore: Johns Hopkins University Press.

CGS (Council of Graduate Schools). n.d.a. "Shaping New Narratives About PhD Careers: A Communications Resource to Advocate for Career Diversity." https://cgsnet.org/wp-content/uploads/2022/02/ShapingNewNarratives2020.pdf.

CGS (Council of Graduate Schools). n.d.b. "Understanding PhD Career Pathways for Program Improvement." Accessed August 4, 2022. https://cgsnet.org/project/understanding-phd-career-pathways-for-program-improvement.

Charles, Susan T., Melissa M. Karnaze, and Frances M. Leslie. 2021. "Positive Factors Related to Graduate Student Mental Health." *Journal of American College Health* 70 (6): 1858–66. https://doi.org/10.1080/07448481.2020.1841207.

Magolda, Marcia B. Baxter. 2008. "Three Elements of Self-Authorship." *Journal of College Student Development* 49, no. 4 (July–August): 269–84.

MLA Commons. n.d. "About Connected Academics." Connected Academics: Preparing Doctoral Students of Language and Literature for a Variety of Careers. Accessed August 4, 2022. https://connect.mla.hcommons.org/about-us/.

Redekopp, Dave E., and Michael Huston. 2020. *Strengthening Mental Health Through Effective Career Development*. Toronto: CERIC.

Simula, Brandy. 2019. "Higher Ed PhD Career Pathways Beyond the Professoriate: Preliminary Study Findings" [Unpublished manuscript]. Last modified December 2019.

APPENDIX A
PhD Characteristics of Essay Contributors

CONTRIBUTOR	PHD DISCIPLINE	PHD-GRANTING INSTITUTION
Barks	Biological Anthropology	Emory University
Bessette	Comparative Literature	University of Alberta, Canada
Boyer	Biblical History	Boston University
Canelli	English	Emory University
Creasap	Sociology	University of Pittsburgh
Debussy	Political Science	University of Connecticut
Dwyer	Ecology	University of California, Davis
Forstie	Sociology	Northwestern University
Hokanson	Biochemistry and Molecular Biophysics	University of Pennsylvania
Hutchins	Comparative Literature	Washington University in St. Louis
Iwema	Neuroscience	SUNY Upstate Medical University
Jacoby	French Language and Literature	University of Maryland
Lodge	English Literature	University of Oregon
McDonald	Genetics and Genomics	Duke University
McWilliams	Education	Indiana University
Partington	English Literature	Emory University
Rideau	Higher Education	Virginia Tech
Rodriguez	Political Science	University of California, Davis
Sikora	Cellular and Molecular Biology	University of Michigan
Silverman	Entomology	University of California, Davis
Wahl	Neuroscience	Rutgers Biomedical Health Sciences and Rutgers University–Newark
Walsh	History	University of Pittsburgh
Wrighting	Genetics	Harvard Medical School

APPENDIX B

Current Employment Characteristics of Essay Contributors

CONTRIBUTOR	CURRENT TITLE	CURRENT EMPLOYER
Barks	Senior Director, STEM Career Communities and Analytics	Grinnell College
Bessette	Assistant Director for Digital Learning	Georgetown University
Boyer	Assistant Director, Graduate Student Career Services	Massachusetts Institute of Technology
Canelli	Assistant Dean of Academic Affairs, Graduate School of Arts and Sciences	Brandeis University
Creasap	Director, Susan Hirt Hagen Center for Civic and Urban Engagement	Wittenberg University
Debussy	Director of External Affairs	Equitas Health
Dwyer	Associate Director for Teaching, Learning, and Inclusion, Center for the Enhancement of Learning and Teaching	Tufts University
Forstie	Education Program Specialist, Center for Educational Innovation	University of Minnesota
Hokanson	Assistant Provost and Assistant Vice President for Research Development and PhD and Postdoctoral Affairs	Boston University
Hutchins	Lecturer and Interim Director of the John Martinson Honors Program	Southern Illinois University Edwardsville
Iwema	Senior UX Strategist	WONDROS/National Institutes of Health
Jacoby	Higher Education Consultant	Barbara Jacoby Consulting
Lodge	Senior Partner Success Manager	PartnerHero Inc.
McDonald	Director of the Biological and Biomedical Sciences Program	University of North Carolina at Chapel Hill
McWilliams	Learning Program Specialist	Denver Public Library

CONTRIBUTOR	CURRENT TITLE	CURRENT EMPLOYER
Partington	Senior Manager, Communications, Department of Family and Preventive Medicine	Emory University School of Medicine
Rideau	Assistant Provost for Faculty Development	Tufts University
Rodriguez	Inclusive Teaching Manager	University of California, Berkeley
Sikora	Associate Dean and Director of Recruiting, Marketing, and Communications, Graduate School	University of Colorado Anschutz Medical Campus
Silverman	Instructional Designer and Lecturer in Women's and Gender Studies	University of Michigan–Dearborn
Wahl	Senior Instructional Design Specialist in the School of Medicine	Virginia Commonwealth University
Walsh	Associate Director of Learning Support Programs	Carnegie Mellon University
Wrighting	Executive Director, ADVANCE Office of Faculty Development	Northeastern University

APPENDIX C

Personal Identities of Essay Contributors

CONTRIBUTOR	RACE/ETHNICITY	GENDER	ADDITIONAL IDENTITIES
Barks	White	Nonbinary	Queer
Bessette	White	Female	First-generation; ADHD; immigrant recent citizen; mother of two
Boyer	White	Female	Cisgender; mother of a one-year-old
Canelli	White	Female	Queer cisgender woman; first-generation college student from Appalachia; trauma survivor with CPTSD and several chronic autoimmune diseases; mother
Creasap	White	Female	Queer woman; first-generation college student from the Midwest
Debussy	White	Female	Lesbian transgender woman from the Deep South; neurodivergent; first-generation college graduate
Dwyer	White, Asian	Female	Cisgender; parent of two young children
Forstie	White	Nonbinary	Queer; parent of a young child
Hokanson	White	Female	Single mom; socioeconomically challenged background; first-generation graduate student
Hutchins	White	Female	First-generation PhD; cisgender; Midwesterner; neurodivergent
Iwema	White	Female	Cisgender
Jacoby	White	Female	Jewish; first-generation college student
Lodge	White	Female	Queer; first-generation; working class

CONTRIBUTOR	RACE/ETHNICITY	GENDER	ADDITIONAL IDENTITIES
McDonald	White	Male	Gay cisgender man
McWilliams	White	Male	Transgender; queer
Partington	White	Female	Stay-at-home-parent for thirteen years
Rideau	Black	Male	Cisgender
Rodriguez	Mexican American	Female	Cisgender
Sikora	American Indian (Chickasaw)	Female	First-generation; from a small town on the Big Island of Hawai`i; full-time working mother
Silverman	White	Female	Cisgender; autism spectrum
Wahl	White	Female	Parent
Walsh	White	Female	Cisgender; full-time working mother of two
Wrighting	Black	Female	Cisgender; full-time working mother of twins

ANNOTATED BIBLIOGRAPHY

Bessette, Lee Skallerup, ed. 2022. *Affective Labor and Alt-Ac Careers*. Lawrence: University Press of Kansas.

Contributors to this volume are academic staff employed in nonteaching roles including educational development, writing centers, technology, research, and academic advising. Their chapters speak to their experiences and consequences of the invisible, affective realm of labor in higher education. At the same time, they demonstrate the significance of that emotional labor for student success.

Cassuto, Leonard. 2015. *The Graduate School Mess: What Caused It and How We Can Fix It*. Cambridge, MA: Harvard University Press.

The author argues that the doctoral curriculum must broaden its definitions of success to allow students to create more fulfilling lives within and beyond the academy, noting that doctoral faculty rarely prepare graduate students for the work that they actually go on to do. Offering advice for building a more student-centered approach, the book follows the student trajectory from admissions to the dissertation and placement, considering the unexamined historical assumptions that frame each stage of graduate education and suggesting new practices to support diverse PhD career outcomes.

Cassuto, Leonard, and Robert Weisbuch. 2021. *The New PhD: How to Build a Better Graduate Education*. Baltimore: Johns Hopkins University Press.

This book is a reimagining of the value of the PhD outside of academic jobs. The authors provide a toolbox for supporting graduate education reform that prepares graduate students for an array of career possibilities. They summarize reform efforts and share innovations in career-diverse graduate education.

Caterine, Christopher L. 2020. *Leaving Academia: A Practical Guide*. Princeton: Princeton University Press.

The author provides advice for grads and scholars in any field for finding employment outside of higher education. Drawing upon interviews with employers as well as professionals who left, the book charts a path for academics seeking a career change.

Fruscione, Joseph, and Kelly J. Baker, eds. 2018. *Succeeding Outside the Academy: Career Paths Beyond the Humanities, Social Sciences, and STEM.* Lawrence: University Press of Kansas.

    Authors in this essay collection offer their perspectives, advice, and cautionary wisdom gleaned from their employment and careers outside the professoriate and higher education. With professions including realtors, freelance editors, writers, and librarians, the authors share their transitions to rewarding possibilities beyond the publish or perish mindset.

Gallagher, Patrick, and Ashleigh Gallagher. 2020. *The Portable PhD: Taking Your Psychology Career Beyond Academia.* Washington, DC: American Psychological Association.

    For graduate students in psychology, readers learn about assumptions of academic culture and explore skills in how to build their networks, navigate different kinds of employment, and communicate their academic skills to hiring managers.

Horinko, Leanne M., Jordan M. Reed, and James M. Van Wyck, eds. 2021. *The Reimagined PhD: Navigating 21st Century Humanities Education.* New Brunswick, NJ: Rutgers University Press.

    Contributing authors in this volume provide new frameworks for graduate students, faculty, and administrators for understanding the current importance of a PhD. Focusing on key graduate experiences, including coursework, mentoring, teaching, research, and professional connections, the book normalizes career preparation incorporated into the graduate curriculum and multiple career possibilities for PhDs.

Kelly, Kevin, Kathryn E. Linder, and Thomas J. Tobin. 2020. *Going Alt-Ac: A Guide to Alternative Academic Careers.* Sterling, VA: Stylus.

    The authors offer practical advice for readers considering employment in non-faculty positions in higher education. Sections in the book include an introduction to what alt-ac means, exploring alt-ac careers, getting started, addressing common challenges, and the alt-ac career life cycle.

Pryal, Katie Rose Guest. 2019. *The Freelance Academic: Transform Your Creative Life and Career.* Chapel Hill, NC: Blue Crow Books.

    The author shares her story of creating her own career, which included a regular column in the *Chronicle of Higher Education*, after leaving employment in academia.

Robbins-Roth, Cynthia, ed. 2005. *Alternative Careers in Science: Leaving the Ivory Tower.* 2nd ed. Cambridge, MA: Academic Press.

Each chapter, authored by a scientist in a profession outside higher education, presents different career tracks for scientists, including job descriptions, expected skills, responsibilities, and advancement possibilities.

Rogers, Katina L. 2020. *Putting the Humanities PhD to Work: Thriving in and Beyond the Classroom.* Durham, NC: Duke University Press.

The author gives practical advice to humanities PhDs about career exploration beyond the academy, offers frameworks for reimagining scholarly success, and invites faculty mentors and advisors as mentors in graduate students' career considerations.

ABOUT THE CONTRIBUTORS

EDITORS

KAREN CARDOZO has provided consulting, coaching, and strategic communication services for individuals and institutions in higher education since 2013. After completing a BA in English from Haverford College (1988), she worked in career services and earned a master's in higher education administration at Harvard (1993). During and after pursuing her PhD in literary studies at the University of Massachusetts Amherst (2005), she held administrative and faculty roles across the Five College Consortium before gaining tenure in interdisciplinary studies at the Massachusetts College of Liberal Arts (2013–2017). Building off her experience leading the career discovery program at Williams College (2012–2013), Cardozo went on to lead career development at Hollins and Northeastern Universities (2018–2021), returning to the Five Colleges as a lecturer in women gender sexuality studies at UMass before launching her business full-time in 2023. She has published intersectional feminist studies of culture, labor, science, trauma, and higher education in *American Studies*, *Journal of Asian American Studies*, *Pedagogy*, *Profession*, and *Signs*, as well as "Academic Labor: Who Cares?" in *Critical Sociology* (2017). Using the holistic framework of authentic and brave career design, her forthcoming book coaches academics at all stages through robust self-assessment and multisector exploration toward meaningful work in a fulfilling life. karencardozophd@gmail.com

KATHERINE KEARNS was the assistant vice provost for student development and director of the Office of Postdoctoral Affairs for the University Graduate School at Indiana University Bloomington from 2019 to 2023. She received a BS in biology from Cornell University (1995) and a PhD in ecology from the University of Georgia (2000). Kearns was a member of the instructional faculty in biology at Boston University, where her professional interests in mentoring graduate students began. In 2005, she joined Instructional Support Services at Indiana University, where she led workshops, did coaching sessions, and facilitated learning communities specifically for the graduate student instructor community. In this position she cultivated communities and resources that promote graduate students' well-being and skill development in scholarly and creative activity, teaching, and preparation for careers in a variety of post-degree professions. Kearns has collaboratively authored articles in *To Improve the Academy* and *Teaching and Learning Inquiry* about the role of communities in graduate student development, especially for students with marginalized identities. She is a coeditor of the book *Teaching as if Learning Matters: Pedagogies of Becoming by Next-Generation Faculty* (Indiana University Press, 2022). katiekearnsphd@gmail.com

SHANNAN PALMA is cofounder and co–executive director of the Autistic Self-Reliance Support Network, cofounder of Independence Through Interdependence Assistive Technologies Inc., and vice president of continuing education for HER Academy. She earned a BA in English, rhetoric and composition, from The Ohio State University (2000) and a PhD in women's, gender, and sexuality studies with a PhD certificate in film and media studies from Emory University (2012). Her dissertation won the 2012 biennial Kore Award for Best Dissertation in Women and Mythology, and her research has been published in *Marvels & Tales: The Journal of Fairy-Tale Studies* and various edited volumes. Palma has appeared on numerous panels advising graduate students on industry and higher ed careers beyond the professoriate. After earning her doctorate, she successfully pivoted her academic expertise to work first in diversity and inclusion and later in marketing and communication at her PhD-granting institution. This path culminated in a hybrid faculty–administrative role in which she founded a graduate program in writing and digital communication at a small liberal arts college in Decatur, Georgia, prior to transitioning into her current roles. In her spare time, Palma co-hosts a podcast, *Once Upon a Patriarchy*, bridging her doctoral research interests with her activism to dismantle oppressive sociocultural systems. shannan.palma@gmail.com

FOREWORD AND AFTERWORD

NATALIE LUNDSTEEN is assistant dean for student affairs at the Anne Burnett Marion School of Medicine at Texas Christian University. For nine years, she was assistant dean for career and professional development at UT Southwestern Medical Center, managing career and professional development programs and resources for postdoctoral researchers and graduate students, and has advised and taught postdocs, graduate students, and alumni at Boston University, MIT, Oxford University, and Stanford University. Lundsteen is a PhD career advice contributor to *Inside Higher Ed*'s weekly *Carpe Careers* blog, coauthor of *ReSearch: A Career Guide for Scientists*, and past president of the Graduate Career Consortium, an international organization comprised of professionals leading career and professional development for postdocs and PhDs. She earned a PhD in education from the University of Oxford in 2011.   n.lundsteen@tcu.edu

TREVOR M. VERROT is the graduate career coach at the Walter Center for Career Achievement in the College of Arts and Sciences at Indiana University Bloomington. By offering one-on-one career coaching, coordinating career development workshops, and facilitating graduate career exploration groups, he provides career and professional development support to graduate students in the arts and sciences. Verrot earned an MPhil in medieval art and architecture from Yale University in 2010.   tmverrot@iu.edu

ESSAY CONTRIBUTORS

SARAH K. BARKS is senior director of STEM career communities and analytics in the Center for Careers, Life, and Service at Grinnell College, where they advise students on careers in STEM fields. Their academic research focused on great ape social cognition and neuroanatomy. Barks earned a PhD in biological anthropology from Emory University in 2010.   barks@grinnell.edu

LEE SKALLERUP BESSETTE is the assistant director for digital learning in the Center for New Designs in Learning and Scholarship at Georgetown University. Her work involves the intersections of technology and pedagogy as they apply to teaching and learning. She is currently the editor of the *National Teaching and Learning Forum* newsletter and recently edited the collection *Affective Labor and Alt-Ac Careers* (University Press of Kansas, 2022). Her writing has appeared in *Inside Higher Ed*, *ProfHacker*, the *Chronicle of Higher Education*, *Educause Review*, and *Women in Higher Education*. Bessette co-hosts a podcast, *All The Things ADHD*, and in whatever spare time she has left, she sews. She has a PhD in comparative literature from the University of Alberta, Canada (2007).   lee.bessette@gmail.com

ALEXIS BOYER is assistant director, graduate student career services, at Massachusetts Institute of Technology, where she advises graduate students pursuing careers in industry and/or academe, plans and facilitates workshops and events, and creates professional development resources. Her professional interests include asynchronous career development resources and working parents, and she also enjoys gardening, paddleboarding, cooking, and spending time with family and friends. Boyer earned a PhD in biblical history from Boston University in 2018. aboyer@mit.edu

ALYSSA STALSBERG CANELLI is assistant dean of academic affairs in the Graduate School of Arts and Sciences at Brandeis University, where she develops academic and curricular policy, supports holistic academic and professional development for graduate students, and triages the administrative or student crisis of the day. She has given multiple invited talks about diverse career pathways for humanities PhD students and the impact of identity on the supervisor–intern dynamic. She volunteers with the First Call program at the Massachusetts Down Syndrome Congress, where she offers nonjudgmental support for parents who have received a diagnosis of trisomy 21. Alyssa earned her PhD in English from Emory University in 2017. alyssacanelli@gmail.com

KIMBERLY CREASAP is currently the director of the Susan Hirt Hagen Center for Civic and Urban Engagement at Wittenberg University, where she leads community-engaged teaching and research initiatives. She is the author of *Making a Scene: Urban Landscapes, Gentrification, and Social Movements in Sweden*, published in 2022 by Temple University Press. Her current research project, "Small Town Pride," focuses on the development of LGBTQ+ civil rights groups in small Midwestern towns. Creasap earned her PhD in sociology from the University of Pittsburgh in 2014. creasapk@wittenberg.edu

DORIAN RHEA DEBUSSY is the inaugural director of external affairs at Equitas Health, which is one of the largest LGBTQ+ and HIV/AIDS–serving healthcare organizations in the country. Rhea is responsible for setting the government and community relations agenda for the agency. She is the lead author of the Modern Military Association of America's 2023 *Freedom to Serve: The Definitive Guide to LGBTQ Military Service*, third edition, and has a book under contract with Columbia University Press. Rhea also currently serves as a lecturer in women's, gender, and sexuality studies at The Ohio State University at Newark. Additionally, she is the founder of the Ace and Aro Alliance of Central Ohio, which is Ohio's first asexual and aromantic organization; a member of the advisory board for the TGX360 Initiative of the OUT Georgia Business Alliance, which is Georgia's first transgender-focused economic empowerment initiative; and an organizational representative to the Public Policy Council of AIDS United, which is a national nonprofit organization dedicated to ending the HIV/AIDS epidemic in the United States. Rhea earned her PhD in political science from the University of Connecticut in 2018.   rheadebussy@equitashealth.com

HEATHER DWYER is an associate director for teaching, learning, and inclusion at the Center for the Enhancement of Learning and Teaching at Tufts University, where she supports instructors across disciplines in their teaching endeavors. Her article "A Mandatory Diversity Workshop for Faculty: Does It Work?" was published in 2020 and "A Call to Interrogate Educational Development for Racism and Colonization" in 2022. She is actively engaged in investigating the ways that educational development reflects and perpetuates racist structures. Heather earned her PhD in ecology from University of California, Davis, in 2014. heather.dwyer@tufts.edu

CLARE FORSTIE is a teaching consultant at the University of Minnesota, where they support graduate students, early-career faculty and instructors, and liberal arts colleagues in making their teaching more effective and inclusive. Clare's most recent book is *Queering the Midwest: Forging LGBTQ Community* (NYU Press, 2022); they have also published numerous articles focused on the social contexts of gender and sexuality. Their teaching, research, and writing addresses the complexities of queer and academic life through multiple critical lenses. Clare earned a PhD in sociology from Northwestern University in 2017.   forst122@umn.edu

SARAH CHOBOT HOKANSON is assistant provost and assistant vice president for research development and PhD and postdoctoral affairs at Boston University, where she develops resources to support faculty in obtaining and leading extramural funding programs and supports all aspects of PhD student and postdoctoral affairs. Her book chapter "Proactive Postdoc Mentoring" was published in 2018, and more recently she published work describing change models in diversity, equity, and inclusion initiatives in "Change Mapping Models to Diversify STEM Faculty as Practiced by Alliances for Graduate Education and the Professoriate," published in 2022. Hokanson is interested in developing inclusive and trainee-centered graduate and postdoctoral training environments through reimagining how higher education is structured. She earned a PhD in biochemistry and molecular biophysics from the University of Pennsylvania School of Medicine in 2010. sch1@bu.edu

JESSICA A. HUTCHINS is a lecturer and interim director of the John Martinson Honors Program at Southern Illinois University Edwardsville. Her academic interests include postcolonial literature, digital humanities, and interdisciplinary education.

She previously worked as director of curriculum and graduate programs in the Division of Biology & Biomedical Sciences at Washington University School of Medicine, integrating humanistic skills and concepts into STEM graduate education. In that role, she developed innovative curricula with funding from the National Institutes of Health and the Burroughs Wellcome Fund. Dr. Hutchins has published on career development training in graduate education, the application of narrative theory to the field of science communication, and gender in postcolonial Caribbean literature. She has also written for *Inside Higher Ed*'s *Carpe Careers* blog and is the editor of the *Texaco Wiki*, a knowledge base on the novel *Texaco* by Patrick Chamoiseau. She earned her PhD in comparative literature from Washington University in St. Louis in 2014. jesshut@siue.edu

CARRIE L. IWEMA is a senior UX strategist with WONDROS and a contractor for the National Institutes of Health, where she focuses on the user experience of researchers in the *All of Us* Research Program. She earned a PhD in neuroscience from SUNY Upstate Medical University (2001) and was a postdoctoral associate at Yale University School of Medicine (2001–2005). She also earned a master's in library science from Southern Connecticut State University (2005) and a UX immersion certificate from CareerFoundry (2022). iwemac@gmail.com

BARBARA JACOBY is a higher education consultant with Barbara Jacoby Consulting. Dr. Jacoby served the University of Maryland for more than forty years in several roles focusing on service-learning, civic engagement, and commuter students. Her current scholarship centers on high-impact educational practices and all forms of experiential learning, with an emphasis on critical reflection, service-learning, civic and community engagement, and the on- and off-campus partnerships that underlie this work. In addition, she focuses on the educational experience of the 85 percent of college students who are variously known as commuter, nontraditional, and adult students. Dr. Jacoby's publications include seven books and many articles and chapters. Her most recent book is *Service-Learning Essentials: Questions, Answers, and Lessons Learned* (Jossey-Bass, 2015). She currently serves as contributing editor for civic engagement for the *Journal of College and Character*. She writes and consults extensively and makes keynote speeches and leads workshops around the world. Dr. Jacoby earned her PhD in French language and literature from the University of Maryland in 1978. bgjacoby@gmail.com

KRISTINE LODGE is a senior partner success manager at PartnerHero Inc., where she is responsible for creating and implementing strategies to support internal and external partner growth. She collaborates with colleagues across the world and helps a variety of organizations achieve their business goals. Lodge previously worked in higher education administration as well as recruiting. She is also the founder of her own coaching business, Incipit Career LLC, where she assists academics and PhDs with career pivots from academia into other industries. Her work on the career transition and development of PhDs has appeared in the Muse and Fast Company. She has been featured on podcasts and in Christopher Caterine's *Leaving Academia: A Practical Guide*. Her interests include PhD career development and career transition as well as LBGTQIA+ community advocacy and support. She also knits, stand-up paddleboards, bakes, and spends time with her wife, two kids, and an opinionated cat. Lodge earned a PhD in English literature with a concentration in medieval studies from the University of Oregon in 2010.   kristi@incipitcareer.com

DAVID A. MCDONALD is the director of the Biological and Biomedical Sciences Program at the University of North Carolina at Chapel Hill, where he supports PhD students in transitioning to graduate school, fostering an inclusive community, and developing strong relationships with mentors. He is the author of multiple articles for the *Carpe Careers* blog for *Inside Higher Ed*. McDonald's interests include advocating for the needs of students and considering how graduate education can better provide the personal and professional development that students need for fulfilling careers. He earned a PhD in genetics and genomics from Duke University in 2013.   david.mcdonald@unc.edu

JACOB MCWILLIAMS completed this chapter while working as a learning program specialist at Denver Public Library. He is currently the learning and development manager at Jefferson Center for Mental Health, a nonprofit that offers behavioral health and substance use services in communities across Colorado. Jacob earned his PhD in learning sciences from Indiana University in 2015. jakemcwilliams14@gmail.com

LEIGH TILLMAN PARTINGTON is communications manager for the Department of Family and Preventive Medicine at Emory University School of Medicine, where she provides faculty development support and internal and external communications expertise. Her interests include unleashing the confident writer hidden within every hesitant writer, reading way past her bedtime, traveling, and spending time with her family. Partington earned her PhD in twentieth century English and Irish literature from Emory University (1999) and an MFA in creative writing from the University of Montana (1994).   leigh.partington@emory.edu

RYAN RIDEAU is the assistant provost of faculty development at Tufts University, where he creates comprehensive and strategic faculty development efforts. He was previously the associate director for teaching, learning, and inclusion at the Center for the Enhancement of Learning and Teaching, also at Tufts. His article "We're Just Not Acknowledged: An Examination of the Identity Taxation of Full-Time Non-Tenure-Track Women of Color Faculty Members" was published in 2021 and "The Experiences of Non-Tenure-Track Faculty Members of Color with Racism in the Classroom" was published in 2020. Rideau is interested in continuing to imagine and work toward the creation of anti-racist and just higher education spaces. He earned his PhD in higher education from Virginia Tech in 2017. Ryan.Rideau@tufts.edu

MARISELLA RODRIGUEZ is the inclusive teaching manager in the Center for Teaching and Learning at the University of California, Berkeley. She partners with campus educators to design and assess equitable and inclusive learning environments. Marisella has authored several publications, including "A Call to Interrogate Educational Development for Racism and Colonization" in 2022 and "Data-Driven Iterative Refinements to Educational Development Services: Directly Measuring the Impacts of Consultations on Course and Syllabus Design" in 2022. In her work as an educational developer, Marisella seeks to explore ways educators can dismantle racist structures in higher education. She earned a PhD in political science at the University of California, Davis, in 2018. marisella@berkeley.edu

KRISTINE M. SIKORA is the associate dean and director of recruitment, marketing, and communications in the Graduate School at the University of Colorado Anschutz Medical Campus, where she develops and implements strategies for the recruitment of graduate students to advanced degree programs, with specific emphasis on initiatives that increase diversity, equity, and inclusion. Her interests include advocating for students from underrepresented backgrounds in STEM and developing innovative methods for prospective student outreach. She also enjoys exploring new creative outlets, reading, movies, and spending time with her family. Sikora earned a PhD in Cellular and Molecular Biology from the University of Michigan Ann Arbor in 2012. kristinesikora@gmail.com

SARAH SILVERMAN is an educator focusing on instructional design, disability studies, and educational technology. She currently teaches women's studies and disability studies at University of Michigan–Dearborn. She previously worked as an instructional designer at the Hub for Teaching and Learning Resources at UM Dearborn, the program facilitator at the Delta Program for Research, Teaching, and Learning at University of Wisconsin–Madison, and a graduate teaching consultant and learning community coordinator at University of California, Davis. Sarah speaks to various higher education audiences on the subjects of neurodiversity and pedagogy against academic surveillance. She received her PhD from UC Davis in 2019. sarahsil@umich.edu

STACEY E. WAHL is the senior instructional designer at the VCU School of Medicine, where she supports faculty to deliver innovative instruction and advance medical and graduate education, while being whole and complete people. She is the author of several scientific publications about oligodendrocyte differentiation and orofacial development. As a medical librarian, Stacey published a paper detailing a successful postdoctoral outreach program, "Partnering with Postdocs: A Library Model for Supporting Postdoctoral Researchers and Educating the Academic Research Community," and won a Best Paper Presentation award for her work "Bringing Postdocs into the Fold: A Targeted Approach to Reaching an Underserved Health Sciences Population." Her interests include using collaboration to push boundaries and provide innovative support to students and faculty, making greeting cards, and marveling at the crazy things cats will do while staring at you like nothing is happening. Stacey earned a dual PhD in biomedical sciences from Rutgers University and Rutgers Biomedical Health Sciences in 2014. Stacey.wahl@vcuhealth.org

KATHARINE (KATIE) P. WALSH is the associate director of learning support programs at Carnegie Mellon University's Student Academic Success Center. At the SASC, Katie manages peer tutors and supplemental instruction leaders, in addition to developing course-aligned workshops and programs. Katie has authored several articles on teaching and learning, including "How Search Committees Assess Teaching" (2022) in *To Improve the Academy* and "Equivalent but Not the Same: Teaching and Learning in Full Semester and Summer Courses" (2019) in *College Teaching*. In addition to her role at the SASC, Katie also teaches courses in the Department of History and Dietrich College's first-year Grand Challenge program. She earned a PhD in history from the University of Pittsburgh in 2014. kpwalsh@andrew.cmu.edu

DIEDRA M. WRIGHTING is executive director of the ADVANCE Office of Faculty Development at Northeastern University. She collaborates with faculty and university leadership to identify faculty development needs and is dedicated to creating dynamic and impactful programming that helps elevate faculty to their highest potential. Her research and recent article, "Teaching Undergraduates to Communicate Science, Cultivate Mentoring Relationships, and Navigate Science Culture," highlights how mentoring relationships foster belonging and persistence in STEM fields. Dr. Wrighting holds a BS in biology from Howard University and a PhD in genetics from Harvard Medical School. She completed her postdoctoral training in diabetes genetics translational research at the Broad Institute of MIT and Harvard.   d.wrighting@northeastern.edu

INDEX

A

AAU (Association of American Universities), 3, 306
ABD (all but dissertation), 105
able-bodiedness, 73–74
abnormal psychology, 117
About Campus (magazine), 153
academia. *See* ambivalence, in academia
academic administration, 26, 95–98
academic affairs, 26, 86, 93, 150, 154, 281, 294; career paths to, 295–97, 300; Graduate School of Arts and Sciences at Brandeis University, 67, 73; LGBTQ+ centers, 300
academic identity, 1, 32, 36, 45, 185–86
academic librarianship, 116
Academy for Excellence in Teaching and Learning, 155
Accelerating Science and Publication in Biology (ASAPbio), 123
accents, spoken, 141, 191–94, 203, 282
activism, 235, 268, 285, 295, 297
activities: academic, 312–13; learning sciences, 264
ADHD, 163, 166–67
adjunct instructors, 132, 254, 263
administration, academic, 26, 95–98
administrators, 109, 288
administrators, BU: career path to, 279–80, 285; changing perspectives, 283–84; with community and social network, 246, 278–79, 282–84; creating sense of belonging for others, 290; evolution of duties, 280; with family, 246, 278–79, 282–84, 286–90; with identity in workplace, 282–83; with perfection and balance, 289; role of, 277–78; 280–82; as social worker, 285–89; with triage rubric, 286; with trust and transparency, 284–85
Advanced People Search, LinkedIn, 59
advice: for academic administration careers, 95–98; for administrators, 289; for boundary spanners, 152–55; from career coaches, 201–2; on career development, 309–17; informational interviews, 61, 202, 316; on life and how to move forward, 189; from peer mentors, 257–59; from pracademic, 156; on queer careers, 301–3; for rediscovering writing and research voice, 164–68; sociological approach to ambivalence, 185–87; for STEM graduate students, 137; work–life balance, 140, 156
advising, 26, 213–14, 312
advisors, 103, 315; career, 206, 210, 212, 215–16, 221; on DEI, 267, 268; dissertation, 35, 71, 238, 251–52; graduate student, 214–15, 251–53, 290; master's thesis, 49, 52; professional development, 67; thesis, 49, 52, 213, 257. *See also* career advisors, in STEM; mentors
advocacy: fatigue, grief and, 271–72; healthcare, 247, 297–98; for transgender rights in athletics, 298; work, 10, 245, 285. *See also* LGBTQ+ advocacy
Afghanistan, 295, 297
African Americans, 86, 97, 194, 233, 234, 269, 270; Black feminists, 242; Black queer women, 79; Office of African-American Affairs, 235. *See also* Black woman scientist
African American studies, 234, 235
Ahmed, Sara, 245

Alfred P. Sloan Foundation, 307
all but dissertation (ABD), 105
Alpha, 4
alt-ac, 3, 305
alumni, networking with, 312, 314–15, 316
Alumni Tool, LinkedIn, 59, 315
ambivalence: research on, 174; as sociological phenomenon, 173, 185–87; tenure track, 171, 175, 186; uncertainty and, 7, 11, 43, 49, 234–37, 243, 255
ambivalence, in academia: as common experience, 141, 171, 185–86; decision-making framework, 140, 185–87; faculty and teaching, 181–83; in/visibility in rural Midwest, 171, 179–81; jumping off tenure-track treadmill, 183–85; with marginalization and privilege, 140, 171; "playing the game," 140, 171, 176–79; social contexts, 172–75
American and New England studies, 172
American Sociology Association, 301
anatomy, human, 136
Andrew W. Mellon Foundation, 77, 307
Anglo Saxons, 190, 197
anthropology, biological, 132, 136
anti-racism, 233–34, 239
Antiracism, Equity, and Inclusion Subcommittee, Tufts University, 239
Arbery, Ahmaud, 233
art historians, 116
articles, 161, 267; books and, 153; peer-reviewed, 95, 160, 164, 166, 167
arts, 61, 67, 73, 87, 91, 221, 268–69. *See also* liberal arts
ASAPbio (Accelerating Science and Publication in Biology), 123
Asia, 149
assessments: institutional research and, 26; self-, 53–54, 316
assistant professors, 17, 24, 30, 75, 101–4, 243, 295–96
Association of American Colleges and Universities, 154
Association of American Medical Colleges Group on Research, Education, and Training, 93
Association of American Universities (AAU), 3, 306
Association of Health Information Professionals, 123
associations: national, 147, 151; professional, 58, 151, 154
athletics, transgender rights in, 298
Atlantic (magazine), 209

B

Baby-Sitters Club series, 163, 167
Baker, Kelly J., 3
basic science: careers beyond, 128; dismissal of, 186; librarians, 116, 121–22; research, 117, 125; transferable skills, 83, 115, 121, 122
Beck, Martha, 205
Becoming Abolitionist (Purnell), 242
Bell, Derrick, 241
belonging, 36, 39, 46, 174, 277, 283, 290
bench research, 118–21, 123–25, 127, 289
bifurcation: of identity, 212; of life, 190, 192, 200
biological anthropology, 132, 136
biological sciences, 86, 90–93
biology, 31, 32, 123
biomedical libraries, 121–22, 127
biomedical science, 19, 22, 51
bioscience, 92, 93–94
BIPOC (Black, Indigenous, and People of Color): community, 299; faculty, 140, 182, 236–37, 241; professionals with racial justice work, 233; with racial identity and belonging, 174; racial inequality and, 182; research on doctoral students, 239; staff, 137, 241; students, 137, 233, 235, 237, 239, 241, 262
Black feminists, 242
Black Lives Matter, 86, 97, 233, 269
Black queer women, 79
Black woman scientist: at career crossroads, 49, 50–52; with destination

mapped, 52–54; emotions and mindset, 54–57; informational interviews, 59–62; mentoring networks, 57–59
Blake, Meredith, 192–93
blogs, 27, 90–91, 159, 162, 164
"body of work," 206
Bolles, Richard, 20
books, 34, 147, 153, 167, 214, 267; contracts with dissertations, 183, 184; on service-learning, 148–49
Boone (Mrs.), 144
Boston University (BU). *See* administrators, BU
boundary spanners, 144, 150, 152–55. *See also* pracademics
boundary-spanning: advice, 152–55; with joyful and balanced life, 189–90; pracademics, 11, 139–40, 143; student affairs and career reflections, 149–55
Brandeis University, 67, 72–73, 77–78
Bridges to the Baccalaureate Program: NIH, 51, 62–63; UMass Boston, 62
British Consulate General, Boston, 279–80, 285
Broad Institute, 49
Brooks, Katherine, 20
BU (Boston University). *See* administrators, BU
Building Professional Connections (Harvard University Faculty of Arts and Sciences Office of Career Services), 61
burnout, 185, 240, 245, 263, 270, 288; student, faculty, and staff, 230; on tenure track, 88–89; from writing and research, 165
buying out of teaching, with grant funds, 22

C

Campus Pride Index, 298
Canadian literature, 160
Canva, 111
Cardozo, Karen, 6
career advisors, 206, 210, 212, 215–16, 221
career advisors, in STEM: academic pathway to, 132–34; advice for graduate students, 137; duties and role of, 132, 134–36; on mentoring, research and teaching, 138; transferable skills of, 131, 132; with work culture, 136–37
career and professional development (CPD) educator, 90, 92–94
career coaches, 76–77, 102, 196–99, 200, 201–2, 308–9
career coaching, 53, 61, 141, 190–91, 305, 307–9, 317
career counselors, 27–28, 74, 76
Career Explorations Working Group (Career Jump Start), 52–53
career paths, 5, 208; academic affairs, 295–97, 300; adjuncting, 263; administrator at BU, 279–80, 285; boundary-spanning, 153–55, 189–90; chaos theory of, 13, 77; contingencies on, 68–73; creating, finding and opening, 8, 13–15, 309–10; crossroads, 49, 50–52, 261; DEI, 262–66; development plan steps on, 316–17; divergent, 44–45, 74–75, 139, 190, 202, 214, 219–20, 258–59, 285, 306; exploring options, 25–26; faculty, 24–25, 44, 171, 308; faculty development, 235–40; healthcare advocacy, 297–98; history, 40–41, 44, 45; humanities in STEM graduate education, 85–87; leaving higher education, 270–72; as limiting phrase, 17; luck on, 146, 225–26, 296; mapping destinations, 52–54; new directions, 22–23; PhD Career Pathways Project, 3, 307; prescribed, 17, 19–20, 22; queer in academia, 28–30; with side gigs, 68–70, 72, 74–75, 89, 201; at single institution, 153–55; with skills charted, 20–21, 29; subject librarians at medical libraries, 82–83, 116–17, 120–22; trail blazing, 17–18, 27–28, 125–27; with transferable skills, networking and professional

career paths (*continued*)
  development, 7; with values identified, 23–24
careers: advice, 95–98, 137, 152–56; advising as, 213–14; beyond basic science, 128; blogs, 27; broader definition for successful, 44–45; GPS metaphor with, 1, 50; Graduate Career Consortium, 93, 318n3; Harvard University Faculty of Arts and Sciences Office of Career Services, 61; Incipit Career, LLC, 199–200; from mommy track to new, 106–7; Navigating Careers in Higher Education series, 5; PhD diversity, 3, 317n1; of pracademics, 149–55; preparation, 7, 86, 93, 307; queer, 294–98, 301–3; research, 120, 316; stories, 196–99; technology, 126; uncertainty about, 49, 234, 235–37; with values identified, 23–24; women with family versus, 71. *See also* well-being, with fulfilling career
career versatility, in PhD education: big picture, 306–9; with career development, 309–17; networking and building community, 258, 314–16; self-knowledge and, 258, 310–11; self-knowledge to guide inquiry, 311–14; steps in career development plan, 316–17
Cassuto, Leonard, 2, 3, 306
Caterine, Christopher, 3
CELT (Center for the Enhancement of Learning and Teaching), Tufts University, 238
Center for New Designs for Learning and Scholarship (CNDLS), Georgetown University, 159
Center for the Enhancement of Learning and Teaching (CELT), Tufts University, 238
centers for teaching and learning (CTL), 31–32, 38–40, 43–44, 153, 238–39, 245, 312

certified mentor trainer, 63
CGS (Council of Graduate School), 3, 307, 317n1
chaos theory, of career paths, 13, 77
Charlton, Brittany, 196
chemistry, 279, 282
Chickering, Arthur, 146
childcare, 210, 279, 290
childhood trauma, 72
chimpanzee research, 11, 132
Chronicle of Higher Education (newspaper and website), 134, 153
Circinus, 4, 12n1
City College of San Francisco, 51
class: elitism and, 41, 125, 138, 174–75, 181–82, 295; teaching with status of second, 36, 37, 39–40, 177–78; working, 141, 189–95, 197–98, 203. *See also* middle class
classism, 141, 262
close readings, 70, 101–2, 106, 108, 113, 213
CNDLS (Center for New Designs for Learning and Scholarship), Georgetown University, 159
code switch, 191, 193, 203
Cohn, Jenea, 96
Colbert, Stephen, 193–94
College of Liberal Arts and Human Sciences, Virginia Tech, 236
College of William and Mary, 103
coming out, LGBTQ+, 29, 141, 190, 195, 297
communications: funding, 111; skills, 85, 94, 102, 124, 134, 208, 224, 284
communications manager, medical school: from mommy track to career as, 106–7; stay-at-home parents with transferable skills, 112; from tenure track to mommy track, 101–6; value of humanities PhDs, 108–12, 113
communities, 173; BIPOC, 299; campus-based faith, 154–55; COVID-19 pandemic and, 257, 268–69; disability, 73–74, 164, 259, 281;

INDEX 343

LGBTQ+, 164, 180–81, 300; life and importance of, 186; loss of, 184; networking and building, 258, 314–16; neurodivergent, 79, 167, 246; queer, 179; as social network, 246, 278–79, 282–84; student affairs, 150–51; supportive, 11. *See also* peer mentoring, graduate students

community college, 40–41, 138, 152, 176

community of practice, 39, 246, 250, 256, 258, 269; learning sciences, 264–65; as toolkit, 253–54

community service, 147–48, 152, 156

commuter students, 146–47, 153

comparative literature, 11, 85, 160, 161

compartmentalization, 72, 79, 283

Complaint! (Ahmed), 245

conferences, 150, 151, 153, 167

Connected Academics, 307

Connected PhD program, 77–78

constellations: of contingencies and possibilities, 67, 76–78; stellar, 4, 12n1

consultants, teaching, 184–85

consultations, service-learning, 148, 149

consulting program, for TAs, 39

contingencies: with absence of necessity, 74; emotional struggles and, 79; with geography and quality of life, 79; key takeaways, 78–79; planning for, 79–80; possibilities and, 67, 76–78; as provision for unforeseen events, 74, 75; with risk thresholds, 78–79; scene 1 on career path, 68–69; scene 2 on career path, 69–73; scene 3 on career path, 73; support networks and, 78–79; as unpredictable future events, 73–74; at work, 73–76

contingent faculty, 159, 161

continuing education, 123

Core Curriculum Webinar #7, 58

Cornell University, 279

Council of Graduate School (CGS), 3, 307, 317n1

courses: faculty development, 39; service-learning, 143, 149, 151, 152

cover letters, 76–77, 183, 213

COVID-19 pandemic, 1, 86, 184, 186, 215, 263; communities and, 257, 268–69; mental health and, 103, 284, 309; skills acquired during, 165–66; work–life balance and, 102–3

CPD (career and professional development) educator, 90, 92–94

creative writing, 103–4, 224, 263

CRMs (customer relationship management systems), 200

CTL. *See* centers for teaching and learning

culture, 8, 10, 33, 124, 245–47, 312. *See also* work culture

curiosity, 83, 134, 165–66, 179, 202, 311–14

curriculum vitae (CV), 20, 25, 57, 165, 183, 268, 316. *See also* résumés

customer relationship management systems (CRMs), 200

CV (curriculum vitae), 20, 25, 57, 165, 183, 268, 316

D

"dark woods" moments, 205

data analysis, 3, 9, 123, 135, 136, 226

Data-Sitters Club, 163, 167

debt, 68, 104, 174, 223

decision-making: ambivalent framework for, 140, 185–87; to navigate career uncertainty, 235–37; self-reflection with, 314; trauma and intuitive, 72; values-driven, 9, 87–90, 139

Defoe, David, 56

DEI. *See* diversity, equity, and inclusion

depression, 90, 245, 270

digital humanities, 69, 71, 167

digital identity, 169

digital learning, 159

Dinner with a Mentor speaker series, 52

Disability and Access Services, BU, 281

disability community, 73–74, 164, 259, 281

disciplinary expertise, 9, 81, 83, 251

disciplinary identity, 155
disciplinary knowledge, 81, 87
disciplinary training, 9, 83
discounts, tuition, 101, 113
disenfranchised grief, 55–56
disillusionment, with graduate school, 37–40
dissertations, 104, 119, 145, 150, 161, 190, 196, 311, 315–16; ABD, 105; advisors, 35, 71, 238, 251–52; birthing, 70; with book contracts, 183, 184; completing, 179; completion fellowship grant, 77; defense committees, 267; nontraditional formats, 78; research, 35, 97, 132, 151, 180; with skills developed, 152; video, 265
diversity, 3, 34, 39, 58, 178–79, 235, 317n1
diversity, equity, and inclusion (DEI), 32, 228–29, 283, 284; career path to, 262–66; job market, 298; leadership and, 268, 269, 270; minority groups with, 10; need for, 261–62, 269–70; promotion of, 18, 29; purpose in higher education, 246, 266–73; role of, 267, 270; university offices and positions, 26; work, 206
doctoral education, 3, 70, 85, 210
doctoral students: first-generation, 198; research on BIPOC, 239
Doka, Kenneth, 55
Down (trisomy 21) syndrome, 72, 79
dreams, 22, 220, 242
dropping out, 35, 37, 75, 101, 105–6, 235

E

educational developers, 31–32, 43–46, 246, 250, 254, 256–58
educational development, 14, 40, 42, 249
elitism, 41, 125, 138, 174–75, 181–82, 295
emails, 60, 61, 110
emotions: baggage, 282–83; with coming out, 297; "dark woods" moments, 205; disillusionment and, 37–40; fatigue, 233, 240–42, 271–72; grief, 55–56, 271–72; with identity shifts, 45–46; isolation, 36, 43, 46, 71, 210, 236, 245, 249, 258, 279; joy, 219, 221–23, 232, 241, 257; with limiting mindsets, 54–57; microaggressions and, 96, 235, 240; processing struggles, 79; self-doubt, 46, 55, 104, 225; self-loathing, 71, 166; shame, 71, 75–76, 79, 187, 191, 201, 272, 293. *See also* burnout; impostor syndrome; mental health
engineering, 90–91
entomology, 249
entrepreneurship, 1, 141, 191–92, 199–201, 203, 280
Equitas Health, 298
equity, 50, 237, 239, 263, 269, 272. *See also* diversity, equity, and inclusion
"The Ever-Tightening Job Market for PhDs" (McKenna), 209
"Expand Your Network" guide, LinkedIn, 59

F

faculty: academic administration with staff roles and, 97; BIPOC, 140, 182, 236–37, 241; burnout, 230; career coaches for, 102; career path, 24–25, 44, 171, 308; contingent, 159, 161; Future Faculty Development Program at Virginia Tech, 237; Harvard University Faculty of Arts and Sciences Office of Career Services, 61; hierarchy between staff and, 95–96, 132, 136–37; life, 19–20, 22, 206, 237; marginalized, 207, 294; NCFDD, 58; positions versus STEM enrollment, 294; recruitment of, 137; research, 18, 19, 20, 90, 281, 307; rural Midwest and almost-, 171, 179–81; salaries, 136; with service-learning, 148–49, 151; with teaching ambivalences, 181–83; trans or nonbinary, 265
faculty development, 3, 14, 101, 143, 152, 156, 169; career uncertainty and path to, 235–40; courses, 39; foundation and

values, 233, 234–35; job searches, 164; LGBTQ+ workshops, 299; listserv, 183; NCFDD, 58; at Northeastern University, 50; private provider, 153; research and mentoring resources, 281; for service-learning, 148; staff, 111; workshops, 151, 299; with writing and research, 140, 159, 162–63
failure, 293–94
faith-based campus communities, 154–55
families: childcare, 210, 279, 290; coming out, 29, 141, 190, 195, 297; duties, 219, 221; fathers, 87, 127, 191, 193, 198–99, 201, 216; influence of, 191–94; lactation policies, 268; life, 67, 70–72, 74–75, 79, 104, 144–45, 159, 161, 163–64, 173–76, 181–82, 191–94, 207, 209–12, 214–16, 224, 233–34, 236–37, 239–40, 242, 246, 278–79, 282–84, 286–90, 296; maternity leave, 214; middle-class, 174, 179, 181, 193, 198–99; mommy track and, 103–7; motherhood, 82, 121, 212, 214–15, 278–79; mothers, 87, 141, 191–92, 197, 200–201; 9/11 and, 105; queer, 15, 71–72, 74–75, 79, 184; stay-at-home parents, 112; tuition discounts for, 101, 113; women with career versus, 71; working-class, 141, 189–95, 197–98, 203
fathers, 87, 127, 191, 193, 198–99, 201, 216. *See also* families
fatigue, emotional: grief, advocacy and, 271–72; racial battle, 233, 240–42
fellowships, 19, 68, 77, 119; CTL, 38, 39–40; digital humanities, 71; diversity, 178–81; research, 45; teaching, 45, 51–52, 155, 171
feral (rogue) librarians, 116, 120, 125
financial concerns: decision-making around, 23, 173, 178–79, 279; of funding, 111; for graduate students, 68–69; identity and, 15, 194; 195–201, 282; 297–98; new opportunities balancing, 28, 113, 123, 124–25, 132–33, 153, 168–69, 312; personal values and priorities

contrasted with, 23–24, 87–89, 105–6, 182–83, 220, 223, 231, 237; risks and, 78, 195–96; side gigs and, 67–75, 200–201; skill-building projects countering, 77; tenure security and, 37, 176, 198–99, 202, 295–96
first-generation students: college, 68, 86–87, 97, 144, 198, 219, 297; graduate, 75, 246
Five Colleges of Ohio, 294
Flaubert, Gustave, 144
Floyd, George, 97, 184, 233, 270
food stamps, PhDs and, 2
401(k), 195
fragmentation, 10, 206
French literature, 139, 143, 144, 149, 152
Friedman School of Nutrition, Tufts University, 239
Fruscione, Joseph, 3
funding, 34, 111, 118, 251–52, 286–87. *See also* grant funding
Future Faculty Development Program, Virginia Tech, 237

G

Gallagher, Ashleigh, 3
Gallagher, Patrick 3
gaps, in existing body of scholarship, 148
Garber, Marjorie, 97
Garriott, Omar, 59
gay people, 18, 29, 196, 297, 300
gender: with campus sexuality center, 179; equity, 50, 263, 272; inclusivity with housing policies, 299; race and, 210; studies, 175, 265, 294, 300; transgender, 11, 183, 246–47, 264–66, 268, 271–73, 298–300; Women & Gender Center at University of Colorado Denver, 262–63, 266, 268, 272
geography: BIPOC and, 140; in/visibility in rural Midwest, 171, 179–81; quality of life and, 79, 156; spoken accents and, 141, 191–94, 203, 282
Georgetown University, 159, 169
gigs, side, 68–70, 72, 74–75, 89, 201

Going Alt-Ac (Kelly, Linder, and Tobin), 3
GPS metaphor, with career, 1, 50
Graduate Career Consortium, 93, 318n3
graduate programs, 7, 33, 51, 118, 147, 190, 302; application fees, 175; choosing, 134–35; navigating, 252–53; tenure-track positions versus students in, 44
graduate school: disillusionment with, 37–40; expectations versus reality, 32–36; identity shifts, 40–44, 45–46; peers, 33–35, 36; "playing the game" with authenticity, 140, 171, 176–79; as professional development opportunity, 17, 20
Graduate School of Arts and Science, Brandeis University, 67, 73
Graduate Student Mental Health and Well-Being project, 205
graduate students: advice for STEM, 137; advisors, 214–15, 251–53, 290; first-generation, 75, 246; organization, 38; recruitment, 206, 220, 225. *See also* peer mentoring, graduate students
graduate surveys, 135–36
The Graduate School Mess (Cassuto), 3
graduate training, 7, 97–98, 305–6, 308, 311, 313, 316
grant funding, 19, 50, 77–78, 91, 95, 132, 281; buying out of teaching time with, 22; fellowship with professional development, 68; from Howard Hughes Medical Institute, 23, 25; jeopardizing, 307; proposals, 109; white, straight, cisgender scholars with, 294; writing, 92, 93, 102, 106–7, 111, 133, 267
Great Migration, 234
grief: advocacy, fatigue and, 271–72; disenfranchised, 55–56
Grogger, Jeffrey, 194

H

Halberstam, Jack, 293–94
happenstance, 8, 80, 163–64, 279
harm, generational, 273
Harvard Extension School, 53
Harvard Medical School, 51
Harvard T.H. Chan School of Public Health Alumni Affairs, 58–59
Harvard University Faculty of Arts and Sciences Office of Career Services, 61
HBCUs (historically Black colleges and universities), 18, 22–25, 177
health, 15, 58–59, 123, 298; NIH, 51, 62–63, 92–93, 277; profession requirements, 136. *See also* mental health
healthcare, 74–75, 195–96, 209, 295, 299; administrators, 109; advocacy, 247, 297–98; insurance, 2, 71, 72, 176, 300
heteronormativity, 293
HigherEdJobs (website), 134
Hillel, 154–55
hiring committees, 34, 175, 266
Hispanic-serving institutions (HSIs), 177
historically Black colleges and universities (HBCUs), 18, 22–25, 177
history: career paths, 40–41, 44, 45; with scarce funding opportunities, 34
homophobia, 192
housing, 145–46, 150, 153, 297, 299
Howard Hughes Medical Institute, 23, 25
How-To Talks by Postdocs, 123
HSIs (Hispanic-serving institutions), 177
humanists, 82, 85–86, 91–92, 94, 98, 209
humanities, 34, 97–98, 103, 145, 168; academic job market in, 86, 89, 104; digital, 69, 71, 167; value of PhDs, 108–12, 113
humanities, in STEM graduate education: advice for academic administration careers, 95–98; application of, 90–94; career path to, 85–87; values-driven decision-making and, 87–90
Human Resources, BU, 281
hybrid/online curriculum designer, 26
hybrid work arrangements, 1, 7, 180

I

identities: academic, 1, 32, 36, 45, 185–86; bifurcation of, 212; crafting blended positions and, 9, 139–41, 311; cultural, 33; digital, 169; disciplinary, 155; with diversity and intersectionality, 39; entrepreneur, 199–201, 203; forging new, 81; honesty about self-, 201; intellectual, 9, 139; LGBTQ+, 196, 264–65, 269; Mexican American, 255; minoritized, 18, 29, 236; multiple, 189; personal, 8–10, 13, 18, 43, 139, 190; queer, 25, 28–30, 190–91, 195–96; queer careers and working across, 302–3; racial, 174, 246; scientist, 50–51, 52, 54, 56, 57; shifts, 9, 40–44, 45–46, 81, 139, 168; undergraduate students, 32–33, 36; in workplace, 282–83. *See also* professional identities

Ikigai self-assessment, 53–54

impostor syndrome, 7, 38, 45, 108; dealing with, 35–36, 112, 219, 225–26, 231, 302; social contexts and, 180

Incipit Career, LLC, 199–200

inclusion, 239, 245. *See also* diversity, equity, and inclusion

Indeed (job search engine), 27, 53

independent researchers and writers: with freedom, 140, 159–63, 168–69; informational interviews with, 160; with life and work reframed on own terms, 163–68, 170; with voices lost and rediscovered, 159, 161–63, 169

Indiana University, 263–64

inequality, 164, 173, 182

information, 116, 123

informational interviews: advice, 61, 202, 316; conducting, 59–62; golden rule of, 59; networking and, 315; queer careers, 301; questions, 60–61; with researchers and writers, 160; résumés and, 60–63

inquiry, self-knowledge guiding, 311–14

Inside Higher Ed (website), 77, 153, 159

inside/outside-the-academy binary, 6–7

institutional research and assessment, 26

institutional structures, with culture, 8, 10, 245–47, 312

Institutional Transformation grant, National Science Foundation, 50

intellectual identity, 9, 139

inter/disciplinary transfer, 9, 81–83, 101, 314

International Students & Scholars Office, BU, 281

international studies, 295

Internet, 108, 162

internships, 78, 154, 167–68, 213–14, 235, 237, 315

intersectionality, 39

intersex people, 299

in/visibility, almost-faculty in rural Midwest, 171, 179–81

isolation, feelings of, 36, 43, 46, 71, 210, 236, 245, 249, 258, 279

J

Jacoby, Barbara, 149

January 6 insurrection (2021), 270, 271

job market, academic, 42, 88, 105, 169, 175, 181, 252, 303, 306–7, 309; economic reality of current, 75–76, 78; "The Ever-Tightening Job Market for PhDs," 209; evolution of, 17, 90; in humanities, 86, 89, 104; student affairs/DEI, 298; teaching effectiveness on, 34; temporary employment services registry, 106; tenure-track, 89, 101, 104, 112–13, 135, 180, 183, 298; transferable skills in, 106–7

job searches: *Chronicle of Higher Education*, 134, 153; by content-based key words, 53; faculty development, 164; HigherEdJobs, 134; LGBTQ+ centers and, 296; luck and, 72–73; queer careers, 301–3; retooling knowledge and skills for, 44;

job searches (*continued*)
  with self-confidence, 302; sites, 27, 53; by skill-based key words, 27, 53; tenure track, 211; terms, 27, 134, 310; word-of-mouth, 154
Jones, S. M., 266
Jossey-Bass, 148
journals, 264; medical, 102; peer-reviewed, 86, 92, 150, 153, 160, 164, 166, 167
joy, 219, 221–23, 232, 241, 257. *See also* life, joyful and balanced

K

Kee, C., 266
Kelly, Kevin, 3
King, Rodney, 234–35
Knefelkamp, Lee, 146, 150, 155
knowledge, 44, 45, 87, 167–68; production, 1, 81–82, 140; self-knowledge, 258, 310–14
Kohlberg, Lawrence, 146
Kolb, David, 146

L

labor, knowledge production as, 81–82
Labov, William, 193
lactation policies, 268
Latinx communities, 79, 266
Lave, Jean, 264
leadership: administrative burden for department, 109–10; DEI and, 268, 269, 270; Graduate School team, 228; marketing, recruitment and, 226; networking with, 93; opportunities or obstacles with changes in, 96; panelists for postdoc office, 284–85; public libraries, 273; student, 235–36; studies, 149, 152; subject librarians with few opportunities for, 125; teaching, mentoring and, 223–24; trans or nonbinary, 265
learning: CELT, 238; CNDLS, 159; CTL, 31–32, 38–40, 43–44, 153, 238–39, 245, 312; digital, 159; fellowships for teaching and, 155; SOTL, 148, 151–52; student, 25, 149–50, 152–53; teaching, being challenged and, 116–17. *See also* service-learning
learning management system (LMS), 86
learning sciences, 263–65
"leaving academe" discourse, 9, 139
"legitimate peripheral participation," 264
lesbians, 70–71, 79, 174, 189–90, 192
letting go, of scholarly output expectations, 164–65
LGBTQ+: Campus Pride Index, 298; centers, 245, 247, 293, 294, 296, 297, 298–301, 302; coming out, 29, 141, 190, 195, 297; community, 164, 180–81, 300; gay people, 18, 29, 196, 297, 300; identity, 196, 264–65, 269; intersex people, 299; lesbians, 70–71, 79, 174, 189–90, 192; nonbinary people, 11, 246, 265–66, 268, 272; Task Force, 296; transgender people, 11, 183, 246–47, 264–66, 268, 271–73, 298–300
LGBTQ+ advocacy: academic affairs, 295–97, 300; advice on queer careers, 301–3; functional roles of, 299–300; healthcare, 297–98; with LGBTQ+ center, 298–301; queer praxis and, 247, 293–94, 298, 303; transitioning to queer careers, 294–98
liaison librarians. *See* subject librarians, at medical libraries
liberal arts: college, 33, 42, 83, 131, 132, 176, 197–98, 236, 294–96, 298; education, 174, 306; training, 97, 311
librarians, 116, 120–22, 125. *See also* subject librarians, at medical libraries
librarianship, 83, 116, 121, 123, 124, 127, 128
libraries, 11, 26, 124; medical, 82, 115, 121–22, 127; public, 166, 261, 271–73
library science, 82, 121–22, 125, 126
life, 8, 13, 149, 152, 186, 205; bifurcation of, 190, 192, 200; Black Lives Matter, 86, 97, 233, 269; with disenfranchised grief, 55–56; faculty, 19–20, 22, 206, 237; family, 67, 70–72, 74–75, 79, 104,

144–45, 159, 161, 163–64, 173–76, 181–82, 191–94, 207, 209–12, 214–16, 224, 233–34, 236–37, 239–40, 242, 246, 278–79, 282–84, 286–90, 296; geography and quality of, 79, 156; reframing work and, 163–68, 170; work–life harmony, 23, 24. *See also* work–life balance

life, joyful and balanced: advice from career coach, 201–2; career stories, 196–99; entrepreneur identity, 199–201, 203; families and, 191–94; middle class and queer with benefits, 195–96; self-value and boundary-spanning, 189–90

Life Kit, NPR, 56

Lilly Teaching Fellow, 155

Linder, Kathryn E., 3

Linked (Garriott and Schifeling), 59

LinkedIn, 14, 27, 58–60, 112, 189, 202, 315

listservs, 178, 183

literature, 92, 117, 134, 148; comparative, 11, 85, 160, 161; French, 139, 143, 144, 149, 152; Québécois, 160, 163, 169–70; transferable skills with degree in, 146–47

LMS (learning management system), 86

luck: on career path, 146, 225–26, 296; happenstance and, 8, 80, 163–64, 279; job searches and, 72–73; making your own, 8, 13, 26

M

Mable, Phyllis, 156

Magolda, Marcia B. Baxter, 317n2

marching band, 116–17, 118

Mare of Easttown (TV show), 192–93

marginalization, 51, 266, 294; privilege and, 140, 171; of students, 206–7, 238. *See also* diversity, equity, and inclusion

marketing, 69, 92, 108–11, 135, 200, 225–30

Martin, Ann M., 167–68

Maslow, Abraham, 1–2

master of library science (MLS) degree, 121–22, 125, 126

master's thesis advisor, 49, 52

maternity leave, 214

MBSH (Minority Biomedical Scientists of Harvard), 51–52

McKenna, Laura, 209

McKinsey & Company, 104

medical journals, 102

medical librarianship, 121

medical libraries, 82, 115, 121–22, 127. *See also* subject librarians, at medical libraries

Medical Library Association (MLA), 123

medical school. *See* communications manager, medical school

medicine, 90–91, 113

medievalist, 141, 196, 197–98, 199

Melman, Bruce, 1

mental health, 10, 89, 212, 234, 245; COVID-19 pandemic and, 103, 284, 309; depression, 90, 245, 270; well-being and, 205, 249, 309. *See also* work–life balance

mentoring: leadership, teaching and, 223–24; LGBTQ+ center with, 297–98; Mutual Mentoring Program at Tufts University, 241, 242; resources for faculty research development, 281; student, 206, 224; teaching, research and, 138. *See also* peer mentoring

mentors, 179, 184, 187, 315; absence of supportive, 36; advisors, 35, 49, 52, 238, 251–52; on ambivalence in academia, 172; BIPOC students with staff, 235–36; of boundary spanners, 155; with burnout, 88–89; certified trainer, 63; cultivating networks for, 57–59; Dinner with a Mentor speaker series, 52; dissertation advisors, 35, 238, 251–52; faculty research, 19, 20, 90; on sociology PhDs, 175; student development theory, 146, 150, 156; to undergraduate students, 51–52

meritocracy, 172

Mexican American identity, 255

microaggressions, 96, 235, 240
microstructures, positive, 10, 245
middle class: families, 174, 179, 181, 193, 198–99; lifestyle, 191, 195–96, 203, 284, 300; upper-, 193, 203
mindsets: emotions with limiting, 54–57; publish or perish, 19, 106, 133, 140, 159–60, 211, 257; scarcity, 167, 271; "ungenerous thinking," 271
minorities: DEI work and, 206; groups, 10, 29, 119, 206; with inequality, 164; sexual, 196; URMs, 8, 14, 52, 57, 86, 110. *See also* BIPOC
minoritized identities, 18, 29, 236
Minority Biomedical Scientists of Harvard (MBSH), 51–52
misogyny, 71, 247, 261, 298
MLA (Medical Library Association), 123
MLA (Modern Language Association), 104, 151, 307
MLS (master of library science) degree, 121–22, 125, 126
Modern Language Association (MLA), 104, 151, 307
mommy track, 101–6
Monday Motivator, 58
motherhood, 82, 121, 212, 214–15, 278–79. *See also* families
mothers, 87, 141, 191–92, 197, 200–201. *See also* families
mountain gorillas, 133
MS (multiple sclerosis), 71
Mutual Mentoring Program, Tufts University, 241, 242
myIDP, 53

N

NASEM (National Academies of Sciences, Engineering, and Medicine), 90–91
national associations, student affairs, 147, 151
National Center for Faculty Development and Diversity (NCFDD), 58
National Institutes of Health (NIH), 51, 62–63, 92–93, 277
National Museum of Natural History, Smithsonian, 133
National Science Foundation, 50, 277, 307
National Zoo, Smithsonian, 133
Nature (magazine), 279
Navigating Careers in Higher Education series, 5
NCFDD (National Center for Faculty Development and Diversity), 58
needs, hierarchy of, 1–2
networking: advice for boundary-spanners, 154–55; with alumni, 312, 314–15, 316; community building and, 258, 314–16; with leaders, 93; LinkedIn tools for, 59; mentors, 57–59; opportunities from, 63; professional development, transferable skills and, 7; queer careers, 301; questions, 26, 316
networks: BU administrators with social, 246, 278–79, 282–84; risk thresholds and support, 78–79
neuroanatomy, 132, 133
neurodivergent communities, 79, 167, 246
neuroscience, 82, 116–18
The New PhD (Weisbuch and Cassuto), 2, 3, 306
Next Gen PhD (Sinche), 57
NIH (National Institutes of Health), 51, 62–63, 92–93, 277
9/11, 82, 101, 105, 119, 295
nonbinary people, 11, 246, 265–66, 268, 272
non-tenure-track contracts, term limits on, 2
Northeastern University, 50
Now What? Composing a Life of Meaning and Purpose (service-learning course), 149, 152
NPR, *Life Kit*, 56

O

Office of African-American Affairs, University of Virginia, 235
Office of Commuter Affairs, UMD, 146–48, 150–51, 156
Office of the Provost, BU, 280, 281, 282, 283, 285, 288
Office of the Provost and Senior Vice President, Tufts University, 239
Office of the Executive Vice President and Provost, Virginia Tech, 237
On Being Included (Ahmed), 245
online/hybrid curriculum designer, 26
online teaching, 186
optic neuritis, 71
organizational skills, 38, 134

P

panelists, postdoc office leaders, 284–85
parents, stay-at-home, 112. *See also* families
PDPA (Professional Development & Postdoctoral Affairs), BU, 280–81, 282
Pedagogical Partnership Program, Tufts University, 241
pedagogy, 39, 159, 241
peer mentoring, graduate students: advice and lessons learned, 257–59; with community of practice as toolkit, 253–54; dissertation feedback, 251–52; measures of success, 251; navigating graduate programs, 252–53; questions, 250; saying yes to new kind of success, 256–57; shaping spaces in higher education, 255–56; TAC Program, 246, 249–50, 253–58
peer review, 1, 93, 123, 151, 162, 251; articles, 95, 160, 164, 166, 167; journals, 86, 92, 150, 153, 160, 164, 166, 167
peers, graduate school experience, 33–35, 36
Perel, Esther, 250
perfection, balance and, 289

performance reviews, 93, 230
Perry, William, 146
personal identity, 8–10, 13, 18, 43, 139, 190
personality tests, 312
personal statements, 102, 107, 110
PhD, 108–13, 125, 145, 198, 239; basic science, 115, 121; career diversity, 3, 317n1; Connected PhD program, 77–78; disciplinary, 86, 175, 246; "The Ever-Tightening Job Market for PhDs," 209; *The New PhD*, 2, 3, 306; *Next Gen PhD*, 57. *See also* career versatility, in PhD education
PhD Career Pathways Project, CGS, 3, 307
PhD Education Initiative, AAU, 3, 306
PI (primary investigator), 118, 121
play, meaningful, 165–66
"playing the game," ambivalence in academia, 140, 171, 176–79
podcasts, 106, 162–63, 165–67, 250
police, 184, 235, 242, 269
political science, 247, 249, 297
Pollak, Lindsey, 1, 5
Posner, Paul L., 144
postdocs, how-to series for, 123
pracademics: from academic to, 143–49; advice from, 156; boundary-spanning, 11, 139–40, 143; career of, 149–55; defined, 144
predoctoral fellowships, 19
predominantly white institutions (PWIs), 174, 177, 236–37, 239
Presidential Awards, 123
presidents, at universities, 262, 265, 269
primary investigator (PI), 118, 121
primate neuroanatomy, 133
privilege, 183, 219, 221–22; marginalization and, 140, 171; race and, 174, 176, 195, 262, 284
professional associations, 58, 151, 154
professional development: advisors, 67; changing culture and practice of, 7, 44;

professional development (*continued*)
CPD educator, 90, 92–94; framework, 67; graduate programs and, 134–35; graduate school as opportunity for, 17, 20; libraries and, 122; opportunities, 38, 40; PDPA at BU, 280–81, 282; questions, 219–20; with skills charted, 21, 29; transferable skills, networking and, 7; undergraduate students, 51, 219–20; workshops, 27. *See also* peer mentoring, graduate students

Professional Development & Postdoctoral Affairs (PDPA), BU, 280–81, 282

professional identities, 10, 43, 69, 73, 190; evolution of, 8, 13, 18, 56, 212; shifting, 9, 41, 46, 139, 185; with social media, 101, 110

professors, 26, 213; assistant, 17, 24, 30, 75, 101–4, 243, 295–96; tenured, 17, 104, 201–2, 295

ProfHacker (website), 159, 168

project management, 206, 224, 226

proposals, grant, 109

protests, 1, 233, 242, 297

psychology, 116, 117, 126

publications, 93, 123, 151

public speaking, 94, 135, 137, 224, 226, 302

public statements, transparency, 269, 284–85

publish or perish mindset, 19, 106, 133, 140, 159–60, 211, 257

pull factors, 14, 31

Purdue University Press, 5

Purnell, Derecka, 242

push factors, 14, 31

PWIs (predominantly white institutions), 174, 177, 236–37, 239

Q

Québécois literature, 160, 163, 169–70

queer: in academia, 28–30; careers, 294–98, 301–3; diversity fellowships, 178–81; families, 15, 71–72, 74–75, 79, 184; identities, 25, 28–30, 190–91, 195–96; middle class with benefits, 195–96; praxis, 247, 293–94, 298, 303; students, 183. *See also* LGBTQ+

The Queer Art of Failure (Halberstam), 293–94

questions: graduate students peer mentoring, 250; informational interviews, 60–61; networking, 26, 316; professional development, 219–20

R

R1 institutions, 73, 176–78, 184, 199, 311

R2 institutions, 176

race, 174, 176, 194–95, 210, 262, 284

racial battle fatigue, 233, 240–42

racial diversity, 34, 235

racial equity, 237, 269

racial identity, 174, 246

racial inequality, 164, 182

racial justice, 207; in medicine, 113; work, 233–35, 237–43

racial realism, 241

racism, 173, 183, 233–35, 239, 241, 245, 261

Recalculating (Pollak), 1

recruitment, 29, 154, 190, 205, 215, 229, 267; graduate students, 206, 220, 225; leadership, marketing and, 226; of staff, 126, 137

recruitment director, 225–26

reimbursement process, 68–69

remote work arrangements, 1

Renn, Kristen A., 271

research: administration, 26; on ambivalence, 174; analysis, 3, 135; Association of American Medical Colleges Group on Research, Education, and Training, 93; basic science, 117, 125; bench, 118–21, 123–25, 127, 289; on BIPOC doctoral students, 239; career, 120, 316; chimpanzee, 11, 132; dissertation, 35, 97, 132, 151, 180; faculty, 18, 19, 20, 90, 281,

307; fellowships, 45; funding, 252; impostor syndrome with, 38; institutional assessment and, 26; LinkedIn, 202; as measure of success, 251; mentoring, teaching and, 138; new ways to, 166; R1 institutions, 73, 176–78, 184, 199, 311; R2 institutions, 176; Responsible Conduct of Research at BU, 280; science, 22, 25, 117, 125, 135; scientists with passion for, 222–23; skills, 7, 18, 20, 25, 91, 97, 102, 113, 126, 133–34, 178, 246; student affairs and, 150; teaching, service and, 81, 109, 313; teaching and, 22, 24–25, 33, 35–36, 37, 45, 105, 149, 176, 178, 262, 296, 312–13; tenure path and, 35; tenure track and, 177; training core manager position, 63; undergraduate students and, 63, 222; with undirected discovery, 124; universities, 18, 22, 35, 41, 43, 102, 104, 138; writing and, 140, 159, 163–68, 170. *See also* independent researchers and writers

Research Development, BU, 280

Responsible Conduct of Research, BU, 280

resting, to rediscover writing and research voice, 165

résumés, 190, 214, 226; building, 20, 51, 91; CVs, 20, 25, 57, 165, 183, 268, 316; informational interviews and, 60–63; with transferable skills, 76–77, 174, 268

Robbins-Roth, Cynthia, 3

rogue: going, 118–20, 124, 125, 127–28; librarians as feral or, 116, 120, 125

A Room of One's Own (Woolf), 106

S

salaries, 28, 72, 280, 294; cuts, 176, 295; for faculty and staff, 136; paid from discretionary funds, 111; with paid time off, 195; race, speech patterns and, 194; for subject librarians, 123, 124–25; substandard, 161; teaching, 88–89

Sandmann, Lorilee, 143

Sanford, Nevitt, 146

San Francisco State University (SFSU), 51

scarcity mindset, 167, 271

Schifeling, Jeremy, 59

scholarship of teaching and learning (SOTL), 148, 151–52

science: ASAPbio, 123; biological, 86, 90–93; biomedical, 19, 22, 51; bioscience, 92, 93–94; College of Liberal Arts and Human Sciences at Virginia Tech, 236; Graduate School of Arts and Science at Brandeis University, 67, 73; Harvard University Faculty of Arts and Sciences Office of Career Services, 61; information, 116; learning, 263–65; library, 82, 121–22, 125, 126; MLS degree, 121–22, 125, 126; NASEM, 90–91; National Science Foundation, 50, 277, 307; neuroscience, 82, 116–18; political, 247, 249, 297; research, 22, 25, 117, 125, 135; social, 135–36, 236, 251, 294; undergraduate students in, 116–17. *See also* basic science

scientific training, 83, 85, 86

scientists: as career advisors in STEM, 136; with curiosity as transferable skill, 81, 134; identity, 50–51, 52, 54, 56, 57; MBSH, 51–52; with passion for research, 222–23; with public speaking and writing, 94. *See also* Black woman scientist; subject librarians, at medical libraries

search terms, on job sites, 27, 310

self-assessment: career development with, 316; Ikigai, 53–54

self-confidence, 302

self-doubt, 46, 55, 104, 225

self-knowledge, 258, 311–14

self-loathing, 71, 166

self-reflection, 67, 73, 219, 271, 273, 309–11, 314

Seneca, 26

service, with teaching and research, 81, 109, 313
service-learning, 154; community-based, 140, 143, 148, 156; community service and, 147–48, 152, 156; courses, 143, 149, 151, 152; faculty with, 148–49, 151; student affairs and, 152, 155
Service-Learning Essentials (Jacoby), 149
sexism, 71, 299
sexuality center, gender and, 179
sexual minorities, 196
sexual orientation, 189, 299
SFSU (San Francisco State University), 51
shame, feelings of, 71, 75–76, 79, 187, 191, 201, 272, 293
"Shaping New Narratives About PhD Careers" (CGS), 317n1
Simula, Brandy, 6, 308
Sinche, Melanie V., 57
"SINner," 280
60 Minutes (TV newsmagazine show), 194
skills: acquired in COVID-19 pandemic, 165–66; charting, 20–21, 29; communication, 85, 94, 102, 124, 134, 208, 224, 284; developing new, 18, 27–28, 32, 39–40, 46, 112, 127–28, 159, 202, 205, 206, 214, 222, 224, 226–27, 258; dissertations and, 152; job searches and retooling knowledge and, 44; job searches by, 27, 53; nontraditional knowledge and, 45; organizational, 38, 134; research, 7, 18, 20, 25, 91, 97, 102, 113, 126, 133–34, 178, 246; side gigs and building, 69, 75, 89; STEM with writing and editing, 9; teaching, 132, 266; technical, 206, 224; toolkit, 38, 44, 227; VIPS, 310, 312; for writing and research, 163. *See also* transferable skills
Slim, Pamela, 206
Smelser, Neil, 173
Smithsonian Institution, 133, 134
social media, 101, 108, 110–11, 162, 163, 166, 315
social sciences, 135–36, 236, 251, 294

sociology, 140, 173, 175, 247, 294–97, 301
SOTL (scholarship of teaching and learning), 148, 151–52
specialization, 7, 169, 196
specialized institutions, 176
speech: accents, 141, 191–94, 203, 282; with race and perception, 194
spending gap, 262
Sponsors and Collaborators, 58
staff, 97, 111, 150, 235–36, 294; BIPOC, 137, 241; burnout, 230; hierarchy between faculty and, 95–96, 132, 136–37; recruitment of, 126, 137
Starchild Team, 12n1
stay-at-home parents, 112. *See also* families
STEM, 9, 11, 51, 57, 125, 126, 230, 279; advice for graduate students in, 137; enrollment versus faculty positions, 294; gender equity in faculty positions, 50; whites with percentage in, 34. *See also* Black woman scientist; career advisors, in STEM; humanities, in STEM graduate education
stipends, 68, 72, 103–5, 117, 199, 222, 251
stories, 190, 196–99
storytelling, 92, 141, 250
student (personnel) affairs: administrators with burnout, 288; career path, 143–49; conferences, 150, 151, 153; DEI offices within, 266; French literature and, 139, 143, 144, 149, 152; housing and, 145–46, 150, 153; International Students & Scholars Office at BU, 281; job market, 298; LGBTQ+ community and, 180–81; national associations, 147, 151; professional associations, 151, 154; reflections on boundary-spanning career, 149–55; service-learning and, 152, 155; student development theory and, 146, 150, 156; university offices and positions, 26. *See also* pracademic
student debt, 68, 104, 174, 223
student development theory, 146, 150, 156
student learning, 25, 149–50, 152–53

students, 126, 183, 224, 230, 236; BIPOC, 137, 233, 235, 237, 239, 241, 262; commuter, 146–47, 153; first-generation, 68, 75, 86–87, 97, 144, 198, 219, 246, 297; in graduate programs versus available tenure-track positions, 44; marginalized, 206–7, 238. *See also* graduate students

subject (liaison) librarians, at medical libraries: with basic science and transferable skills, 83, 115, 121, 122; benefits, 122–24, 127–28; career path of, 82–83, 116–17, 120–22; drawbacks, 124–25; "going rogue," 118–20, 124, 125, 127–28; salaries, 123, 124–25; scientists as, 115–16, 121; as trail blazers, 125–27; work–life balance for, 123–24

summer programs, 35, 51, 63, 220

surveys: graduate, 135–36; STEM enrollment versus faculty positions, 294

T

TAC (Teaching Assistant Consultant) Program, 246, 249–50, 253–58

TAs (teaching assistants), 34–40, 69, 86, 178, 223, 246, 249

Task Force, LGBTQ+, 296

Taylor, Breonna, 233, 270

teaching, 34, 87, 138, 152, 159, 175, 186, 239; adjunct instructors and, 132, 254, 263; anti-racist practices workshop, 233–34; CELT, 238; consultants, 184–85; with faculty ambivalences, 181–83; fellowships, 45, 51–52, 155, 171; learning, being challenged and, 116–17; mentoring, leadership and, 223–24; non-tenure-track positions, 145, 183; passion for, 35–36, 38–39, 116–17, 118, 161, 169, 178; research, service and, 81, 109, 313; research and, 22, 24–25, 33, 35–36, 37, 45, 105, 149, 176, 178, 262, 296, 312–13; roles, 26, 41, 104; salaries, 88–89; second-class status of, 36, 37, 39–40, 177–78; skills, 132, 266; SOTL, 148, 151–52; stipends, 103, 105; tenure track and, 179, 181–83. *See also* centers for teaching and learning

Teaching Assistant Consultant (TAC) Program, 246, 249–50, 253–58

teaching assistants (TAs), 34–40, 69, 86, 178, 223, 246, 249

technical skills, 206, 224

technology, 126, 159

temporary employment services registry, university, 106

tenure, 1, 17, 22, 37, 201, 262

tenure track: ambivalence, 171, 175, 186; available positions versus graduate students, 44; burnout and, 88–89; going rogue, 118–20; instability of, 296; job market, 89, 101, 104, 112–13, 135, 180, 183, 298; job search, 211; leaving, 176, 183–85, 279, 317; to mommy track, 101–6; non-tenure-track positions, 2, 43, 145, 149, 183, 257; R1 positions, 184; research-oriented, 177; teaching-oriented, 179, 181–83; traditional path, 31, 34–35, 38, 44, 45, 46, 73, 76, 137, 161, 202, 251, 295, 297

termination, 268

term limits, on non-tenure-track contracts, 2

terrorism, 82, 101, 105, 119, 295

thesis advisors, 49, 52, 213, 257

"Three Elements of Self-Authorship" (Magolda), 317n2

time: informational interviews and being on, 61, 62; for rediscovering writing and research voice, 168; salaries with paid time off, 195

Title IX, 299

Tobin, Thomas J., 3

toolkits: community of practice as, 253–54; MLA, 307; professional opportunities and building, 46; skills, 38, 44, 227

toxicity, 75, 96, 122, 263, 264

training, 9, 63, 83, 85, 86, 251, 267; graduate, 7, 97–98, 305–6, 308, 311, 313, 316;

training *(continued)*
  transferable skills and, 81–82, 89, 91, 92–94
transferable skills, 7, 57, 112, 219, 231, 302, 311; in academic job market, 106–7; basic science, 83, 115, 121, 122; boundary-spanning, 139–40, 271; of career advisors in STEM, 131, 132; curiosity as, 83, 134; developing new, 226–27; with literature degree, 146–47; for résumés, 76–77, 174, 268; training and, 81–82, 89, 91, 92–94
Transfer to Terp program, UMD, 151
transgender people, 11, 183, 246–47, 264–66, 268, 271–73, 298–300
transmisogyny, 247, 298
transparency, trust and, 284–85
trauma, 10, 70, 72, 245
triage rubric, 286
trisomy 21 (Down) syndrome, 72, 79
trust, 284–86
Tufts University, 238–39, 241–42
tuition, 101, 104, 113, 172, 222

U

UMass Boston, 62
UMD (University of Maryland), 144–52, 154, 156
uncertainty, 7, 11, 43, 49, 234–37, 243, 255. *See also* ambivalence
undergraduate students, 31, 35, 52, 88, 103, 116–17, 162; professional development, 51, 219–20; research and, 63, 222; "successful" identity of, 32–33, 36
underrepresented minorities (URMs), 8, 14, 52, 57, 86, 110
undirected discovery, research with, 124
unemployment, 196, 279
"ungenerous thinking" mindset, 271
universities, 3, 26, 106, 154, 261, 306; HBCUs, 18, 22–25, 177; presidents, 262, 265, 269; research, 18, 22, 35, 41, 43, 102, 104, 138
University of California, Davis, 249

University of Colorado Denver, 225, 262–63, 266, 268, 272
University of Connecticut, 297
University of Hawai`i at Mānoa, 221
University of Maryland (UMD), 144–52, 154, 156
University of Michigan, 223, 225
University of Montana, 103
University of Oxford, 297
University of Pennsylvania, 279
University of Pittsburgh, 295
University of Virginia, 235
URMs (underrepresented minorities), 8, 14, 52, 57, 86, 110
user experience (UX) strategy, 126

V

value, 108–12, 113; of being seen, 180; self-, 189–90; of self-knowledge, 258, 310–11
values: decision-making driven by, 9, 87–90, 139; faculty development with foundation and, 233, 234–35; with humanities in STEM graduate education, 87–90; identifying career, 23–24; personal, 10, 202, 205–7, 311; purpose aligned with, 245
values, interests, personality, and skills (VIPS), 310, 312
videos, dissertation, 265
violence, 234–35, 270, 271
VIPS (values, interests, personality, and skills), 310, 312
Virginia Tech, 236–37, 238
voices: accents, 141, 191–94, 203, 282; finding, 215–16, 224–26; inner, 205, 289; losing scholarly, 210–12; rediscovering writing and research, 159, 161–69; speaking softly, 213–14; whispering, 212–13

W

waivers, tuition, 104, 172
Weisbuch, Robert, 2, 3, 306
well-being, 205, 249, 298, 309

well-being, with fulfilling career: finding balance, 228–30; finding joy, 219, 221–23; finding strengths, 223–24; finding stride, 226–28; finding voice, 224–26; maintaining momentum, 230–32
Wenger, Etienne, 264
What Color Is Your Parachute? (Bolles), 20
Where Should We Begin? (Perel), 250
whiteness, 179, 234, 273, 294
whites, 34, 176, 194, 235, 300; privilege, 195, 262, 284; PWIs, 174, 177, 236–37, 239
white supremacy, 173, 261
Whitt, Kelly Kizer, 12n1
Winslet, Kate, 192–93
women, 57, 102, 295; lesbians, 70–71, 79, 174, 189–90, 192; motherhood, 82, 121, 212, 214–15, 278–79; mothers, 141, 191–92, 197, 200–201. *See also* Black woman scientist
Women & Gender Center, University of Colorado Denver, 262–63, 266, 268, 272
women's studies, 41, 174
Women's Studies Department, UMD, 154
Woolf, Virginia, 106
word-of-mouth job leads, 154
work: contingencies at, 73–76; hybrid arrangements, 1, 7, 180; identities at, 282–83; knowledge production as labor, 81–82; reframing life and, 163–68, 170

work culture: academic hierarchies influencing, 95–96; career advisors in STEM with, 136–37; collegial, 175; hours per week, 123, 172; with implicit messages, 96, 98n1; reframing life and, 163–68, 170; substandard, 161, 271; termination, 268; toxic, 96, 122
working class, 141, 189–95, 197–98, 203
work–life balance, 18, 95, 105, 111, 113, 202, 220, 223, 312; advice, 140, 156; burnout with lack of, 88–89; COVID-19 pandemic and, 102–3; harmony in, 23, 24, 169; personal values and cultivating, 10, 205–7, 311; prioritizing, 83, 137; research career with, 120; for subject librarians, 123–24. *See also* well-being
workshops, 167, 312; anti-racist teaching practices, 233–34; career paths, 208; for careers outside professoriate, 213; faculty development, 151, 299; for identifying transferable skills, 57; professional development, 27; service-learning, 148; STEM careers, 135
writing, 9, 25, 94, 101, 153, 199, 214; blogging and, 162, 164; creative, 103–4, 224, 263; grant, 92, 93, 102, 106–7, 111, 133, 267; personal statements, 102, 107, 110; research and, 140, 159, 163–68, 170; service-learning and, 148, 149. *See also* independent researchers and writers

Printed in the USA
CPSIA information can be obtained
at www.ICGtesting.com
CBHW072255110424
6795CB00010B/912